The Novel :
Modern Essays
in Criticism

PRENTICE-HALL ENGLISH LITERATURE SERIES
Maynard Mack, *Editor*

Prentice-Hall International, Inc., *London*
Prentice-Hall of Australia, Pty. Ltd., *Sydney*
Prentice-Hall of Canada, Ltd., *Toronto*
Prentice-Hall of India Private Ltd., *New Delhi*
Prentice-Hall of Japan, Inc., *Tokyo*

Edited by
ROBERT MURRAY DAVIS, comp.
University of Oklahoma

The Novel:
Modern Essays
in Criticism

Prentice-Hall, Inc., Englewood Cliffs, New Jersey

Library of Congress Catalog Card Number: 69–12625

Printed in the United States of America

Current Printing (last number):
10 9 8 7 6 5 4 3 2 1

Preface

Perhaps the most valuable body of criticism of fiction in the twentieth century deals with problems of form and technique. Other approaches have merits that should not be ignored, but anyone who takes more than a passing interest in the novel as an art form must consider what a novel is and how it works. Such considerations are relevant to the work of any novelist in any period. Even if the approach through form and technique is to be qualified or transcended, as in some degree it must, it can never be entirely ignored or superseded.

The essays in this volume have been selected not only to acquaint the student with statements that are historically important and with major critical concepts of fictional technique, but also to demonstrate that no theory is incapable of refinement. To this end, the emphasis tends to fall upon statements by critics rather than novelists; upon recent critics who develop earlier ideas rather than the critics who first adumbrated those ideas; and upon writing that can serve in some measure as a model of style as well as of thought.

The essays can be usefully studied in any fashion, but the collection as arranged has a form. The first two essays provide a useful contrast in approach between that of the individual creator, full of the sense of his form's promise, and that of the historical scholar, who sees the novel not only as a product of craft and vision, an organic whole, but also as part of a tradition, an artifact and a piece of evidence. The next three essays deal with problems of genre and illustrate most clearly the process by which a critical theory can be refined and extended. More particular aspects of the novel are treated in the next nine essays, although it should become increasingly clear that the divisions are artificial and that each aspect involves all of the others. The essays by Marcus and

Wain represent a type that has become almost a subgenre: the "whither the novel" essay. Both are far removed from the confidence and enthusiasm of James. They have the humbling but salutary implication that if the novel is to be saved, novelists rather than critics will save it; they suggest to the historically-minded the plight of neo-classical critics of the epic, who found themselves with a fully developed critical method and no epics on which to use it—merely some refractory and unaccountable pieces of writing. Leslie Fiedler, who has the last but not the final word, returns the discussion to the individual sensibility and its vital apprehension of experience.

The comment that follows each essay is intended not to outline the overt statement of the essay but to show its relationship to trends in modern criticism as well as to other essays in the volume and to suggest extensions and modifications. Most of the comments contain suggestions for further reading on a particular issue, probably more useful to the student than a separate bibliography because they are more pointed and more selective.

Obviously, there are far more essays of merit than could be presented here. Theoretical works that deal in part with other genres or art forms, such as Joseph Frank's "Spatial Form in Modern Literature" and George Bluestone's "Time in Film and Fiction," have been omitted in order to focus more sharply upon the technique of fiction. European criticism has been left untouched in an attempt to reduce the number and range of works used for illustration in the essays.

The assistance of the librarians of Loyola University (Chicago), the University of California (Santa Barbara), and the University of Oklahoma has been valuable throughout the preparation of this book. Many of my colleagues have made suggestions or asked useful questions; those of Martha Banta and William Holtz were the most thorough and the most searching.

Contents

Introduction

In 1948, even as René Wellek and Austin Warren wrote that the criticism of fiction was inferior both in quantity and quality to the criticism of poetry, a number of critics and scholars were doing work that made necessary a qualification if not a denial of that judgment. In fact, 1948 can be seen as a turning point for the modern criticism of fiction, for in that year Mark Schorer's "Technique as Discovery"—one of the most extreme statements of the formalist position—was published in the *Hudson Review* and almost immediately reprinted in one of the first important anthologies of fiction criticism, *Forms of Modern Fiction: Essays Collected in Honor of Joseph Warren Beach* (edited by William Van O'Connor). Less widely known but even more important because of its greater range and its large bibliography, *Critiques and Essays on Modern Fiction, 1920–1951*, edited by John W. Aldridge, came four years later. By this time scholarly journals devoted entirely to fiction had begun to appear: *Nineteenth Century Fiction* in 1949 (it had been *The Trollopian* since 1945); *Modern Fiction Studies* in 1955; *Critique,* devoted to recent fiction, in 1956; *Studies in Short Fiction* in 1963; *Novel: A Forum on Fiction* in 1967; *Studies in the Novel,* announced but not yet published; and a number of other journals devoted to fiction as well as other topics, such as *Wisconsin Studies in Contemporary Literature* and *Essays in Criticism*. It might not be presumptuous to say that the criticism of fiction has grown in more than bulk since 1948.

The use of 1948 as a turning point does not imply that no valuable work was done before. Later critics obviously drew upon the theories of their predecessors, sometimes merely inflating them, but sometimes developing and extending them. At least as important as their theories was the early critics' clearing of ground for serious discussion. James, Conrad, and Ford argued again and again that the novel was an art form at least the equal of any, that the artist's method rather than his subject matter was the proper subject for the critic, and that an understanding of form was essential to anything like a full appreciation of the novel. Their arguments must be seen in context (a context outlined in Beach's introduction to the 1954 edition of his *The Method of Henry James*). Today, in different situations, we may need different emphases. Yet the issues presented in James's "The Art of Fiction," Conrad's "Preface to *The Nigger of the Narcissus*," and Ford's *Joseph Conrad: A Personal Remembrance* are still relevant to the modern theorist. By the 1920's, critics could assume an audience that took the novel seriously and were interested in formal rather than ethical standards, and, drawing upon the criticism as well as the novels of their predecessors, they moved to analysis and classification. Percy Lubbock's *The Craft of Fiction* (1921) stressed the importance of point of view; E. M. Forster's *Aspects of the Novel* (1927) emphasized the need for vitality as well as formal arrangement; Edwin Muir's *The Structure of the Novel* (1928) classified novels by formal effects as well as subject matter. All of these critics tended to speak in broad terms and make rough distinctions and sometimes to prescribe the best methods for novelists of past and future.

Relatively speaking, there was little theoretical criticism of the novel in the 1930's—the work of Beach and R. P. Blackmur's collection of and valuable introduction to James's prefaces to the New York edition of his novels are two obvious exceptions. Critics tended to concentrate on theme rather than on form, on practical criticism—evaluation and analysis—rather than on more abstract matters. Yet even during this period the New Critics had begun to extend to fiction the critical methods they had developed to deal with poetry; in the middle and late 1940's, most notably in the work of Mark Schorer, Robert Wooster Stallman, and Ray B. West, Jr.—the last two associated with the *Western Review*—and of scores of other critics, the theories were publicized and developed. The collections edited by O'Connor and Aldridge represent the high tide of aggressive formalism, though Aldridge could foresee the time when a shift of emphasis from form to matter and from analysis to evaluation would be necessary to redress the critical balance.

Reaction against formalist theories was swift and emphatic. Opponents maintained that the stuff of fiction differed radically from the stuff of poetry and, in more concrete terms, objected that the formalist emphasis made certain texts into untouchable classics, denied the validity of other fictional methods, and undervalued novels and writers who had superior claims to attention. The theoretical split that resulted (only its terms and examples are new; the debate is ancient) underlies a good deal of modern criticism: on the one hand, the conception of the novel as an autonomous artifact, a created object whose form is its content, which appeals primarily to the aesthetic sense of the reader; on the other, the mimetic view of the novel as a presentation of life, a product of the author's vision of the outer world rather than his technique, which appeals to the ethical and emotional perceptions of the reader—or to the whole man, the aesthetic sense being subordinated or denied. Some have gone so far as to link the former view with political conservatism or reaction, the latter with liberalism or humanism. Whether true or not, the charges help to account for the heat generated in the dispute.

Although recent critics have in general accepted one of these theoretical positions, they have tended to be more tolerant of opposition and to see that certain approaches—though not major premises—must be adapted to the kind of novel under discussion, that *War and Peace, The Ambassadors,* and *Candide* simply cannot be seen in the same terms, though they may be subjected to the same scale of values. This realization has not stifled debate, and it has made critics aware of the importance of examining a work not merely in terms of its own merits or of its conformity to certain preconceptions, often concealed, about what a novel must be but in terms of its genre and of the author's rhetorical strategy. These last two ways of viewing fiction are not identical, but both emphasize the importance of the author, restoring him to a central position as shaper and craftsman that formalists would deny him on the grounds that the completed work is primary in importance and that the mimetic school tends to subordinate to the reality represented. In addition, the rhetorical approach—Wayne Booth's *The Rhetoric of Fiction* is the seminal work—regards the novel as a process rather than as an artifact. Clearly it is both, but the degree of emphasis has important implications for the practice as well as the theory of criticism that Malcolm Bradbury and others are only beginning to work out and that may represent a major new approach to the criticism of fiction.

If Henry James was right in saying that discussion is a sign of health, then the criticism of fiction is not only healthy but flourishing. There seems to be a feeling that several critics may be on the verge of major theoretical statements as important as Wayne Booth's and Northrop Frye's; the new journal *Novel* is a sign and hopefully an agent of a more coherent, more psychologically valid, and more flexible theory of fiction. Yet there are still other, less hopeful signs. The most impressive parts of two recent statements by David Lodge and Malcolm Bradbury are the summaries of theoretical and practical shortcomings of previous critics; their own positive contributions extend our knowledge far less than one could hope. Moreover, there is the problem of the sheer bulk of criticism and especially the proliferation of terminology that results. Students of the novel generally agree that a central body of definitions is needed; there is less agreement about the form it should take.

It may be objected that such work smacks of prescription and methodology. Certainly it is true that no awareness of previous criticism, no amount of consistency in critical theory, and no devisable method of dealing with fiction or anything else will avail the reader who cannot respond with sensitivity and taste. Significant new criticism, like significant new fiction, will be the product not of planning or hope but of a major talent. Still, though genius we cannot attain, method we can, and surely it is better to use what light we have than wait darkling for sudden and total illumination.

From the Preface to
The Portrait of a Lady

HENRY JAMES

. . .

Trying to recover here, for recognition, the germ of my idea, I see that it must have consisted not at all in any conceit of a "plot," nefarious name, in any flash, upon the fancy, of a set of relations, or in any one of those situations that, by a logic of their own, immediately fall, for the fabulist, into movement, into a march or a rush, a patter of quick steps; but altogether in the sense of a single character, the character and aspect of a particular engaging young woman, to which all the usual elements of a "subject," certainly of a setting, were to need to be superadded. Quite as interesting as the young woman herself, at her best, do I find, I must again repeat, this projection of memory upon the whole matter of the growth, in one's imagination, of some such apology for a motive. These are the fascinations of the fabulist's art, these lurking forces of expansion, these necessities of upspringing in the seed, these beautiful determinations, on the part of the idea entertained, to grow as tall as possible, to push into the light and the air and thickly flower there; and, quite as much, these fine possibilities of recovering, from some good standpoint on the ground gained, the intimate history of the business—of retracing and reconstructing its steps and stages. I have always fondly remembered a remark that I heard fall years ago from the lips of Ivan Turgenieff in regard to his own experience of the usual origin of the fictive picture. It began for him almost always with the vision of some person or persons, who hovered before him, soliciting him, as the active or

Reprinted from the Preface to *The Portrait of a Lady*, Volume III, *The Novels and Tales of Henry James*.

1

passive figure, interesting him and appealing to him just as they were and by what they were. He saw them, in that fashion, as *disponibles,* saw them subject to the chances, the complications of existence, and saw them vividly, but then had to find for them the right relations, those that would most bring them out; to imagine, to invent and select and piece together the situations most useful and favourable to the sense of the creatures themselves, the complications they would be most likely to produce and to feel.

"To arrive at these things is to arrive at my 'story,' " he said, "and that's the way I look for it. The result is that I'm often accused of not having 'story' enough. I seem to myself to have as much as I need—to show my people, to exhibit their relations with each other; for that is all my measure. If I watch them long enough I see them come together, I see them *placed,* I see them engaged in this or that act and in this or that difficulty. How they look and move and speak and behave, always in the setting I have found for them, is my account of them—of which I dare say, alas, *que cela manque souvent d'archi-tecture.* But I would rather, I think, have too little architecture than too much—when there's danger of its interfering with my measure of the truth. The French of course like more of it than I give—having by their own genius such a hand for it; and indeed one must give all one can. As for the origin of one's wind-blown germs themselves, who shall say, as you ask, where *they* come from? We have to go too far back, too far behind, to say. Isn't it all we can say that they come from every quarter of heaven, that they are *there* at almost any turn of the road? They accumulate, and we are always picking them over, selecting among them. They are the breath of life—by which I mean that life, in its own way, breathes them upon us. They are so, in a manner prescribed and imposed—floated into our minds by the current of life. That reduces to imbecility the vain critic's quarrel, so often, with one's subject, when he hasn't the wit to accept it. Will he point out then which other it should properly have been?—his office being, essentially *to* point out. *Il en serait bien embarrassé.* Ah, when he points out what I've done or failed to do with it, that's another matter: there he's on his ground. I give him up my 'architecture,' " my distin-guished friend concluded, "as much as he will."

So this beautiful genius, and I recall with comfort the gratitude I drew from his reference to the intensity of suggestion that may reside in the stray figure, the unattached character, the image *en disponibilité.* It gave me higher warrant than I seemed then to have met for just that blest habit of one's own imagination, the trick of investing some conceived or encountered individual, some brace or group of individuals, with the germinal property and authority. I was myself so much more antecedently conscious of my figures than of their setting— a too preliminary, a preferential interest in which struck me as in general such a putting of the cart before the horse. I might envy, though I couldn't emulate, the imaginative writer so constituted as to see his fable first and to make out its agents afterwards: I could think so little of any fable that didn't need its agents positively to launch it; I could think so little of any situation that didn't depend for its interest on the nature of the persons situated, and thereby on their way of taking it. There are methods of so-called presentation, I believe—among novelists who have appeared to flourish—that offer the situation as indifferent to that support; but I have not lost the sense of the value for me, at the time, of the admirable Russian's testimony to my not needing, all superstitiously, to try and perform any such gymnastic. Other echoes from the same source linger with me, I confess, as unfadingly—if it be not all indeed one much-embracing echo. It was impossible after that not to read, for one's uses, high lucidity into the tormented and disfigured and bemuddled question of the objective value, and even quite into that of the critical appreciation, of "subject" in the novel.

One had had from an early time, for that matter, the instinct of the right estimate of such values and of its reducing to the inane the dull dispute over the "immoral" subject and the moral. Recognising so promptly the one measure of the worth of a given subject, the question about it that, rightly answered, disposes of all others—is it valid, in a word, is it genuine, is it sincere, the result of some direct impression or perception of life?—I had found small edification, mostly, in a critical pretension that had neglected from the first all delimitation of ground and all definition of terms. The air of my earlier time shows, to memory, as darkened, all round, with that vanity—unless the difference today be just in one's own final impatience, the lapse of one's attention. There is, I think, no more nutritive or suggestive truth in this connexion than that of the perfect dependence of the "moral" sense of a work of art on the amount of felt life concerned in producing it. The question comes back thus, obviously, to the kind and the degree of the artist's prime sensibility, which is the soil out of which his subject springs. The quality and capacity of that soil, its ability to "grow" with due freshness and straightness any vision of life, represents, strongly or weakly, the projected morality. That element is but another name for the more or less close connexion of the subject with some mark made on the intelligence, with some sincere experience. By which, at the same time, of course, one is far from contending that this enveloping air of the artist's humanity—which gives the last touch to the worth of the work—is not a widely and wondrously varying element; being on one occasion a rich and magnificent medium and on another a comparatively poor and ungenerous one. Here we get exactly the high price of the novel as a literary form—its power not only, while preserving that form with closeness, to range through all the differences of the individual relation to its general subject-matter, all the varieties of outlook on life, of disposition to reflect and project, created by conditions that are never the same from man to man (or, so far as that goes, from man to woman), but positively to appear more true to its character in proportion as it strains, or tends to burst, with a latent extravagance, its mould.

The house of fiction has in short not one window, but a million—a number of possible windows not to be reckoned, rather; every one of which has been pierced, or is still pierceable, in its vast front, by the need of the individual vision and by the pressure of the individual will. These apertures, of dissimilar shape and size, hang so, all together, over the human scene that we might have expected of them a greater sameness of report than we find. They are but windows at the best, mere holes in a dead wall, disconnected, perched aloft; they are not hinged doors opening straight upon life. But they have this mark of their own that at each of them stands a figure with a pair of eyes, or at least with a field-glass, which forms, again and again, for observation, a unique instrument, insuring to the person making use of it an impression distinct from every other. He and his neighbours are watching the same show, but one seeing more where the other sees less, one seeing black where the other sees white, one seeing big where the other sees small, one seeing coarse where the other sees fine. And so on, and so on; there is fortunately no saying on what, for the particular pair of eyes, the window may *not* open; "fortunately" by reason, precisely, of this incalculability of range. The spreading field, the human scene, is the "choice of subject"; the pierced aperture, either broad or balconied or slit-like and low-browed, is the "literary form"; but they are, singly or together, as nothing without the posted presence of the watcher—without, in other words, the consciousness of the artist. Tell me what the artist is, and I will tell you of what he has *been* conscious. Thereby I shall express to you at once his bound-less freedom and his "moral" reference.

All this is a long way round, however, for my word about my dim first move toward *The Portrait,* which was exactly my grasp of a single character—an acquisition I had made, moreover, after a fashion not here to be retraced. Enough that I was, as seemed to me, in complete possession of it, that I had been so for a long time, that this had made it familiar and yet had not blurred its charm, and that, all urgently, all tormentingly, I saw it in motion and, so to speak, in transit. This amounts to saying that I saw it as bent upon its fate—some fate or other; *which,* among the possibilities, being precisely the question. Thus I had my vivid individual—vivid, so strangely, in spite of being still at large, not confined by the conditions, not engaged in the tangle, to which we look for much of the impress that constitutes an identity. If the apparition was still all to be placed how came it to be vivid?—since we puzzle such quantities out, mostly, just by the business of placing them. One could answer such a question beauti-fully, doubtless, if one could do so subtle, if not so monstrous, a thing as to write the history of the growth of one's imagination. One would describe then what, at a given time, had extraordinarily happened to it, and one would so, for instance, be in a position to tell, with an approach to clearness, how, under favour of occasion, it had been able to take over (take over straight from life) such and such a constituted, animated figure or form. The figure has to that extent, as you see, *been* placed—placed in the imagination that detains it, preserves, protects, enjoys it, conscious of its presence in the dusky, crowded, heterogeneous back-shop of the mind very much as a wary dealer in precious odds and ends, competent to make an "advance" on rare objects confided to him, is conscious of the rare little "piece" left in deposit by the reduced, mysterious lady of title or the specula-tive amateur, and which is already there to disclose its merit afresh as soon as a key shall have clicked in a cupboard-door.

That may be, I recognise, a somewhat superfine analogy for the particular "value" I here speak of, the image of the young feminine nature that I had had for so considerable a time all curiously at my disposal; but it appears to fond memory quite to fit the fact—with the recall, in addition, of my pious desire but to place my treasure right. I quite remind myself thus of the dealer resigned not to "realise," resigned to keeping the precious object locked up indefinitely rather than commit it, at no matter what price, to vulgar hands. For there *are* dealers in these forms and figures and treasures capable of that refinement. The point is, however, that this single small corner-stone, the conception of a certain young woman affronting her destiny, had begun with being all my outfit for the large building of *The Portrait of a Lady.* It came to be a square and spacious house—or has at least seemed so to me in this going over it again; but, such as it is, it had to be put up round my young woman while she stood there in perfect isolation. That is to me, artistically speaking, the circumstance of interest; for I have lost myself once more, I confess, in the curiosity of analysing the structure. By what process of logical accretion was this slight "personality," the mere slim shade of an intelligent but presumptuous girl, to find itself endowed with the high attributes of a Subject? —and indeed by what thinness, at the best, would such a subject not be vitiated? Millions of presumptuous girls, intelligent or not intelligent, daily affront their destiny, and what is it open to their destiny to *be,* at the most, that we should make an ado about it? The novel is of its very nature an "ado," an ado about something, and the larger the form it takes the greater of course the ado. Therefore, consciously, that was what one was in for—for positively organising an ado about Isabel Archer.

One looked it well in the face, I seem to remember, this extravagance; and with the effect precisely of recognising the charm of the problem. Challenge any such problem with any intelligence, and you immediately see how full it is of substance; the wonder being, all the while, as we look at the world, how absolutely, how inordinately, the Isabel Archers, and even much smaller female fry, insist on mattering. George Eliot has admirably noted it—"In these frail vessels is borne onward through the ages the treasure of human affection." In *Romeo and Juliet* Juliet has to be important, just as, in *Adam Bede* and *The Mill on the Floss* and *Middlemarch* and *Daniel Deronda,* Hetty Sorrel and Maggie Tulliver and Rosamond Vincy and Gwendolen Harleth have to be; with that much of firm ground, that much of bracing air, at the disposal all the while of their feet and their lungs. They are typical, nonetheless, of a class difficult, in the individual case, to make a centre of interest; so difficult in fact that many an expert painter, as for instance Dickens and Walter Scott, as for instance even, in the main, so subtle a hand as that of R. L. Stevenson, has preferred to leave the task unattempted. There are in fact writers as to whom we make out that their refuge from this is to assume it to be not worth their attempting; by which pusillanimity in truth their honour is scantly saved. It is never an attestation of a value, or even of our imperfect sense of one, it is never a tribute to any truth at all, that we shall represent that value badly. It never makes up, artistically, for an artist's dim feeling about a thing that he shall "do" the thing as ill as possible. There are better ways than that, the best of all of which is to begin with less stupidity.

It may be answered meanwhile, in regard to Shakespeare's and to George Eliot's testimony, that their concession to the "importance" of their Juliets and Cleopatras and Portias (even with Portia as the very type and model of the young person intelligent and presumptuous) and to that of their Hettys and Maggies and Rosamonds and Gwendolens, suffers the abatement that these slimnesses are, when figuring as the main props of the theme, never suffered to be sole ministers of its appeal, but have their inadequacy eked out with comic relief and underplots, as the playwrights say, when not with murders and battles and the great mutations of the world. If they are shown as "mattering" as much as they could possibly pretend to, the proof of it is in a hundred other persons, made of much stouter stuff, and each involved moreover in a hundred relations which matter to *them* concomitantly with that one. Cleopatra matters, beyond bounds, to Antony, but his colleagues, his antagonists, the state of Rome and the impending battle also prodigiously matter; Portia matters to Antonio, and to Shylock, and to the Prince of Morocco, to the fifty aspiring princes, but for these gentry there are other lively concerns; for Antonio, notably, there are Shylock and Bassanio and his lost ventures and the extremity of his predicament. This extremity indeed, by the same token, matters to Portia—though its doing so becomes of interest all by the fact that Portia matters to *us*. That she does so, at any rate, and that almost everything comes round to it again, supports my contention as to this fine example of the value recognised in the mere young thing. (I say "mere" young thing because I guess that even Shakespeare, preoccupied mainly though he may have been with the passions of princes, would scarce have pretended to found the best of his appeal for her on her high social position.) It is an example exactly of the deep difficulty braved—the difficulty of making George Eliot's "frail vessel," if not the all-in-all for our attention, at least the clearest of the call.

Now to see deep difficulty braved is at any time, for the really addicted artist, to feel almost even as a pang the beautiful incentive, and to feel it verily in such sort as to wish the danger intensified. The difficulty most worth tackling can only be for him, in these conditions, the greatest the case permits of. So I remember feeling here (in presence, always, that is, of the particular uncertainty of my ground), that there would be one way better than another—oh, ever so much better than any other!—of making it fight out its battle. The frail vessel, that charged with George Eliot's "treasure," and thereby of such importance to those who curiously approach it, has likewise possibilities of importance to itself, possibilities which permit of treatment and in fact peculiarly require it from the moment they are considered at all. There is always the escape from any close account of the weak agent of such spells by using as a bridge for evasion, for retreat and flight, the view of her relation to those surrounding her. Make it predominantly a view of *their* relation and the trick is played: you give the general sense of her effect, and you give it, so far as the raising on it of a superstructure goes, with the maximum of ease. Well, I recall perfectly how little, in my now quite established connexion, the maximum of ease appealed to me, and how I seemed to get rid of it by an honest transposition of the weights in the two scales. "Place the centre of the subject in the young woman's own consciousness," I said to myself, "and you get as interesting and as beautiful a difficulty as you could wish. Stick to *that*—for the centre; put the heaviest weight into *that* scale, which will be so largely the scale of her relation to herself. Make her only interested enough, at the same time, in the things that are not herself, and this relation needn't fear to be too limited. Place meanwhile in the other scale the lighter weight (which is usually the one that tips the balance of interest) : press least hard, in short, on the consciousness of your heroine's satellites, especially the male; make it an interest contributive only to the greater one. See, at all events, what can be done in this way. What better field could there be for a due ingenuity? The girl hovers, inextinguishable, as a charming creature, and the job will be to translate her into the highest terms of that formula, and as nearly as possible moreover into *all* of them. To depend upon her and her little concerns wholly to see you through will necessitate, remember, your really 'doing' her."

So far I reasoned, and it took nothing less than that technical rigour, I now easily see, to inspire me with the right confidence for erecting on such a plot of ground the neat and careful and proportioned pile of bricks that arches over it and that was thus to form, constructionally speaking, a literary monument. Such is the aspect that today *The Portrait* wears for me: a structure reared with an "architectural" competence, as Turgenieff would have said, that makes it, to the author's own sense, the most proportioned of his productions after *The Ambassadors*—which was to follow it so many years later and which has, no doubt, a superior roundness. On one thing I was determined; that, though I should clearly have to pile brick upon brick for the creation of an interest, I would leave no pretext for saying that anything is out of line, scale or perspective. I would build large—in fine embossed vaults and painted arches, as who should say, and yet never let it appear that the chequered pavement, the ground under the reader's feet, fails to stretch at every point to the base of the walls. That precautionary spirit, on re-perusal of the book, is the old note that most touches me: it testifies so, for my own ear, to the anxiety of my provision for the reader's amusement. I felt, in view of the possible limitations of my subject, that no such provision could be excessive, and the development of the latter was simply the general form of that earnest quest. And I find indeed that this is the only account I can give myself of the evolution of the fable: it is all under the head thus named that I conceive the needful accretion as having taken place, the right complications as having started. It was naturally of the essence that the young woman should be herself complex; that was rudimentary—or was at any rate the light in which Isabel Archer had originally dawned. It went, however, but a certain way, and other lights, contending, conflicting lights, and of as many different colours, if possible, as the rockets, the Roman candles and Catherine-wheels of a "pyrotechnic display," would be employable to attest that she was. I had, no doubt, a groping instinct for the right complications, since I am quite unable to track the footsteps of those that constitute, as the case stands, the general situation exhibited. They are there, for what they are worth, and as numerous as might be; but my memory, I confess, is a blank as to how and whence they came.

I seem to myself to have waked up one morning in possession of them—of Ralph Touchett and his parents, of Madame Merle, of Gilbert Osmond and his daughter and his sister, of Lord Warburton, Caspar Goodwood and Miss Stackpole, the definite array of contributions to Isabel Archer's history. I recognised them, I knew them, they were the numbered pieces of my puzzle, the concrete terms of my "plot." It was as if they had simply, by an impulse of their own, floated into my ken, and all in response to my primary question: "Well, what will she *do?*" Their answer seemed to be that if I would trust them they would show me; on which, with an urgent appeal to them to make it at least as interesting as they could, I trusted them. They were like the group of attendants and entertainers who come down by train when people in the country give a party; they represented the contract for carrying the party on. That was an excellent relation with them—a possible one even with so broken a reed (from her slightness of cohesion) as Henrietta Stackpole. It is a familiar truth to the novelist, at the strenuous hour, that, as certain elements in any work are of the essence, so others are only of the form; that as this or that character, this or that disposition of the material, belongs to the subject directly, so to speak, so this or that other belongs to it but indirectly—belongs intimately to the treatment. This is a truth, however, of which he rarely gets the benefit—since it could be assured to him, really, but by criticism based upon perception, criticism which is too little of this world. He must not think of benefits, moreover, I freely recognise, for that way dishonour lies: he has, that is, but one to think of—the benefit, whatever it may be, involved in his having cast a spell upon the simpler, the very simplest, forms of attention. This is all he is entitled to; he is entitled to nothing, he is bound to admit, that can come to him, from the reader, as a result on the latter's part of any act of reflexion or discrimination. He may *enjoy* this finer tribute—that is another affair, but on condition only of taking it as a gratuity "thrown in," a mere miraculous windfall, the fruit of a tree he may not pretend to have shaken. Against reflexion, against discrimination, in his interest, all earth and air conspire; wherefore it is that, as I say, he must in many a case have schooled himself, from the first, to work but for a "living wage." The living wage is the reader's grant of the least possible quantity of attention required for consciousness of a "spell." The occasional charming "tip" is an act of his intelligence over and beyond this, a golden apple, for the writer's lap, straight from the wind-stirred tree. The artist may of course, in wanton moods, dream of some Paradise (for art) where the direct appeal to the intelligence might be legalised; for to such extravagances as these his yearning mind can scarce hope ever completely to close itself. The most he can do is to remember they *are* extravagances.

All of which is perhaps but a gracefully devious way of saying that Henrietta Stackpole was a good example, in *The Portrait,* of the truth to which I just adverted—as good an example as I could name were it not that Maria Gostrey, in *The Ambassadors,* then in the bosom of time, may be mentioned as a better. Each of these persons is but wheels to the coach; neither belongs to the body of that vehicle, or is for a moment accommodated with a seat inside. There the subject alone is ensconced, in the form of its "hero and heroine," and of the privileged high officials, say, who ride with the king and queen. There are reasons why one would have liked this to be felt, as in general one would like almost anything to be felt, in one's work, that one has one's self contributively felt. We have seen, however, how idle is that pretension, which I should be sorry to make too much of. Maria Gostrey and Miss Stackpole then are cases, each, of the light *ficelle,* not of the true agent; they may run beside the coach "for all they are worth," they may cling to it till they are out of breath (as poor Miss Stackpole all so visibly does), but neither, all the while, so much as gets her foot on the step, neither ceases for a moment to tread the dusty road. Put it even that they are like the fishwives who helped to bring back to Paris from Versailles, on that most ominous day of the first half of the French Revolution, the carriage of the royal family. The only thing is that I may well be asked, I acknowledge, why then, in the present fiction, I have suffered Henrietta (of whom we have indubitably too much) so officiously, so strangely, so almost inexplicably, to pervade. I will presently say what I can for that anomaly—and in the most conciliatory fashion.

A point I wish still more to make is that if my relation of confidence with the actors in my drama who *were,* unlike Miss Stackpole, true agents, was an excellent one to have arrived at, there still remained my relation with the reader, which was another affair altogether and as to which I felt no one to be trusted but myself. That solicitude was to be accordingly expressed in the artful patience with which, as I have said, I piled brick upon brick. The bricks, for the whole counting-over—putting for bricks little touches and inventions and enhancements by the way—affect me in truth as well-nigh innumerable and as ever so scrupulously fitted together and packed-in. It is an effect of detail, of the minutest; though, if one were in this connexion to say all, one would express the hope that the general, the ampler air of the modest monument still survives. I do at least seem to catch the key to a part of this abundance of small anxious, ingenious illustration as I recollect putting my finger, in my young woman's interest, on the most obvious of her predicates. "What will she 'do'? Why, the first thing she'll do will be to come to Europe; which in fact will form, and all inevitably, no small part of her principal adventure. Coming to Europe is even for the 'frail vessels,' in this wonderful age, a mild adventure; but what is truer than that on one side—the side of their independence of flood and field, of the moving accident, of battle and murder and sudden death—her adventures are to be mild? Without her sense of them, her sense *for* them, as one may say, they are next to nothing at all; but isn't the beauty and the difficulty just in showing their mystic conversion by that sense, conversion into the stuff of drama or, even more delightful word still, of 'story'?" It was all as clear, my contention, as a silver bell. Two very good instances, I think, of this effect of conversion, two cases of the rare chemistry, are the pages in which Isabel, coming into the drawing-room at Gardencourt, coming in from a wet walk or whatever, that rainy afternoon, finds Madame Merle in possession of the place, Madame Merle seated, all absorbed but all serene, at the piano, and deeply recognises, in the striking of such an hour, in the presence there, among the gathering shades, of this personage, of whom a moment before she had never so much as heard, a turning-point in her life. It is dreadful to have too much, for any artistic demonstration, to dot one's i's and insist on one's intentions, and I am not eager to do it now; but the question here was that of producing the maximum of intensity with the minimum of strain.

The interest was to be raised to its pitch and yet the elements to be kept in their key; so that, should the whole thing duly impress, I might show what an "exciting" inward life may do for the person leading it even while it remains perfectly normal. And I cannot think of a more consistent application of that ideal unless it be in the long statement, just beyond the middle of the book, of my young woman's extraordinary meditative vigil on the occasion that was to become for her such a landmark. Reduced to its essence, it is but the vigil of searching criticism; but it throws the action further forward than twenty "incidents" might have done. It was designed to have all the vivacity of incident and all the economy of picture. She sits up, by her dying fire, far into the night, under the spell of recognitions on which she finds the last sharpness suddenly wait. It is a representation simply of her motionlessly *seeing,* and an attempt withal to make the mere still lucidity of her act as "interesting" as the surprise of a caravan or the identification of a pirate. It represents, for that matter, one of the identifications dear to the novelist, and even indispensable to him; but it all goes on without her being approached by another person and without her leaving her chair. It is obviously the best thing in the book, but it is only a supreme illustration of the general plan. As to Henrietta, my apology for whom I just left incomplete, she exemplifies, I fear, in her superabundance, not an element of my plan, but only an excess of my zeal. So early was to begin my tendency to *overtreat,* rather than undertreat (when there was choice or danger) my subject. (Many members of my craft, I gather, are far from agreeing with me, but I have always held overtreating the minor disservice.) "Treating" that of *The Portrait* amounted to never forgetting, by any lapse, that the thing was under a special obligation to be amusing. There was the danger of the noted "thinness"—which was to be averted, tooth and nail, by cultivation of the lively. That is at least how I see it today. Henrietta must have been at that time a part of my wonderful notion of the lively. And then there was another matter. I had, within the few preceding years, come to live in London, and the "international" light lay, in those days, to my sense, thick and rich upon the scene. It was the light in which so much of the picture hung. But that *is* another matter. There is really too much to say.

※※※※

James's prefaces to the New York edition of his novels, in which he gave final form to the work he wished to preserve, were, he wrote to William Dean Howells, "a sort of plea for Criticism, for Discrimination, for Appreciation on other than infantile lines—as against the so almost universal Anglo-Saxon absence of these things. . . . They ought. . .to form a sort of comprehensive manual or *vade mecum* for aspirants in our arduous profession."* These two goals—critical plea and writer's manual—may seem different, if not contradictory, but James believed that full appreciation of a novel demands not merely consideration of its vision but, primarily and sometimes almost exclusively, of the means by which the author shaped and embodied his vision. He was particularly aware of the need for more thorough discussion, more conscious theory, and more precise terms of description. Ever since "The Art of Fiction" (1884), he had insisted that the novel was not merely the commodity that many producers and consumers seemed to think it, but the form of art with the widest possibilities and the greatest promise.

---

* Percy Lubbock, ed., *The Letters of Henry James* (New York: Charles Scribner's Sons, 1920), II, 99.

His influence on critical attitudes toward the novel as an art form, on theories of the form, and on methods of writing, describing, and evaluating individual novels and whole subgenres has been profound and lasting. It is now widely conceded that the novel is the dominant literary form of the twentieth century. Though some critics feel that its vitality—if not its sway—is diminishing, many others (like Leslie Fiedler in this volume) write about novels when they profess to be writing about all forms of literature. The aesthetic and formal approach to the novel advocated by James inspired the work of influential critics such as Joseph Warren Beach, Percy Lubbock, Mark Schorer, and to some extent, Fiedler. James's example is also the basis for studies of particular aspects of technique. For instance, characters and their functions in the novel, points of view and focus, and different kinds of narrative method, all singled out by James as important subjects, are discussed at greater length in the essays by Harvey, Friedman, Booth, O'Grady, and Lutwack.

James's theories, however, have never been without opposition. E. M. Forster dismissed as unimportant his theories about point of view; later critics denounced his emphasis upon technique and the consequent tendency of his followers to undervalue Tolstoy and Dickens. Some, like W. J. Harvey in this volume and Marvin Mudrick in *Yale Review*,* argue that his method in *The Portrait of a Lady* is incompatible with true novelistic method and that the meditation of Isabel, far from being what James calls "obviously the best thing in the book," is the chief sign of his evasion of the novelist's responsibility. Other critics, most notably Northrop Frye, Wayne Booth, and Robert Scholes and Robert Kellogg, less anxious to advance a particular theory or the work of a particular school, have not rejected the novels or the critical methods of James; but they have sought to broaden the scope of discussion from the novel to prose fiction in general and from relatively narrow prescriptive rules to critical principles based upon the practice of writers outside the frame of reference created or implied by James. Nevertheless, that frame of reference stands, and it furnishes thesis or antithesis for most modern criticism.

James's example as a novelist and his practice as a critic are discussed by Percy Lubbock in *The Craft of Fiction*;† by Morris Roberts in *Henry James's Criticism*,‡ a summary and analysis

---

* L (December 1960), 202–18.
† New York: Viking Press, 1957.
‡ Cambridge: Harvard University Press, 1929.

of James's major critical essays; and by R. P. Blackmur in his introduction to James's *The Art of the Novel,** which collects all the prefaces to the New York edition. *The Notebooks of Henry James,* edited by F. O. Matthiessen and Kenneth Murdock,† show him in the process of planning his novels rather than explaining them in retrospect. See especially the notes for *The Portrait of a Lady,* pages 15-19.

---

* New York: Charles Scribner's Sons, 1934.
† New York: George Braziller, Inc., 1955.

The Narrative Tradition

ROBERT SCHOLES and ROBERT KELLOGG

For the past two centuries the dominant form of narrative literature in the West has been the novel. In writing about the Western
narrative tradition we will in one sense, therefore, necessarily be
describing the heritage of the novel. But it will not be our intention
to view the novel as the final product of an ameliorative evolution,
as the perfected form which earlier kinds of narrative—sacred myth,
folktale, epic, romance, legend, allegory, confession, satire—were all
striving, with varying degrees of success, to become. Instead, our
intention will be almost the opposite. We hope to put the novel in its
place, to view the nature of narrative and the Western narrative
tradition whole, seeing the novel as only one of a number of narrative
possibilities. In order to attempt this it has been necessary to take long
views, to rush into literary areas where we can claim some interest and
competence but not the deep knowledge of the specialist, and perhaps
to generalize overmuch in proportion to the evidence we present. For
these and other excesses and exuberances, we apologize, hoping only
that the result will justify our temerity in having undertaken such an
elaborate project.

The object of this study of narrative art is not to set a new vogue,
in either literature or criticism, but to provide an antidote to all
narrow views of literature, ancient or modern. In any age in which
criticism flourishes, and ours is certainly such an age, a conflict between
broad and narrow approaches to literary art is sure to arise. An age
of criticism is a self-conscious age. Its tendency is to formulate rules,
to attempt the reduction of art to science, to classify, to categorize,
and finally to prescribe and proscribe. Theoretical criticism of this

sort is usually based on the practice of certain authors, whose works become classics in the worst sense of the word: models of approved and proper literary performance. This kind of narrowing down of the literature of the past to a few "classic" models amounts to the construction of an artificial literary tradition. Our purpose in this work is to present an alternative to narrowly conceived views of one major kind of literature—which we have called narrative.

By narrative we mean all those literary works which are distinguished by two characteristics: the presence of a story and a story-teller. A drama is a story without a story-teller; in it characters act out directly what Aristotle called an "imitation" of such action as we find in life. A lyric, like a drama, is a direct presentation, in which a single actor, the poet or his surrogate, sings, or muses, or speaks for us to hear or overhear. Add a second speaker, as Robert Frost does in "The Death of the Hired Man," and we move toward drama. Let the speaker begin to tell of an event, as Frost does in "The Vanishing Red," and we move toward narrative. For writing to be narrative no more and no less than a teller and a tale are required.

There is a real tradition of narrative literature in the Western world. All art is traditional in that artists learn their craft from their predecessors to a great extent. They begin by conceiving of the possibilities open to them in terms of the achievements they are acquainted with. They may add to the tradition, opening up new possibilities for their successors, but they begin, inevitably, within a tradition. The more aware we are—as readers, critics, or artists—of the fullness and breadth of the narrative tradition, the freer and the sounder will be the critical or artistic choices we make. For mid-twentieth-century readers a specific problem must be overcome before a balanced view of the narrative tradition becomes attainable. Something must be done about our veneration of the novel as a literary form.

With Joyce, Proust, Mann, Lawrence, and Faulkner, the narrative literature of the twentieth century has begun the gradual break with the narrative literature of the immediate past that characterizes all living literary traditions. Specifically, twentieth-century narrative has begun to break away from the aims, attitudes, and techniques of realism. The implications of this break are still being explored, developed, and projected by many of the most interesting living writers of narrative literature in Europe and America. But, by and large, our reviewers are hostile to this new literature and our critics are unprepared for it, for literary criticism is also influenced by its conception of tradition.

Rather than pick out one or a dozen reviewers to exemplify the hostility of contemporary criticism to much that is best in contemporary narrative art, we can take as an example a great scholar and critic, whose views are now acknowledged to be among the most influential in our graduate schools of literature (where the teachers, critics, and even the reviewers of the future are being developed) and whose attitude toward modern literature, for all the learning and sensitivity with which he presents it, is surprisingly similar to that of the most philistine weekly reviews. This scholar-critic is Erich Auerbach, whose book *Mimesis,* in its paperback, English language version, is one of the two or three most widely read and currently influential books in its field. And its field is a broad one: Western narrative literature. It is a great book, but Auerbach's single-minded devotion to realistic principles leaves him unwilling or unable to come to terms with twentieth-century fiction, and especially with such writers as Virginia Woolf, Proust, and Joyce. He finds *Ulysses* a "hodgepodge," characterized by "its blatant and painful cynicism, and its uninterpretable symbolism," and he asserts that along with it, "most of the other novels which employ multiple reflection of consciousness also leave the reader with an impression of hopelessness. There is often something confusing, something hazy about them, something hostile to the reality which they represent."

Auerbach's dissatisfaction with post-realistic fiction is echoed by the dissatisfactions of lesser men, which we meet on nearly every page of current literary reviews and journals, where much of the best contemporary writing is treated with hostility or indifference. And current attitudes toward contemporary literature also carry over into current attitudes toward the literature of the past. The tendency to apply the standards of nineteenth-century realism to all fiction naturally has disadvantages for our understanding of every other kind of narrative. Spenser, Chaucer, and Wolfram von Eschenbach suffer from the "novelistic" approach as much as Proust, Joyce, Durrell, and Beckett do. In order to provide a broader alternative to the novelistic approach to narrative, we must break down many of the chronological, linguistic, and narrowly conceived generic categories frequently employed in the discussion of narrative. We must consider the elements common to all narrative forms—oral and written, verse and prose, factual and fictional—as these forms actually developed in the Western world. While fairly rare, an undertaking of this sort is not without precedent.

Such, in fact, was the aim of the first book in English wholly devoted to the study of the narrative tradition, Clara Reeve's *The Progress of Romance through Times, Countries, and Manners,* which was published in 1785. Clara Reeve, confronted by the common eighteenth-century prejudice against romance, endeavored to provide a pedigree for the form, to show especially that "the ancients" employed it, and to distinguish it from its follower, the novel, without prejudice to either form. Her distinction, indeed, is the one preserved in our dictionaries today, and it is still employed by critics who make any pretensions to discriminating among narrative forms:

> I will attempt this distinction, and I presume if it is properly done it will be followed,—if not, you are but where you were before. The Romance is an heroic fable, which treats of fabulous persons and things.—The Novel is a picture of real life and manners, and of the times in which it is written. The Romance in lofty and elevated language, describes what never happened nor is likely to happen.—The Novel gives a familiar relation of such things, as pass every day before our eyes, such as may happen to our friend, or to ourselves; and the perfection of it, is to represent every scene, in so easy and natural a manner, and to make them appear so probable, as to deceive us into a persuasion (at least while we are reading) that all is real, until we are affected by the joys or distresses of the persons in the story, as if they were our own.

Along with this clear and useful formulation, Miss Reeve made half-hearted attempts at some other categories: a miscellaneous group of "original or uncommon" stories, which included such "modern" works as *Gulliver's Travels, Robinson Crusoe, Tristram Shandy,* and *The Castle of Otranto;* and another class of "tales and fables," which included everything from fairy tales to *Rasselas.* She also struggled with the problem of separating the Epic from the Romance, tackling such formidable considerations as the Ossianic question. (She hesitated, saying *Fingal* was "an Epic, but not a Poem" and finally located Ossian with the romances.) She made it clear throughout that a romance might be in either verse or prose, but felt that an epic must be poetical. She was also disposed to think of epic as a term of praise, so that a really fine poetic romance such as Chaucer's Knight's Tale (the example is hers) would deserve the title of epic.

For her time, and considering the limits of her education, Clara

Reeve was astonishingly well informed and free from prejudice. Her veneration for "the ancients" and her moralistic approach to literary achievement were shared by greater minds than her own. Until quite recently, in fact, very few attempts to deal with narrative literature in her comprehensive way have been made; and her knowledge, balance, and good sense would benefit many a modern book reviewer, could he attain them. Still, the difficulties Clara Reeve encountered in 1785 may be instructive for us in the present. After novel and romance she had trouble reducing other narrative forms to order— and so have modern critics. But even more troublesome is her tendency to attach a value judgment to a descriptive term like "epic." One of the greatest difficulties arising in modern criticism stems from a tendency to confuse descriptive and evaluative terminology. "Tragic" and "realistic," for example, are normally applied to literary works as terms of praise. Such usage can be found in the book and theater review pages of nearly any of our periodicals. A serious drama can be damned for its failure to be "tragic." A narrative can be damned as "unrealistic." But the greatest obstacle to an understanding of narrative literature in our day is the way notions of value have clustered around the word "novel" itself. One reason Clara Reeve could see the progress of romance with such a relatively unprejudiced eye was the fact that she lived before the great century of the realistic novel, the nineteenth.

But now, in the middle of the twentieth century, our view of narrative literature is almost hopelessly novel-centered. The expectations which readers bring to narrative literary works are based on their experience with the novel. Their assumptions about what a narrative should be are derived from their understanding of the novel. And this is true whether the reader is a professor of contemporary literature or a faithful subscriber to one of those ladies' magazines which regale their readers with contemporary fiction. The very word "novel" has become a term of praise when applied to earlier narratives. We are told on dust-jackets and paperback covers that such diverse works as Chaucer's *Troilus and Criseyde,* Geoffrey of Monmouth's *History of the Kings of Britain,* and Homer's *Odyssey* are "the first novel." But if we take these designations seriously, we are bound to be disappointed. Judged as a "novelist" even Homer must be found wanting.

The novel-centered view of narrative literature is an unfortunate one for two important reasons. First, it cuts us off from the narrative literature of the past and the culture of the past. Second, it cuts us off from the literature of the future and even from the advance guard of our own day. To recapture the past and to accept the future we must, literally, put the novel in its place. To do this we need not part with any of our appreciation of realistic fiction. When the novel is in its place the achievements of such as Balzac, Flaubert, Turgenev, Tolstoy, and George Eliot will not lose any of their luster. They may even shine more brightly.

The novel, let us remember, represents only a couple of centuries in the continuous narrative tradition of the Western world which can be traced back five thousand years. Two hundred years of considerable achievement, of course; modern Europe has nothing to be ashamed of where its production of narrative literature is concerned, whatever its failings in other spheres; but still, only two hundred years out of five thousand. The purpose of this study is to examine some of the lines of continuity in this five-thousand-year tradition by considering some of the varieties of narrative literature, by discerning patterns in the historical development of narrative forms, and by examining continuing or recurring elements in narrative art. Our task is incomparably easier than Clara Reeve's. Though the need for a broad approach to narrative art is as pressing now as it was in 1785, the intellectual developments of the intervening years have brought many more of the necessary tools to hand.

From various sources we have learned more in the last hundred years about the pre-history of literature and about pre-modern literature than was ever known before. Vital information that was simply not available to the literary historians and critics of the eighteenth and nineteenth centuries is now available to us. The anthropologists, beginning with Frazer in *The Golden Bough,* have given us priceless information about the relationship between literature and culture in primitive society, opening the way to such literary studies as Jessie Weston's *From Ritual to Romance.* The psychologists—Jung even more than Freud—have given us equally important insights into the ways in which literature is related to an individual's mental processes, making possible a new and fruitful school (despite some excesses) of literary studies—archetypal criticism. The students of oral literature, such as Parry and Lord, have enabled us for the first time to perceive how written and oral literatures are differentiated and what the oral heritage of written narrative actually is. Literary scholars like the classicists Murray and Cornford and the Hebraist Theodore Gaster have shown ways in which some of the new extra-literary knowledge can enhance our understanding of literature. Historians of art and literature, such as Erwin Panofsky and D. W. Robertson, Jr., have made the attitudes and world view of our cultural ancestors more intelligible to us than ever before. And such a brilliant critical synthesizer as Northrop Frye has shown us how it is possible to unite cultural and literary study in such a way as to approach closer to a complete theory of literature than ever before.

Deriving what we could from the example as well as from the techniques and discoveries of such men as these, we have attempted to formulate a theory which would, as clearly and economically as possible, account for the varieties of narrative form and the processes that produce them and govern their interrelationships. Faced with the facts of history, with the various kinds of narrative which have been recognized and classified—often according to different and conflicting systems—and with the "influences," affinities, and correspondences which have been observed, we have tried to do justice to both the intractabilities of fact and the mind's lust for system and order. Our results, with their full and proper range of illustrations and qualifications, are developed in the following chapters. In the remainder of this chapter, we offer a kind of "argument" or gloss for the more elaborate exposition to come. It is a minimal, stripped-down version of our view of the narrative tradition, representing not *a priori* convictions which have shaped our study but rather a pattern we found emerging in the course of it.

The evolution of forms within the narrative tradition is a process analogous in some ways to biological evolution. Man, considering himself the end of an evolutionary process, naturally sees evolution as a struggle toward perfection. The dinosaur, could he speak, might have another opinion. Similarly, a contemporary novelist can see himself as the culmination of an ameliorative evolution; but Homer, could he speak, might disagree. Yet the epic poem is as dead as the dinosaur. We can put together a synthetic epic with a superficial resemblance to the originals, just as we can fabricate a museum dinosaur; but the conditions which produced the originals have passed. God will never recover that lost innocence which He displayed in the creation of those beautiful monsters, nor will man ever again be able to combine so innocently materials drawn from myth and history, from experience and imagination.

Of course, the evolutionary analogy breaks down. The *Iliad* is as great a wonder as a live dinosaur would be. Individual literary works do not always die off, though their forms may cease to be viable. Nor is their reproduction a matter of natural selection. Literary evolution is in some ways more complex than biological evolution. It is a kind of cross between a biological and a dialectical process, in which different species sometimes combine to produce new hybrids, which can in turn combine with other old or new forms; and in which one type will beget its antitype, which in turn may combine with other forms or synthesize with its antitypical originator.

To find a satisfactory means of ordering and presenting the complex processes at work in the evolution of narrative forms is a difficult task. The solution here presented is a compromise between the chaotic and the schematic. It is not offered as a simulacrum of the actual conscious or unconscious mental processes of narrative artists but as a handy way of reducing such processes to manageable terms. Its main purpose is to reveal, by clarifying them, the principal relationships which do exist and have existed historically among the major forms of narrative literature.

Written narrative literature tends to make its appearance throughout the Western world under similar conditions. It emerges from an oral tradition, maintaining many of the characteristics of oral narrative for some time. It often takes that form of heroic, poetic narrative which we call epic. Behind the epic lie a variety of narrative forms, such as sacred myth, quasi-historical legend, and fictional folktale, which have coalesced into a traditional narrative which is an amalgam of myth, history, and fiction. For us, the most important aspect of early written narrative is the fact of the tradition itself. The epic story-teller is telling a traditional story. The primary impulse which moves him is not a historical one, nor a creative one; it is *re*-creative. He is retelling a traditional story, and therefore his primary allegiance is not to fact, not to truth, not to entertainment, but to the *mythos* itself—the story as preserved in the tradition which the epic story-teller is re-creating. The word *mythos* meant precisely this in ancient Greece: a traditional story.

In the transmission of traditional narrative it is of necessity the outline of events, the plot, which is transmitted. Plot is, in every sense of the word, the articulation of the skeleton of narrative. A myth, then, is a traditional plot which can be transmitted. Aristotle saw plot (*mythos* is his word) as the soul of any literary work that was an imitation of an action. Sacred myth, a narrative form associated with religious ritual, is one kind of mythic narrative; but legend and folktale are also mythic in the sense of traditional, and so is the oral epic poem. One of the great developmental processes that is unmistakable in the history of written narrative has been the gradual movement away from narratives dominated by the mythic impulse to tell a story with a traditional plot. In Western literature we can trace this movement twice: once in the classical languages and again in the vernacular languages. In the course of this evolutionary process narrative literature tends to develop in two antithetical directions. A proper understanding of the growth of the two great branches of narrative which emerge as the traditional impulse declines in power is essential to a true appreciation of the evolution of narrative forms. To understand this development properly we must take into account both the nature of the separation between the two great branches of narrative and the interaction and recombination of the two.

The two antithetical types of narrative which emerge from the epic synthesis may be labeled the *empirical* and the *fictional*. Both can be seen as ways of avoiding the tyranny of the traditional in story-telling. Empirical narrative replaces allegiance to the *mythos* with allegiance to reality. We can subdivide the impulse toward empirical narrative into two main components: the *historical* and the *mimetic*. The historical component owes its allegiance specifically to truth of fact and to the actual past rather than to a traditional version of the past. It requires for its development means of accurate measurement in time and space, and concepts of causality referable to human and natural rather than to supernatural agencies. In the ancient world empirical narrative manifests itself first through its historical component as writers like Herodotus and Thucydides carefully distinguish their work from Homeric epic. The mimetic component owes its allegiance not to truth of fact but to truth of sensation and environment, depending on observation of the present rather than investigation of the past. It requires for its development sociological and psychological concepts of behavior and mental process, such as those which inform the characterization of the Alexandrian Mime. Mimetic forms are the slowest of narrative forms to develop. In the ancient world we find the strongest mimetic elements in the Theophrastian Character (a narrative counterpart of the dramatic Mime), in such a realistic "idyll" as Theocritus' *Adoniazusae* (No. 15), and in such a passage as the Dinner at Trimalchio's in Petronius. Mimetic narrative is the antithesis of mythic in that it tends toward plotlessness. Its ultimate form is the "slice of life." Biography and autobiography are both empirical forms of narrative. In biography, which is developed first, the historical impulse dominates; in autobiography, the mimetic.

The *fictional* branch of narrative replaces allegiance to the *mythos* with allegiance to the ideal. We can subdivide the impulse toward fictional narrative into two main components also: the *romantic* and the *didactic*. The writer of fiction is set free from the bonds of tradition and the bonds of empiricism as well. His eye is not on the external world but on the audience, which he hopes to delight or instruct, giving it either what it wants or what he thinks it needs. While empirical narrative aims at one or another kind of truth, fictional narrative aims at either beauty or goodness. The world of romance is the ideal world, in which poetic justice prevails and all the arts and adornments of language are used to embellish the narrative. Where mimetic narrative aims at a psychological reproduction of mental process, romantic narrative presents thought in the form of rhetoric. As the general titles of the two great branches of narrative imply (empirical and fictional) they represent, within the world of narrative literature, an opposition akin to the scientific and the artistic approaches to ultimate truth. In the ancient world, Greek romance, with its alliance between the rhetorical and the erotic, typifies romantic narrative. In the movement from the *Odyssey* to the *Argonautica* we can see the epic becoming more literary and fictional, moving toward such pure romance as the *Aethiopica*. In a modern language such a progression as the *Chanson de Roland,* Chrétien's *Perceval,* and the *Grand Cyrus* reveals the same pattern of evolution.

The didactic subdivision of fiction we may call *fable,* a form which is ruled by an intellectual and moral impulse as romance is ruled by an esthetic one. The human intellect being what it is, fable tends toward brevity in narrative, and is inclined to lean heavily on romance for narrative articulation if the narrative artist has anything like a sustained flight in mind. Aesop's fables are typical of the form, but in its usual combination with romance Xenophon's *Cyropaedia* and the narrative allegories of the Middle Ages and Renaissance are major examples. So-called Menippean satire is fable combined with anti-romance, Lucian's *True History* beginning as a parody of Odysseus' adventures. Literary epic moves from romantic to didactic narrative in Vergil, who did not become Dante's guide in the *Commedia* by accident. Didactic and romantic narrative seek one another out for mutual support and for justification in the face of attacks such as

Plato's attack on poetry in the *Republic*. Sidney's *Defense* of literature is made from the fictional side of the great division we have been considering. He defends literature as presenting an ideal, or "golden," world and as instructing through delight. But Fielding's account of his practice in his Preface to *Joseph Andrews* and elsewhere is made from the empirical side of the line, on the basis of his work's truth to general human nature, though he certainly intended to provide delight and instruction as well.

We have been considering the breakdown of the epic synthesis into two antithetical components. We must now consider briefly the new synthesis in narrative which has been the main development in post-Renaissance narrative literature. This was a gradual process, beginning at least as early as Boccaccio, but it is most obviously discernible in Europe during the seventeenth and eighteenth centuries. The new synthesis can be seen clearly in a writer like Cervantes, whose great work is an attempt to reconcile powerful empirical and fictional impulses. From the synthesis he effected, the novel emerges as a literary form. The novel is not the opposite of romance, as is usually maintained, but a product of the reunion of the empirical and fictional elements in narrative literature. Mimesis (which tends to short forms like the Character and "slice of life") and history (which can become too scientific and cease to be literature) combine in the novel with romance and fable, even as primitive legend, folktale, and sacred myth originally combined in the epic, to produce a great and synthetic literary form. There are signs that in the twentieth century the grand dialectic is about to begin again, and that the novel must yield its place to new forms just as the epic did in ancient times, for it is an unstable compound, inclining always to break down into its constituent elements. The disintegration of the novel is much too complicated to consider here in detail, but we can note that it is reflected in the extreme measures taken by such as Joyce and Proust to counteract it, in the return to romance of Isak Dinesen and Lawrence Durrell, in the reduction of naturalism to absurdity by Samuel Beckett, in the rise of science fiction and the nightmare novels of Céline and Hawkes, and even in the best-seller list, which tends to fragment into sociological narrative and spy-adventure tales, Mary McCarthy and Ian Fleming inevitably reminding us of fiction's ancient heritage from Theophrastian Character and Greek romance.

In its instability the novel partakes of the general nature of narrative. Poised between the direct speaker or singer of lyric and the direct presentation of action in drama; between allegiance to reality and to the ideal; it is capable of greater extremes than other forms of literary art, but pays the price for this capability in its capacity for imperfection. The least formal of disciplines, it offers a domain too broad for any single work to conquer, and it continually provokes literary compromise and subterfuge. The greatest narratives are inevitably those in which the most is attempted. Narrative literature provides, as William Faulkner observed, opportunities for cautious success or glorious failure. It has been, historically, the most various and changeable of literary disciplines, which means that it has been the most alive. For all its imperfections it has been—from the epic to the novel—the most popular and influential kind of literature, seeking the widest audience in its culture and being more responsive to extra-literary influences than other kinds of literature. . . .

※※※

Henry James's Preface to *Portrait of a Lady* is the oldest essay reprinted in this volume; Scholes and Kellogg's "The Nature of Narrative," the most recent. The contrast between their attitudes toward fiction and their means of analyzing it shows a good deal about the major shifts that have taken place in the interests, materials, and methods of modern criticism of fiction. James is not only a critic but a polemicist: advancing his own theories and practices, correcting the errors of his contemporaries and immediate predecessors, and attempting to influence his successors. His perspective is thus limited, for he wishes to focus sharply on the immediate problem. Robert Scholes, best known for his critical and scholarly work on James Joyce, and Robert Kellogg, a specialist in medieval literature, bring to the study of fiction both the scholar's perspective and the modern critic's impatience with a predecessor whose theory and example have become for his followers rigid and imposing monuments. To restore vitality to criticism and to make James's novels a part of rather than the end of a tradition, Scholes and Kellogg, like other modern critics, attack his theories by shifting or broadening the perspective, by finding virtues in methods he disliked and limitations in his own, and by raising new questions about the means and ends of fiction.

The approach to literature taken by Scholes and Kellogg represents a departure not only from the "novel-centered" view of James, Rahv, Harvey, Booth, and Friedman but from the theoretical basis of the New Criticism (now more than thirty years old). Two of the basic tenets of the latter school are, first, the capability of the work of art to be judged apart from biographical, social, and historical considerations (including any opinions that the author may have expressed about it) and apart from its effect on its audience; and, second, the more generally and sometimes unconsciously accepted corollary that the critic should confine himself to a close examination of the text of the work. The followers of the New Critics were to some degree reacting against the excessive concern of literary historians for facts about the lives of artists and about their works as merely biographical or historical documents at the expense of concern for and response to the work of art itself. Opponents of the New Criticism—Rahv and Harvey are the chief examples in this volume—reject its emphasis on form and insist that other considerations, mimetic adequacy to the world of our sensory and ethical perceptions being the most prominent, are far more important. Critics and scholars more recent than either group have begun to insist that the context of a work of art is at least as important as its text, that context cannot, in fact, be separated from the text. Context may include generic, historical, biographical, sociological, rhetorical, philosophical, or bibliographical considerations. According to these critics, no body of relevant information should be excluded; all are ways of seeing the artist's relation to formal and intellectual movements. Used tactfully, these methods can lead to an understanding of not only the work's meaning but the way in which the artist confronts reality by and in the work of art.

Like any other method, this one can be abused. Interest in facts, ideas, and theories can lead the critic away from the work as a work of art—the specific concern of the critic as distinct from the moralist, psychologist, or sociologist—and the reader away from a total response, not merely intellectual or emotional or aesthetic, to the literary work. For example, the generic approach emphasized by Scholes and Kellogg can lead to empty methodizing. Labeling a book as a fictional didactic or an empirical mimetic form of narrative says nothing about its quality or how it, individually, is to be read. More basically, it could be argued that although genres other than the novel have their virtues and their claims to attention, they are not relevant to the reader, who has a set of expectations for a novel, but cannot, without a good deal of scholarly assistance, understand and fully participate in the conventions and therefore the experience of works in other genres. The relevance of a genre as well as the fact of its existence must be established.

Of these objections Scholes and Kellogg are fully aware. As they practice it, the approach through genre proves both valuable and necessary: valuable, because it enables readers to understand and appreciate other forms of narrative, the newest as well as the oldest; necessary, because it forces critics to examine their preconceptions about the function and value of the novel and of all art. Examined preconceptions often become first principles; unexamined ones, mere prejudices.

The strict new critical view of the autonomy of the work of art is presented in "The Intentional Fallacy" and "The Affective Fallacy," both written in collaboration by W. K. Wimsatt and Monroe C. Beardsley and reprinted in Wimsatt's *The Verbal Icon: Studies in the Meaning of Poetry.** For Wimsatt's further development, clarification, and defense of his views, see *Hateful Contraries: Studies in Literature and Criticism,*† particularly "Horses of Wrath," an analytical survey of modern critical theories. New methods of blending criticism and scholarship are given an interesting theoretical defense by E. D. Hirsch, Jr., in "Objective Interpretation."‡ An excellent evaluation and extension of the argument presented in *The Nature of Narrative* and David Lodge's *Language of Fiction*§ can be found in Malcolm Bradbury's review, "The Language Novelists Use."||

---

* Lexington: University of Kentucky Press, 1954.
† Lexington: University of Kentucky Press, 1965.
‡ *PMLA,* LXXV (September 1960), 463–79.
§ New York: Columbia University Press, 1966.
|| *Kenyon Review,* XXIX (January 1967), 123–36.

Specific Continuous Forms (Prose Fiction)

NORTHROP FRYE

In assigning the term fiction to the genre of the written word, in which prose tends to become the predominating rhythm, we collide with the view that the real meaning of fiction is falsehood or unreality. Thus an autobiography coming into a library would be classified as non-fiction if the librarian believed the author, and as fiction if she thought he was lying. It is difficult to see what use such a distinction can be to a literary critic. Surely the word fiction, which, like poetry, means etymologically something made for its own sake, could be applied in criticism to any work of literary art in a radically continuous form, which almost always means a work of art in prose. Or, if that is too much to ask, at least some protest can be entered against the sloppy habit of identifying fiction with the one genuine form of fiction which we know as the novel.

Let us look at a few of the unclassified books lying on the boundary of "non-fiction" and "literature." Is *Tristram Shandy* a novel? Nearly everyone would say yes, in spite of its easygoing disregard of "story values." Is *Gulliver's Travels* a novel? Here most would demur, including the Dewey decimal system, which puts it under "Satire and Humor." But surely everyone would call it fiction, and if it is fiction, distinction appears between fiction as a genus and the novel as a species of that genus. Shifting the ground to fiction, then, is *Sartor Resartus* fiction? If not, why not? If it is, is *The Anatomy of Melancholy* fiction? Is it a literary form or only a work of "non-fiction" written with "style"? Is Borrow's *Lavengro* fiction?

Everyman's Library says yes; the World's Classics puts it under "Travel and Topography."

The literary historian who identifies fiction with the novel is greatly embarrassed by the length of time that the world managed to get along without the novel, and until he reaches his great deliverance in Defoe, his perspective is intolerably cramped. He is compelled to reduce Tudor fiction to a series of tentative essays in the novel form, which works well enough for Deloney but makes nonsense of Sidney. He postulates a great fictional gap in the seventeenth century which exactly covers the golden age of rhetorical prose. He finally discovers that the word novel, which up to about 1900 was still the name of a more or less recognizable form, has since expanded into a catchall term which can be applied to practically any prose book that is not "on" something. Clearly, this novel-centered view of prose fiction is a Ptolemaic perspective which is now too complicated to be any longer workable, and some more relative and Copernican view must take its place.

When we start to think seriously about the novel, not as fiction, but as a form of fiction, we feel that its characteristics, whatever they are, are such as make, say, Defoe, Fielding, Austen, and James central in its tradition, and Borrow, Peacock, Melville, and Emily Bronte somehow peripheral. This is not an estimate of merit: we may think *Moby Dick* "greater" than *The Egoist* and yet feel that Meredith's book is closer to being a typical novel. Fielding's conception of the novel as a comic epic in prose seems fundamental to the tradition he did so much to establish. In novels that we think of as typical, like those of Jane Austen, plot and dialogue are closely linked to the conventions of the comedy of manners. The conventions of *Wuthering Heights* are linked rather with the tale and the ballad. They seem to have more affinity with tragedy, and the tragic emotions of passion and fury, which would shatter the balance of tone in Jane Austen, can be safely accommodated here. So can the supernatural, or the suggestion of it, which is difficult to get into a novel. The shape of the plot is different: instead of manoeuvering around a central situation, as Jane Austen does, Emily Bronte tells her story with linear accents, and she seems to need the help of a narrator, who would be absurdly out of place in Jane Austen. Conventions so different justify us in regarding *Wuthering Heights* as a different form of prose fiction from the novel, a form which we shall here call the romance. Here again we have to use the same word in several different contexts, but romance seems on the whole better than tale, which appears to fit a somewhat shorter form.

The essential difference between novel and romance lies in the conception of characterization. The romancer does not attempt to create "real people" so much as stylized figures which expand into psychological archetypes. It is in the romance that we find Jung's libido, anima, and shadow reflected in the hero, heroine, and villain respectively. That is why the romance so often radiates a glow of subjective intensity that the novel lacks, and why a suggestion of allegory is constantly creeping in around its fringes. Certain elements of character are released in the romance which make it naturally a more revolutionary form than the novel. The novelist deals with personality, with characters wearing their *personae* or social masks. He needs the framework of a stable society, and many of our best novelists have been conventional to the verge of fussiness. The romancer deals with individuality, with characters *in vacuo* idealized by revery, and, however conservative he may be, something nihilistic and untamable is likely to keep breaking out of his pages.

The prose romance, then, is an independent form of fiction to be distinguished from the novel and extracted from the miscellaneous heap of prose works now covered by that term. Even in the other heap known as short stories one can isolate the tale form used by Poe, which bears the same relation to the full romance that the stories of Chekhov or Katherine Mansfield do to the novel. "Pure" examples of either form are never found; there is hardly any modern romance that could not be made out to be a novel, and vice versa. The forms of prose fiction are mixed, like racial strains in human beings, not separable like the sexes. In fact the popular demand in fiction is always for a mixed form, a romantic novel just romantic enough for the reader to project his libido on the hero and his anima on the heroine, and just novel enough to keep these projections in a familiar world. It may be asked, therefore, what is the use of making the above distinction, especially when, though undeveloped in criticism, it is by no means unrealized. It is no surprise to hear that Trollope wrote novels and William Morris romances.

The reason is that a great romancer should be examined in terms of the conventions he chose. William Morris should not be left on the side lines of prose fiction merely because the critic has not learned to take the romance form seriously. Nor, in view of what has been said about the revolutionary nature of the romance, should his choice of that form be regarded as an "escape" from his social attitude. If Scott has any claims to be a romancer, it is not good criticism to deal only with his defects as a novelist. The romantic qualities of *The Pilgrim's Progress,* too, its archetypal characterization and its revolutionary approach to religious experience, make it a well-rounded example of a literary form: it is not merely a book swallowed by English literature to get some religious bulk in its diet. Finally, when Hawthorne, in the preface to *The House of the Seven Gables,* insists that his story should be read as romance and not as novel, it is possible that he meant what he said, even though he indicates that the prestige of the rival form has induced the romancer to apologize for not using it.

Romance is older than the novel, a fact which has developed the historical illusion that it is something to be outgrown, a juvenile and undeveloped form. The social affinities of the romance, with its grave idealizing of heroism and purity, are with the aristocracy.... It revived in the period we call Romantic as part of the Romantic tendency to archaic feudalism and a cult of the hero, or idealized libido. In England the romances of Scott and, in less degree, the Brontes, are part of a mysterious Northumbrian renaissance, a Romantic reaction against the new industrialism in the Midlands, which also produced the poetry of Wordsworth and Burns and the philosophy of Carlyle. It is not surprising, therefore, that an important theme in the more bourgeois novel should be the parody of the romance and its ideals. The tradition established by *Don Quixote* continues in a type of novel which looks at a romantic situation from its own point of view, so that the conventions of the two forms make up an ironic compound instead of a sentimental mixture. Examples range from *Northanger Abbey* to *Madame Bovary* and *Lord Jim.*

The tendency to allegory in the romance may be conscious, as in *The Pilgrim's Progress,* or unconscious, as in the very obvious sexual mythopoeia in William Morris. The romance, which deals with heroes, is intermediate between the novel, which deals with men, and the myth, which deals with gods. Prose romance first appears as a late development of Classical mythology, and the prose Sagas of Iceland follow close on the mythical Eddas. The novel tends rather to expand into a fictional approach to history. The soundness of Fielding's instinct in calling *Tom Jones* a history is confirmed by the general rule that the larger the scheme of a novel becomes, the more obviously its historical nature appears. As it is creative history, however, the novelist usually prefers his material in a plastic, or roughly contemporary state, and feels cramped by a fixed historical pattern. *Waverley* is dated about sixty years back from the time of writing and *Little Dorrit* about forty years, but the historical pattern is fixed in the romance and plastic in the novel, suggesting the general principle that most "historical novels" are romances. Similarly a novel becomes more romantic in its appeal when the life it reflects has passed away: thus the novels of Trollope were read primarily as romances during the Second World War. It is perhaps the link with history and a sense of temporal context that has confined the novel, in striking contrast to the worldwide romance, to the alliance of time and Western man.

Autobiography is another form which merges with the novel by a series of insensible gradations. Most autobiographies are inspired by a creative, and therefore fictional, impulse to select only those events and experiences in the writer's life that go to build up an integrated pattern. This pattern may be something larger than himself with which he has come to identify himself, or simply the coherence of his character and attitudes. We may call this very important form of prose fiction the confession form, following St. Augustine, who appears to have invented it, and Rousseau, who established a modern type of it. The earlier tradition gave *Religio Medici, Grace Abounding,* and Newman's *Apologia* to English literature, besides the related but subtly different type of confession favored by the mystics.

Here again, as with the romance, there is some value in recognizing a distinct prose form in the confession. It gives several of our best prose works a definable place in fiction instead of keeping them in a vague limbo of books which are not quite literature because they are "thought," and not quite religion or philosophy because they are Examples of Prose Style. The confession, too, like the novel and the romance, has its own short form, the familiar essay, and Montaigne's *livre de bonne foy* is a confession made up of essays in which only the continuous narrative of the longer form is missing. Montaigne's scheme is to the confession what a work of fiction made up of short stories, such as Joyce's *Dubliners* or Boccaccio's *Decameron,* is to the novel or romance.

After Rousseau—in fact in Rousseau—the confession flows into the novel, and the mixture produces the fictional autobiography, the *Künstler-roman,* and kindred types. There is no literary reason why the subject of a confession should always be the author himself, and dramatic confessions have been used in the novel at least since *Moll Flanders.* The "stream of consciousness" technique permits of a much more concentrated fusion of the two forms, but even here the characteristics peculiar to the confession form show up clearly. Nearly always some theoretical and intellectual interest in religion, politics, or art plays a leading role in the confession. It is his success in integrating his mind on such subjects that makes the author of a confession feel that his life is worth writing about. But this interest in ideas and theoretical statements is alien to the genius of the novel proper, where the technical problem is to dissolve all theory into personal relationships. In Jane Austen, to take a familiar instance, church, state, and culture are never examined except as social data, and Henry James has been described as having a mind so fine that no idea could violate it. The novelist who cannot get along without ideas, or has not the patience to digest them in the way that James did, instinctively resorts to what Mill calls a "mental history" of a single character. And when we find that a technical discussion of a theory of aesthetics forms the climax of Joyce's *Portrait,* we realize that what makes this possible is the presence in that novel of another tradition of prose fiction.

The novel tends to be extroverted and personal; its chief interest is in human character as it manifests itself in society. The romance tends to be introverted and personal: it also deals with characters, but in a more subjective way. (Subjective here refers to treatment, not subject matter. The characters of romance are heroic and therefore inscrutable; the novelist is freer to enter his characters' minds because he is more objective.) The confession is also introverted, but intellectualized in content. Our next step is evidently to discover a fourth form of fiction which is extroverted and intellectual.

We remarked earlier that most people would call *Gulliver's Travels* fiction but not a novel. It must then be another form of fiction, as it certainly has a form, and we feel that we are turning from the novel to this form, whatever it is, when we turn from Rousseau's *Emile* to Voltaire's *Candide,* or from Butler's *The Way of All Flesh* to the Erewhon books, or from Huxley's *Point Counterpoint* to *Brave New World.* The form thus has its own traditions, and, as the examples of Butler and Huxley show, has preserved some integrity even under the ascendancy of the novel. Its existence is easy enough to demonstrate, and no one will challenge the statement that the literary ancestry of *Gulliver's Travels* and *Candide* runs through Rabelais and Erasmus to Lucian. But while much has been said about the style and thought of Rabelais, Swift, and Voltaire, very little has been made of them as craftsmen working in a specific medium, a point no one dealing with a novelist would ignore. Another great writer in this tradition, Huxley's master Peacock, has fared even worse, for, his form not being understood, a general impression has grown up that his status in the development of prose fiction is that of a slapdash eccentric. Actually, he is as exquisite and precise an artist in his medium as Jane Austen is in hers.

The form used by these authors is the Menippean satire, also more rarely called the Varronian satire, allegedly invented by a Greek cynic named Menippus. His works are lost, but he had two great disciples, the Greek Lucian and the Roman Varro, and the tradition of Varro, who has not survived either except in fragments, was carried on by Petronius and Apuleius. The Menippean satire appears to have developed out of verse satire through the practice of adding prose interludes, but we know it only as a prose form, though one of its recurrent features (seen in Peacock) is the use of incidental verse.

The Menippean satire deals less with people as such than with mental attitudes. Pedants, bigots, cranks, parvenus, virtuosi, enthusiasts, rapacious and incompetent professional men of all kinds, are handled in terms of their occupational approach to life as distinct from their social behavior. The Menippean satire thus resembles the confession in its ability to handle abstract ideas and theories, and differs from the novel in its characterization, which is stylized rather than naturalistic, and presents people as mouthpieces of the ideas they represent. Here again no sharp boundary lines can or should be drawn, but if we compare a character in Jane Austen with a similar character in Peacock we can immediately feel the difference between the two forms. Squire Western belongs to the novel, but Thwackum and Square have Menippean blood in them. A constant theme in the tradition is the ridicule of the *philosophus gloriosus*. ...The novelist sees evil and folly as social diseases, but the Menippean satirist sees them as diseases of the intellect, as a kind of maddened pedantry which the *philosophus gloriosus* at once symbolizes and defines.

Petronius, Apuleius, Rabelais, Swift, and Voltaire all use a loose-jointed narrative form often confused with the romance. It differs from the romance, however (though there is a strong admixture of romance in Rabelais), as it is not primarily concerned with the exploits of heroes, but relies on the free play of intellectual fancy and the kind of humorous observation that produces caricature. It differs also from the picaresque form, which has the novel's interest in the actual structure of society. At its most concentrated the Menippean satire presents us with a vision of the world in terms of a single intellectual pattern. The intellectual structure built up from the story makes for violent dislocations in the customary logic of narrative, though the appearance of carelessness that results reflects only the carelessness of the reader or his tendency to judge by a novel-centered conception of fiction.

The word "satire," in Roman and Renaissance times, meant either of two specific literary forms of that name, one (this one) prose and the other verse. Now it means a structural principle or attitude, what we have called a *mythos*. In the Menippean satires we have been discussing, the name of the form also applies to the attitude. As the name of an attitude, satire is, we have seen, a combination of fantasy and morality. But as the name of a form, the term satire, though confined to literature (for as a *mythos* it may appear in any art, a cartoon, for example), is more flexible, and can be either entirely fantastic or entirely moral. The Menippean adventure story may thus be pure fantasy, as it is in the literary fairy tale. The Alice books are perfect Menippean satires, and so is *The Water-Babies,* which has been influenced by Rabelais. The purely moral type is a serious vision of society as a single intellectual pattern, in other words a Utopia.

The short form of the Menippean satire is usually a dialogue or colloquy, in which the dramatic interest is in a conflict of ideas rather than of character. This is the favorite form of Erasmus, and is common in Voltaire. Here again the form is not invariably satiric in attitude, but shades off into more purely fanciful or moral discussions, like the *Imaginary Conversations* of Landor or the "dialogue of the dead." Sometimes this form expands to full length, and more than two speakers are used: the setting then is usually a *cena* or symposium, like the one that looms so large in Petronius. Plato, though much earlier in the field than Menippus, is a strong influence on this type, which stretches in an unbroken tradition down through those urbane and leisurely conversations which define the ideal courtier in Castiglione or the doctrine and discipline of angling in

Walton. A modern development produces the country-house weekends in Peacock, Huxley, and their imitators in which the opinions and ideas and cultural interests expressed are as important as the lovemaking.

The novelist shows his exuberance either by an exhaustive analysis of human relationships, as in Henry James, or of social phenomena, as in Tolstoy. The Menippean satirist, dealing with intellectual themes and attitudes, shows his exuberance in intellectual ways, by piling up an enormous mass of erudition about his theme or in overwhelming his pedantic targets with an avalanche of their own jargon. A species, or rather sub-species, of the form is the kind of encyclopaedic farrago represented by Athenaeus' *Deipnosophists* and Macrobius' *Saturnalia*, where people sit at a banquet and pour out a vast mass of erudition on every subject that might conceivably come up in a conversation. The display of erudition had probably been associated with the Menippean tradition by Varro, who was enough of a polymath to make Quintilian, if not stare and gasp, at any rate call him *vir Romanorum eruditissimus.* The tendency to expand into an encyclopaedic farrago is clearly marked in Rabelais, notably in the great catalogues of torcheculs and epithets of codpieces and methods of divination. The encyclopaedic compilations produced in the line of duty by Erasmus and Voltaire suggest that a magpie instinct to collect facts is not unrelated to the type of ability that has made them famous as artists. Flaubert's encyclopaedic approach to the construction of *Bouvard et Pecuchet* is quite comprehensible if we explain it as marking an affinity with the Menippean tradition.

This creative treatment of exhaustive erudition is the organizing principle of the greatest Menippean satire in English before Swift, Burton's *Anatomy of Melancholy*. Here human society is studied in terms of the intellectual pattern provided by the conception of melancholy, a symposium of books replaces dialogue, and the result is the most comprehensive survey of human life in one book that English literature had seen since Chaucer, one of Burton's favorite authors. We may note in passing the Utopia in his introduction and his "digressions," which when examined turn out to be scholarly distillations of Menippean forms: the digression of air, of the marvellous journey; the digression of spirits, of the ironic use of erudition; the digression of the miseries of scholars, of the satire on the *philosophus gloriosus*. The word "anatomy" in Burton's title means a dissection or analysis, and expresses very accurately the intellectualized approach of his form. We may as well adopt it as a convenient name to replace the cumbersome and in modern times rather misleading "Menippean satire."

The anatomy, of course, eventually begins to merge with the novel, producing various hybrids including the *roman à these* and novels in which the characters are symbols of social or other ideas, like the proletarian novels of the thirties in this century. It was Sterne, however, the disciple of Burton and Rabelais, who combined them with greatest success. *Tristram Shandy* may be, as was said at the beginning, a novel, but the digressing narrative, the catalogues, the stylizing of character along "humor" lines, the marvellous journey of the great nose, the symposium discussions, and the constant ridicule of philosophers and pedantic critics are all features that belong to the anatomy.

A clearer understanding of the form and traditions of the anatomy would make a good many elements in the history of literature come into focus. Boethius' *Consolation of Philosophy,* with its dialogue form, its verse interludes and its pervading tone of contemplative irony, is a pure anatomy, a fact of considerable importance for the understanding of its vast influence. *The Compleat Angler* is an anatomy because of its mixture of prose and verse, its rural *cena* setting, its dialogue form, its deipnosophistical interest in food, and its gentle Menippean raillery of a society which considers everything more important than fishing and yet has discovered very few better things to do. In nearly every period of literature there are many romances, confessions, and anatomies that are neglected only because the categories to which they belong are unrecognized. In the period between Sterne and Peacock, for example, we have, among romances, *Melmoth the Wanderer*; among confessions, Hogg's *Confessions of a Justified Sinner*; among anatomies, Southey's *Doctor,* Amory's *John Buncle,* and the *Noctes Ambrosianae.*

To sum up then: when we examine fiction from the point of view of form, we can see four chief strands binding it together, novel, confession, anatomy, and romance. The six possible combinations of these forms all exist, and we have shown how the novel has combined with each of the other three. Exclusive concentration on one form is rare: the early novels of George Eliot, for instance, are influenced by the romance, and the later ones by the anatomy. The romance-confession hybrid is found, naturally, in the autobiography of a romantic temperament, and is represented in English by the extroverted George Borrow and the introverted De Quincey. The romance-anatomy one we have noticed in Rabelais; a later example is *Moby Dick,* where the romantic theme of the wild hunt expands into an encyclopaedic anatomy of the whale. Confession and anatomy are united in *Sartor Resartus* and in some of Kierkegaard's strikingly original experiments in prose fiction form, including *Either/Or.* More comprehensive fictional schemes usually employ at least three forms: we can see strains of novel, romance, and confession in *Pamela,* of novel, romance, and anatomy in *Don Quixote,* of novel, confession, and anatomy in Proust, and of romance, confession, and anatomy in Apuleius.

I deliberately make this sound schematic in order to suggest the advantage of having a simple and logical explanation for the form of, say, *Moby Dick* or *Tristram Shandy.* The usual critical approach to the form of such works resembles that of the doctors in Brobdingnag, who after great wrangling finally pronounced Gulliver a *luses naturae.* It is the anatomy in particular that has baffled critics, and there is hardly any fiction writer deeply influenced by it who has not been accused of disorderly conduct. The reader may be reminded here of Joyce, for describing Joyce's books as monstrous has become a nervous tic. I find "demogorgon," "behemoth," and "white elephant" in good critics; the bad ones could probably do much better. The care that Joyce took to organize *Ulysses* and *Finnegans Wake* amounted nearly to obsession, but as they are not organized on familiar principles of prose fiction, the impression of shapelessness remains. Let us try our formulas on him.

If a reader were asked to set down a list of the things that had most impressed him about *Ulysses,* it might reasonably be somewhat as follows. First, the clarity with which the sights and sounds and smells of Dublin come to life, the rotundity of the character-drawing, and the naturalness of the dialogue. Second, the elaborate way that the story and characters are parodied by being set against archetypal heroic patterns, notably the one provided by the *Odyssey.* Third, the revelation of character and incident through the searching use of the stream-of-consciousness technique. Fourth, the constant tendency to be encyclopaedic and exhaustive both in technique and in subject matter, and to see both in highly intellectualized terms. It should not be too hard for us by now to see that these four points describe elements in the book which relate to the novel, romance, confession, and anatomy respectively. *Ulysses,* then, is a complete prose epic with all four forms employed in it, all of practically equal importance, and all essential to one another, so that the book is a unity and not an aggregate.

This unity is built up from an intricate scheme of parallel contrasts. The romantic archetypes of Hamlet and Ulysses are like remote stars in a literary heaven looking down quizzically on the shabby creatures of Dublin obediently intertwining themselves in the patterns set by their influences. In the "Cyclops" and "Circe" episodes particularly there is a continuous parody of realistic patterns by romantic ones which reminds us, though the irony leans in the opposite direction, of *Madame Bovary.* The relation of novel and confession techniques is similar; the author jumps into his characters' minds to follow their stream of consciousness, and out again to describe them externally. In the novel-anatomy combination, too, found in the "Ithaca" chapter, the sense of lurking antagonism between the personal and intellectual aspects of the scene accounts for much of its pathos. The same principle of parallel contrast holds good for the other three combinations: of romance and confession in "Nausicaa" and "Penelope," of confession and anatomy in "Proteus" and "The Lotos-Eaters," of romance and anatomy (a rare and fitful combination) in "Sirens" and parts of "Circe."

In *Finnegans Wake* the unity of design goes far beyond this. The dingy story of the sodden HCE and his pinched wife is not contrasted with the archetypes of Tristram and the divine king: HCE is himself Tristram and the divine king. As the setting is a dream, no contrast is possible between confession and novel, between a stream of consciousness inside the mind and the appearances of other people outside it. Nor is the experiential world of the novel to be separated from the intelligible world of the anatomy. The forms we have been isolating in fiction, and which depend for their existence on the commonsense dichotomies of the daylight consciousness, vanish in *Finnegans Wake* into a fifth and quintessential form. This form is the one traditionally associated with scriptures and sacred books, and treats life in terms of the fall and awakening of the human soul and the creation and apocalypse of nature. The Bible is the definitive example of it; the Egyptian Book of the Dead and the Icelandic Prose Edda, both of which have left deep imprints on *Finnegans Wake,* also belong to it.

✻✻✻✻

This essay (in its earlier version, "The Four Forms of Prose Fiction") * has been the most important influence on the generic approach to prose fiction in recent criticism. In the first place, Frye defended the idea of genre and insisted that it could be used "not so much to classify as to clarify...traditions and affinities, thereby bringing out a large number of literary relationships that would not be noticed as long as there were no context established for them." (*Anatomy of Criticism,* pp. 247–48.) Second, he provided a set of terms with which to label works and make it possible for later critics to divest themselves of preconceptions based on the realistic novel.

However useful it may be, Frye's essay does not go far enough in analyzing and judging. He notes that the four types almost inevitably overlap, but for the most part he leaves unexplored the effects possible with mixed forms. Scholes and Kellogg, who acknowledge a major debt to Frye, extend the discussion of this point in *The Nature of Narrative* and broaden the historical perspective to put the discussion of fictional forms into a clearer, if more limited, context. In *The Plot of Satire,*† Alvin B. Kernan demonstrates that satire has its own patterns of development and is far from the "loose-jointed narrative form" that Frye rather casually describes. Further study needs to be devoted to the historical development of forms other than the novel. Granted that they explore areas of experience other than the mimetic and that they should not be judged in terms of the novel, but what are those areas? How should they be judged? Traditional means of analysis and explication, some of which are discussed in other essays in this volume, can be used to supplement generic criticism, but future theorists need to develop means of dealing with the forms that Frye has described.

The most important supplement to this essay is the whole of *Anatomy of Criticism.* Among the more valuable chapters for the student of fiction are Frye's discussion of fictional modes in "Historical Criticism: Theory of Modes" and of "The Mythos of Winter: Irony and Satire." Evaluations of the strengths and limitations of his method are presented in *Northrop Frye in Modern Criticism,* edited by Murray Krieger.‡

---

* *Hudson Review,* II (Winter 1950), 582–95.
† New Haven: Yale University Press, 1965.
‡ New York: Columbia University Press, 1966.

The Novel as a Genre

MAURICE Z. SHRODER

When we speak of "the novel" in general terms, we are—willingly or unwillingly—accepting the assumption that genre has more than a theoretical reality. Presumably, then, we should be able to offer a description of that genre, to say what a novel is and what distinguishes it from other forms of prose fiction. Yet students of literature—and even so eminent a witness as E. M. Forster—seem to be uneasy with any definition of the novel more elaborate than the formulae familiar to authors of literary manuals. The novel, according to such handbooks, is merely "a fictional narrative in prose, of substantial length"; but so, one may add, are the prose *Lancelot, Pilgrim's Progress,* Ballanche's *Orphée,* and *Finnegans Wake,* none of which could qualify as novels were we to compare them with *Don Quixote* or *Madame Bovary, The Egoist* or *The Ambassadors,* "fictional narratives, etc." that are unquestionably novels and nothing else.

The reluctance to provide more explicit and more substantial descriptions of the novel may reflect the admirable desire to avoid the pitfalls of prescriptive theories of genre. But Aristotle's reflections on tragedy have outlasted those "rules" that later critics dredged from the *Poetics;* and Aristotle's attempt at description should remain our example. We must really face the facts of critical responsibility, and we must either drop such general categories as "the novel," "the romance," and so on, or be prepared to offer justifications for such terms, in the form of more extensive descriptions and discussions. This is not a matter of mere academic quibbling; the question is, as Humpty Dumpty neatly puts it to Alice, "which is to be master"—the words we use or we who use them. Especially in the criticism of literature, when we do not define our terms as precisely as possible, we invite exactly that form of bamboozling in which Humpty Dumpty himself indulges.

An adequate definition of the novel would, of course, have to be totally comprehensive, exhaustive, and infallible. It would have to borrow at once from the history of literature, the study of external form, and the study of the fictional matter of novels in general. I cannot pretend that the pages which follow are any more than a suggestion of the direction such a study might take; I am, indeed, more interested in the matter of the novel and in the testimony provided by literary history than I am in questions of external form, specific novelistic techniques and the stylistic peculiarities of individual novelists. My reason is a simple one. The realities of genre underlie individual and external variations—an eclogue is an eclogue in unrhymed iambic pentameter or in alexandrine couplets; and just as we look, in an eclogue, for characteristic imagery and a vision of the world peculiar to the genre, so in examining the novel we should look first at the matter which is susceptible to a variety of shapes. Like any narrative form, the novel has a typical action, with thematic value, which is peculiarly its own.

The matter of the novel—the theme that has informed the genre from *Don Quixote* onward—is relatively uncomplicated. The novel records the passage from a state of innocence to a state of experience, from that ignorance which is bliss to a mature recognition of the actual way of the world. In the less loaded terms of Lionel Trilling, the novel deals with a distinction between appearance and reality. It is not necessarily a question of ontological subtleties: the reality to which the novel appeals is that to which it is historically connected, the reality of bourgeois life, of business, and of the modern city. The first Falstaff, as he stands on the field of Shrewsbury, the thought of money metaphorically coloring his speech—as he questions the value of such aristocratic absolutes as chivalric honor and resolves to be a live coward—Falstaff embodies the sensibility that will make the novel possible. The great expectations of the young Hotspur find ironic responses in the lost illusions of the old Sir John. The protagonist of the novel follows the same pattern of disillusionment—which Harry Levin sees as a major part of what we call realism—from potential fulfillment to actual accomplishment, from a hopeful naïveté to a resigned wisdom.

Thematically, then, the novel distinguishes itself from the romance, in which the protagonist proves himself a hero, actually fulfills his heroic potentiality. *Vanity Fair*—"A Novel Without a Hero"—is rather an exemplary case than an exception. The protagonist of a novel is likely to be an "anti-hero," an "unheroic hero," as Raymond Giraud calls him—a Miniver Cheevy or a Walter Mitty who is able to elaborate his dreams of glory only by ignoring the material realities of his station and his times.

The action of the novel (which receives various episodic developments, as it informs the particular intrigue or plot of any given novel) is essentially a reworking of the basic action of romance—that familiar story which Joseph Campbell discusses, in *The Hero With a Thousand Faces*, as the "monomyth," and to which Northrop Frye, in his *Anatomy of Criticism*, gives the more descriptive name of "the quest." A young man goes forth to discover his own nature and the nature of the world; he is often in search of his name, his father, in search of a mysterious treasure. The completion of the quest proves the young man, if he is the protagonist of a romance, to be what he, and the author, and we the readers knew from the start that he was —a hero. In the novel, the "going forth" may be metaphorical rather than actual; but the voyage often provides the novelistic framework, and the protagonist's movement is always from a narrow environment to a broader one. He may move in space, like Dickens' Pip, from the English countryside to London, and like Balzac's Lucien de Rubempré, from the provinces to Paris; he may move rather in time, with Austen's Emma or Proust's Marcel, from the restricted awareness of childhood to the wider experience of maturity. The goal of the quest—the name and the treasure—may or may not be achieved; but the protagonist of the novel is likely to discover, with Falstaff, that there is no future for heroism, that he himself is a perfectly ordinary man, with the experience and the knowledge that suit his station. The magic name itself proves to be merely an inaccurate pseudonym: Don Quixote, the Knight of the Sad Countenance, is really Alonso Quixano; Lucien de Rubempré—the young "aristocrat"—was born Lucien Chardon.

Although Don Quixote dies with his boots off and Lucien hangs himself in prison, this is not to say that all romances end happily, while all novels end unhappily, that romances incline toward comedy and novels toward tragedy. The hero of a romance may realize his heroic potential only in death—the triumph of the *Liebestod* at the close of the Tristan legend is perhaps our most familiar example. The protagonist of a novel, on the other hand, may—like Elizabeth Bennet and Tom Jones, Eugène de Rastignac and Pierre Bezukhov—live happily ever after; yet all these protagonists succeed only because they have let fall their illusions and their pride. Such a fall, in a novel, is a happy one, since it represents the completion of that educational process with which the novel deals, an education into the realities of the material world and of human life in society.

In other words, the *Bildungsroman* is not merely a special category: the theme of the novel is essentially that of formation, of education. The terms of the education are themselves important, since the process described in the novel is analogous to that described in two other fictional forms, which serve perhaps as the boundaries between which the novelistic sensibility functions. At one extreme stands the romance, with its tale of triumphant adventure and its heroic protagonist. At the other extreme stand such *contes philosophiques* as *Candide* and *Gulliver's Travels,* tales which depend on protagonists who are incredibly naïve and largely unheroic, which deal in the disillusionments one suffers in trying to apply systems to the unsystematic realities of life. The novel, as the French critic Gustave Kahn suggested, is perhaps more like the *conte philosophique* than like the romance, in that it records a similar process of disillusionment; but while philosophical tales cast such disillusionment in ideological terms, novels treat it experientially, in the terms of quotidian reality. Both the novel and the philosophical tale, however, reject that "spirit of romance" which sees the world through a haze of imaginative and subjective interpretation, colored at the least by sentimentality and transformed at the most by the poetry of legend and of myth.

Ortega y Gasset put the matter succinctly in his first book, the recently translated *Meditations on Quixote.* "The myth," Ortega wrote, "is always the starting point of all poetry, including the realistic, except that in the latter we accompany the myth in its descent, in its fall. This collapse of the poetic is the theme of realistic poetry" (p. 144). "Myth" in this context means primarily the thorough transformation—and perhaps elevation—of reality through imaginative projection; the process of the novel (as all critics would, I think, agree) is one of "demythification," the formal or generic equivalent to the experiential disillusionment of the novel's protagonist. Were we to define "myth" in the more limited sense in which it applies to the epic, it would be possible to consider the novel the epic of the modern world, or (in Fielding's phrase) "a comic epic in prose."

The mock-heroic passages in *Tom Jones* strengthen the argument, as do such isolated cases as Thackeray's theories of the epic novel and Rémy de Gourmont's reference to *L'Education sentimentale* as the French *Odyssey*—and *Ulysses* would of course fall in line to continue the process into the twentieth century. Nevertheless, the general testimony of literary history suggests that the novel more surely derived from its immediate predecessor, the romance of the Middle Ages and of the Renaissance, than from the epic. The mockepic—written more often in verse than in prose—all but disappeared with neoclassicism; the mock-romance—a *Roman comique* or a *Roman bourgeois*—is a crucial step in the development of the novel, an imitation of Cervantes' example. Formally or generically, then, the novel is an "anti-romance"—the term, after all, originally designated Sorel's *Berger extravagant,* which literally began where *Don Quixote* left off, with a reduction to the absurd of pastoral romance. Useful as the concept of "demythification" is, however, it is somewhat misleading: it is a critical category, while the terms of the novel are experiential. In such terms, what is revealed as illusory—as mere imaginative projection, "myth" in the pejorative sense of the word—is not quite another genre, the romance, and another literary mode than the realistic (what we are forced to call both the romantic and the romanesque). It is rather the state of mind that evokes and informs that genre and that mode, what we might call (and in so doing avoid the double adjective) the "romance sensibility."

At the root of the romance sensibility lies as active—or, in terms of the novel's process of demythification and disillusionment, an *over-active*—imagination. Jane Austen's Emma Woodhouse, for whom romance takes on the popular associations of love and marriage, calls herself an "imaginist"; and her education involves the recognition that the reality of her world is not identical with her wishes and fancies. Flaubert's Emma Bovary suffers from a more critical form of the same disorder, which Jules de Gaultier labeled *le Bovarysme,* a divorce form reality so great that it renders Madame Bovary incapable of accepting her limitations and resigning herself to the dreary provincial towns in which she lives. At its most extreme, the romance sensibility simply turns into madness, imaginative monomania —the spirit of a Don Quixote, which peoples the world with giants and maidens, transforms the world into a theatre for adventure. Don Quixote sees an army with banners in every flock of sheep; it is thus not surprising to find Stendhal's Fabrice del Dongo, after the disillusionment of Waterloo, his own devastating initiation into reality, seeing only a flock of sheep in the retreating and bedraggled French army. But Stendhal is far from finished with his young protagonist: Fabrice's reaction is one of adolescent cynicism, an overstatement as illusory and potentially as dangerous as Don Quixote's romanesque hyperbole. The sensibility that produces novels—I think of Falstaff catechizing himself on the plains of Shrewsbury—asks questions instead of making contrary statements. In what is perhaps the most thoroughly emblematic scene in Cervantes' novel, Don Quixote loudly proclaims that a group of windmills are giants. The adequate response to such a statement is not the contrary assertion, that giants are merely windmills. It is the question asked by the unwilling squire, Sancho Panza: "What giants?" In that crucial question, the innocent Sancho makes explicit the distinction between the novel and the romance.

In the opposition of Don Quixote and Sancho Panza, Cervantes translated into human terms the literary and technical distinctions between his book and the romances he parodied. Don Quixote is the incarnation of the romance sensibility which (while it may be madness) "mythifies," renders the world more poetic and more adventurous. His manner is one of naïveté, a curious combination of innocence and ignorance. Sancho, on the other hand (while just as naïve, and while he may represent so many attitudes that in the second part of *Don Quixote* his nature and his role become increasingly problematic), generally speaks with the voice of the belly and calls his errant master back to reality. He, too, should remind us of a familiar character from the canon of romance, the *vilain,* the comic rustic whose unlovely person and gross personality represent all that is otherwise excluded from the idealized romanesque world. The function of this figure, C. S. Lewis suggests in *The Allegory of Love,* was to serve as "a sop to Silenus"—to give the readers of a romance something to laugh at, to preserve them from the temptation to question and perhaps to mock the romanesque vision itself. But while the *vilain* of romance was more often than not an episodic or a minor character, Sancho Panza accompanies his master to the center of the stage, and his voice is as insistent as is that of the old knight. His call is often a coarse one; his presence often reduces Don Quixote's misadventures to the level of the most crude burlesque; and Byron's reaction—"Cervantes smiled Spain's chivalry away"—is justifiable, if not historically accurate.

But Sancho's quiet question, "What giants?" is not an instance of burlesque: it is the interrogative understatement that complements and confounds Don Quixote's hyperbolic assertion. Sancho, in the episode of the windmills, does not initially reveal the truth of the situation directly and crudely—Byron himself is far less subtle in *Don Juan,* his reductions of romance far more emphatic. The peasant squire simply questions the romanesque premise, the highly-colored overstatement of his master. Without knowing it, Sancho is playing the *eiron* (self-depreciator) to Don Quixote's *alazon* (self-deceiver): Cervantes has recreated the basic comic opposition indicated by Francis Cornford and exhaustively analyzed by Northrop Frye, the opposition of the overly-modest quester after truth and the cocksure pretender.

The *eiron,* however, deliberately understates his side of the case, and, while Sancho may qualify as a true *eiron* when he sits in judgment during his term as governor of the Isle Barataria, his irony in the windmill episode is totally unconscious. Cervantes, on the other hand, is consciously ironic: it is he, after all, who puts the revealing question in Sancho's mouth. The irony of Cervantes, which colors the entire atmosphere of *Don Quixote,* is the most authentic and the most powerful of ironies, that which Aristotle discusses in the *Nicomachean Ethics.* Like Aristotle's *eiron,* Cervantes simulates ignorance: he reaches truth rather by indirection than by dramatic revelation. His novel—and the paradigm he established surely is, as Harry Levin has indicated, the route to realism—does indeed begin in burlesque and parody, in the confounding of illusion through a confrontation with reality in its most ludicrous and most solid forms. But to pass from the first book of *Don Quixote* to the second, from the absurd imitation of knightly romance to the ambiguous adventures in the Cave of Montesinos and on the magic horse Clavileño, is to move from burlesque to irony. We may note the same progression in the fiction of seventeenth-century France, as we turn from Sorel and Scarron to Madame de La Fayette's ironic treatment of a romanesque situation in *La Princesse de Clèves;* and the sequence of Jane Austen's works—from *Love and Freindship* through *Northanger Abbey* to *Mansfield Park* and *Emma*—illustrates the same development. The progression may be an automatic one if, as David Worcester asserts in *The Art of Satire,* the two modes are relatively lower and higher points on the same scale, irony involving a more subtle contrast of appearance and reality, a more ambiguous form of incongruity, than does burlesque. And irony would thus be singularly appropriate to the purposes of the novel as a genre: the novel treats of disillusionment, of disenchantment, and irony, as Vladimir Jankélévitch writes in *L'Ironie,* "enables us never to be disenchanted, for the simple reason that it resists enchantment" (p. 25). The pleasure we take in seeing an *alazon* shocked out of his illusions—the enchantment of his own imagination—is the pleasure of irony: even the simplest verbal irony depends on the contrast of appearance and reality.

The novel would then seem to be an essentially ironic fictional form, occupying a middle position between the non-ironic romance and the philosophical tale, which is ironic, but in ways often different from those of the novel. The novel shares with the romance an emphasis on human situations rather than on ideas: both deal in experiential reality rather than theoretical questions. The novel shares with the *conte philosophique* a distrust of the romance sensibility, the sentimental and mythopoeic attitudes that make romances the enchanting and illusory works they are. Like the philosophical tale, too, the novel has a certain didactic purpose: irony has always been one of the major devices of the rhetor, a device by which the speaker separates his audience into the shrewd and the gullible. Within the total audience is an intelligent elite that responds to the rhetor's irony, that understands from the first that Brutus is anything but honorable, that divines the real set of moral values behind the apparent one. In other words, the novel may be a far less "popular" form than we usually assume—far less popular, surely, than the romance, courtly, bourgeois, or historical. Romance persisted (and persists) even after the birth and eventual triumph of the novel, simply by adapting its methods and matter to the fancies of a different social order. It had, after all, survived the late medieval questioning of the secular ethos of courtly romance that resulted in the various Grail cycles. Romance reflects an eternal tendency of the human mind that goes all but unaffected by historical change. In a society of *vilains*—Falstaffs and Sancho Panzas—the heroine of romance is a servant-girl and the hero an orphaned newsboy; but Pamela and Horatio Alger, and the responses they awaken in us, hark back to the codes of Laudine and Yvain. The function of romance has not changed, its action has not changed, although the externals of romanesque setting and intrigue have undergone a great alteration. Romance is essentially escapist literature; it appeals to the emotions and imagination of the reader, invites him to marvel at an enchanted world of triumphant adventure —and the triumph may be the slaying of a dragon or the unmasking of a corrupt sheriff. The novel, however, leads the reader back to reality by questioning the basis of romance; and the more sophisticated, the more subtle, or the more devastating the process becomes (as it becomes, in various ways, in Stendhal, and James, and Flaubert), the less "popular" the novel is likely to be, the more limited the audience that savors the novelist's irony.

This may well be the result of the nature of novelistic irony, which is more a matter of attitude and of moral orientation than of style. The irony of the philosophical tale—that of Voltaire, let us say, in *Candide*—is largely verbal, and it is the rare reader who does not respond to the oxymoron, hyperbole, and litotes characteristic of such a style. This irony falls under the heading of *tropes,* figures of speech; but the irony of the novel is rather a figure of thought, in the broadest sense. The distinction is at least as old as the *Institutio Oratoria,* and Quintilian's example of the ultimate in irony is the life and manner of Socrates. The Socratic method of apparently innocent questioning— which Sancho Panza adopts as he confronts the windmills—is the method which underlies the irony and the realism of the novel.

However, a further distinction must be made, and the figure of Falstaff is once again useful. Falstaff at Shrewsbury plays the role of the *eiron* as he questions such enchanting abstractions as honor; but Falstaff is an *alazon* as well, a boaster, heir to the long tradition of the *miles gloriosus,* the braggart soldier. Similarly, in relation to romances, all novels are ironic, in that they repeat Sancho Panza's questioning of the romanesque premise, but some novels are clearly more intrinsically ironic than others. Gustave Kahn wrestled with this problem in a brief essay he wrote on the irony of Stendhal and on irony in the French novel in general. There is clearly a contrast, wrote Kahn, between the ironic description of the battle of Waterloo in *La Chartreuse de Parme* and the overblown presentation of the battlefield in *La Débâcle:* Zola's hyperbolic evocation is more reminiscent of Hugo's apocalyptic Romanticism than of Stendhal's detached understatement. Kahn's solution was to distinguish the Stendhalian *roman ironique* from the Romantic or Naturalistic *roman lyrique.* The first term is just enough, but the second unfortunately introduces a new unknown quality; and a better set of terms may be those Harry Levin has used to qualify the ironic manner of Stendhal and the more Romantic method of Balzac, "deflationary" and "inflationary." Romance, perhaps, depends on the art of inflation: the romanesque world is one in which every youth is a hero, every antagonist an ogre, every maiden a masterpiece of nature. Novels are relatively more or less "deflationary": Balzac "deflates" more than does George Sand, Flaubert "deflates" more than does Balzac. An equivalent trio of English novelists might be composed of Walter Scott, Dickens, and James. The question is not merely one of chronology, although these two lists might seem to suggest that the history of modern fiction is the record of a progression from an inflationary to a deflationary manner. On the other hand, the movement from burlesque to irony that appeared as early as *Don Quixote* may be another aspect of the same development.

In the early chapters of *Don Quixote,* Sancho Panza calls his master back to reality; but as they travel through Spain, the knight's imagination fertilizes his squire's mind—and by the time they mount the wooden Clavileño, Sancho is as capable of producing hyperbolic fabrications as is Don Quixote. Cervantes, on the other hand, has become progressively more reticent, less willing to tell us the facts, more prone to force his readers to arrive at the truth by their own efforts of understanding. Cervantes' manner in the second book of *Don Quixote* suggests the manner which triumphs in the nineteenth century, when the novel definitively becomes the vehicle for literary realism. The irony of his novel, and of later novels, arises less from the presence of an *alazon-eiron* pair like Don Quixote and Sancho Panza, than from the novelist's attitude toward the characters and the fictional world he creates. While (as Ian Watt has indicated) the rise of the novel reflects the rise of the middle class and the spread of the bourgeois ethic, the bourgeois himself receives ironic treatment in the nineteenth-century novel, and M. Homais recalls Don Quixote as much as he does Sancho Panza. It is Flaubert's attitude that counts, and not the social status and intellectual baggage of M. Homais.

The literary *alazon* writes advertisements for himself; he is, in Gustave Kahn's sense, a "lyric" author, no matter what genre he produces. His characters and his world are likely to be the projections of his own wish-dreams, his own imaginative transformations of the humdrum world about him. The "inflationary" novelist—a Balzac or a Zola—deals in a reality familiar to us all, but rendered almost hallucinatory. The real Vidocq becomes the diabolical Vautrin; all of Balzac's characters, Baudelaire remarks, have the genius of their calling and their station. While the romancer transports us to a never-never land of fancy, where all our dreams of glory may be realized,

Balzac overloads his reality and loudly proclaims that "all is true." But he protests too much. The "deflationary"—that is, the more ironic—novelist is more likely to disclaim responsibility, to apologize for the story he tells us and the way he tells it. I think of the elaborate fiction Cervantes invents, by which he shifts responsibility for his story to the Arabian chronicler, Cide Hamete Benengeli; of Stendhal's false modesty, as he feigns shock at the morals and motives of his passionate Italians; of Gide's review of the characters in *Les Faux-monnayeurs,* his pretense that he has followed Bernard and Olivier wherever they chose to lead him. As the novelist continues this process, he arrives at what one usually thinks of as the extremity of the realistic method: like Flaubert, like Verga, he disappears completely from his novel, suppresses all explicit moral judgment, and lets his characters fend for themselves. Yet while understating his responsibility and his personality, the ironic novelist remains in complete control. The hero of a romance may run away with his story; the protagonist of a novel is always held more tightly in check. Accepting as we do the theory that the novel tends to approximate a slice of life itself, to represent "real" men and women in "real" situations, it may seem paradoxical to suggest that the closing words of *Vanity Fair*—"Come, children, let us shut up the box and the puppets, for our play is played out" —only make explicit what is implicit in every novel. The novelist is a puppeteer, the novel is a puppet show—and the patented collapsible ending of *La Chartreuse de Parme,* the comic resolution of the intrigue in *Tom Jones,* are merely more obvious examples of a common situation.

What I am suggesting—and what it may not be necessary to state so baldly—is that the heir to Socrates is not Sancho Panza but Cervantes, that the novelist is the *eiron,* while his protagonist (the "imaginist," the romance sensibility in a real world) is an *alazon* who learns, through disillusionment, that he is not a hero after all. Unlike the inflationary novelist, who advertises his characters (if not himself), the deflationary novelist, the ironic author, *appears* to allow his characters to magnify themselves, but is in reality subtly and silently reducing them to their actual stature.

To look at the matter in another light, the novelist is the god of his fictional universe, observing and controlling his characters from above. Hardy, when he invented a "President of the Immortals" in *Tess of the d'Urbervilles,* in no way altered the narrative manner, the general authorial attitude that we find in *The Return of the*

Native—but he did, consciously or unconsciously, reveal to us the sense of that attitude, the fact that the malicious deity rebuked by Eustacia Vye was in truth Thomas Hardy himself. Zola, too, in doting the Rougons and the Macquarts with their dreadful heredity, was more like a vengeful god cursing a human house than like the indifferent and objective experimental scientist he somewhat belatedly claimed to be. Flaubert and Joyce, in comparing the novelist to a god absent from his own creation, provide two more examples; but we must not be taken in by that emphasis on absence, any more than we should by Zola's pretense at objectivity, by the similar claims associated with realism as a whole. A novelist's hand may ultimately be less apparent than that of the author who openly dispenses poetic justice to his various characters. Novelists are rather like the god of Tolstoy's parable: they see the truth, but wait. The *alazon* confounds himself by his own pretensions; the *eiron* has only to lead him on. And we have no less an authority than Pascal—relying, indeed, on the Fathers of the Church—to tell us that irony is appropriate for God. In the eleventh of his *Lettres provinciales,* Pascal wrote that the Lord's first words to Adam, after the expulsion of Adam and Eve from Eden, constituted an ironic discourse: "Behold, the man is become as one of us." Adam might take God's words to refer solely to his illgained knowledge of good and evil; but the price of that knowledge has been the fall into mortality. Once again we return to that basic theme of the novel, the ironic distinction between the state of innocence (a special variety of ignorance and of moral blindness) and the state of experience. The protagonist of the novel is another Adam, driven out of the paradise of childhood and his own imagination, that paradise which is the country of romance. The novelist plays the role of a god who (like Hardy's Will) may be neither malevolent nor benevolent, but who is constantly ironic.

That the situation of Adam may provoke at once the laughter of the gods and the lamentations of men may help to explain why the novel, with its roots in comedy and comic devices, often approximates tragedy. Irony, after all, modulates between comedy and tragedy— it is, according to J. A. K. Thompson's *Irony,* "the trembling equipoise between jest and earnest" (p. 166). The reason, as Francis Cornford pointed out, is that the comic fault of *alazoneia* is equivalent to the tragic *hybris.* The braggart Falstaff and the over-confident Othello are comic and tragic versions of the same figure, the man blinded to reality by his own pretensions. Thus Don Quixote may be both a grotesque caricature and—for the Romantics—the martyred saint of the imagination. Meredith's Sir Austin Feverel reminds us, in his naïve reliance on the virtues of "the System," of Molière's mono-maniacs; but the figure of Sir Austin, at the end of *The Ordeal of Richard Feverel,* is that of a man whose pride has been the cause of madness and death and desolation. Meredith's theory of comedy is perhaps rather a theory of irony, with the Tragic Spirit as one of its Muses. Similarly, the ambiguity of our reactions to Emma Bovary and to Clym Yeobright, to Frédéric Moreau and to Olive Chancellor —are they pretentious fools? or is their plight a reflection of the human condition, with all the potentiality for tragic revelation that phrase suggests?—is dictated by the ambiguous nature of the ironic method and manner. If the novel seems to us so successful a vehicle for a realistic picture of the world, it may be that we see in the ambiguous irony of the novel the most accurate reflection of the unsure "realities" of human life. Hardy's title —*Life's Little Ironies*—reflects what may be the general consensus, that life *is* ironic, that only an ironic fiction could reproduce the moral complexities of life. "Now we see through a glass, darkly"—and only the oblique and ironic revelation of the truth is possible for us.

It would follow then that as the novel becomes more thoroughly comic or more thoroughly tragic, it passes beyond irony and beyond realism into a new area of fictive expression, open to more cosmic and more reflective visions of the world. This would seem to be consistent with the development of fiction in the late nineteenth and early twentieth centuries. Irony in the nineteenth century (in prose and in verse) served a specific purpose: it was the mode of reaction to the overstatements of Romanticism, self-advertisement and rampant sentimentality, the "spirit of romance" in one of its most emphatic manifestations.

> We had fed the heart on fantasies,
> The heart's grown brutal from the fare—

these lines from Yeats might serve as a motto for the mid-century reaction of such French authors as Flaubert, Baudelaire, and Leconte de Lisle. While certain statements of Matthew Arnold are similar to those of his French contemporaries, the reaction in England had come earlier, with Byron and Peacock—even, to a degree, with Jane Austen

—and was less embittered, less violent. But once having made its point, the ironic manner that produced the great realistic novels had no place to go. (Were it not for the subsistence of Romanticism itself throughout the nineteenth century, it would even be surprising to find in Flaubert and Twain and Turgenev methods and lessons which we can trace back to Cervantes, Madame de La Fayette, and Fielding.) Once Flaubert moved from the individual case of Emma Bovary to the generation of Frédéric Moreau, he had gone as far as his variety of realism could carry him. Thus the last decades of the nineteenth century are marked by a change in fiction, the tendency either to become more emphatically psychological, to look for ironies deeper within the individual sensibility, or to become more openly "cosmic," to see all men as blind pretenders and truth as the prerogative of an omniscient god. The methods and the concerns of realistic fiction continue to appear in novels of the early—and, one should add, of the middle—twentieth century, just as the romance survived the coming of the novel: François Mauriac and C. P. Snow are only two of the living novelists writing in the nineteenth-century manner. But the concern for point of view in James, the stream of consciousness in Virginia Woolf, the subtle analyses of the conscious and unconscious mind in Gide and Proust reflect changes in our attitude toward the nature of reality that had of necessity to affect modern fiction. We associate these new developments with the work of such men as Bergson and Freud; we might look to Sir J. G. Frazer for an equivalent to other changes in the nature of fiction. With such authors as Zola and Hardy, the novel opens itself to a process that we might call remythification," the tendency to see human life in terms of myth and legend, to appropriate the processes and effects which earlier novelists had avoided as the province of poetry. The pattern for many early novelists was to begin with a parody of romance and to end as realists. The pattern that becomes increasingly obvious after 1900 is a curious reversal of Cervantes' paradigm: Joyce and Mann, for example, begin in realism and end in mythopoeia. As realism had burlesqued romance, so the authors of the new fiction turned the processes of realistic novels themselves into objects of ridicule. Proust's pastiches of his predecessors, his caricature of the realistic novelist—that detached *poseur* who, when questioned on his cold aloofness, responds, "J'observe!"—are exemplary, as is Joyce's burlesque of catalogue realism in the "Ithaca" chapter of *Ulysses*.

I am not trying to suggest that by the early twentieth century, fiction had completed a perfect circle. This would be far from the truth. The ironic matter of the novel (corresponding as it did to certain changes in the social order, in science, and in philosophy) left ineradicable effects on the nature of fiction: Proust's Marcel grows from the age of names to the age of things, Joyce's *Ulysses* is set in a modern city, and Joyce's use of myth is in itself often ironic. But if we are to deal with the various forms of fiction in terms of their essential qualities, we must recognize that the ironic realism of the novel from Cervantes to the late nineteenth century gives way to other fictional modes in the twentieth. We may be forced to continue to use the term "novel" for the fiction of the twentieth century, as French has been forced to employ the word *roman* for both the romance and the novel; but we must recognize that our expectations may be wrong—as wrong as they often are when we turn from the fiction of England and of France to that of other countries, even in the nineteenth century. The novel was at one moment the dominant form of fiction in England and in France; this seems to have been less surely so in, let us say, America and Russia. "The American novel" is a phrase we use almost indiscriminately; were we to follow Richard Chase and to distinguish the American novel from the American romance (in all likelihood a form both more abundant and more accurately a reflection of the American imagination), we might discover that we had cleared up an unfortunate critical confusion, one that Nathaniel Hawthorne noted in his preface to *The House of the Seven Gables*. And, while there is indeed a tradition of ironic fiction in Russia (a tradition represented by Gogol, Goncharov, Saltykov, Turgenev, and Chekhov), the more impressive works of Dostoevsky and Tolstoy belong rather to the body of literature that E. M. Forster calls "prophetic fiction"—novels, perhaps, but not novels of the stricter sort deriving from *Don Quixote*. As Forster says, one needs a different set of tools to examine such fiction, and so it often is with English and French literature of our own century. Brunetière's theory of the evolution of genres, since it confused evolution and progress, was incorrect; but genres do change, and as the novel grew out of the romance through the ironic attitude and manner that we call realism, so—as our views of reality have changed, and as the ironic fiction that depicted the contrast of appearance and reality has made its point—something new has grown out of the novel.

❋❋❋

Shroder not only offers useful advice to the maker of generic definitions but illustrates the way in which the various sources of information—"the history of literature, the study of external form, and the study of the fictional matter of novels in general"—can be separated only in theory. In describing the novel's characteristic theme, he reveals a pattern or internal form that gives structure to the novel; and in contrasting the characteristic tone of the romance to that of the novel, he discusses authorial attitude and point of view and then considers mutations in narrative form that lead to the end of old genres and the rise of new ones.

This essay can be usefully compared not only to those that discuss genre (does, for example, his division of prose fiction into three forms render superfluous Frye's term "confession"?) but to those at the end of the volume. John Wain attributes the decline of the novel to an exhaustion of formal possibilities; Steven Marcus, to attenuated subject matter; whereas Shroder believes that shifts in mode away from the ironic toward the tragic and comic lead to new possibilities and even to new forms. Leslie Fiedler's assertion that the artist, by whom he means the novelist, must say "No! In Thunder" seems to contradict Shroder's view that the novelist rejects appearance and pretence to embrace an undefined reality that is not subject to the corrosive effects of irony, but they may be describing different stages of the same process. It may be that in newer or merely altered forms the narrative artist does not deflate but expands, becomes prophet rather than ironist.

Nature and Forms
of the Lyrical Novel

RALPH FREEDMAN

I

The concept of the lyrical novel is a paradox. Novels are usually associated with storytelling: the reader looks for characters with whom he can identify, for action in which he may become engaged, or for ideas and moral choices he may see dramatized. Lyrical poetry, on the other hand, suggests the expression of feelings or themes in musical or pictorial patterns. Combining features of both, the lyrical novel shifts the reader's attention from men and events to a formal design. The usual scenery of fiction becomes a texture of imagery, and characters appear as *personae* for the self. Lyrical fiction, then, is not defined essentially by a poetic style or purple prose. Every novel may rise to such heights of language or contain passages that contract the world into imagery. Rather, a lyrical novel assumes a unique form which transcends the causal and temporal movement of narrative within the framework of fiction. It is a hybrid genre that uses the novel to approach the function of a poem. Not surprisingly, the expectations of a reader who has been brought up on more traditional standards for the novel are often frustrated, for the symbolic patterns he encounters seem to him antithetical to the very method on which narrative is built.

Essentially, what distinguishes lyrical from non-lyrical writing is a different concept of *objectivity*. It is a truism that the novel is not always realistic in the sense of being a "truthful" reproduction of

From Ralph Freedman, *The Lyrical Novel: Studies in Herman Hesse, André Gide, and Virginia Woolf*. Reprinted by permission of Princeton University Press. Copyright © 1963.

external life. But its main tradition (the tradition we think of when "novel" comes to mind) separates the experiencing self from the world the experiences are about. Moll Flanders, David Copperfield, Ivan Karamazov, Hans Castorp—all these figures exist in and by virtue of a world, a milieu to which they react. Man confronts other men in love and hostility; he gropes his way through the labyrinth of his own and other societies or measures his wit against the dangers of nature; he pits his moral or amoral sense against the values of others, rebels against historical currents in which he is caught or exemplifies their norms. Objectivity is achieved through the dramatic and narrative form which develops these actions. An artist will naturally remold them for aesthetic or ideological reasons, but the plot— i.e., the display of interaction between man and world in time—is usually also a measure of the novel's design. *Tom Jones* is the *locus classicus* of this form, for Fielding sought precisely such differentiating criteria which would be distinctive of the novel.[1] But novels as different from one another as Jane Austen's *Emma*, Flaubert's *Madame Bovary*, Thackeray's *Vanity Fair*, or Zola's *Germinal*, all seek to abstract an objective quality from the encounter between self and other, man and the universe beyond him.

The lyrical novel, by contrast, seeks to combine man and world in a strangely inward, yet aesthetically objective, form. This is not to say that lyrical writers are uninterested in the questions of human conduct that concern all fiction, but they view these questions in a different light. Their stages are not those on which men usually perform in the novel, but independent designs in which the awareness of men's experiences is merged with its objects. Rather than finding its *Gestalt* in the imitation of an action, the lyrical novel absorbs action altogether and refashions it as a pattern of imagery. Its tradition is neither didactic nor dramatic, although features of both may be used, but poetic in the narrow sense of "lyrical." A lyrical poem's form objectifies not men and times but an experience and a theme for which men and their lives, or places and events, have been used. Similarly, lyrical novels such as Goethe's *Werther*, Hölderlin's *Hyperion*, or Djuna Barnes' *Nightwood* reflect the pleasure and pain or the dying of men as extended lyrics. Their objectivity lies in a form uniting

---

[1] See R. S. Crane, "The Concept of Plot and the Plot of *Tom Jones*," *Critics and Criticism* (Chicago: University of Chicago Press, 1952), pp. 616–47. See also Wayne C. Booth, *The Rhetoric of Fiction* (Chicago: University of Chicago Press, 1961), pp. 215–19.

self and other, a picture that detaches the writer from his *persona* in a separate, formal world.

We have so far discussed the lyrical novel as if it were an impermeable genre whose well-defined function leaves no room for ambiguity. But it should be obvious that the range and variety of lyrical fiction, from Hölderlin's dithyrambs to the later Gide's formal severity, preclude so rigid a definition of its form. The most obvious types may be easily identified, but others blur with normal narrative structures, and limits cannot be simply drawn. Most works of fiction, as Northrop Frye has shown, are composed of various elements, drawing on what we usually designate as novel, romance, confession, and satire.[2] Similarly, lyrical fiction crosses boundaries between types and methods of narrative, now showing itself in the romance, now in the confession, and often even in the conventional novel. Lyrical novels are determined not by any preordained form but by poetic manipulation of narrative types which writers have found ready-made or have constructed within an existing tradition of the novel.

Since the features of individual novels vary with their ingredients, an analysis must artificially separate their narrative and lyrical components. Some novels are more lyrical than others, and the unique organization of each work depends on its composition. But it is not merely a sliding scale of different elements that distinguishes these novels, nor a mere combination or compound, but also an internal conflict, a precarious balance of different, sometimes antithetical, techniques which creates a poetic effect. It is our purpose to show how a particular genre has emerged from an aggregate of such complex techniques, defining a mood, a type of literary sensibility, a way of approaching knowledge. For this reason, we shall first isolate purely lyrical qualities before turning to their more involved juxtapositions with other narrative forms.

II

A passage from a novel almost purely lyrical may distill some of the crucial characteristics of the genre. Rainer Maria Rilke's lengthy prose fragment, *Die Aufzeichnungen des Malte Laurids Brigge* (1910), draws a picture of outer squalor and inner despair by filtering it through the mind of the poet's double, Malte, a sensitive young

---

[2] *Anatomy of Criticism* (Princeton: Princeton University Press, 1957), pp. 315–25 *passim*.

Dane in Paris. Conceived as a journal, the book imposes its images upon the prose discourse of narrative fiction, but at the same time it marshals them in a "formal" progression whose inevitability and depth betray the hand of a great lyrical poet. In the following scene, Malte, pursued by anxiety, fastens his fear on a person, an object:

> I knew at once that my idea was worthless. The dedication of his misery, unlimited by any caution or dissimulation, surpassed my means of understanding. I had grasped neither the angle of his posture's decline nor the horror with which the underside of his eye-lids constantly seemed to fill him. I had never thought of his mouth, which was indrawn like the opening of a sewer.... I had stopped walking, and while I saw everything almost at once, I felt that he was wearing a different hat and a Sunday necktie; it was patterned obliquely in yellow and violet squares, and as for the hat, it was a cheap straw hat with a green band. There is, of course, no significance in these colors, and it is petty that I have remembered them. I only want to say that they clung to him like the utmost softness of a bird's underside. He himself took no pleasure in it, and who of all people (I looked around) was allowed to think this get-up was for him?
>
> My God, it occurred to me with violence, thus *art* thou. There are proofs for thy existence.... And... now they are shown to me. This is thy taste; herein thou takest thy pleasure....

A description moving toward great intensity in the first paragraph is elucidated by a statement in the second. Two images introduce this development. The first of these expresses inner horror plastically: dread wells up within the underside of the eyelids, which express the entire character of the person before him. This graphic picture is underscored by the second image: the comparison of the man's mouth to an *Ablauf* (translated as "sewer"), a combination of toilet and gutter used in this book to suggest a hideous identity of filth and elimination, degradation and sexuality. The second part of the passage intensifies these images with an unexpected shift. Bright, tasteless colors liken the man to a strutting peacock. The two sets are combined both by an explicit statement and by implicit imagery. Asking himself why he remembers all these details, the poet answers himself by making a further comparison: the colors are like "the utmost softness of a bird's underside." The image denotes softness of shade as well as of texture; it links the impression of the man as a whole with the underside of his eyelids and bears out the suggestion that the horror "constantly seems to fill him." Transforming the localized eyelids into the bird representing the whole man, the passage reaches a point of concentration. But the horror evoked by soft, pliant sensuality is at once turned into its opposite. The gay colors are only for God's pleasure, and yet what dubious pleasure it is. In the contrapuntal exclamation, *My God . . .*, the poet draws the difficult conclusion. The man's very hideousness serves to celebrate his creator. Hence, he proves the existence of God. Rilke concludes Malte's soliloquy with the reflection:

> That we would only learn to hold out before all things and not to judge. Which are the hard things? Which are the gracious ones? Thou alone knowest.

Breaking off abruptly, Rilke then turns to Malte's condition as a poor young man in Paris by referring to a new overcoat. The initial point of view is reestablished.[3]

The surprising thing about this passage is that it "works" both as a narrative and as a poem. Rilke shows himself a master of description, exposing the minutest details relevant to his hero's psyche. We see the strutting, sensuous man before us with his declining posture, gelatinous eyelids, and the toothless hollow of his mouth, the garish hat and necktie, and we know he has become the epitome of Malte's sexual dread. But at the same time the power of imagery acts through a peculiar medium of its own. Malte comprehends the man ahead of him as an image of human existence and of the knowledge of God. Clarifying statements and a movement of images have distilled this recognition from an otherwise commonplace occurrence. Pictorially, the images are not as intricately ordered as in Rilke's descriptive poems such as "Der Panther." The absence of verbal structuring sets it off from self-portraits in verse such as "Der Dichter" or from the tight, metaphorical rhetoric of the *Sonette an Orpheus*. Nor is there an inexorable progression as we find it, for example, in the movement from Angel to lovers in the second of the *Duineser Elegien*. Yet the lyrical prose we have considered uses similar methods to intensify feeling and theme, ordering all parts retroactively in a total image.

Conventionally, the lyric, as distinct from epic and drama, is seen either as an instantaneous expression of a feeling or as a spatial form. The reader approaches a lyric the way an onlooker regards a picture: he sees complex details in juxtaposition and experiences them as a whole. In Pound's famous phrase, the very notion of the image is

---

[3] *Die Aufzeichnungen des Malte Laurids Brigge, Gesammelte Werke* (Leipzig: Insel-Verlag, 1930), V, 246–47.

defined as the rendering of "an emotional and intellectual complex in an instant of time."[4] Yet as a lyrical poem moves from image to image, it also follows its own inimitable progression, acting through variations and expansions of themes, changes in rhythm, and elaborations of images to reach a point of greatest intensity at which the poet's vision is realized. Kenneth Burke has called such a movement a *qualitative* progression; Wolfgang Kayser aptly named it a *lyrical process*.[5] Time and action may be simulated, but the point of the poem's language is to reach a specific intensity by modulations of images.

In lyrical poetry, the process we have described is decisive. It exemplifies "lyrical" objectivity. But we have already seen that in lyrical novels such a progression exists in conjunction with narrative. Indeed, the tension peculiar to lyrical novels rests on this deliberate ambiguity. We follow in Malte's footsteps as if he were an ordinary character of fiction. We enter into his scene, expect time to pass, events to occur. But at the same time we know that this movement is a blind for a more decisive lyrical progression. The mere use of prose and the skillful handling of narrative have directed our attention to succession in time only to discover that we have actually entered into the rather different rhetoric of images. Lyrical novels (*Malte Laurids* included) exploit the expectation of narrative by turning it into its opposite: a lyrical process.

These distinctions assume that narrative progression is determined entirely by consecutive time. This is obviously an over-simplification: such rudimentary narrative hardly exists even in the simplest forms of detective fiction. Most novels buttress their characters' actions with meaningful schemes of encounters and images. But the distinction makes sense as a way of isolating narrative progression, just as the "lyrical process" is a way of isolating qualitative progression. As Jacques Rivière recognized in the "Roman d'aventure," narrative is the surge toward that which does not yet exist. In lyrical poetry, by contrast, events are contained in one another. Consecutiveness is simulated by

---

4 "A Few Don'ts," *Poetry,* I, 6 (March 1913), cited from *The Literary Essays of Ezra Pound,* ed. T.S. Eliot (New York: New Directions, 1955), p. 4. Note the use made of this concept by Joseph Frank in defining "spatiality" in modern literature. "Spatial Form in Modern Literature," *Sewanee Review,* LIII (1945), 221–46, 433–56, 643–53.

5 See *Das sprachliche Kunstwerk. Eine Einführung in die Literaturwissenschaft* (Bern: A. Francke, 1951), pp. 160–62ff.

lyrical language: its surge toward greater intensity reveals not new events but the significance of existing events. Actions are turned into scenes which embody recognitions.[6] There exists, then, a qualitative difference between novels such as *Madame Bovary,* which use imagery to develop a character's progressive "conversation with life," and novels such as *Malte Laurids Brigge,* which utilize modes of narrative movement to function as lyrical poetry.

Within its purpose of weaving a fabric of images, the lyrical novel, unlike lyrical poetry, depends on the base of the novel. It shares with the form it exploits the common purpose of narrative, i.e., to enact what Wellek and Warren have called the writer's "fictional world" in order to communicate it to an audience.[7] A decisive difference between the two forms, however, is the *locus* of that world. In conventional narratives, the outer world is the thing. It is placed beyond both writer and reader, interposing between them and the theme. In the lyrical mode, such a world is conceived, not as a universe in which men display their actions, but as a poet's vision fashioned as a design. The world is reduced to a *lyrical point of view,* the equivalent of the poet's "I": the lyrical self. In the masquerade of the novel, this point of view is the poet's *mask* as well as the source of his consciousness, whether it appears as one or more disguised *personae* or in the more direct function of the diarist, the confessor, or first-person narrator.

The hero of *Malte Laurids Brigge* acts from such a lyrical point of view. Countless perceptions impose themselves upon him. At one point, buttons on a tray of notions offered for sale by an old woman writhe toward him. Remembering a delirium of his childhood, Malte recalls buttons on his bedclothes threatening to crush him. In Paris, an electric streetcar, ringing wildly, races over his prostrate body. A sewage pipe on the remaining wall of an old building creeps toward him like a hideous snake. His dying grandfather in Denmark is symbolically transformed into the bell that tolls his time as he becomes an image of death itself. Malte's passive awareness absorbs all these objects and transforms them into images. He *mirrors* the world as he sees it and so lends it a specific color or shape, distorting or even

---

6 "Le Roman d'aventure," *La Nouvelle Revue française* (July–December, 1913). Cf. Henri Bonnet, *Roman et poésie. L'Esthétique des genres* (Paris: Librairie Nizet, 1951), pp. 67–69. Bonnet defines the poem by its plasticity, harmony, tonality; the novel by its temporal progression.

7 *Theory of Literature* (New York: Harcourt Brace, 1949), pp. 222–25.

displacing it. His function in the novel, to cite Joseph Frank, is *self-reflexive*. Depicting experience and enacting it through a progression of images, the hero renders himself as a symbolic vision.

The passive protagonist's point of view draws the contours of the lyrical novel. The individual encounters absorbed by the *persona* of *Malte Laurids* only seem to be scattered at random. Actually they cohere as a texture, intermingling past and present, occult and real events, mythical and historical figures with persons in the hero's life. The cruelly realistic Parisian hospital is treated on the same level as the mysterious Abelone of Malte's childhood. Images, then, include not only objects and scenes but also characters, who exist as image-figures within the protagonist's lyrical point of view. Made credible by the form of the notebook, which does not need to distinguish between levels of time and reality, the figures of persons and things become part of an exquisitely woven pattern of tapestry, an artificial "world." The writer aims for the effect of lyrical poetry: to use whatever scene, characterization, action in time, and corresponding techniques are the *donnés* of the novel within which he works, not in the development of a fictional world, but in the rendering of objects, sensations, even ideas, with immediacy.

Lyrical immediacy is different from the immediacy of narrative action as we find it, for example, in the battle scenes of *War and Peace*. It is an immediacy of portraiture, an availability of themes and motifs to the reader's glance without the interposition of a narrative world. The form, the world, the sensibility of the poet evolve in the qualitative progression of the lyric, counterpointing, distorting, but always present in other forms of narrative.

III

We have so far endeavored to isolate peculiarly lyrical qualities and have chosen for this purpose an unusually pure example of the genre. There have, of course, been other novels equally lyrical: De Quincey's *Dream Fugue,* for example, or Gide's *Nourritures terrestres*. But wherever lyricism is pervasive in a work of narrative prose, critics have doubted that such works are actually novels rather than extended prose poems. Our discussion of *Malte Laurids* has provided, I believe, some criteria by which its status as a novel can be measured. It is a work trading on the expectations of narrative: on description and even action in particular scenes and, in the book as a whole, on the novel of personal confession. Indeed, even this purest form of the lyrical novel could not be considered entirely outside its narrative context. The narrative directly affects the lyrical techniques and lends them the weight of their complexity. Similarly, as we shall see, *Les Nourritures terrestres* becomes an exciting experiment precisely because the loose array of disjointed images is fused with an underlying plot of the novel of education.

Narrative, then, is by no means irrelevant to the lyrical novel. It is used by the perverse poet as the object of his deformations. The hallmark of lyrical fiction is not the form of the narrative but the manner in which it is used. Actually, as we noted, lyrical novels appear in a variety of traditional forms, and it is the critic's task to investigate precisely how the lyrical qualities we have isolated function within their context. For example, diaries and letters were originally a means of promoting verisimilitude. Defoe so assures us in his introduction to *Moll Flanders*. Richardson's *Pamela*, Laclos' *Liaisons dangéreuses*, or Tieck's *Geschichte des Herrn William Lovell* uses letters to depict feelings and actions, but their attention is focused on an external world of events into which their protagonists' discoveries are projected. But the same form can also become an effective way of presenting a hero's sensibility directly and of allowing him to act as a lyrical point of view. The author is identical with the hero, who portrays himself in his missives or journals. Rousseau pointed the way for such a lyrical usage of these forms without himself writing a complete lyrical novel. St. Preux's fervent exchange of letters in the opening phases of *La Nouvelle Héloïse* holds out the promise of a lyrical novel which is not fulfilled in the remainder of the book. The *Confessions* actually come closer to poetic fiction (as Friedrich Schlegel aptly perceived), but, of course, this book was not intended as a novel. Beyond Rousseau, however, a distinct type of lyrical novel extends from *Werther*, Sénancour's *Obermann*, and *Hyperion* to Gide's *Cahiers d' André Walter* and Rilke's *Malte Laurids*. In all these novels, a hero mirrors himself in significant figures and scenes through which his life is expressed.

A similar situation occurs in a narrative form which, far more intensely than letters and diaries, exploits the hero's inner life. Although both the interior monologue and the stream of consciousness have often been identified with poetic fiction, they share with the confession and the epistolary form an original narrative intention. By itself the direct depiction of the mind's content does not entail a lyrical form. The very notion of Dos Passos' "camera eye," for example, indicates that it can also be used to illuminate precisely all figures within the hero's perception. Indeed, the stream of consciousness can be an intensified device of naturalism, supporting the effort to get at the heart of the external conditions of man by sifting all details that pass through the protagonist.

In a lyrical use of the stream of consciousness, by contrast, a design of images and motifs emerges from associations of the mind. The most obvious early example is Sterne's *Tristram Shandy,* which seems to turn a semblance of the stream of consciousness in a "poetic" direction. To be sure, it is richly bedecked with vivid characters, full of satiric jibes at men and affairs. Its unity as a design is open to question and, in fact, rather resembles a haphazardly patched quilt. But Tristram's compound of comic scenes, memories, and tales told by others, seems to produce a loose and disjointed web displacing the external world and revealing the narrator's mind as he struggles to compose his book. Although it was most influential for the lyrical novel, especially in Germany, *Tristram Shandy* itself is ambivalent, lacking many of the characteristics of lyrical technique. But it is part of its comic effect that it plays on the possibilities of association and memory, on the one hand to divert the reader from its avowed intention of presenting Tristram's "life and opinions" and, on the other, to draw that identity of narrator and subject which was to become a hallmark of lyrical design. In his *Sentimental Journey,* Sterne actually wrote a lyrical novel, a "picture album," as Virginia Woolf once described it, "of the human soul." Without using the stream of consciousness, this small book describing a "journey of the mind" abstracts the mental impression from the concrete world and renders it in a coherent form.

In our time, the stream of consciousness has been used far more self-consciously as a means of phychological exploration and as an aesthetic device. Joyce's *Ulysses* comes to mind, but, like *Tristram Shandy,* it points the way to lyrical fiction rather than being a lyrical novel itself. The novel is built on an obvious counterpoint. On the one hand, we encounter the epic quest through the concrete world of Dublin, but, on the other, we observe the filtering of that quest through the conscious and unconscious stream. This contrast implies a semblance of lyricism. A narrator exposes himself while ostensibly reflecting the world of his perception. Instead of one narrator (including in himself the monologues of others), we encounter three equally important interior monologues which together create a web of motifs.

Bloom, Stephen, and Molly function as a triple lyrical self, a divided point of view. Their monologues transform the streets of the city, its tower, library, and bawdy-house, into a significant design which uses the way stations of the epic quest to lend it symbolic weight. A "lyrical process" based on the quest seems to move toward a moment of recognition in each of the characters, to be unified in the end by the novel's resolution as a whole. In many ways, then, *Ulysses* seems to use both the quest and the stream of consciousness for a lyrical purpose. But the Homeric scheme and the thesis novel underlying the work pull it also in different directions. The juggling of lyrical technique is only one aspect among many of this complex work, which extends from a parody of literature and language to a concise dramatization of men and events.

Proust's *À la recherche du temps perdu* likewise opens the interior monologue to a poetic version of the novel. In many ways, these novels seem even more pertinently lyrical than *Ulysses*. No epic structure establishes a consecutive order to which levels of time must conform. The plot bends with the modulations of memory. The opening pages of the overture state clearly that Marcel has absorbed the worlds of present and past and renders them as a design. Self and world appear undivided, and Marcel suggests a lyrical point of view. Yet Proust breaks out of the lyrical mode. Scene upon scene turns to an enactment of life and manners, thicknesses of history, psychological terror observed and externalized until the world being created is not tapestry like *Malte Laurids* or quilt like *Tristram Shandy,* but society itself in which men move, succeed, and die. Even more than *Ulysses,* Proust's novels become narrative explorations of personal and social lives as they are viewed from an over-all perspective.

An accomplished juxtaposition of the lyrical form with the stream of consciousness occurs in many novels by Virginia Woolf. As we shall see, the ruminations of her individual characters are part of a "public" monologue in which they share, a monologue spoken in the language and couched in the imagery of the omniscient author. This method is especially useful in her purely lyrical novel, *The Waves,* in which an artful design is composed of the soliloquies of several characters. Leon Edel's interesting observation that psychological novelists usually set out seeking verisimilitude and conclude as symbolists cannot be applied to the form itself. "What begins as an attempt to click the mind's shutter and catch the images of outer reality impinging upon it, ends up as an impressionist painting."[8] This is quite true of Virginia Woolf, but it does not necessarily apply to all stream of consciousness novelists. Dos Passos, Proust, or Joyce take different attitudes toward the stream of consciousness. The desire to enhance truthful observation may be one purpose; the refashioning of mental imagery into a texture of lyrical poetry may be another. Often they are intermingled, but whether one form or the other is used depends on the author's purposes and sometimes even on the limits of his talent.

Lyrical fiction, however, is not confined to such narrative forms as the journal, confession, interior monologue or stream of consciousness, which reflect the contents of men's minds. Perhaps the most influential form of the lyrical novel has been suggested by the picaresque, the episodic romance, and the allegorical quest. Although these forms are not inherently poetic, they were so conceived by German romantic critics, and in this guise they have influenced various types of the lyrical novel. Both the Spanish picaresque and *Don Quixote* were seen as romantic forms in which a portrait of life is created by the adventures of a wandering protagonist. In *Tom Jones* and *Humphry Clinker,* the method retains its narrative purpose, but in Novalis' *Heinrich von Ofterdingen* it is lyrically conceived. The hero's time-bound adventures are transformed into a sequence of image-scenes that mirror the nature of the protagonist's quest and represent it symbolically. The progression required by the narrative genre is converted into a lyrical progression produced by the elaboration of pictures and scenes. This adaptation of the episodic structure to poetry has produced incisive types of lyrical novels, variously intermingled with ingredients of the novel of adventure, from the German symbolic novel of the romantic age to *Moby Dick* and *The Heart of Darkness.* Especially in the German literary tradition, the episodic romance is one of the most widespread types of lyrical fiction. The hero, as the poet's mask, wanders through worlds of symbolic encounters.

The emphasis on the protagonist as the poet's mask is inevitable in a genre which depends on the analogy between the lyrical "I" of verse poetry and the hero of fiction. Since the formal presentation of a self is a "self-reflexive" method, most lyrical novels indeed seem to require a single point of view. But actually the tradition of lyrical

---

8 *The Psychological Novel, 1900–1950* (New York: Lippincott, 1955), p. 185.

fiction is considerably more generous; it is capable of including many
novels which feature several important characters or suggest a pano-
ramic form. *Wuthering Heights,* for example, is intensely lyrical in its
imagery and language, yet its design conforms to that of an objective
novel which is not confined to a single figure. The narrator, Nellie
Dean, is no replica of the author; her consciousness does not contain
the two lovers as if they were images. Rather, Heathcliff and
Catherine create between them an aura of passion upon which Nellie
Dean comments. Their intense feelings, which counterpoint her narrow
perspective, are reflected in the images of nature, uniting inner and
outer worlds. The lyrical perspective is created by the concealed
author, who manipulates both the narrator's limited vision and the
lovers' poetic scenery.

A more usual variation is the pattern of soliloquists. In a straightfor-
ward narrative, as, for example, in Joyce Cary's trilogies, different
aspects of a drama may be viewed by several first-person narrators
whose versions of identical circumstances enhance the complexity of
the novel. By analogy, in lyrical novels several monologues may be
contrasted or paired in patterns of interlocking images. A lyrical novel
like *The Waves* draws its aesthetic rearrangement of time and life from
such a pattern of formal soliloquies, each of which reshapes an individual world. In *Les Faux-Monnayeurs,* Gide created a design of
image-scenes viewed by various figures, including the author. The
novel's form is made up of a pattern of these sequences which acts
both through the cumulative motion of the "lyrical process" and
through several juxtaposed levels of awareness. These forms use narrative means to project modes perfectly familiar in lyrical poetry. In
verse, too, different "voices" can be reflected against each other, as
Yeats has done effectively, or different *personae* can enact a stylized
lyrical drama, as they do occasionally in Eliot or Auden. Lyrical novels,
then, possess widely ranging possibilities of objectification. Their reper-
toire of possible techniques includes many variations of narrative form
which they use in the manner of lyrical poetry, extending from a pure
stream of consciousness to a controlled pattern of figures and scenes
manipulated by an omniscient author. Epistolary novels and confessions, picaresques and novels of education have contributed to corresponding forms of lyricism. The novel of manners may furnish a base
for the lyrical novel as much as the novel of adventure. But the
precise nature of the poetic world it substitutes for time, cause, and
place cannot always be described. It may include subconscious imagery

and monologues, but it may also consist of patterns of symbolic encounters or a canvas of complementing figures. Its defining characteristics vary with the author's traditions, his country and time, with his personal sensibility and genius. But whatever form is used, his point of view is crystallized in his protagonists, who transform their perceptions into a network of images.

IV

A final question concerns the motive of lyrical novelists. Why should writers use storytelling, figures and scenes, the movement of time, however distorted or grotesque, to create a poetic world? Very likely, this way of manipulating the narrative genre is a peculiar dodge of *romanciers manqués*. And indeed, poetic spirits from Novalis to Gérard de Nerval and André Gide seem to have suffered from a lack of sturdiness with which to meet external life. But such an explanation is too simple, for it does not illuminate the importance of the genre or its persistence. Prose allegories, poetic idylls and picaresques, the use of fairy tale, dream, distortion and fantasy, of mental association and dithyrambs in prose—all these have subverted the novel since its beginnings, supplanting narrative with lyrical objectivity.

It would not, then, be enough to say that Sterne's *Sentimental Journey* or Nerval's *Aurélia,* the lyrical novels of Hermann Broch and Hermann Hesse, of André Gide and Virginia Woolf represent failures of personal sensibility, constructs of pathetic minds unable to create concrete worlds. As compensations for failure they may indeed bear witness to the personal tragedies of writers. But the very ambivalence of novelist and poet which requires these compensations has often converted "failure" into magnificent achievement. At the same time, the lyrical version of the novel has also been ideologically conditioned. To the extent that the empirical idealism of the eighteenth century and the transcendental idealism of the nineteenth have offered an appropriate climate for the fusion of self and world, writers have followed in the footsteps of thinkers. Whether as poets, as philosophers, or as bystanders baffled at the intellectual display of their times, they have sought to eliminate the disjunction of self and world in the very genre that seems most to require their separation.

These reflections about the form of lyrical novels, and the motives of their authors, give rise to the conclusion that a critical method for their scrutiny must be historically conditioned. Distinguishing characteristics are rooted in different ways of thinking about the novel, which in turn are deeply embedded in the literary tradition of each country. Although our main purpose is to investigate three distinct kinds of the contemporary lyrical novel, we would do well to relate each of these types to its corresponding literary milieu, which may define not only the nature of the form but also the impulse behind it. From the ambiguous relationship between narration and lyricism we can distill a general significance for the novel: the challenge of reconciling the "inner" and the "outer" with each other and with the exigencies of art.

✻✦✻✦✻

One of the more interesting and perhaps more fruitful tendencies in modern criticism is the displacement of the scholarly "influence study" (which seeks to demonstrate as objectively as possible the debt of one author to another) by the partly scholarly, partly critical discussion of trend, subgenre, or artistic method. The advantages of the latter approach are at least threefold: it can establish a case without straining evidence and overworking conjecture; it enables the critic to compare artists whose work cannot be connected by external evidence; and most important, it deals in more fundamental terms than does the influence study with the way in which the artistic process seems to work. An artist borrows methods not because he admires them per se, but because he wishes to solve a common artistic problem, to embody a similar vision.

This being the case, it can be argued further that Freedman's method of classifying and defining genres (or methods—the distinction is not entirely clear) according to the form, the shape given to experience in a realized work of art, may be more generally useful than approaches that emphasize subject matter or tone. Discussions of the international novel, the novel of violence, and the radical novel or the comic, tragic, and satiric novel are valuable to the literary historian; but the formal approach, more closely linked to the particular work and the individual novelist's sensibility, may serve better as a method of analysis and discrimination.

Freedman's essay demonstrates still another use of the generic approach: apologia for a form that has been neglected or attacked. Logically, such a defense may be unnecessary or irrelevant, but in modern criticism of fiction any method other than that of the realistic novel is likely to be violently attacked on grounds that are not always clear. Some critics seem to feel that the novel is essentially a manly form—Freedman is placating this attitude in his concession that "poetic spirits...seem to have suffered from a lack of sturdiness with which to meet external life"—and they regard as suspicious, and very likely as effete, any writer who does not exhibit the proper bluffness in dealing with experience. In its crudest form, this attitude is found among reviewers for mass-circulation magazines and newspapers, but it may underlie the view, met in more intellectually respectable journals, that the methods of fiction and the methods of poetry are entirely distinct. The work of critics who hold this view tends to be characterized negatively by an absence of concern for and discussion of poetry, the purity or autonomy of which they accept and dismiss, and positively by attacks on the theories and methods—or works and pomps—of Henry James.

Some critics, not necessarily a different group, reject other forms and defend the novel on ideological grounds. They value the liberal attitude toward the world and regard the novel as the form that uniquely expresses that attitude. In an understandable if logically inadmissible confusion, they seek to defend the attitude by defending its form of expression.

Although they might reject some or all of these premises, many critics accept the view that the novel is concerned with empirical data—Shroder, Harvey, Marcus, Rahv, and Wain are a few in this volume. Others believe that there is a link between the novel and particular ways of perceiving and evaluating the world, a theory underlying many of the essays on the death or transmutation of the novel. For the most detached and most comprehensive view of the effect of changing attitudes upon literary form, see Joseph Frank's "Spatial Form in Modern Literature."*

---

* Originally published in *Sewanee Review*, LIII, Nos. 2, 3, and 4 (Spring, Summer, and Autumn 1945); reprinted in expanded form in *The Widening Gyre: Crisis and Mastery in Modern Literature* (New Brunswick, N.J.: Rutgers University Press, 1963.

Technique as Discovery

MARK SCHORER

I

Modern criticism, through its exacting scrutiny of literary texts, has demonstrated with finality that in art beauty and truth are indivisible and one. The Keatsian overtones of these terms are mitigated and an old dilemma solved if for beauty we substitute form, and for truth, content. We may, without risk of loss, narrow them even more, and speak of technique and subject matter. Modern criticism has shown us that to speak of content as such is not to speak of art at all, but of experience; and that it is only when we speak of the *achieved* content, the form, the work of art as a work of art, that we speak as critics. The difference between content, or experience, and achieved content, or art, is technique.

When we speak of technique, then, we speak of nearly everything. For technique is the means by which the writer's experience, which is his subject matter, compels him to attend to it; technique is the only means he has of discovering, exploring, developing his subject, of conveying its meaning, and, finally, of evaluating it. And surely it follows that certain techniques are sharper tools than others, and will discover more; that the writer capable of the most exacting technical scrutiny of his subject matter, will produce works with the most satisfying content, works with thickness and resonance, works which reverberate, works with maximum meaning.

We are no longer able to regard as seriously intended criticism of poetry which does not assume these generalizations; but the case for fiction has not yet been established. The novel is still read as though its content has some value in itself, as though the subject matter of fiction has greater or lesser value in itself, and as though technique

From *Hudson Review,* I (1948). Reprinted by permission of Mark Schorer.

were not a primary but a supplementary element, capable perhaps of not unattractive embellishments upon the surface of the subject, but hardly of its essence. Or technique is thought of in blunter terms from those which one associates with poetry, as such relatively obvious matters as the arrangement of events to create plot; or, within plot, of suspense and climax; or as the means of revealing character motivation, relationship, and development; or as the use of point of view, but point of view as some nearly arbitrary device for the heightening of dramatic interest through the narrowing or broadening of perspective upon the material, rather than as a means toward the positive definition of theme. As for the resources of language, these, somehow, we almost never think of as a part of the technique of fiction— language as used to create a certain texture and tone which in themselves state and define themes and meanings; or language, the counters of our ordinary speech, as forced, through conscious manipulation, into all those larger meanings which our ordinary speech almost never intends. Technique in fiction, all this is a way of saying, we somehow continue to regard as merely a means to organizing material which is "given" rather than as the means of exploring and defining the values in an area of experience which, for the first time *then,* are being given.

Is fiction still regarded in this odd, divided way because it is really less tractable before the critical suppositions which now seem inevitable to poetry? Let us look at some examples: two well-known novels of the past, both by writers who may be described as "primitive," although their relative innocence of technique is of a different sort— Defoe's *Moll Flanders* and Emily Bronte's *Wuthering Heights;* and three well-known novels of this century—*Tono Bungay,* by a writer who claimed to eschew technique; *Sons and Lovers,* by a novelist who, because his ideal of subject matter ("the poetry of the immediate present") led him at last into the fallacy of spontaneous and unchangeable composition, in effect eschewed technique; and *A Portrait of the Artist as a Young Man,* by a novelist whose practice made claims for the supremacy of technique beyond those made by anyone in the past or by anyone else in this century.

Technique in fiction is, of course, all those obvious forms of it which are usually taken to be the whole of it, and many others; but for the present purposes, let it be thought of in two respects particularly: the uses to which language, as language, is put to express the quality of the experience in question; and the uses of point of view not only as a mode of dramatic delimitation, but more particularly, of thematic definition. Technique is really what T. S. Eliot means by "convention"—any selection, structure, or distortion, any form or rhythm imposed upon the world of action; by means of which—it should be added—our apprehension of the world of action is enriched or renewed. In this sense, everything is technique which is not the lump of experience itself, and one cannot properly say that a writer has no technique or that he eschews technique, for, being a writer, he cannot do so. We can speak of good and bad technique, of adequate and inadequate, of technique which serves the novel's purpose, or disserves.

II

In the prefatory remarks to *Moll Flanders,* Defoe tells us that he is not writing fiction at all, but editing the journals of a woman of notorious character, and rather to instruct us in the necessities and the joys of virtue than to please us. We do not, of course, take these professions seriously, since nothing in the conduct of the narrative indicates that virtue is either more necessary or more enjoyable than vice. On the contrary, we discover that Moll turns virtuous only after a life of vice has enabled her to do so with security; yet it is precisely for this reason that Defoe's profession of didactic purpose has interest. For the actual morality which the novel enforces is the morality of any commercial culture, the belief that virtue pays—in worldly goods. It is a morality somewhat less than skin deep, having no relation to motives arising from a sense of good and evil, least of all, of evil-*in*-good, but exclusively from the presence or absence of food, drink, linen, damask, silver, and time-pieces. It is the morality of measurement, and without in the least intending it, *Moll Flanders* is our classic revelation of the mercantile mind: the morality of measurement, which Defoe has completely neglected to measure. He fails not only to evaluate this material in his announced way, but to evaluate it at all. His announced purpose is, we admit, a pious humbug, and he meant us to read the book as a series of scandalous events; and thanks to his inexhaustible pleasure in excess and exaggeration, this element in the book continues to amuse us. Long before the book has been finished, however, this element has also become an absurdity; but not half the absurdity as that which Defoe did not intend at all— the notion that Moll could live a rich and full life of crime, and yet, repenting, emerge spotless in the end. The point is, of course, that she has no moral being, nor has the book any moral life. Everything is external. Everything can be weighed, measured, handled, paid for in gold, or expiated by a prison term. To this, the whole texture of the novel testifies: the bolts of goods, the inventories, the itemized accounts, the landlady's bills, the lists, the ledgers: all this, which taken together comprises what we call Defoe's method of circumstantial realism.

He did not come upon that method by any deliberation: it represents precisely his own world of value, the importance of external circumstance to Defoe. The point of view of Moll is indistinguishable from the point of view of her creator. We discover the meaning of the novel (at unnecessary length, without economy, without emphasis, with almost none of the distortions or the advantages of art) in spite of Defoe, not because of him. Thus the book is not the true chronicle of a disreputable female, but the true allegory of an impoverished soul —the author's; not an anatomy of the criminal class, but of the middle class. And we read it as an unintended comic revelation of self and of a social mode. Because he had no adequate resources of technique to separate himself from his material, thereby to discover and to define the meanings of his material, his contribution is not to fiction but to the history of fiction, and to social history.

The situation in *Wuthering Heights* is at once somewhat the same and yet very different. Here, too, the whole novel turns upon itself, but this time to its estimable advantage; here, too, is a revelation of what is perhaps the author's secret world of value, but this time, through what may be an accident of technique, the revelation is meaningfully accomplished. Emily Bronte may merely have stumbled upon the perspectives which define the form and the theme of her book. Whether she knew from the outset, or even at the end, what she was doing, we may doubt; but what she did and did superbly we can see.

We can assume, without at all becoming involved in the author's life but merely from the tone of somnambulistic excess which is generated by the writing itself, that this world of monstrous passion, of dark and gigantic emotional and nervous energy, is for the author, or was in the first place, a world of ideal value; and that the book sets out to persuade us of the moral magnificence of such unmoral passion. We are, I think, expected, in the first place, to take at their own valuation these demonic beings, Heathcliff and Cathy: as special creatures, set apart from the cloddish world about them by their heightened capacity for feeling, set apart, even, from the ordinary objects of human passion as, in their transcendental, sexless relationship, they identify themselves with an uncompromising landscape and cosmic force. Yet this is absurd, as much of the detail that surrounds it ("Other dogs lurked in other recesses") is absurd. The novelist Emily Bronte had to discover these absurdities to the girl Emily; her technique had to evaluate them for what they were, so that we are persuaded that it is not Emily who is mistaken in her estimate of her characters, but they who are mistaken in their estimate of themselves. The theme of the moral magnificence of unmoral passion is an impossible theme to sustain, and what interests us is that it was device— and this time, mere, mechanical device—which taught Emily Bronte that, the needs of her temperament to the contrary, all personal longing and reverie to the contrary, perhaps—that this was indeed not at all what her material must mean as art. Technique objectifies.

To lay before us the full character of this passion, to show us how it first comes into being and then comes to dominate the world about it and the life that follows upon it, Emily Bronte gives her material a broad scope in time, lets it, in fact, cut across three generations. And to manage material which is so extensive, she must find a means of narration, points of view, which can encompass that material, and, in her somewhat crude concept of motive, justify its telling. So she chooses a foppish traveler who stumbles into this world of passionate violence, a traveler representing the thin and conventional emotional life of the far world of fashion, who wishes to hear the tale: and for her teller she chooses, almost inevitably, the old family retainer who knows everything, a character as conventional as the other, but this one representing not the conventions of fashion, but the conventions of the humblest moralism. What has happened is, first, that she has chosen as her narrative perspective those very elements, conventional emotion and conventional morality, which her hero and heroine are meant to transcend with such spectacular magnificence; and second, that she has permitted this perspective to operate throughout a long period of time. And these two elements compel the novelist to see what her unmoral passions come to. Moral magnificence? Not at all; rather, a devastating spectacle of human waste; ashes. For the time of the novel is carried on long enough to show Heathcliff at last an emptied man, burned out by his fever ragings, exhausted and will-less, his passion meaningless at last. And it goes even a little further, to Lockwood, the fop, in the graveyard, sententiously contemplating headstones. Thus in the end the triumph is all on the side of the cloddish world, which survives.

Perhaps not all on that side. For, like Densher at the end of *The Wings of the Dove,* we say, and surely Hareton and the second Cathy say, "We shall never be again as we were!" But there is more point in observing that a certain body of materials, a girl's romantic day-dreams, have, through the most conventional devices of fiction, been pushed beyond their inception in fancy to their meanings, their conception as a written book—that they, that is, are not at all as they were.

III

Technique alone objectifies the materials of art; hence technique alone evaluates those materials. This is the axiom which demonstrates itself so devastatingly whenever a writer declares, under the urgent sense of the importance of his materials (whether these are autobiography, or social ideas, or personal passions)—whenever such a writer declares that he cannot linger with technical refinements. That art will not tolerate such a writer H. G. Wells handsomely proves. His enormous literary energy included no respect for the techniques of his medium, and his medium takes its revenge upon his bumptiousness. "I have never taken any very great pains about writing. I am outside the hierarchy of conscious and deliberate writers altogether. I am the absolute antithesis of Mr. James Joyce. . . . Long ago, living in close conversational proximity to Henry James, Joseph Conrad, and Mr. Ford Madox Hueffer, I escaped from under their immense artistic preoccupations by calling myself a journalist." Precisely. And he escaped—he disappeared—from literature into the annals of an era.

Yet what confidence! "Literature," Wells said, "is not jewelry, it has quite other aims than perfection, and the more one thinks of 'how it is done' the less one gets it done. These critical indulgences lead along a fatal path, away from every natural interest towards a preposterous emptiness of technical effort, a monstrous egotism of artistry, of which the later work of Henry James is the monumental warning. 'It,' the subject, the thing or the thought, has long since disappeared in these amazing works; nothing remains but the way it has been 'manipulated.' " Seldom has a literary theorist been so totally wrong; for what we learn as James grows for us and Wells disappears, is that without what he calls "manipulation," there *is* no "it," no "subject" in art. There is again only social history.

The virtue of the modern novelist—from James and Conrad down—is not only that he pays so much attention to his medium, but that, when he pays most, he discovers through it a new subject matter, and a greater one. Under the "immense artistic preoccupations" of James and Conrad and Joyce, the form of the novel changed, and with the technical change, analogous changes took place in substance, in point of view, in the whole conception of fiction. And the final lesson of the modern novel is that technique is not the secondary thing that it seemed to Wells, some external machination, a mechanical affair, but a deep and primary operation; not only that technique *contains* intellectual and moral implications, but that it *discovers* them. For a writer like Wells, who wished to give us the intellectual and the moral history of our times, the lesson is a hard one: it tells us that the order of intellect and the order of morality do not exist at all, in art, except as they are organized in the order of art.

Wells's ambitions were very large. "Before we have done, we will have all life within the scope of the novel." But that is where life already is, within the scope of the novel; where it needs to be brought is into novels. In Wells we have all the important topics in life, but no good novels. He was not asking too much of art, or asking that it include more than it happily can; he was not asking anything of it—as art, which is all that it can give, and that is everything.

A novel like *Tono Bungay,* generally thought to be Wells's best, is therefore instructive. "I want to tell—*myself,*" says George, the hero, "and my impressions of the thing as a whole"—the thing as a whole being the collapse of traditional British institutions in the twentieth century. George "tells himself" in terms of three stages in his life which have rough equivalents in modern British social history, and this is, to be sure, a plan, a framework; but it is the framework of Wells's abstract thinking, not of his craftsmanship, and the primary demand which one makes of such a book as this, that means be discovered whereby the dimensions of the hero contain the experiences he recounts, is never met. The novelist flounders through a series of literary imitations—from an early Dickensian episode, through a kind of Shavian interlude, through a Conradian episode, to a Jules Vernes vision at the end. The significant failure is in that end, and in the way that it defeats not only the entire social analysis of the bulk of the novel, but Wells's own ends as a thinker. For at last George finds a purpose in science. "I decided that in power and knowledge lay the salvation of my life, the secret that would fill my need; that to these things I would give myself."

But science, power and knowledge, are summed up at last in a destroyer. As far as one can tell Wells intends no irony, although he may here have come upon the essence of the major irony in modern history. The novel ends in a kind of meditative rhapsody which denies every value that the book had been aiming toward. For of all the kinds of social waste which Wells has been describing, this is the most inclusive, the final waste. Thus he gives us in the end not a novel, but a hypothesis; not an individual destiny, but a theory of the future; and not his theory of the future, but a nihilistic vision quite opposite from everything that he meant to represent. With a minimum of attention to the virtues of technique, Wells might still not have written a good novel; but he would at any rate have established a point of view and a tone which would have told us what he meant.

To say what one means in art is never easy, and the more intimately one is implicated in one's material, the more difficult it is. If, besides, one commits fiction to a therapeutic function which is to be operative not on the audience but on the author, declaring, as D. H. Lawrence did, that "One sheds one's sicknesses in books, repeats and presents again one's emotions to be master of them," the difficulty is vast. It is an acceptable theory only with the qualification that technique, which objectifies, is under no other circumstances so imperative. For merely to repeat one's emotions, merely to look into one's heart and write, is also merely to repeat the round of emotional bondage. If our books are to be exercises in self-analysis, then technique must—and alone can—take the place of the absent analyst.

Lawrence, in the relatively late Introduction to his *Collected Poems*, made that distinction of the amateur between his "real" poems and his "composed" poems, between the poems which expressed his demon directly and created their own form "willy-nilly," and the poems which, through the hocus pocus of technique, he spuriously put together and could, if necessary, revise. His belief in a "poetry of the immediate present," poetry in which nothing is fixed, static, or final, where all is shimmeriness and impermanence and vitalistic essence, arose from this mistaken notion of technique. And from this notion, an unsympathetic critic like D. S. Savage can construct a case which shows Lawrence driven "concurrently to the dissolution of personality and the dissolution of art." The argument suggests that Lawrence's early, crucial novel, *Sons and Lovers,* is another example of meanings confused by an impatience with technical resources.

The novel has two themes: the crippling effects of a mother's love on the emotional development of her son; and the "split" between kinds of love, physical and spiritual, which the son develops, the kinds represented by two young women, Clara and Miriam. The two themes should, of course, work together, the second being, actually, the result of the first: this "split" is the "crippling." So one would expect to see the novel developed, and so Lawrence, in his famous letter to Edward Garnett, where he says that Paul is left at the end with the "drift towards death," apparently thought he had developed it. Yet in the last few sentences of the novel, Paul rejects his desire for extinction and turns towards "the faintly humming, glowing town," to life—as nothing in his previous history persuades us that he could unfalteringly do.

The discrepancy suggests that the book may reveal certain confusions between intention and performance.

The first of these is the contradiction between Lawrence's explicit characterizations of the mother and father and his tonal evaluations of them. It is a problem not only of style (of the contradiction between expressed moral epithets and the more general texture of the prose which applies to them) but of point of view. Moral and Lawrence are never separated, which is a way of saying that Lawrence maintains for himself in this book the confused attitude of his character. The mother is a "proud, *honorable* soul," but the father has a "small, *mean* head." This is the sustained contrast; the epithets are characteristic of the whole; and they represent half of Lawrence's feelings. But what is the other half? Which of these characters is given his real sympathy—the hard, self-righteous, aggressive, demanding mother who comes through to us, or the simple, direct, gentle, downright, fumbling, ruined father? There are two attitudes here. Lawrence (and Morel) loves his mother, but he also hates her for compelling his love; and he hates his father with the true Freudian jealousy, but he also loves him for what he is in himself, and he sympathizes more deeply with him because his wholeness has been destroyed by the mother's domination, just as his, Lawrence-Morel's, has been.

This is a psychological tension which disrupts the form of the novel and obscures its meaning, because neither the contradiction in style nor the confusion in point of view is made to right itself. Lawrence is merely repeating his emotions, and he avoids an austerer technical scrutiny of his material because it would compel him to master them. He would not let the artist be stronger than the man.

The result is that, at the same time that the book condemns the mother, it justifies her; at the same time that it shows Paul's failure, it offers rationalizations which place the failure elsewhere. The handling of the girl, Miriam, if viewed closely, is pathetic in what it signifies for Lawrence, both as man and artist. For Miriam is made the mother's scape-goat, and in a different way from the way that she was in life. The central section of the novel is shot through with alternate statements as to the source of the difficulty: Paul is unable to love Miriam wholly, and Miriam can love only his spirit. The contradictions appear sometimes within single paragraphs, and the point of view is never adequately objectified and sustained to tell us which is true. The material is never seen as material; the writer is caught in it exactly as firmly as he was caught in his experience of it. "That's how women are with me," said Paul. "They want me like mad, but they don't want to belong to me." So he might have said, and believed it; but at the end of the novel, Lawrence is still saying that, and himself believing it.

For the full history of this technical failure, one must read *Sons and Lovers* carefully and then learn the history of the manuscript from the book called *D. H. Lawrence: A Personal Record,* by one E. T., who was Miriam in life. The basic situation is clear enough. The first theme—the crippling effects of the mother's love—is developed right through to the end; and then suddenly, in the last few sentences, turns on itself, and Paul gives himself to life, not death. But all the way through, the insidious rationalizations of the second theme have crept in to destroy the artistic coherence of the work. A "split" would occur in Paul; but as the split is treated, it is superimposed upon rather than developed in support of the first theme. It is a rationalization made from it. If Miriam is made to insist on spiritual love, the meaning and the power of theme one are reduced; yet Paul's weakness is disguised. Lawrence could not separate the investigating analyst, who must be objective, from Lawrence, the subject of the book; and the sickness was not healed, the emotion not mastered, the novel not perfected. All this, and the character of a whole career, would have been altered if Lawrence had allowed his technique to discover the fullest meaning of his subject.

A Portrait of the Artist as a Young Man, like *Tono Bungay* and

Sons and Lovers, is autobiographical, but unlike these it analyzes its material rigorously, and it defines the value and the quality of its experience not by appended comment or moral epithet, but by the texture of the style. The theme of *A Portrait,* a young artist's alienation from his environment, is explored and evaluated through three different styles and methods as Stephen Dedalus moves from childhood through boyhood into maturity. The opening pages are written in something like the stream of consciousness of *Ulysses,* as the environment impinges directly on the consciousness of the infant and the child, a strange, opening world which the mind does not yet subject to questioning, selection, or judgment. But this style changes very soon, as the boy begins to explore his surroundings, and as his sensuous experience of the world is enlarged, it takes on heavier and heavier rhythms and a fuller and fuller body of sensuous detail, until it reaches a crescendo of romantic opulence in the emotional climaxes which mark Stephen's rejection of domestic and religious values. Then gradually the style subsides into the austerer intellectuality of the final sections, as he defines to himself the outlines of the artistic task which is to usurp his maturity.

A highly self-conscious use of style and method defines the quality of experience in each of these sections, and, it is worth pointing out in connection with the third and concluding section, the style and method evaluate the experience. What has happened to Stephen is, of course, a progressive alienation from the life around him as he progressed in his initiation into it, and by the end of the novel, the alienation is complete. The final portion of the novel, fascinating as it may be for the developing aesthetic creed of Stephen-Joyce, is peculiarly bare. The life experience was not bare, as we know from *Stephen Hero;* but Joyce is forcing technique to comment. In essence, Stephen's alienation is a denial of the human environment; it is a loss; and the austere discourse of the final section, abstract and almost wholly without sensuous detail or strong rhythm, tells us of that loss. It is a loss so great that the texture of the notation-like prose here suggests that the end is really all an illusion, that when Stephen tells us and himself that he is going forth to forge in the smithy of his soul the uncreated conscience of his race, we are to infer from the very quality of the icy, abstract void he now inhabits, the implausibility of his aim. For *Ulysses* does not create the conscience of the race; it creates our consciousness.

In the very last two or three paragraphs of the novel, the style changes once more, reverts from the bare, notative kind to the romantic prose of Stephen's adolescence. "Away! Away! The spell of arms and voices: the white arms of roads, their promise of close embraces and the black arms of tall ships that stand against the moon, their tale of distant nations. They are held out to say: We are alone—come." Might one not say that the austere ambition is founded on adolescent longing? That the excessive intellectual severity of one style is the counterpart of the excessive lyric relaxation of the other? And that the final passage of *A Portrait* punctuates the illusory nature of the whole ambition?

For *Ulysses* does not create a conscience. Stephen, in *Ulysses,* is a little older, and gripped now by guilt, but he is still the cold young man divorced from the human no less than the institutional environment. The environment of urban life finds a separate embodiment in the character of Bloom, and Bloom is as lost as Stephen, though touchingly groping for moorings. Each of the two is weakened by his inability to reach out, or to do more than reach out to the other. Here, then, is the theme again, more fully stated, as it were in counterpoint.

But if Stephen is not much older, Joyce is. He is older as an artist not only because he can create and lavish his Godlike pity on a Leopold Bloom, but also because he knows now what both Stephen and Bloom mean, and *how much,* through the most brilliant technical operation ever made in fiction, they can be made to mean. Thus *Ulysses,* through the imaginative force which its techniques direct, is like a pattern of concentric circles, with the immediate human situation at its center, this passing on and out to the whole dilemma of modern life, this passing on and out beyond that to a vision of the cosmos, and this to the mythical limits of our experience. If we read *Ulysses* with more satisfaction than any other novel of this century, it is because its author held an attitude toward technique and the technical scrutiny of subject matter which enabled him to order, within a single work and with superb coherence, the greatest amount of our experience.

IV

In the United States during the last twenty-five years, we have had many big novels but few good ones. A writer like James T. Farrell apparently assumes that by endless redundancy in the description of the surface of American Life, he will somehow write a book with the scope of *Ulysses*. Thomas Wolfe apparently assumed that by the mere disgorging of the raw material of his experience he would give us at last our epic. But except in a physical sense, these men have hardly written novels at all.

The books of Thomas Wolfe were, of course, journals, and the primary role of his publisher in transforming these journals into the semblance of novels is notorious. For the crucial act of the artist, the unique act which is composition, a sympathetic editorial blue pencil and scissors were substituted. The result has excited many people, especially the young, and the ostensibly critical have observed the prodigal talent with the wish that it might have been controlled. Talent there was, if one means by talent inexhaustible verbal energy, excessive response to personal experience, and a great capacity for auditory imitativeness, yet all of this has nothing to do with the novelistic quality of the written result; until the talent is controlled, the material organized, the content achieved, there is simply the man and his life. It remains to be demonstrated that Wolfe's conversations were any less interesting as novels than his books, which is to say that his books are without interest as novels. As with Lawrence, our response to the books is determined, not by their qualities as novels, but by our response to him and his qualities as a temperament.

This is another way of saying that Thomas Wolfe never really knew what he was writing *about*. Of Time and the River is merely a euphemism for Of a Man and his Ego. It is possible that had his conception of himself and of art included an adequate respect for technique and the capacity to pursue it, Wolfe would have written a great novel on his true subject—the dilemma of romantic genius; it was his true subject, but it remains his undiscovered subject, it is the subject which *we* must dig out for him, because he himself had neither the lamp nor the pick to find it in and mine it out of the labyrinths of his experience. Like Emily Bronte, Wolfe needed a point of view beyond his own which would separate his material and its effect.

With Farrell, the situation is opposite. He knows quite well what his subject is and what he wishes to tell us about it, but he hardly needs the novel to do so. It is significant that in sheer clumsiness of style, no living writer exceeds him, for his prose is asked to perform no service beyond communication of the most rudimentary kind of fact. For his ambitions, the style of the newspaper and the lens of the documentary camera would be quite adequate, yet consider the diminution which Leopold Bloom, for example, would suffer, if he were to be viewed from these, the technical perspectives of James Farrell. Under the eye of this technique, the material does not yield up enough; indeed, it shrinks.

More and more writers in this century have felt that naturalism as a method imposes on them strictures which prevent them from exploring through all the resources of technique the full amplifications of their subjects, and that thus it seriously limits the possible breadth of aesthetic meaning and response. James Farrell is almost unique in the complacency with which he submits to the blunt techniques of naturalism; and his fiction is correspondingly repetitive and flat.

That naturalism had a sociological and disciplinary value in the nineteenth century is obvious; it enabled the novel to grasp materials and make analyses which had eluded it in the past, and to grasp them boldly; but even then it did not tell us enough of what, in Virginia Woolf's phrase, is "really real," nor did it provide the means to the maximum of reality coherently contained. Even the Flaubertian ideal of objectivity seems, today, an unnecessarily limited view of objectivity, for as almost every good writer of this century shows us, it is quite as possible to be objective about subjective states as it is to be objective about the circumstantial surfaces of life. Dublin, in *Ulysses,* is a moral setting: not only a city portrayed in the naturalistic fashion of Dickens' London, but also a map of the modern psyche with its oblique and baffled purposes. The second level of reality in no way invalidates the first, and a writer like Joyce shows us that, if the artist truly respects his medium, he can be objective about both at once. What we need in fiction is a devoted fidelity to every technique which will help us to discover and to evaluate our subject matter, and more than that, to discover the amplifications of meaning of which our subject matter is capable.

Most modern novelists have felt this demand upon them. André Gide allowed one of his artist-heroes to make an observation which considerably resembles an observation we have quoted from Wells. "My novel hasn't got a subject. . . . Let's say, if you prefer it, it hasn't got *one* subject. . . . 'A slice of life,' the naturalist school said. The great defect of that school is that it always cuts its slice in the same direction; in time, lengthwise. Why not in breadth? Or in depth? As for me I should like not to cut at all. Please understand; I should

like to put everything into my novel." Wells, with his equally large
blob of potential material, did not know how to cut it to the novel's
taste; Gide cut, of course—in every possible direction. Gide and others.
And those "cuts" are all the new techniques which modern fiction
has given us. None, perhaps, is more important than that inheritance
from French symbolism which Huxley, in the glittering wake of Gide,
called "the musicalization of fiction." Conrad anticipated both when
he wrote that the novel "must strenuously aspire to the plasticity of
sculpture, to the colour of painting, and to the magic suggestiveness
of music—which is the art of arts," and when he said of that early
but wonderful piece of symbolist fiction, *Heart of Darkness*, "It was
like another art altogether. That sombre theme had to be given a
sinister resonance, a tonality of its own, a continued vibration that,
I hoped, would hang in the air and dwell on the ear after the last
note had been struck." The analogy with music, except as a metaphor,
is inexact, and except as it points to techniques which fiction can
employ as fiction, not very useful to our sense of craftsmanship. It
has had an approximate exactness in only one work, Joyce's final
effort, and an effort unique in literary history, *Finnegan's Wake,* and
here, of course, those readers willing to approach the "ideal" effort
Joyce demands, discovering an inexhaustible wealth and scope, are
most forcibly reminded of the primary importance of technique to
subject, and of their indivisibility.

The techniques of naturalism inevitably curtail subject and often
leave it in its original area, that of undefined social experience. Those
of our writers who, stemming from this tradition, yet, at their best,
achieve a novelistic definition of social experience—writers like the
occasional Sherwood Anderson, William Carlos Williams, the occasional Erskine Caldwell, Nathanael West, and Ira Wolfert in *Tucker's
People,* have done so by pressing naturalism far beyond itself, into
positively gothic distortions. The structural machinations of Dos Passos
and the lyrical interruptions of Steinbeck are the desperate maneuvers
of men committed to a method of whose limitations they despair.
They are our symbolists *manqué,* who end as allegorists.

Our most accomplished novels leave no such impression of desperate
and intentional struggle, yet their precise technique and their determination to make their prose work in the service of their subjects have
been the measure of their accomplishment. Hemingway's *The Sun Also
Rises* and Wescott's *The Pilgrim Hawk* are works of art not because

they may be measured by some external, neo-classic notion of form, but because their forms are so exactly equivalent with their subjects, and because the evaluation of their subjects exists in their styles.

Hemingway has recently said that his contribution to younger writers lay in a certain necessary purification of the language; but the claim has doubtful value. The contribution of his prose was to his subject, and the terseness of style for which his early work is justly celebrated is no more valuable, as an end in itself, than the baroque involutedness of Faulkner's prose, or the cold elegance of Wescott's. Hemingway's early subject, the exhaustion of value, was perfectly investigated and invested by his bare style, and in story after story, no meaning at all is to be inferred from the fiction except as the style itself suggests that there is no meaning in life. This style, more than that, was the perfect technical substitute for the conventional commentator; it expresses and it measures that peculiar morality of the stiff lip which Hemingway borrowed from athletes. It is an instructive lesson, furthermore, to observe how the style breaks down when Hemingway moves into the less congenial subject matter of social affirmation: how the style breaks down, the effect of verbal economy as mute suffering is lost, the personality of the writer, no longer protected by the objectification of an adequate technique, begins its offensive intrusion, and the entire structural integrity slackens. Inversely, in the stories and the early novels, the technique was the perfect embodiment of the subject and it gave that subject its astonishing largeness of effect and of meaning.

One should correct Buffon and say that style is the subject. In Wescott's *Pilgrim Hawk,* a novel which bewildered its many friendly critics by the apparent absence of subject, the subject, the story, is again in the style itself. This novel, which is a triumph of the sustained point of view, is only bewildering if we try to make a story out of the narrator's observations upon others; but if we read his observations as oblique and unrecognized observations upon himself the story emerges with perfect coherence, and it reverberates with meaning, is as suited to continuing reflection as the greatest lyrics.

The rewards of such respect for the medium as the early Hemingway and the occasional Wescott have shown may be observed in every good writer we have. The involutions of Faulkner's style are the perfect equivalent of his involved structures, and the two together are the perfect representation of the moral labyrinths he explores, and of the ruined world which his novels repeatedly invoke and in which these labyrinths exist. The cultivated sensuosity of Katherine Anne Porter's style has charm in itself, of course, but no more than with these others does it have aesthetic value in itself; its values lie in the subtle means by which sensuous details become symbols, and in the way that the symbols provide a network which is the story, and which at the same time provides the writer and us with a refined moral insight by means of which to test it. When we put such writers against a writer like William Saroyan, whose respect is reserved for his own temperament, we are appalled by the stylistic irresponsibility we find in him, and by the almost total absence of theme, or defined subject matter, and the abundance of unwarranted feeling. Such a writer inevitably becomes a sentimentalist because he has no means by which to measure his emotion. Technique, at last, is measure.

These writers, from Defoe to Porter, are of unequal and very different talent, and technique and talent are, of course, after a point, two different things. What Joyce gives us in one direction, Lawrence, for all his imperfections as a technician, gives us in another, even though it is not usually the direction of art. Only in some of his stories and in a few of his poems, where the demands of technique are less sustained and the subject matter is not autobiographical, Lawrence, in a different way from Joyce, comes to the same aesthetic fulfilment. Emily Bronte, with what was perhaps her intuitive grasp of the need to establish a tension between her subject matter and her perspective upon it, achieves a similar fulfilment; and, curiously, in the same way and certainly by intuition alone, Hemingway's early work makes a moving splendor from nothingness.

And yet, whatever one must allow to talent and forgive in technique, one risks no generalization in saying that modern fiction at its best has been peculiarly conscious of itself and of its tools. The technique of modern fiction, at once greedy and fastidious, achieves as its subject matter not some singleness, some topic or thesis, but the whole of the modern consciousness. It discovers the complexity of the modern spirit, the difficulty of personal morality, and the fact of evil—all the untractable elements under the surface which a technique of the surface alone can not approach. It shows us—in Conrad's words, from *Victory*—that we all live in an "age in which we are camped like bewildered travellers in a garish, unrestful hotel," and while it puts its hard light on our environment, it penetrates, with its sharp weapons, the depths of our bewilderment. These are not two things, but only an adequate technique can show them as one. In a realist like Farrell, we have the environment only, which we know from the newspapers; in a subjectivist like Wolfe, we have the bewilderment only, which we record in our own diaries and letters. But the true novelist gives them to us together, and thereby increases the effect of each, and reveals each in its full significance.

Elizabeth Bowen, writing of Lawrence, said of modern fiction, "We want the naturalistic surface, but with a kind of internal burning. In Lawrence every bush burns." But the bush burns brighter in some places than in others, and it burns brightest when a passionate private vision finds its objectification in exacting technical search. If the vision finds no such objectification, as in Wolfe and Saroyan, there is a burning without a bush. In our committed realists, who deny the resources of art for the sake of life, whose technique forgives both innocence and slovenliness—in Defoe and Wells and Farrell, there is a bush but it does not burn. There, at first glance, the bush is only a bush; and then, when we look again, we see that, really, the thing is dead.

�֎�֎✎

"Technique as Discovery" is one of the central essays in modern criticism of the novel because it states most explicitly and emphatically the formalist attitude toward fiction, in which the unit is the word, the embodiment the technique, and the end result an aesthetic whole that is valid in its own terms. However, although he is a formalist, Schorer is not an aesthete, and even such theoretical adversaries as Philip Rahv can find common ground in Schorer's view that technique is valuable only insofar as it produces "works with the most satisfying content, works with thickness and resonance, works which reverberate, works with maximum meaning," although they might reject his definition of these terms.

Still, a number of Schorer's assumptions and judgments can be questioned. Underlying the view that the best work has the most "thickness and resonance" is the assumption that the most complex work is the best, an assumption that accounts for the New Critical bias toward James and the metaphysicals, for example, and the devaluation of Fielding and Spenser. Historically and generically oriented critics like Frye and Scholes and Kellogg are likely to question this position.

Furthermore, on at least two occasions Schorer seems to

violate the implications of his own critical premises that the novel should be approached through its style and technique and that external evidence should be used to confirm rather than determine evaluations of the work. He seems to assume, for example, that because H. G. Wells often announced his belief in progress, the end of *Tono Bungay* is therefore without irony; and he relies to a considerable extent for his evaluation of *Sons and Lovers* on Lawrence's independent statement of the theme (apparently forgetting that Lawrence elsewhere said "Trust the tale, not the teller") and on the testimony of E. T., the model for the character of Miriam and hardly a disinterested witness. Some critics, although indebted to Schorer, are more consistent. David Lodge, for example, has shown in *Language of Fiction* that Wells's novel should be judged not as novel but as confession and that, in terms of style, it is both coherent and impressive as a work of art; and H. M. Daleski, in *The Forked Flame: A Study of D. H. Lawrence,** has argued, with close textual analysis of key passages, that *Sons and Lovers* is artistically unified and that its weaknesses, though real, are marginal.

Most of the objections to Schorer's essay, however, seek not to qualify particular judgments but to overthrow his assertion of the primacy of style. In this volume, Rahv, Harvey, and Marcus regard "satisfying content," "thickness and resonance," and "maximum meaning" as being to some extent independent of style and technique. Their essays continue a debate which has not yet been and probably cannot be resolved. In addition to these essays, see Philip Rahv's "Notes on the Decline of Naturalism," which rejects naturalism in terms similar to Schorer's. Rahv, however, defends realism, making reality "the discipline of fiction, much in the same sense that syllabic structure functions as the discipline of verse."† The opening section of Lodge's *Language of Fiction* contains a clear and adroitly outlined discussion of the major issues of this debate.

---

* Evanston, Ill.: Northwestern University Press, 1965.

† "Notes on the Decline of Naturalism," Philip Rahv, *Image and Idea.* Copyright 1949 by Philip Rahv. Reprinted by permission of New Directions Publishing Corporation.

Toward a
Formalist Criticism of Fiction

WILLIAM HANDY

I

The real contribution of the New Critics lies not so much in their providing a method for examining a poem as in their providing an account of the essential *structure* possessed by all lyric poems. Once a sense of the basic stuff of the poem is grasped, the method to be followed in analyzing it presents itself quite naturally and unmistakably. "A poem," Mr. Ransom tells us, "is a *logical structure* having a *local texture.*" He then proceeds to distinguish these two basic elements. He determines the "logical structure" of the poem by formulating a statement of its argument; and he isolates the "local texture" by focusing on "the devices which are, precisely, its [poetry's] means of escaping from prose."

Ransom is not fashioning some sort of arbitrary structure for the poem when he makes his distinction between its logical and nonlogical elements. What he has discerned is basic to the poem as a symbolic formulation. For verification he turned first to Hegel, later to Kant. In one of his more famous essays, "Criticism as Pure Speculation," he declares:

> He [Hegel] seems to make the handsomest concessions to realism by offering to knowledge a kind of universal which was not restricted to the usual abstracted aspects of the material, but included all aspects, and was a concrete universal. The concreteness in Hegel's handling was not honestly, or at any rate not fairly, defined. It was always represented as being in process of pointing up and helping out the universality. He could look at a work of art and report all its substance as almost assimilated to a ruling "idea." But at least Hegel

From *Texas Studies in Literature and Language,* III (Spring 1961). Reprinted by permission of The University of Texas Press.

seemed to distinguish what looked like two ultimate sorts of substance there, and stated the central esthetic problem as the problem of relating them.

Here is what Ransom means by "ontological criticism": the recognition that in the symbols of art there are "two ultimate sorts of substance" and that "the concrete esthetic problem is the problem of relating them." That is, every work of art, in whatever medium, characteristically possesses a universal aspect, which makes possible a concept of the work, and a particular aspect, which offers a *presentation* of meaning far in excess of what its concept is able to render.

In another of his key essays, "Poetry: A Note in Ontology," Ransom makes a distinction similar to that of the Hegel passage, this time relating his theory to Kant's aesthetics. His immediate concern is for the fundamental kinds of subject matter a poem may emphasize: "things" and "ideas." His point is the basic difference in the being of the symbols representing things and the being of the symbols representing ideas. His opening paragraph states:

> A poetry may be distinguished from a poetry by virtue of subject-matter [i.e., things and ideas] and subject-matter may be differentiated with respect to its ontology, or the reality of its being. An excellent variety arises recently out of this differentiation, and thus perhaps criticism leans upon ontological analysis as it was meant to do by Kant.

Kant called for a distinction to be made between the "Understanding," the faculty which reduces its object to a concept in order to classify it, and the "Imagination," the faculty which maintains its object in a presentation in order to know it as it is—undistorted by logical reduction. Kant insisted that the kinds of being represented by the two forms of the judgment were ontologically distinct.

His insistence has its echo in modern criticism in Ransom's final chapter of *The World's Body,* "Wanted: An Ontological Critic." Ransom's meaning is clear: He wishes a critic who approaches the literary work with an awareness of its fundamental structure as a distinctly *aesthetic* judgment—one which exceeds the capacity of a logical judgment by offering a concrete presentation of the texture of experience.

Ransom's critical practice is based upon his theory of the ontological structure of the poem. The steps in the process of relating his theory to his practice may be summarized as follows:

1. Every poem has a paraphrasable content, the argument or plot of the poem.

2. The important considerations for criticism are located not in the paraphrase but in the "texture" of the poem.

3. The texture is composed of devices or forms through which a concrete presentation of meaning is achieved. Some of the more common devices of concretion which have received special emphasis by various schools of modern criticism include: the symbol, the image, paradox, irony, ambiguity, myth, tone, and the like.

4. Critical procedure means the close analysis of these formal devices, because it is in the special use of language, in the *form* it receives, that literary art becomes a unique kind of knowledge.

5. Close analysis presupposes, first, the sensibility to "re-create" (Theodore M. Greene's term for the initial critical act) the work, i.e., to experience it as a presentation; second, the humility to allow the work to speak its own meanings through its own form without imposing critical preconceptions upon it; and third, the full realization that the critical task is forever one of discovery.

II

The movement from the poem to the story is not different in kind. The lyric poem, like the painting, testifies to man's capacity to formulate his world in concrete presentations which render the full unabstracted bodiness or texture of the experience. The work of fiction accomplishes all this but adds a new dimension; it testifies to man's capacity to experience his experience in time. On the surface, the work of fiction appears quite different from the lyric poem. Fiction is concerned with a particular world and particular characters, presented through a succession of scenes which are constructed to develop a central action. Yet the essential structure of fiction—what Ransom would call its "ontological" structure—is basically the same as that of poetry.

When we consider the ontological structure of fiction, it is immediately apparent that the most basic unit of *presentation* is the scene. Other presentational elements abound in a work of fiction, the concrete portrayal of character, the concrete description of the world of the action; but the presentational unit which, more than any other characteristic, distinguishes fiction as a unique literary form, is its formulation of experience as a succession of scenes. The *scene* in fiction may be viewed as analogous to the *image* in poetry. From an ontological point of view both the scene and the image possess the same fundamental characteristics:

1. Both *present* rather than predicate about.
2. Both comprise a single configuration of multiple meaning.

3. Both intend to formulate the particularity, the texture of experience.

4. Both are directed primarily to sense—not to abstract intellection.

5. Both exceed the concept in containing more meaning than a concept can, by its inherent nature, formulate.

The fictional scene, then, no less than the poetic image, represents the literary artist's attempt at, in Eliot's words, "transmuting ideas into sensations." When Stephen Spender wrote the following passage in his fine essay on poetic creation, "The Making of a Poem," he had, primarily, ontological considerations in mind. And the amazing fact is that if we substitute "fiction" for "poetry" in the first line and "scenes" for "images" in the second, the truth of the passage is as evident as in its original sense. My point is of course the analogous, even homologous role played by "images" in the poem and "scenes" in the novel. Mr. Spender writes:

> That is the terrifying challenge of poetry. Can I think out the logic of images? How easy it is to explain here the poem that I would have liked to write! How difficult it would be to write it. For writing it would imply living my way through the imaged experience of all these ideas, which here are mere abstractions...

Spender's observations recall T. S. Eliot's simple statement of the same Coleridgean insight: "There is a logic of the imagination as well as a logic of concepts." The suggestion I wish to make is that from both a creative and a re-creative (critical) standpoint, fiction possesses the same ontological structure as poetry. The writer must "think out the logic" of his scenes with a logic which springs from his image-making faculty. The reader, confronted with a symbolic pattern similar to his daily experience—a progression of individual scenes—responds to the pattern with the expectancy that it will be fully as comprehensible as his daily experience. Actually he anticipates much more. The succession of scenes which are given form in a fictional work constitutes a much more meaningful pattern than one's experience, because they constitute not merely a representation of experience but a *judgment about* experience.

Again, T. S. Eliot's famous concept of the "objective correlative," although most often applied to the understanding of poetry, is fully as applicable to the understanding of fiction. Indeed Eliot conceived the idea while examining a work of drama, which would suggest that its original use was closer to fiction than to poetry. The fact is, Eliot's "objective correlative" is an ontological distinction in Ransom's fullest sense, and applies with equal validity to all forms of literary art. Eliot wrote:

> The only way of expressing emotion in the form of art is by finding an "objective correlative"; in other words, a set of objects, a situation, a chain of events which shall be the formula of that particular emotion; such that when the external facts, which must terminate in sensory experience are given, the emotion is immediately evoked.

Ransom would have preferred Eliot to have written something like "artistic meaning" for "emotion" in his opening sentence, but the "ontological" intention of the passage is the same in either case. The form that the selected or "discovered" "set of objects, situation, chain of events" must be presented in is, of course, the scene. The poem imposes no such demand, but the poem is not, as is fiction, concerned with life in action; the poem is a still life; the work of fiction is life in motion, life experienced not merely in space, but in time.

Pound was closer to a structural definition of the basic literary unit when he described the image as "that which presents an intellectual and emotional complex in an instant of time." Here the term "presents" differentiates the artistic unit from the conceptual unit of expository prose—again a distinction which is ontological in nature. When we recall that Pound was not defining merely a single image—one of the many which constitute a poem—but was also considering the entire poem as a single image, then we may draw the analogy with the *scene* of fiction. At once Pound's definition may be seen to encompass a broader scope and perform a more fundamental service than in its restricted application to the poem. The scene in Pound's ontological sense is also an image and performs the same service for fiction that the image performs for the poem. Consider the treatment of scene in any of Hemingway's novels or short stories. I choose Hemingway because Pound's teachings had a great influence on the young Hemingway who was in Paris learning to become a writer. His associates and teachers included Sherwood Anderson and Gertrude Stein. Concerning the relationship Malcolm Cowley quotes Hemingway as commenting: "Ezra was right half the time, and when he was wrong, he was so wrong you were never in any doubt about it." In his sharply delineated scenes, in his careful fashioning of every line to get the most out of every presentational unit, in his insistence that writing is a process of "getting it right," Hemingway constructs prose poems. His concern is always with the expressionistic qualities which are generated in literary art. One cannot help but draw the parallel to the same concern for expressionism in literature that defines the writing of another of Pound's pupils, T. S. Eliot. For both, the presentational unit must itself do the work, and with that sense of immediacy of meaning that Pound continually insisted upon.

In "The Short Happy Life of Francis Macomber" the opening scene is characteristic of Hemingway's technique, in which, following Pound's teachings, meaning is *presentational* and *immediate*:

> It was now lunch time and they were all sitting under the double green fly of the dining tent pretending that nothing had happened.
> "Will you have lime juice or lemon squash?" Macomber asked.
> "I'll have a gimlet," Robert Wilson told him.
> "I'll have a gimlet too. I need something," Macomber's wife said.
> "I suppose it's the thing to do," Macomber agreed. "Tell him to make three gimlets."
> The mess boy had started them already, lifting the bottles out of the canvas cooling bags that sweated wet in the wind that blew through the trees that shaded the tents.
> "What had I ought to give them?" Macomber asked.
> "A quid would be plenty," Wilson told him. "You don't want to spoil them."
> "Will the headsman distribute it?"
> "Absolutely."

If we were to mark off the scenes in the story by drawing a line between them, the first line would be drawn here.

Much of the impact of Hemingway's writing depends on the sharp demarcation between scenes. For example, the tone shift which accompanies the next scene captures the full sense of the contrast one experiences when the immediacy of a present experience is broken by a sudden shift to a past experience presented in reflection. Hemingway's second scene begins:

> Francis Macomber had, half an hour before, been carried on the arms and shoulders of the cook, the personal boys, the skinner and the porters. The gunbearers had taken no part in the demonstration.

Within the frame of the individual scene each language unit functions expressively or in Susanne Langer's term "non-discursively" to present an aspect of the total work—a thematic meaning, an attitude, a relationship—that is essential to the total meaning of the work. For example in the opening scene Hemingway presents not only the world of the action and the characters involved but he also suggests the tension of the situation, the relationship between the characters and the all important fact that the subject matter is to concern not so much action and event as it is individual human values.

While it is unquestionably true that fiction does not offer its succession of scenes with the same degree of objective presentation that occurs in the drama, yet the apparently discursive passages, such as description, narrative summary, and even author commentary, take on a presentational character when they are woven into the context of a scene.

III

From an ontological point of view a scene is a way of giving form to the way we actually encounter experience in the process of daily living. Each successive experience, however inconsequential, is an encounter, a confrontation, with an expressive presentation. In his recent work, *Adonis and the Alphabet,* Aldous Huxley writes:

> Whether we like it or not, we are amphibians, living simultaneously in the world of experience and the world of notions, in the world of direct apprehension of Nature, God and ourselves, and the world of abstract, verbalized knowledge about these primary facts. Our business as human beings is to make the best of both these worlds.

It is the sciences which not only provide us with the "notions" and the "knowledge," but at the same time testify as one kind of symbolic form to man's impulse to abstraction. It is the arts, on the other hand, which remind us that one portion of our living experience is "the world of direct apprehension of Nature." They also testify to a knowledge impulse—the desire to give symbolic form to concrete, individual experience.

Perhaps in the bombardment of our sensibilities by the shapes and colors and sounds of ever changing experience, we attend but little to individual presentations. That is, we make little effort to "understand" them. Perhaps we unconsciously perform a cognition sufficient to classify them so that we maintain some sort of order and orientation even as we go about experiencing the myriad variety of our presentational experience.

Something like this must occur when we read fiction. The appeal fiction has for us must in part come from the satisfaction that here is a symbolic formulation whose business it is to give a more adequate account of the way human experience actually unfolds, not when it is known about or "understood" merely, but when it is experienced in the course of human living.

In the novel, as in life, presented scene follows presented scene. They are ordered here, of course, not haphazard, because they are *informed* with human purpose. Even Joyce's *Ulysses* possesses an integrating principle which must be recognized if the work is to make meaningful reading. Or consider the presentational scenes which make up the daily round of experience for Faulkner's Benjy in *The Sound and the Fury*. The thirty-three-year-old idiot experiences the conglomeration of disparate experience which comprises his restricted world without sufficient cognitive power to classify and relate the ever-changing shapes and events that continue to register upon his consciousness. But even Benjy has some powers of abstraction. In some vague way those experiences which remind him of his sister, whom he loves with a deep, childlike devotion, are integrated in his mind. The integration is initiated by a cognition, which itself springs from Benjy's values. The reader, once aware of Benjy's pathetic situation as an adult idiot who possesses a touching, however limited, sensibility, follows the main line of the action—seeing the world as Benjy sees it, a confused welter of kaleidoscopic experiences—having meaning only as they are related to his vague memory and longing for his sister, the only one, it is gradually realized, who responded to Benjy as an individual human being.

For social or external purposes, Caddie is a fallen woman driven by misshapen values toward a life of prostitution. For existential or inner purposes, Caddie is recognized as one so capable of love that she alone grants Benjy his individual being. Only for her he is not a concept. Thus when the informed reader is confronted with Benjy's experience —the scenes of life as Benjy experiences them—the whole formulation is fiction of great significance. The integrating principle is love, Benjy's for Caddie, and the ironic justification of Benjy's value judgment concerning his sister gives a new dimension to experience, a new knowledge in a new form, because through Faulkner's fictional form we are made aware of the validity of Benjy's judgment concerning his sister. Were it not for seeing her through Benjy's values, we could not know that she was also a saint.

Form in fiction is an embodiment of meaning, just as it is in poetry, not merely a framework for content. In Ransom's ontological sense, a work is made up of many *forms*, large and small, some structural, some imagistic, some ethical, all testifying to the truth so essential to the theory of Kant and Coleridge that man experiences his life concretely through his imaging faculty, as well as abstractly through his conceptualizing one.

In fiction as well as poetry, the ontology or reality of its being as a symbolic form suggests the approach criticism must take. Since the essential power of the fictional work resides in its *texture,* in the *forms* through which the artist constructs and relates his scenes, criticism becomes a matter of consciousness, of bringing to awareness the nondiscursive meaning embodied in the scenes. Character, action, world must as in poetry be concretely presented. But what makes the fictional form unique is its imitation of the way we encounter life's experience, as a succession of presentations to which we provide some integration, sometimes only to maintain orientation, sometimes to give meaning and even value to the events that pass over consciousness. But just as knowledge of life's "presentations" is a process of becoming aware—of providing a meaningful abstraction in a concept of our experience, so, too, knowledge of literature's "presentations" is a repetition of the same process. Criticism of art as well as of life is consciousness after experience; it is the discovery of meaning in a presentation.

※※※

Whether in praise or blame, it has frequently been said that formalist critics of the novel have transferred to the analysis of fiction methods originally developed for analyzing lyric poetry. Schorer does so, of course, and Handy is more open and more systematic than Schorer in making such a transference. Unlike Schorer, however, he believes that the terminology and the approach need modification before they can be applied to fiction. And unlike Joseph Frank in "Spatial Form in Modern Literature" (see p. 74), he does not seem to think that the novel can be profitably seen in spatial terms; it remains a process, a progression, not an "image" in the same way that a lyric poem is an image—though he does not seem quite aware of the distinction that he implies.

Except in these matters, Handy follows the New Critics' line of argument quite closely. The view that art—especially poetry—is a special kind of knowledge is one of the major premises in the defense of literature against the encroachments of science. This theory is implied in Handy's view that form is an embodiment of meaning and accounts for his and Schorer's emphasis on technique. Some critics, of course, do not see the need for a theoretical defense of literature. Those oriented to the view of the novel as an imitation of reality, like Rahv and Harvey, tend to be pragmatic. They concede the weight of objections to any theory which would divorce content and form, and they

respond to these objections by arguing that the novelist appre-
hends reality and reproduces it—not re-creates it—through the
power of his vision, insight, or imagination. For them, technique
in Schorer's and Handy's sense does not exist, though techniques
do. Nevertheless, divergent though these two theories are, they
have in common an implied (in Handy's case an explicit) concern with ontology, for both are based on the view that ways
of knowing reality are linked to ways of reproducing it.

Handy's essay is useful for its treatment of broad theoretical
issues, but he leaves the way open for specific application of
his approach, and certain points are open to objection. Specifically, the term "scene" may not be entirely adequate for his
purposes, and in any case it needs clearer definition. Further,
one might ask in what sense the quotation from the second
"scene" of "The Short Happy Life of Francis Macomber" is
"presentational" and whether it in fact is "presented in reflection." These questions center on fundamental issues of point of
view and narrative methods in fiction, and they suggest that the
how as well as the *what* of fiction must always be considered.
Further still, is the example fairly chosen? Assuming that
Handy's method works for the fiction of Hemingway, Faulkner,
and Joyce, would it be fruitful if applied to the work of writers
who do not construct "prose poems"? Finally, and more broadly,
does a poem or a painting or a novel really and fully "formulate
[man's] world in concrete presentations which render the full
unabstracted bodiness or texture of the experience"?

Erich Auerbach's *Mimesis: The Representation of Reality in
Western Literature,* translated by Willard Trask,* is a pioneering
attempt to relate the artist's perception of reality to his technique, and in *Character and the Novel* W. J. Harvey exhibits
an admittedly pragmatic and unsystematic interest in ontological
questions. Simon O. Lesser deals in more detail with the psychological appeal of fiction to the reader in *Fiction and the
Unconscious.*† E. M. Forster's chapter on plot in *Aspects of the
Novel* raises in clearest form the objections to using the terms of
drama to describe fiction.

---

* Garden City, N.Y.: Doubleday Anchor Books, 1957.
† Boston: Beacon Hill Press, 1957.

Fiction and
the Criticism of Fiction

PHILIP RAHV

The novel is at the present time universally recognized as one of the greater historic forms of literary art. Its resources and capacities appear to be commensurate with the realities and consciousness of the modern epoch, and its practitioners, having inherited a good many of the functions once exercised by poetry and the drama, no longer feel the slightest need to engage in the kind of apologetics that were quite common even as late as a hundred years ago, when in respectable quarters novel-writing and novel-reading were still looked upon as activities falling below the level of true cultural aspiration. But if the novel was then still widely regarded as a thing somewhat effeminate and moonshiny, fit mainly for the consumption of young ladies, it was at the same time quickly impressing itself upon the mind of the age as a newfangled form full of rude plebeian energy, unruly, unpredictable, and ungovernable in its appropriation of materials from unprocessed reality—"the conscience of a blackened street impatient to assume the world." Much of the life the novel contains is defined by these contrary reactions, one pointing to its origin in romance and the other to its revitalization through the new principle of realism.

Among the last apologies for the novel—an apology in which we fully sense, however, the surge of confidence and power generated by the phenomenal rise of this relatively new genre—is the preface that the Goncourt brothers wrote for their novel *Germinie Lacerteux* (1864). "Now that the novel," they observed, "is broadening, growing, beginning to be a great, serious, impassioned living form of literary study and social research, now that by means of analysis and

Reprinted from *The Myth and the Powerhouse* by Philip Rahv, by permission of Farrar, Straus & Giroux, Inc. Copyright © 1956, 1965 by Philip Rahv.

psychological inquiry it is turning into contemporary moral history, now that the novel has imposed upon itself the investigations and duties of science, one may again make a stand for its liberties and privileges." This memorable formulation is in the main still acceptable to us. The one dated element in it is of course the reference to science, a reference all too patently of its period and linked to the development of the naturalistic school in French fiction. At the time not a few writers were so impressed by the triumphs of scientific method as to want to borrow some of its magic for themselves, yet at bottom it was not so much a matter of faith in science (though doubtless that played its part too) as of an intention to gain prestige for the novel by means of an honorific association. But apart from that the formulation I have cited has scarcely lost its cogency. The one question arising in connection with it is whether it is still necessary at this late date again to make a stand for the novel's liberties and privileges. So far as the intelligent reader at large is concerned such a stand may well be redundant. But it is not in the least redundant, I think, so far as some present-day critics of fiction are concerned and the reading practices to which they have been habituating us.

My argument rests on a premise that most of us will surely accept, and that is that twentieth-century criticism has as yet failed to evolve a theory and a set of practical procedures dealing with the prose medium that are as satisfactory in their exactness, subtlety, and variety as the theory and procedures worked out in the past few decades by the critics of poetry. It may well be, as is so frequently said, that in art there is no such thing as progress. But then, criticism is only partially an art, so little of an art perhaps as to admit in some periods not only change, as all the arts do, but also gradual development toward a more accurate knowledge. One is certainly disposed to think so when comparing the present state of poetry criticism with its state, say, forty or fifty years ago. The criticism of poetry has of late acquired a rich consciousness which may be defined objectively as the self-consciousness of the medium—an historic acquisition that, acting as a force in its own right, has already considerably affected the writing of poetry and may be expected to affect it even more in the near future.[1]

In fiction the prevailing situation is quite different. Is it not a

---

[1] Let us keep in mind, though, that the sway of consciousness is by no means an unmixed blessing. At the heart of consciousness there is always equivocation. One can do no more than hope that this heightened and elabo-

curious fact that while we have had in this century novelists as fully accomplished in their metier as the poets we all esteem are in theirs, none of these novelists have made a contribution to the theory of fiction that comes anywhere near what the poets have attained in their critical forays? You can go through all the essays of Thomas Mann, for instance, without finding anything of really clinching interest for students of the novel as a form; and Mann is surely an exceptionally intellectual and selfconscious artist. Nor will you find, in this respect, any truly close insights in Joyce or Proust. Both *A Portrait of the Artist as a Young Man* and *Ulysses* contain some discussions of aesthetic structure on a fairly abstract level, and these are of no help to us if we are on the lookout for the differentia distinguishing the prose narrative from the other verbal arts. In Proust you encounter a metaphysical theory of the aesthetic meaning of time that generalizes the author's creative experience, but it scarcely yields the kind of concrete illumination of the novelistic form that we gain in poetic theory from the discursive writings of poet-critics like Valéry, Eliot, Pound, Empson, Ransom, and Tate. As for American novelists of our time such as Fitzgerald, Wolfe, Faulkner, and Hemingway, they have influenced fictional modes solely through their practice, steering clear of theoretical divagations. Henry James differs of course from the novelists I have mentioned by virtue of his unusual effort to formulate in critical terms his fascination with method and technique. But James, like Flaubert, is not a novelist of our age. Chiefly he belongs to that heroic period of the past century when the novel fought and won its fight for recognition as an autonomous literary genre making good its claims to the status of high art. At present, however, the practitioners of fiction appear to lack sufficient motive to engage in the analytic study of problems specific to their medium. Such studies are mostly left to professional critics and scholars.

The authority of fact often proves irresistible. I am inclined to think that it is precisely the fact of signal progress that we have witnessed in the criticism of poetry that accounts in some ways for the observable lag in the criticism of fiction. We must beware of

---

rated awareness of the poetic medium, which is after all a kind of wisdom or self-knowledge, will not soon provide us with another melancholy illustration of Hegel's famous dictum that the owl of Minerva begins its flight only when the shades of night are gathering. Not that I in the least associate myself with Edmund Wilson's thesis that verse is a "dying technique." Still, we know that in this world nothing comes free, and one wonders what the price of so intense a consciousness will turn out to be in this instance.

taking a simplistic view of progress. In criticism, as in any other sphere, it is never a unilinear, harmonious forward movement in which every critical concern is equally well served. On the contrary, progress is necessarily an uneven and irregular process: the advantage gained at one point is ordinarily paid for by regress or loss at another point. And to entertain some such notion of what progress comes to in reality is to understand why the very success of the poetry critics has of late begun to exert an influence on the criticism of prose which is far from salutary. For the commanding position assumed by poetic analysis has led to the indiscriminate importation of its characteristic assumptions and approaches into a field which requires generic critical terms and criteria of value that are unmistakably its own. Just as Zola, the Goncourt brothers, and other pioneers of the naturalist school associated the novel with science for the sake of the prestige that this conjunction seemed to confer upon their literary ambitions, so now critics of fiction are attempting to assimilate it to the poem, thus impeding an adequate inspection of the qualities and effects of the prose medium. This effort to deduce a prosaics from a poetics is *au fond* doomed to fail, for it is simply not the case that what goes for a microscopic unit such as the lyric poem goes equally well for the macroscopic compositions of the writer of narrative prose.

In this paper I wish to isolate three biases that can be traced directly or indirectly to this recent infection of the prose sense by poetics. The first bias is manifested in the current obsession with the search for symbols, allegories, and mythic patterns in the novel—a search conducted on the unanalyzed assumption that to locate such symbols in a fictional work is somehow tantamount to a demonstration of its excellence. The fact that the same symbols and patterns are just as easily discoverable in the worst as in the best novels counts for nothing among the pursuers of this type of research. The second bias, even more plainly deriving from the sensibility of poetry, is the one identifying style as the "essential activity" of imaginative prose, an identification that confuses the intensive speech proper to poetry with the more openly communicative, functional, and extensive language proper to prose. The third bias is that of technicism, which may be defined as the attempt to reduce the complex structure and content of the novel to its sum of techniques, among which language is again accorded a paramount place. This third bias, which includes the second and exceeds it, is epitomized in Mark Schorer's well-known essay "Technique as Discovery," presenting in summary form an extreme version of the formalist tendency that has played a leading role in the poetics of our time. Mr. Schorer makes no bones about his indebtedness to the theorists of poetry. In the course of his argument he states this to be the fact, not once but repeatedly, evidently unaware that so large an indebtedness in itself poses a problem and points to predicament.

In examining this bias toward symbolism, allegory and mythic patterning in the reading of fiction, one is first of all struck by its debilitating effect on the critical mind. There was a time not so long ago when it was clearly understood among us that allegory is an inferior mode scarcely to be compared to symbolism in imaginative efficacy; it was also understood that myth and symbol are by no means synonymous terms. But by now all such elementary though essential distinctions have gone by the board. The younger critics have taken to using all three terms almost interchangeably and always with an air of offering an irrefutable proof of sensibility, with the result that they have been nearly emptied of specific meaning and turned into little more than pretentious counters of approbation.[2] But the more these terms lose their reference to anything concrete beyond themselves, the easier becomes their conversion into verbal symbols in their own right, symbols of admission and belonging to a school at present academically and critically dominant. And if you add to this sacred triad the famed pair of paradox and irony your initiation is well nigh complete.

An example is wanted. There is Mr. Robert W. Stallman, for instance, who rather unnerves one with his literal passion for up-to-date notions in criticism. In an essay on Stephen Crane, he writes that

> ...like Conrad, Crane puts language to poetic uses, which, to define it, is to use language reflexively and to use language symbolically. It is the works which employ this reflexive and symbolic use of language that constitute what is permanent of Crane. It is the language of symbol and paradox; the wafer-like sun [the reference is to Crane's memorable sentence in *The Red Badge of Courage:* "The red sun was pasted in the sky like a wafer"]; or in "The Open Boat" the paradox of "cold,

---

2 The word "myth" in particular is being put to such multiple and varied use these days—as when people speak of the myth of racial superiority, or of the myth of the proletariat, or of the mythology of Americanism—that if any sense at all is to be made of the mythic concern in literature, then the least a critic can do is to discriminate sharply between the broad, popular, loosely analogical employment of the term and what Robert Graves rightly, I think, calls the "true myth," which he defines as "the reduction to narrative shorthand of ritual mime."

comfortable sea-water," an image which calls to mind the poetry of W. B. Yeats with its fusion of contradictory emotions. This single image evokes the sensation of the whole experience of the men in the boat. . . . What is readily recognizable in this paradox of "cold, comfortable sea-water" is that irony of opposites which constitutes the personality of the man who wrote it.[3]

And preceding this paragraph with its wholesale disgorgement of shibboleths lifted from contemporary poetry criticism, there is a passage in which Mr. Stallman bares his fixation on the sentence previously quoted ("The red sun was pasted in the sky like a wafer"), in which he professes to see the "key to the symbolism of the whole novel." Why? Because the initials, J. C., of Jim Conklin, the tall, spectral soldier who dies in so grotesque a fashion, ineluctably suggests to Mr. Stallman that he represents Jesus Christ. Thus *The Red Badge of Courage,* which is something of a *tour de force* as a novel and which is chiefly noted for the advance it marks in the onset of realism on the American literary scene, is transmogrified into a religious allegory. All that is lacking in this analysis to give it the final certification of the *Zeitgeist* is the word "myth." Observe, too, that the evidence for this thesis is drawn, not from a study of the narrative progression of Crane's novel as a whole, but from a single image and the amalgam of the initials of the tall soldier's name with the name of Jesus Christ. It is entirely characteristic of Mr. Stallman's approach (and of the critical school to which he is attached) that it never even occurs to him that to speak of "the symbolism of the whole novel" is perhaps in this case a piece of sheer gratuity, that the novel is actually "about" what it seems to be, war and its impact on human beings moved by pride, bravado, fear, anxiety, and sudden panic. If it is symbolic, it is in the patent sense in which all good art, in so far as it opens out to the world at large by transcending its immediate occasions and fixed, exclusive meanings, can be said to be symbolic. But to attribute a symbolic character to Crane's novel in this universal sense has nothing whatever to do with Mr. Stallman's idea of symbolism, an idea indistinguishable from the "fallacy of misplaced concreteness," systematically applied to works of literature.

The absurdity of Mr. Stallman's reading of Crane becomes all too apparent when you look up the text to check on his quotations. He professes to see a poetic paradox in the phrase "cold, comfortable

---

3 Cf. "Stephen Crane," p. 269, in *Critiques and Essays in Modern Fiction,* edited by John W. Aldridge (New York, 1952).

sea-water," but in point of fact within the context of the story the juxtaposition of "cold" and "comfortable" cannot strike us as paradoxical but rather as wholly natural. The situation is that the four shipwrecked men in the tiny boat—the captain, the correspondent, the oiler, and the cook—are dog-tired, not having slept for two days. It is night, and three of them are sleeping in the water-drenched bottom of the boat while the correspondent is rowing:

> The wind became stronger, and sometimes a wave raged out like a mountain cat, and there was to be seen the sheen and sparkle of a broken crest.
> The captain, in the bow, moved on his water-jar and sat erect. "Pretty long night," he observed to the correspondent. . . .
> "Did you see that shark playing around?"
> "Yes, I saw him. He was a big fellow all right."
> . . . Later the correspondent spoke into the bottom of the boat. "Billie!" There was a slow and gradual disentanglement. "Billie, will you spell me?"
> "Sure," said the oiler.
> As soon as the correspondent touched the cold, comfortable sea-water in the bottom of the boat and had huddled close to the cook's life-belt he was deep in sleep.

Now obviously the water *in* the boat feels "comfortable" as against the waves beating *at* the boat, pictured throughout the story as black, menacing, sinister. In contrast the water at the bottom of the boat, in which the men have been sleeping, seems positively domesticated. Hence the adjective "comfortable." Only by carefully sequestering the phrase "cold, comfortable sea-water" from its context can you make it out to be paradoxical.

As for the sentence ending Chapter IX of *The Red Badge of Courage*—"The [red] sun was pasted in the sky like a wafer"—it would seem to me that the verb "pasted" is quite as important to its effect as the substantive "wafer." Moreover, in the first edition of the novel "wafer" was preceded by "fierce," a modifier hardly suggestive of the Christian communion. Crane liked to speak of himself as an impressionist, and as a stylist he was above all concerned with getting away from the morbidly genteel narrative language of his time; the daring colloquialism "pasted in the sky" must have appealed to him on the well-known avant-garde principle of "make it new." More particularly, this concluding sentence of Chapter IX illustrates perfectly what Conrad described as "Crane's unique and exquisite faculty . . . of disclosing an individual scene by an odd simile." Conrad's remark has the aptitude of close critical observation, whereas Mr. Stallman's farfetched religious exegesis is mere *Zeitgeist* palaver.

No wonder that this critic is quite as partial to allegory as he is to symbolism. Thus in a study of Conrad he claims that "The Secret Sharer" is a double allegory—"an allegory of man's moral conscience and...of man's aesthetic conscience. The form of 'The Secret Sharer,' to diagram it, is the form of the capital letter L—the very form of the captain's room. (It is hinted at again in the initial letter of Leggatt's name.) One part of the letter L diagrams the allegory of the captain's divided soul, man in moral isolation and spiritual disunity. The other part of the letter represents the allegory of the artist's split soul. . . . The captain stands at the angle of the two isolations and the two searches for selfhood."[4] It is the inescapable logic of this obsession with symbols and allegories that it is bound to decline into a sort of mechanistic cabala that scrutinizes each sign and letter of the printed page for esoteric or supernal meanings. The plain absurdity of Mr. Stallman's reading of "The Secret Sharer" should not, however, deter us from recognizing that this mode, which he carries to an extreme, is a fairly representative one nowadays and that it is greatly favored by abler critics who at times still manage to retain some sense of proportion. My concern is not with Mr. Stallman's absurdities as such. I cite him only because his very excess brings to light the fantastication inherent in the approach he shares with a good many other people.[5]

What, at bottom, is the animating idea behind this exaltation of symbolism in current critical practice? As I see it, its source is not directly literary but is to be traced to an attitude of distaste toward the actuality of experience—an attitude of radical devaluation of the actual if not downright hostility to it; and the symbol is of course readily available as a means of flight from the actual into a realm where the spirit abideth forever. If the typical critical error of the thirties was the failure to distinguish between literature and life, in

4 Cf. "Life, Art, and 'The Secret Sharer,' " p. 241 in *Forms of Modern Fiction,* edited by William Van O'Connor (Minneapolis, 1948).

5 The payoff of the rage for symbolism is surely Mr. Charles Feidelson's recent book, *Symbolism and American Literature,* the fundamental assumption of which is that "to consider the literary work as a piece of language is to regard it as a symbol, autonomous in the sense that it is quite distinct both from the personality of the author and the world of pure objects, and creative in the sense that it brings into existence its own meaning." In this curious work the interest in symbolism has quite literally consumed the interest in literature.

the present period that error has been inverted into the failure to perceive their close and necessary relationship. Hence the effort we are now witnessing to overcome the felt reality of art by converting it into some kind of schematism of spirit; and since what is wanted is spiritualization at all costs, critics are disposed to purge the novel of its characteristically detailed imagination working through experiential particulars—the particulars of scene, figures and action: to purge them, that is to say, of their gross immediacy and direct empirical expressiveness. It is as if critics were saying that the representation of experience, which is the primary asset of the novel, is a mere appearance; the really and truly real is to be discovered somewhere else, at some higher level beyond appearance. The novel, however, is the most empirical of all literary genres; existence is its original and inalienable datum; its ontology, if we may employ such a term in relation to it, is "naïve," common-sensical, positing no split between appearance and reality. "The supreme virtue of a novel," as Henry James insisted, "the merit on which all its other merits...helplessly and submissively depend," is its truth of detail, its air of reality or "solidity of specification." "If it be not there, all other merits are as nothing, and if these be there, they owe their effect to the success with which the author has produced the illusion of life." It is an illusion in the sense that what is recounted has not really happened but has been imagined by the author; but this cannot mean that it is an illusion in relation to itself too, that the novel dreams itself, as it were. There is not some other novel, composed of spiritual and moral integers, hovering somewhere behind the illusion of life with which the novelist has sought to infuse his fictive world. We are of course free to interpret that world and to approach it from different angles and on different levels. But to interpret a fiction is one thing; to dissolve it is something else again, and we do dissolve it when treating it as a mere appearance, of the senses only, of interest only to the extent that it provides a domicile for symbols, supersensible forms comparable to Plato's Ideas. Such a notion has little in common with the literary theory of symbolism, though on the surface it may look like a logical extension of it. It belongs rather to metaphysics. The obsession with symbolization is at bottom expressive of the reactionary idealism that now afflicts our literary life and that passes itself off as a strict concern with aesthetic form.

This is not to say, to be sure, that fiction excludes symbolization. On the contrary, works of fiction abound in symbolic devices and the more significant among them have symbolic import. But when we speak of the symbolic import of a novel what we have in mind is nothing more mysterious than its overplus of meaning, its suggestiveness over and above its tissue of particulars, the actual representation of which it is comprised; and that is scarcely the same thing as treating these particulars as "clues" which it is the ingenious critic's task to follow up for hidden or buried meanings that are assumed to be the "real point" of the text under examination. In the long run this procedure cannot but make the text itself dispensable; it ceases to be of use once you have extracted the symbols it contains. The text, however, is not a container, like a bottle; it is all there is; and the symbol-hunting critics are unwittingly reasserting the dichotomy of form and content which they ostensibly reject. *Moby Dick*, for instance, is a work of which certain basic elements, such as the whale, the sea and the quest, have both symbolic and direct representational value. There is no consensus among commentators as to what the symbolic value of those elements comes to in specific, exact terms; and it is a proof of the merit of this work that no such consensus is in fact possible. The narrative, not being an allegory, has no meanings that can be mentally tabulated and neatly accounted for. Its symbols are integrally a part of its fictive reality, and it is precisely their organic character that renders them immune to purely intellectual specification.

One should also be on the lookout against mistaking the creative intent of the conscious symbolic device employed by many modern writers. A novella like *Death in Venice,* in which the symbolic device is used again and again and always with exemplary control, will serve as a splendid example. One device in it is the introduction of a series of figures playing the part of "messengers" to Aschenbach (e.g., the "stranger with the pilgrim air" who appears at the very opening of the narrative and the gondolier who ferries him like Charon over to the Lido) whose function is at once to warn the hero and to foretell his doom. This function, however, has no independent "meaning"; it falls rather within the sphere of the technique devised to vivify our sense of the basic theme, which is the relationship between Aschenbach and Tadzio. This as well as the other symbolic devices to which Mann has recourse belong more to the compositional than to the thematic element of the novella. Mann succeeds in it to the degree in which he convinces us that the relationship between Aschenbach and Tadzio with its tragic consummation is actual and that it *is* what it appears to be. Hence it can be said that whatever symbolic value we may discover in the story is incremental, so to speak, to its actuality. It is a value, in other words, gained in the process of the story's actualization; it had no prior claim to existence and least of all can it lay claim to being its rationale. Nor is it its "essence," but rather a gift freely offered as the story comes to life, and in this sense it is more gratuitous than necessary. This would explain why it is so tractable, that is, why it is open to varying and contradictory interpretations. For anything a fiction might conceivably be a symbol of is inevitably far less compelling than what it immediately is in its felt unity of reality and appearance. To convert the experience it embodies into a symbol pure and simple is to empty it of its palpable substance. Thus what the objection to the excessive critical emphasis on symbolism comes down to is that, in making for a split between spirit and sense, it goes so far in conceptualizing the literary object as to drain it of its existential qualities.

The second bias in the contemporary idea of the prose medium is that of language, a bias which John Crowe Ransom not so long ago brought out into the open in committing himself to the view that "fiction, in being literature, will have style as its essential activity." In dealing with this view we know exactly where we stand, for Mr. Ransom's candor leaves us in no doubt as to its origin. In his essay, "The Understanding of Fiction," he is quite explicit on that point, declaring that "following that criticism of poetry which has made such a flourish in our time," he brings to fiction "a set of procedural biases gained elsewhere. . . ." And he goes on to say that since "the criticism of poetry has been an intensive one, concentrating for the most part upon the linguistic detail of the lyric passage," he would like to begin by citing "a few passages. . .from reputable fictions, as an indication of the sort of fixed images or exempla, which I carry around with me, and from which I must start; they will not be poetry but they will be like fictional analogues of lyrical moments." He then proceeds to quote a paragraph from Jane Austen, several paragraphs from *Daisy Miller,* and a paragraph consisting of just sixteen lines from *War and Peace,* taken from the chapter portraying Napoleon coming upon Prince Andrey as he lies wounded on the battlefield. The conclusion Mr. Ransom implicitly comes to is that Tolstoy is not so good a writer as Jane Austen and Henry James. The author of *War and Peace,* he remarks, "does not possess fully the technical advantages of a style. For concentration he substitutes repetition. . . ."

Now quite apart from the fact that the passages from Jane Austen and James are quoted as they wrote them while the passage from Tolstoy is given in translation, the procedure adopted by Mr. Ransom, that of citing sixteen lines from a novel of nearly twelve-hundred pages, does not seem to justify itself from the standpoint of critical method. A passage so brief might be cited to illustrate some special usage but scarcely the over-all effects of a narrative style, for such effects are secured not locally, in the short run, but in the long run, by accumulation and progression. Moreover, for the purpose of my argument here, it is not in the least necessary for me to dispute Mr. Ransom's judgment of the comparative value of the three prose styles he has examined. Let me grant him his judgment—that Tolstoy is inferior as a stylist. What is not acceptable, however, is the implicit estimate of the three novelists involved in this judgment. We cannot but suspect the relevance of a standard the application of which elevates the author of *Mansfield Park* above the author of *War and Peace*. To my mind, *War and Peace* and *Anna Karenina* are both greater works of literature than any of Jane Austen's or James's novels; and if I am right in this respect (I imagine that most qualified readers of fiction would probably agree with me), then perhaps it is the test chosen by Mr. Ransom, the criterion of language or style in the poetry sense of the term, which is at fault. In applying other criteria—character creation, for instance, or the depth of life out of which a novelist's moral feeling springs, or the capacity in constructing a plot (plot, that is, in the Aristotelian sense as the soul of an action) to invest the contingencies of experience with the power of the inevitable—we shall be persuaded soon enough that Tolstoy far outranks Jane Austen. Plainly the difficulty is with the linguistic criterion, which when applied unilaterally is likely to expose us to false valuations, such as that of ranking Turgenev above both Tolstoy and Dostoevsky (for Turgenev is generally admitted to be a better stylist than either of his coevals), or a storyteller like Ivan Bunin above his contemporary Chekhov. In the same way, if we turn to American fiction for examples, few would deny that Dos Passos is a better writer of prose than Dreiser; but is he on that account also the superior novelist? I think not. Dreiser's fictive world, for all his sloppiness as a stylist, is far more solid and meaningful than that of Dos Passos.

Mr. F. R. Leavis is another critic who, coming to prose with habits of mind acquired in the study of poetry, adopts a view similar to that of Mr. Ransom. He, too, is a great believer in "exemplifying," as he calls it; and he has noted that while it is easier to cite examples from poetry, prose demands the same approach even if it does not admit it quite so readily. "With the novel it is so much harder to apply in a critical method the realization that everything the novelist does is done with words, here, here, and here, and that he is to be judged as an artist (if he is one) for the same kind of reason as a poet is. Poetry works by concentration; for the most part, success or failure is obvious locally. . . . But prose depends ordinarily on cumulative effect, in such a way that a page of a novel that is on the whole significant may appear undistinguished or even bad. . . ." But though Mr. Leavis is fully aware of the hazard involved in transferring the poetry critic's method of local exemplification to the study of narrative prose, he nevertheless comes out in its favor because he sees no alternative. The trouble lies, I think, in his reluctance to draw a sharp enough distinction in principle between prosaic and poetic speech. Is it really the case that language plays the same role in both media? In looking to narrative prose for "fictional analogues of lyrical moments," as Mr. Ransom does, are we not in effect ignoring the crucial differences between the use to which language is put in poetry as against its use in prose and hence denying the latter the status of a separate genre?

The approach to the prose medium I am disputing is not an isolated one. It is deeply imbedded in the history of modern literary critcism and scholarship. More or less the same approach was advocated by the extreme wing of the Russian formalists, who were also inclined to over-react to the undeniable fact that fiction is made up of words, just like poetry. In the controversy that developed around this issue, it was the more moderate formalist Victor Zhirmunsky who was in the right, I believe, when he protested against the superstition of the word by which his colleagues appeared to have been overcome. According to Zhirmunsky's theory, a novel and a lyric poem are not to be equated as works of verbal art because the relation in them between theme and composition is quite different. Words in a novel, say, by Tolstoy, or Stendhal, are closer to everyday speech and openly communicative in function, whereas in a poem the verbalization is wholly determined by the aesthetic design and is in that sense an end in itself. There is such a thing, to be sure, as a purely formal prose, in which the elements of style and composition dominate (as in the work of Leskov, Remizov and Biely), but it is precisely the "ornamentalism" of such prose that basically differentiates it from the narrative language of novelists like Stendhal, Tolstoy, or Dostoevsky, who achieve expressiveness chiefly through extensive rather than intensive verbal means.

I might add that "ornamental prose" is a technical term in Russian criticism which does not at all mean the same thing as "ornate prose." As D. S. Mirsky explains in his *History of Russian Literature,* "ornamental" prose fiction "is not necessarily marked by conventionally uplifted diction." It may be crudely realistic or even blatantly coarse. It is mainly distinguished by the fact that it keeps the reader's attention fixed on the small detail: the words, their sounds, their rhythm. "It is the opposite of Tolstoy's or Stendhal's analytical prose. It is the declaration of independence by the smaller unit. . . . Ornamental prose has a decided tendency to escape the control of the larger unit, to destroy the wholeness of the work." I suppose that in English the work of Virginia Woolf would to some extent correspond to what the Russians mean by "ornamental" prose fiction, as would a novel like *Nightwood;* and among the younger American novelists there are not a few "ornamental" writers of prose to whom the test of local exemplification would apply, for the effects they seek depend almost entirely on stylization, on the perceptibility, to borrow a phrase favored by the formalists, of the mode of expression. But the norms of the novel are scarcely those of ornamentation, or of art-prose, a related term employed by the German critic Ernst Robert Curtius in a fine critical passage comparing Balzac and Flaubert:

> Balzac's creative power equals that of the greatest writers. Is he their equal also as an artist? It is evident that Balzac cannot be weighed in the scale of Flaubert's art-ideal. This ideal is that of art for art's sake. To Flaubert the value of a work hinges upon the quality of style, the faultless purity of language, the rhythms of the paragraphs and the music of the prose. His ideal was to transmute reality into imperishable verbal substance. He called it: *faire du réel écrit.* Flaubert's language is art-prose in the sense in which one speaks of the art-prose of the Greeks and Romans. That was for Flaubert an inner necessity, which had its psychological grounds. An author like Balzac, in whom a world of living figures strains toward the light, cannot possibly write that way and has no need to do so. The artificial linking of artistry and the novel, for which Flaubert is responsible and which degenerates into a mannerism in the Goncourt brothers, leads to a blind alley.

The norms of the novel cannot accommodate a declaration of independence by the smaller unit, the word, the phrase, the sentence or the paragraph. Normatively the language of the novel does not possess the autonomous value that it has in poetry. It only intermittently lends itself to that verbal play characteristic of poetic speech, a play which uncovers the phonic texture of the word while at the same time releasing its semantic potential. In prose the relation between the word or sign and its referent is more firmly fixed and necessarily conventionalized than in poetry, where this relation is continually maneuvered so as to exploit the discord no less than the concord of sign and referent. Why is it, asks Susanne Langer in her book *Feeling and Form,* that the lyric poem is of all literary genres the one most directly dependent on verbal means—the sound and evocative power of words, meter, alliteration, rhyme, and other rhythmic devices, such as repetition, archaisms, and grammatical distortion? Her answer is that "the motif. . .of a lyric is usually nothing more than a thought, a vision, a mood, or a poignant emotion, which does not offer a very robust framework for the creation of a piece of virtual history. . . . The lyric poet uses every quality of language because he has neither plot nor fictitious characters, nor, usually, any intellectual argument to give his poem continuity. The lure of verbal preparation and fulfillment has to do nearly everything. . . ." Admitting that Miss Langer somewhat overstates her case, what she is saying on the whole is so self-evident as to be hardly more than a truism. It is a truism, however, which poetry critics, carried away by the simultaneous turn toward dramatic speech and intellectual elaboration in modern verse, are inclined to forget, with the result that they almost never stress the radical difference between the illusion of life or air of reality created in a poem and that created in a story or a novel or a play. Actually, the dramatic as well as the narrative (epic) resources of the modern poetic medium are extremely limited and the imagery it employs, however dramatic its impact on its own chosen ground, is no substitute for the bodying forth of character in action.

The late Christopher Caudwell is the critic who has made the most of the difference between poetic and prosaic language. In his book *Illusion and Reality* he wrote that the "poetic word is the logos, the word-made-flesh, the active will ideally ordering, whereas the novel's word is the sign, the reference, the conversationally pointing gesture." And again: "Painting, poetry and melody all have this in common—the timeless universal quality of the human genus rather than the interesting complications and subcomplications of a group of human individuals." It seems to me that he gets to the bottom of the distinction we are seeking to define when he says that "poetry concentrates on the immediate affective associations of the word," whereas the story goes first to "the object or entity symbolized by the word" in order to draw its associations from that. "The poem and the story both use sounds which awake images of outer reality and affective reverberations; but in poetry the affective associations are organized by the structure of the language, while in the novel they are organized by the structure of the outer reality portrayed. . . . Hence the hero of the novel is not like the 'hero' of poetry, a universal common 'I,' but a real concrete individual." The reader of the poem lives in the words of the poem and identifies with the poet, while the reader of the novel does not identify with the novelist but immerses himself instead in his fictive world, in which he finds "a more or less consistent mock-reality that has sufficient stuff in it" to stand between him and external reality. This means that the emotional associations in the novel are attached not to its words but to the mock-reality which they bring into being. "That is why rhythm, 'preciousness' and style are alien to the novel; why the novel translates so well; why novels are not composed of words. They are composed of scenes, actions, *stuff,* and people, just as plays are. A 'jewelled' style is a disadvantage to the novel because it distracts the eye from the things and people to the words—not as words, as black outlines, but as symbols to which a variety of feeling-tone is directly attached. . . ." There are of course poetic passages in novels (as in Melville and Lawrence) as there are novelistic passages in poetry, but that in no way changes the characteristics of the two genres.

It seems to me that in Caudwell's formulation, which I have summed up all too briefly, we get at last to the root of the matter. It is the only theory which brings to bear a fundamental principle of explanation telling us why poetry is the form most indissoluble from its language while fiction is translatable with but minor loss to the integrity of the text. It explains why we are able to recognize Dostoevsky's greatness as a novelist at the same time that we are not in the least impressed by his stylistic powers. He is in fact a most indifferent stylist, but that hardly bothers us in reading him, for once we are caught up by the moving current of mock-reality in his narratives we cease noticing the words as such: the language becomes a kind of transparent envelope or medium through which we watch the action. Stendhal is another novelist of the first order whose stylistic gifts are unimpressive. Valéry goes so far as to speak of his "negligence, the wilful negligence, the contempt for all the formal qualities of style." But if so many of us have been drawn into Stendhal's fictive world and utterly won by it, it must be that the word *stylist,* or even the word *writer,* and the word *novelist* are not really synonymous. Sartre once observed that the poet is a writer who refuses to "utilize" language. An admirable formula, and the obverse of it would be that the novelist is a writer who is more often than not perfectly willing to utilize language. And if he is also a fine stylist, that is something thrown into the bargain. This bargain may inspire us with gratitude, but that is hardly a sufficient basis for an aesthetic of prose.

For the poet the major problem is always style, which it seldom is for the novelist. If you look into the working notebooks of two novelists so vastly different as James and Dostoevsky you are struck by the fact that verbal stylization is never among the difficulties they wrestle with. In their private notebooks both writers are talking to themselves, as it were, talking in an effort to define their subject, that above all, and further to see their way through the plot, the complications of the intrigue, the arrangement of scenes, the temporal sequence, the narrative perspective or point of view, and so on. The language in which all these things are to be embodied they take more or less for granted. In the notebook outlining the scenario of *Crime and Punishment* Dostoevsky is greatly worried by such problems as whether to tell the story in the first or third person, i.e., whether to let Raskolnikov tell the story in the form of a diary or whether to adopt the stance of the omniscient author; he has not as yet made up his mind whether Raskolnikov is to commit suicide or repent and go to Siberia to expiate his crime; and his entire conception of the novel changes upon deciding to introduce the Marmeladov family into the plot. These are clearly problems of theme and structure, exclusively, never of stylization. When he repeatedly complained that because of his poverty, the material pressure he was under to write rapidly in order to meet the monthly schedule of the periodicals in which his work was serialized, he could never turn in a performance as finished as that of Turgenev's for example, he did not mean that given more time he would apply himself to improving his diction and sentence structure. What he had in mind, rather, is that with less pressure on him he would have been able to organize his plots and design his scenes more carefully. He would have been able, in other words, to construct a more powerful and convincing illusion of life, a fictive world of superior consistency drawn more accurately to scale.

All that we can legitimately ask of a novelist in the matter of language is that it be appropriate to the matter in hand. What is said must not stand in a contradictory relation to the way it is said, for that would dispel the illusion of life and with it the credibility of the fiction. A Dostoevskyean story cannot be appropriately told in the style, say, of Dreiser, as that style is too cumbersome and the pace too slow. Dostoevsky's style has a kind of headlong, run-on quality which suits perfectly the speed of narration and the dramatic impetuosity of the action. But in itself, if we set out to examine it in small units, it is not rewarding. The principle of Dostoevsky's language is velocity; once it has yielded him that it has yielded nearly everything that his dramatic structure requires of it. The exact opposite of Dostoevsky is a novelist like Proust, whose themes and structures are undramatic and who must therefore secure his effects primarily through stylization. Proust's themes are essentially poetic-ironic rather than dramatic— memory, the intermittences of the heart, nostalgia for childhood, the vocation of the artist, illusion and disillusion with the great social world. There is of course action in Proust, but this action is rendered undramatically, in a mode shifting from analytic meditation to rhapsody and back again; and meditation and rhapsody are closely allied to the poetic medium. The intrinsic nature of Proust's themes and his conception of them as "enchanted realms," as he put it, in which "the dust of reality is mixed with magic sand," are such that they demand a master of language for their realization. It is pointless, however, to ask of a novelist whose themes do not require such an intensive stylistic effort that he captivate us through language when he is quite capable of captivating us through other means.

So far as Mr. Mark Schorer's essay "Technique as Discovery" is concerned, I think I have already dealt with it to the extent that it uniquely puts emphasis on style as an element of novelistic technique. For the rest, what is mainly to be objected to in Mr. Schorer's approach is his exclusive and almost vindictive emphasis on technique which leads him to say that "when we speak of technique in the novel we speak of nearly everything." His notion is that because technique objectifies the materials of art it also *ipso facto* evaluates them in a moral and intellectual sense. To me this formulation represents a monistic scheme, a violent simplification that leaves out of account any number of problems, such as that of creative personality, of the conditioned historical outlook prompting writers to settle upon some techniques while rejecting others, and the problem of the personal and unforeseen which, as Malraux has noted, is always present in our experience of a masterpiece. If by some chance the text of *Hamlet* had been lost to us, we would plainly be unable to imagine it despite all our accumulated knowledge of Shakespeare's techniques. And how are we to reconcile Mr. Schorer's point of view with Proust's precept that style is essentially a matter not of technique but of vision? The implication of that precept is that the technique of a true artist is dictated by an inner need and can be imitated only superficially. Vision is inimitable.

In a way everything Mr. Schorer says about the importance of technique is true, but true only in the trite sense that the novelist cannot render a single scene without some kind of technique, adequate or inadequate. But does Mr. Schorer really intend us to understand him in this altogether obvious manner? He remarks that if Thomas Wolfe had had the right sort of respect for technique and the ability to pursue it he would have written "a great novel on his true subject —the dilemma of romantic genius." Plausible as this sounds, does it actually mean anything more than if Wolfe had been a different kind of man he would have written different books? Tautologies are not insights. There is something anterior to technique and that is sensibility. Wolfe's sensibility was such that he was unable to conceive of the subject of romantic genius in a genuinely novelistic spirit; all he could do is spill the subject rather than express it; and the sensibility of Wolfe is not something he could alter. Sensibility can be cultivated under the appropriate conditions but it can scarcely be learned as a technique is learned. Let us beware of regarding technique as some sort of gimmick which it takes a certain amount of intelligence to master, after which the writer is at liberty to "create" to the top of his bent. One detects in such ideas an unconscious predisposition toward scientism, toward purely manipulative notions of the creative process and a tendency to subject it to rationalization. Let us recall T. S. Eliot's statement about Massinger—that he was a brilliant master of technique without being in any profound sense an artist. This can only mean that even though without technique we can do nothing in art, technique is not nearly enough.

※○※○※

Philip Rahv's essay, delivered as a lecture in 1955 and first published in 1956, is one of the major counterattacks on new critical approaches to the novel. Whether one accepts his position or not, he presents a useful warning, particularly to the neophyte, against certain critical excesses. Perhaps most important are his attacks on theories that claim exclusive authority in approaching the novel and his insistence that the novel is not only a work of art but a reflection of life. Finally, arguing in more general terms, he demonstrates that a critical position cannot be entirely divorced from ethics, politics, and philosophy.

Rahv's argument, however, has weaknesses as well as strengths. His discussion of allegory exhibits what may be called a provincialism of period that confuses rather than clarifies some of the issues. Critics and scholars who take longer views and who are less bound to the novel as a form and to realism as a mode— Scholes and Kellogg, for example—use allegory as a descriptive term rather than as a shibboleth and have demonstrated that allegory as well as symbolism can be organic to a mature and complex work of art. Moreover, most of Rahv's support for his major thesis, that certain approaches to the novel are not salutary, seems to be based on the view that the abuse of a critical position is sufficient demonstration that it is not to be used. Furthermore, in opposing these theories categorically, he has obscured the fact that he and his opponents agree on many points. For example, Schorer probably would not deny that "the felt reality of art" is important, since he talks in terms of "thickness and resonance"; certainly he does not regard technique as "some sort of gimmick." Granted that Schorer's "technique" is not clearly defined; the term that Rahv would substitute, "sensibility," seems no clearer.

Both Rahv and his opponents advance categorically exclusive arguments: in Rahv's case, opposing the language of fiction to the language of poetry, allegory to symbol, and perhaps—the underlying premises are not clearly defined—reality to art. It is possible, however, to answer Rahv's objections to certain critical tendencies without taking up an antagonistic position. To his strictures against "the obsession with the search for symbols, allegories, and mythic patterns in the novel" one might respond that these patterns can—though not inevitably—contribute to the resonance of the novel and for that matter help to convey "the depth of life out of which a novelist's moral feeling springs." Mythic patterns are one possible means of giving dimension to character, and they can further the understanding and imaginative participation of the reader. Symbolic patterns can be one means of satisfying the reader's aesthetic desire for order. Both of these defenses assume the validity of his, and Henry James's, distinction between compositional thematic elements, between the subject—a "grasp of a single character" in *Portrait of a Lady* or a relationship in *Death in Venice*—and the means of embodying it, such as a *ficelle* or the recurring motif of the stranger.

To Rahv's argument on language it might possibly be conceded that language is not *the* essential activity of fiction, but surely it is *an* essential activity. Perhaps, as David Lodge has argued in refutation of Caudwell and Rahv, literary language is a continuum rather than a series of radically discontinuous types. Rahv's argument might be tested by analysis of similar words or situations or emotions as they are embodied in lyric poetry and in prose. More to the immediate point, many of the novelists that Rahv praises (Tolstoy and Stendahl are major examples) are discursive rather than dramatic, analytic rather than presentational in any obvious sense, so that "solidity of specification" may be rather more complex a matter than Rahv conceives—or than Handy and Schorer do, for that matter.

Finally, to Rahv's argument against technicism, no reply is possible, except that no responsible critic would argue that the novel is simply the sum of its techniques. The formalists stress the organic quality of the work of art; and an organism is not merely a sum.

Several essays in Lionel Trilling's *The Liberal Imagination** are relevant to Rahv's essay and the controversies in which it participates. Trilling shows both in "Reality in America" and "Manners, Morals, and the Novel" the unduly honorific nature of the term "reality." He argues in "Art and Fortune" that T. S. Eliot's critical disciples discount ideas in literature and thus predict the death of the novel and that the poetic bias of criticism displaces rather than supplements the critical theories of Flaubert and James. David Lodge's *Language of Fiction*

* New York: Viking Press, 1950.

examines the implications of the controversy more thoroughly than either Schorer or Rahv. Robert Wooster Stallman refutes some and rejects all of Rahv's arguments in "Fiction and Its Critics: A Reply to Mr. Rahv,"* an essay reprinted in expanded form in *The Houses that James Built and Other Literary Studies.*†

* *Kenyon Review,* XIX (Spring 1957), 290–99.
† East Lansing: Michigan State University Press, 1961.

Character and
the Context of Things

W. J. HARVEY

I

The present essay derives from the thesis that whereas in life we are allowed only intrinsic knowledge of self and only contextual knowledge of others (knowledge, that is, formed from the perception of relationships), fiction allows us both kinds of knowledge. It is concerned to examine the simplest of such contexts; namely, the relation of people to the world of inanimate objects.

II

> When you've lived as long as I you'll see that every human being has his shell and that you must take the shell into account. By the shell I mean the whole envelope of circumstances. There's no such thing as an isolated man or woman; we're each of us made up of some cluster of appurtenances. What shall we call our "self"? Where does it begin? Where does it end? It overflows into everything that belongs to us—and then it flows back again. I know a large part of myself is in the clothes I choose to wear. I've a great respect for *things*! One's self—for other people—is one's expression of one's self; and one's house, one's furniture, one's garments, the books one reads, the company one keeps—these things are all expressive.

Madame Merle's excursion into metaphysics raises a great many questions about the nature of character—indeed, more than character, for without her viewpoint what would become of our old thematic friend, Appearance and Reality? But she also states with finality the most obvious *function* in fiction of the various relationships assumed to

From *Essays in Criticism,* **XIII** (1963). Reprinted by permission of the editors of *Essays in Criticism.*

exist between people and objects. This function is to create settings
which, as Wellek and Warren observe, "may be viewed as metonymic,
or metaphoric, expressions of character." This function has so often
been the object of critical attention that I shall not discuss it further
here. My concern is with some less obvious and more problematical
aspects of the relations established between mind and things.

We may begin with a passage from the superb eleventh chapter of
Our Mutual Friend, which describes a dinner party at the Podsnaps:

> Mr. and Mrs. Veneering, and Mr. and Mrs. Veneering's bran-new
> bride and bridegroom, were of the dinner company; but the Podsnap
> establishment had nothing else in common with the Veneerings. Mr.
> Podsnap could tolerate taste in a mushroom man who stood in need
> of that sort of thing, but was far above it himself. Hideous solidity
> was the characteristic of the Podsnap plate. Everything was made to
> look as heavy as it could, and to take up as much room as possible.
> Everything said boastfully, "Here you have as much of me in my
> ugliness as if I were only lead; but I am so many ounces of precious
> metal worth so much an ounce;—wouldn't you like to melt me down?"
> A corpulent straddling epergne, blotched all over as if it had broken
> out in an eruption rather than been ornamented, delivered this address
> from an unsightly silver platform in the centre of the table. Four silver
> wine-coolers, each furnished with four staring heads, each head obtru-
> sively carrying a big silver ring in each of its ears, conveyed the
> sentiment up and down the table, and handed it on to the pot-bellied
> silver salt-cellars. All the big silver spoons and forks widened the
> mouths of the company expressly for the purpose of thrusting the
> sentiment down their throats with every morsel they ate.

It is not enough to say that the dinner table is merely metonymic,
that it simply reflects or symbolizes the qualities of Podsnappery. The
passage may begin in that way but any sense of equivalence is soon
overtaken by a livelier fantastication of the prose. The objects in a
sense *become* Podsnap and his guests; in the sustained exuberance of
the conceit, salt-cellar and spoon live a life of their own far more
intense than that of the assembled company, who suffer for a moment
the unnatural reverse of becoming merely objects. All critics have
remarked on Dickens's power of animating the inanimate world;
none better than R. H. Horne who in an early essay compares him
with Hogarth:

> There is a profusion and prodigality of character in the works of
> these two artists. A man, woman, or child, cannot buy a morsel of
> pickled salmon, look at his shoe, or bring in a mug of ale; a solitary
> object cannot pass on the other side of the way; a boy cannot take
> a bite at a turnip or hold a horse; a by-stander cannot answer the

simplest question; a dog cannot fall into a doze; a bird cannot whet his bill; a pony cannot have a peculiar nose, nor a pig one ear, but out peeps the first germ of "a character." Nor does the ruling tendency and seed-filled hand stop with such as these; for inanimate objects become endowed with consciousness and purpose, and mingle appropriately in the background of the scene. Sometimes they even act as principals, and efficient ones too. . . .

The good thing about Horne's comment is the way in which he connects two main characteristics of Dickens's fictional world. The Dickensian qualities of abundance and prodigality are such that, moving with him through his imaginatively crowded world, we seem continually to be bumping into things. This is a world of perpetual small collisions. At a pinch, we might say that this was an objective quality of his age, that a Victorian drawing room, for example, literally was crowded with objects. But it was also a quality of his imagination since this dense world of things is also alive; it has a comic or malign energy of its own. Dickens's imagination is primitive, animistic. I think we misread him slightly if we take his quickening power as merely conceit or metaphor or symbol; I believe this inanimate world was, for him, literally alive. There is nothing very odd in this; when a pencil breaks or we stub our toe in the dark we often have, in a transient way, this primitive sense of objects stubbornly leading a mysterious life of their own, a life which sometimes thwarts or obtrudes into ours. Most of us have vestigial terrors which are the feeble descendants of a magical view of the world. This primitive, animistic sense of things not just as "out-there," opaque, other-than-us, but also as alive, hostile or benevolent, is only one end of a whole scale of relationships between mind and the world of objects. Up and down this scale the novelist may range at will. Its center—that which we take to be both norm and normal—is surely represented in fiction by Tolstoy, in whose work, as F. G. Steiner says, in his *Tolstoy or Dostoevsky,* "Physical objects derive their *raison d'être* and solidity from the human context." Mr. Steiner at this point in his argument is contrasting Tolstoy's humanistic attitude to the world of things with that of Flaubert; he quotes from *Madame Bovary* the famous description of Charles's schoolboy cap:

> It was a headgear of composite order, containing elements of an ordinary hat, a hussar's busby, a lancer's cap, a sealskin cap and a nightcap; one of those wretched things whose mute hideousness suggests unplumbed depths, like an idiot's face. Ovoid and stiffened with

whalebone, it began with three convex strips; then followed alternating lozenges of velvet and rabbit's fur, separated by a red band; then came a kind of bag, terminating in a cardboard-lined polygon intricately decorated with braid. From this hung a long, excessively thin cord, ending in a kind of tassel of gold netting. The cap was new; its peak was shiny.

The object here is more truly metonymic, but Mr. Steiner is surely right to dismiss those critics who load this passage with tremendous symbolic import. While it may throw *some* light on Charles's character it also communicates a kind of linguistic desperation in the face of a contingent and multitudinous world of objects—as though the author has said to himself, "At least I will pin *this* down in a definitive manner." By contrast Tolstoy moves freely and confidently through his imagined world which seems denser, of greater plenitude, precisely because he does not lavish his attention on detail in the way that Flaubert does. Tolstoy is lord of creation—at least of his creation— and things retreat before him to their humble place in a centrally human world.

If we travel further down the scale of mind-thing relationships, from the primitive imagination of Dickens, through the human centrality of Tolstoy, past the desperation of Flaubert, then we arrive at something like this:

"We went back to look for Minta's brooch," he said, sitting down by her. "We"—that was enough. She knew from the effort, the rise in his voice to surmount a difficult word that it was the first time he had said "we." "We" did this, "we" did that. They'll say that all their lives, she thought, and an exquisite scent of olives and oil and juice rose from the great brown dish as Martha, with a little flourish, took the cover off. The cook had spent three days over that dish. And she must take great care, Mrs. Ramsay thought, diving into the soft mass, to choose a specially tender piece for William Bankes. And she peered into the dish, with its shiny walls and its confusion of savoury brown and yellow meats, with its bay leaves and its wine, and thought: This will celebrate the occasion—a curious sense rising in her, at once freakish and tender, of celebrating a festival, as if two emotions were called up in her, one profound—for what could be more serious than the love of man for woman, what more commanding, more impressive, bearing in its bosom the seeds of death; at the same time these lovers, these people entering into illusion glittering eyed, must be danced round with mockery, decorated with garlands.

"It is a triumph," said Mr. Bankes, laying his knife down for a moment. He had eaten attentively. It was rich; it was tender. It was perfectly cooked.

There is here, as in Flaubert, a desperation in face of the world of objects. But whereas Flaubert reacts by attempting to capture the thing in itself, objective, in all its bizarre detail, Virginia Woolf tries to pin the thing down at the moment when it deliquesces into the consciousness of her characters. The sensuous richness of so much of her prose is not, as it might at first seem, her tribute to a crowded world of autonomous objects since for her all things ultimately become mind-stuff, entering the glow of that "luminous halo" which is her metaphor for life itself. Virginia Woolf is perhaps too often a naïve Berkeleyan since *esse percipi est* is only one side of the equipoise between mind and the world of objects. The other side is our sense that objects *resist* our attention, that they remain opaque, stubbornly themselves. This sense is abundant in Dickens—it is one source of his metaphoric richness—but is deficient in Virginia Woolf. To dine with the Podsnaps is to surrender to a world of things sensed as living a life of its own; to dine with the Ramsays is to celebrate a triumph of mind over matter. For in the passage I have quoted from *To the Lighthouse,* the book as well as the dinner has been beautifully cooked. Behind the perfection of the Boeuf-en-Daube, with its subtle blend of ingredients, is Mrs. Ramsay's triumph in blending and reconciling the human ingredients of her dinner party; Mr. Bankes pays tribute to both successes. And behind Mrs. Ramsay, of course, stands Virginia Woolf triumphantly blending the elements of life into her art. The extreme self-consciousness of this process is evident— "this will celebrate the occasion," Mrs. Ramsay thinks. This is one reason why Virginia Woolf's novels, though containing many striking and beautiful effects, are in the last analysis irritating. The metaphoric vivacity of Dickens's prose only enhances the independence of the objects described; Virginia Woolf, by contrast, allows the external world too little freedom. The sensibility of her characters too easily digests whatever it encounters. We are left with facts of mind where sometimes we hunger for simple, brute facts. Moreover—this is a different but related complaint—the mind which thus transmutes is far too limited, allowing little dramatic variety; most of her characters metamorphose the world in strikingly similar ways. The results achieved are rich but narrow; intensity is purchased at too great a cost. After so much Boeuf-en-Daube one hungers for plain bread-and-cheese.

If we go still further in our scale of mind-thing relationships, beyond Virginia Woolf, then we encounter something like Roquentin's famous confrontation with the chestnut tree:

> Absurdity; another word; I struggle against words; down there I touched the thing. But I wanted to fix the absolute character of this absurdity here. A movement, an event in the tiny coloured world of men is only relatively absurd: by relation to the accompanying circumstances. A madman's ravings, for example, are absurd in relation to the situation in which he finds himself, but not in relation to his delirium. But a little while ago I made an experiment with the absolute or the absurd. This root—there was nothing in relation to which it was absurd. Oh, how can I put it into words? Absurd: in relation to the stones, the tufts of yellow grass, the dry mud, the tree, the sky, the green benches. Absurd, irreducible; nothing—not even a profound, secret upheaval of nature—could explain it. Evidently I did not know everything, I had not seen the seeds sprout, or the tree grow. But faced with this great wrinkled paw, neither ignorance nor knowledge was important; the world of explanations and reasons is not the world of existence. A circle is not absurd, it is clearly explained by the rotation of a straight segment around one of its extremities. But neither does a circle exist. This root, on the other hand, existed in such a way that I could not explain it. Knotty, inert, nameless, it fascinated me, filled my eyes, brought me back unceasingly to its own existence. In vain to repeat: "This is a root"—it didn't work any more. I saw clearly that you could not pass from its function as a root, as a breathing pump, *to that,* to this hard and compact skin of a sea lion, to this oily, callous, headstrong look. The function explained nothing: it allowed you to understand generally that it was a root, but not *that one* at all. This root, with its colour, shape, its congealed movement, was...below all explanation. Each of its qual- ities escaped it a little, flowed out of it, half solidified, almost became a thing; each one was *in the way* in the root and the whole stump now gave me the impression of unwinding itself a little, denying its existence to lose itself in a frenzied excess. I scraped my heel against this black claw: I wanted to peel off some of the bark. For no reason at all, out of defiance, to make the bare pink appear absurd on the tanned leather; to *play* with the absurdity of the world. But, when I drew my heel back, I saw that the bark was still black.

This passage, which perhaps suffers more than the others in being wrenched from its context, is really the extension of an insight which has come to Roquentin a few pages earlier, when he ponders the seat of a tramcar in which he is traveling:

> Things are divorced from their means. They are there, grotesque, headstrong, gigantic and it seems ridiculous to call them seats or say anything at all about them: I am in the midst of things, nameless

things. Alone, without words, defenceless, they surround me, are beneath me, behind me, above me. They demand nothing, they don't impose themselves; they are there.

It is clear, even from these short extracts, that part of *La Nausée* is concerned with dramatizing the struggle of a mind to leap through the void that separates it from the world of things and to make sense of a totally senseless universe. The desperation of both the effort and the inevitable defeat is to be sensed in the language, particularly in its quality of powerful but slightly sinister metaphor. The thing, the tree-root, can be named but the name is divorced from the thing; that its "absolute character" can never be fixed is shown by the drastic metamorphoses it undergoes—a breathing pump, a sea-lion, a black claw. The prose oscillates between that and a kind of abstraction— "a circle is not absurd"—which enacts, I suppose, the effort of the mind to come to terms with the vigour and plenitude of an external world totally subversive of all logic. Even to speak in these terms is to do the passage an injustice, since what appears as metaphorical is also, in a sense, literal. In a world where, as Roquentin says, "the essential thing is contingency," where no necessary or stable relation-ships are to be discerned, which is sensed primarily as a viscous flux, such metamorphoses are not impossible. Why, in this totally random world, should a root *not* become a black claw or the seat of a tramcar change into the upturned belly of a dead donkey? The prose does more than play with such questions; behind it is a serious and sophisticated philosophy. Yet, oddly enough, our scale of mind-thing relationships seems almost to be circular, with its extremes meeting; the philosophic imagination of Sartre seems much more akin to the primitive imagination of Dickens than to anything else we have encountered.

III

Alienation has unfortunately become something of a cant word in many kinds of intellectual discourse, including literary criticism. But it is the right and inevitable word if we are to see the passages I have quoted as representative rather than arbitrary. Its primary connotations are, of course, social; it directs us to such topics as the replacement of community by mass or the breakdown in communica-tion between the artist and any coherent audience. If its efforts have been primarily social so, we may agree, was its cause; I see little to quarrel with in the Marxist thesis that alienation is a product of complex industrial and capitalist societies. But a contributary cause was certainly the decline of a theology in which man's relation to his world was given stability by being part of a divinely-ordered cosmos. We need not discuss how the breakdown of this world-view was related to social and economic changes. But we should notice that one of the series of correspondences supposed to exist between microcosm and macrocosm presupposed a stable relation between the world of things and man's mind,

> that ocean where each kind
> Does straight its own resemblance find.

At first the grandeur and order of the Newtonian universe buttressed the coherence and stability of this world view. But as the idea of rational man living in a rational universe crumbles, as scientific laws turn into mere high-order probabilities, as the possibility of certain knowledge dwindles and as the necessary turns into the contingent, so the novelist comes to inhabit an exciting but unstable world. I am not, of course, suggesting a simple relationship between intellectual cause and imaginative response; no doubt there is a cultural time-lag and no doubt diffusion means distortion. But gradually man's view of his world changes and gradually this affects the novelist's response; we move from confidence to uncertainty, from stability to flux, from the assurance that we know what is normal to Roquentin's sense of the absurd. The effects of this breakdown—of alienation—are discernible in every aspect of life, including man's relation to the world of things.

The breakdown usually takes one of two forms. There is the common Romantic nightmare—particularly acute in Coleridge—of the material world when the creative mind fails in its seminal function; a universe of little things, dry, disconnected, dead. But it is the second kind of alienation that I wish to stress, one denounced by Carlyle and Ruskin, not to speak of Marx himself. This is the view of man as victim of the cash-nexus and the industrial jungle; man as reduced to the status of a mere thing, an extension of the lever or the loom; man as an object to be manipulated and exploited.

Most novelists view with abhorrence this reduction of man to thing. This is partly because most of them write from within a liberal world view with its respect for people as autonomous beings, as ends-in-themselves. But this respect is also inherent in the nature of their craft; acutely aware of the dangers of creating puppets, they must strive to give at least the illusion of autonomy to their characters. Hence most of them react sharply to this aspect of alienation; manipulation of other people, the reduction of man to object, quickly become objects of attack in their fiction. This is certainly what happens in the extract quoted from *Our Mutual Friend*, constituting the important difference between Dickens and Sartre. For Dickens's primitive imagination of the world is given moral point and direction by a mind that is, in the last analysis, in confident control, whereas Sartre's protagonist is helpless in face of a totally contingent world of objects.

It is rare for the problems thus raised to be intellectually formulated by the novelist. Indeed, it is quite possible—witness most English novels—to rest in a kind of comfortable empiricism, to concern oneself with particular, limited human and social situations, and to be entirely unaware that any larger problem exists. Alienation most often manifests itself as a diffused and undefined pressure to which the novelist responds obliquely. As one might expect, an important set of responses is religious in nature; yet these produce surprisingly few really great novels. There is a kind of neo-Platonic response in which objects are placed and given significance by being the symbolic manifestation of a transcendental reality. This, of course, is the descendant of the traditional Christian metaphysic; what is new is that the god is veiled and ambiguous; reality may be divine or diabolic. Of this kind of reaction Melville and Kafka are perhaps the major representatives. As against this, by believing that the divine is also totally immanent, one may simultaneously celebrate God and life in all its particularity; parts of Tolstoy's work are here the best example. Finally, one can accept the entire contingency of the phenomenal world as it is humanly experienced and leap, like Kierkegaard, across the void between the breakdown of reason and the acceptance of faith. I cannot recall any great novel which dramatizes this position; Dostoevsky comes closest, I suppose, but does not quite fit into this or into any other category. Roquentin makes part of the journey and comes to the edge of the void, to the absurd; but he can go no further since God is absent from his universe. Sartre, to be sure, subsequently makes the leap to a total faith. But this is irrelevant to his fiction; indeed, perhaps it killed him as a novelist.

The significant reaction, in fact, has not been so much religious as aesthetic. One thinks, for example, of characters like Mrs. Ramsay whose sensibility works on the raw data of her experience in a typically aesthetic way, composing relationships into harmony, translating her gastronomic triumph into a symbolic celebration of human love. One thinks of all those novelists—the Mrs. Ramsays of that craft—who have written novels exploring the preconditions necessary to the writing of a novel. One thinks of the rise of the *bildungsroman*. Most significant of all, perhaps, one thinks of Roquentin's faint hope of escape from the world of nausea; he, too, however feebly, can rejoice, having to construct something on which to rejoice. Why can Roquentin hope that the writing of a novel will make some sense of his life? Because the work of art—viewed as a self-sufficient artefact—is a necessary and not a contingent thing. It is a thing wrenched from the chaotic flux of the experienced world; it has its own laws and its own firm structure of relationships; it can, like a system of geometry, be held to be absolutely true within its own conventionally established terms.

Many modern novelists have found consolation in this view which has consequently affected their creative practice. While few novels can be derived from it in any philosophically rigorous sense, it is clearly no accident that autonomy theories of art have concurrently become dominant. Connected with these theories there is another kind of aesthetic response to the fact of alienation which is important to the substance and the implied values of many modern novels. In an autonomy theory of art the cardinal sin is didacticism. By this I mean any attempt on the part of either writer or reader to *use* the work of art. On this theory the artefact both arouses and completes emotion; the aesthetic state is one of stasis. Kinetic responses—those which carry over from the artefact to life—are at best irrelevant and at worst vitiating since the work of art is a sufficient end in itself, containing its own values. In the post-Kantian, liberal ethic endorsed by most novelists, the human being has much the same status as that accorded the work of art by this type of aesthetic. Man is an end in himself; we must respond to him as an autonomous being; the cardinal sin is to use or to manipulate him, to reduce him to a mere thing. The fields of aesthetics and ethics have a common frontier; thus one may easily understand how many novelists will therefore dramatize the moral substance of their novels in aesthetic terms. Aesthetic value becomes a metaphor for moral value; if man, in his alienated state, is reduced to a thing, then the novelist responds by asserting that he is at any rate a very special *kind* of thing—a work of art. Ethical discrimination merges into aesthetic discrimination;

good taste becomes nearly synonymous with good sense and right feeling.

Here again, Virginia Woolf is a relevant example, especially if one sees her as sharing an ethos derived from G. E. Moore:

> By far the most valuable things, which we know or can imagine, are certain states of consciousness, which may be roughly described as the pleasures of human intercourse, and the enjoyment of beautiful objects. No one, probably, who has asked himself the question, has ever doubted that personal affection and the appreciation of what is beautiful in Art or Nature, are good in themselves; nor, if we consider strictly what things are worth having purely for their own sakes, does it appear probable that any one will think that anything else has nearly so great a value as the things which are included under these two heads.

But it is probably Henry James who has most consistently, richly and subtly exploited this interplay between aesthetics and ethics. Let us examine briefly, therefore, some aspects of *The Portrait of A Lady*.

IV

In the education of Isabel Archer no lesson is more bitter or more important than this recognition of what Osmond and Madame Merle have done to her:

> She saw, in the crude light of that revelation which had already become a part of experience and to which the very frailty of the vessel in which it had been offered her only gave an intrinsic price, the dry staring fact that she had been an applied handled hung-up tool, as senseless and convenient as mere shaped wood and iron. (Chapter 52).

This perfect example of the sin against human autonomy—of use and exploitation, of the person reduced to a thing—gains part of its force from a context of imagery which persistently renders human experience in aesthetic terms. This is particularly true when applied to Isabel herself; thus, early in the novel, her cousin Ralph thinks of her:

> "A character like that," he said to himself—"a real little passionate force to see at play is the finest thing in nature. It's finer than the finest work of art—than a Greek bas-relief, than a great Titian, than a Gothic cathedral. It's very pleasant to be so well treated where one had least looked for it. I had never been more blue, more bored, than for a week before she came; I had never expected less that anything pleasant would happen. Suddenly I received, by the post, to hang on

my wall—a Greek bas-relief to stick over my chimney-piece. The key of a beautiful edifice is thrust into my hand, and I'm told to walk in and admire." (7).

As Isabel is seen in aesthetic terms, so she sees others; thus Lord Warburton is "a hero of romance" (7) and in Caspar Goodwood "she saw the different fitted parts of him as she had seen, in museums and portraits, the different fitted parts of armoured warriors—in plates of steel handsomely inlaid with gold." (13). So her moral life, too, is defined in these terms; of her relation with Madame Merle, "it was as if she had given to a comparative stranger the key to her cabinet of jewels. These spiritual gems were the only ones of any magnitude that Isabel possessed." (19). The notion of the key is, of course, recurrent and related to the persistent image of the house, both conveying the basic themes of independence, invasion and possession. Similarly when Ralph tells Isabel, "Don't question your conscience so much—it will get out of tune like a strummed piano," (21), his simile perhaps gains a resonance from the literal, emphasized fact of Madame Merle's skill at the piano; she *plays* on Isabel as well.

This brings us to Madame Merle and Osmond, and to one of the central problems confronting James in this novel. Madame Merle and Osmond must be made to *seem* fine and impressive, at least in Isabel's eyes; otherwise her sensibility will be coarsened and her value as moral agent diminished. If she is to be deceived then at least she must be taken in by a very good imitation of the real thing. But she *is* deceived; Madame Merle and Osmond must be seen by the reader only as *seeming* what Isabel actually takes them to be. James's major techniques for solving this problem are not relevant here, but clearly the problem *is* closely related to the view of human beings as aesthetic objects. Thus many critics have noticed the limiting qualifications in James's description of Madame Merle: "Of painting she was devotedly fond, and made no more of brushing in a sketch than of pulling off her gloves." (19). Similarly, Osmond *appears* a fine aesthetic object:

> He suggested, fine coin as he was, no stamp nor emblem of the common mintage that provides for general circulation; he was the elegant complicated medal struck off for a special occasion. (22).

But the fine coin proves to have too great an admixture of base alloy; Osmond is like the precious coffee-cup flawed by a minute crack. (49). The human failure is suggested in aesthetic terms; thus Madame Merle admits that "his painting's pretty bad" (19); thus Rosier (whose testimony we tend to trust since he sacrifices Art for Life by selling his bibelots) thinks that much of Osmond's taste is bad (37); Ralph, while allowing to Isabel that Osmond is "the incarnation of taste," comes as near as he can to savagery by telling her, "you were meant for something better than to keep guard over the sensibilities of a sterile dilettante." (34). Osmond himself reveals his human-aesthetic flaw. He dismisses Madame Merle thus; "Oh, the imagination of women! It's always vulgar, at bottom. You talk of revenge like a third-rate novelist." (49). Yet within a few pages he too becomes the third-rate novelist:

> Osmond turned slightly pale; he gave a cold smile.
> "That's why you must go then? Not to see your cousin, but to take a revenge on me."
> "I know nothing about revenge."
> "I do," said Osmond. "Don't give me an occasion." (51).

Naturally these two predators regard Isabel in similar terms:

> What could be a happier gift in a companion than a quick, fanciful mind which saved one repetitions and reflected one's thought on a polished, elegant surface? Osmond hated to see his thought reproduced literally—that made it look stale and stupid; he preferred it to be freshened in the reproduction even as "words" by music. His egotism had never taken the crude form of desiring a dull wife; this lady's intelligence was to be a silver plate, not an earthen one—a plate that he might heap up with rich fruits, to which it would give a decorative value, so that talk might become for him a sort of served dessert. He found the silver quality in this perfection in Isabel; he could tap her imagination with his knuckle and make it ring. (35).

Even before this Isabel has conceived of herself in a like way:

> She only felt older—ever so much, and as if she were "worth more" for it, like some curious piece in an antiquary's collection. (32).

This, of course, is precisely what she is destined to become; part of the tragedy of her relationship with Osmond is in the metamorphosis from "silver plate" to "an applied handled hung-up tool, as senseless and convenient as mere shaped wood and iron."

The examples I have quoted in this brief analysis are not isolated; such imagery is dense in *The Portrait of A Lady*. It is a concern, moreover, which persists through much of James's work; one thinks of *The Princess Casamassima* and *The Tragic Muse*. From it James derives many of his most beautiful effects; I can think of few more lyrical passages in his work than his description of Strether's walk through the French countryside in the eleventh book of *The Ambassadors*. Yet in the margins of this translation of human experience into aesthetic terms there remains a faint question mark. How adequate, after all, to the complexity of life is this view of human relationships as a matter of conoisseurship? If Osmond regards Isabel as a work of art, so do Ralph and Lord Warburton; if Osmond regards his daughter thus, so does Rosier. But unlike them, Osmond has a base and improper aesthetic sense; unlike them, he wants to *use* the work of art. It is precisely in these terms that James achieves the desired moral discrimination and, in doing so, achieves also a masterpiece. Nevertheless, the question remains; the balance between aesthetic vehicle and moral tenor is a precarious one; the traffic between the two areas is often equivocal and ambiguous. This is the reason, surely, why the attitude of the Ververs to their captive Prince has caused so much critical debate.

For a symbol of this mingled strength and weakness, this combination on the reader's part of admiration and marginal doubt, we may turn to another novelist. Aschenbach in *Death in Venice* is truly representative of many writers whose dilemma and response I have tried to describe. His artistic life has been dedicated to the wrenching of a classic order out of the delirium and flux of life. Yet behind the order lies the dream of a Dionysiac revel; life reasserts itself, fascinating, corrupt, chaotic, a jungle. In face of this, "his art, his moral sense, what were they in the balance beside the boons that chaos might confer?...Knowledge is all-knowing, understanding, forgiving; it takes up no position, sets no store by form. It has compassion with the abyss —it *is* the abyss."

Yet before he plunges into the abyss of life, immersing himself for the last time in the destructive element, Aschenbach once more asserts his identity and dignity as an artist, "and fashioned his little essay after the model Tadzio's beauty set; that page and a half of choicest prose, so chaste, so lofty, so poignant with feeling, which would shortly be the wonder and admiration of the multitude."

It is a heroic stance, compelling respect and compassion. The artist for the last time tames the multitudinous seas, before breaking his magic staff and drowning into life. Yet even here we hear the whisper of our marginal doubt. Do we ever really believe in that page and a half of exquisite prose? Is the purity of the aesthetic response ever adequate to the challenge of a corrupt, contingent, chaotic world? Can a last-ditch defense ever become a proper base for further explanation?

✼✼✼✼

Although he is aware that division is not always practical, W. J. Harvey prefers, in this essay and even more explicitly in *Character and the Novel,** to ally himself critically with Rahv as opposed to Schorer, to extol the method of Tolstoy as opposed to that of James, and to judge the novel in terms of its adequacy in reflecting experience as opposed to its adequacy as art—in other words, to accept "mimetic" rather than "autonomy" theories of the novel. Like other critics of the mimesis school, notably Erich Auerbach and Ian Watt, he emphasizes the influence on technique resulting from the individual artist's perception of reality, as conditioned by his age. For example, Watt holds that the novel arose when "the study of the particulars of experience by the individual investigator"† could be assumed to produce valid results; Philip Rahv comments on the novel's "naive ontology"; and Shroder holds that the novel's characteristic subject is the divorce between appearance and reality— reality as defined by the novelist. Frequently a corollary to this position is the view that, in Harvey's terms, "the novel is the distinct art form of liberalism."

Like Harvey's "scale of relationships between mind and the world of objects"—such scales are used throughout *Character and the Novel*—this kind of statement can be either a useful description of what in fact occurs or a prescription, giving coherence to or paralyzing the critic's approach. Although Harvey sometimes approaches prescription, as in the final paragraphs of this essay, his practical criticism is generally not doctrinaire. In fact, his judgments often concur with those of David Lodge, who follows Schorer. Thus, though Harvey maintains that the language of fiction cannot sustain the intense analysis given to that of poetry, he does not exclude such analysis, as his discussion of metaphor in *Portrait of a Lady* demonstrates. His objection that Virginia Woolf allows the external world too little freedom is echoed by Lodge's view that Woolf's stylistic devices

---

* Ithaca, N.Y.: Cornell University Press, 1965.
† *The Rise of the Novel* (Berkeley: University of California Press, 1957), p. 12.

"might be used as evidence for alleging certain important limitations in her art."* And though Harvey's school of criticism
tends to uphold the virtue of the nineteenth century French and
Russian novelists—partly in conscious attempts to redress critical
judgments—he, like Lodge, gives the highest kind of praise to
the eleventh book of James's *The Ambassadors.*

This kind of agreement does not mean, of course, that the
ideal criticism will be a kind of bland theoretical ecumenism.
However much they borrow each other's methods, the formalist
and mimetic approaches remain fundamentally distinct. It might
be argued—as recent theorists seem increasingly inclined to do—
that different kinds of literature, even different kinds of novels,
demand different approaches, and that theoretical statements
should be used as explanations rather than as slogans in a
critical holy war.

The most useful supplementary reading to Harvey's essay is
his book, which examines clearly and with remarkably little
rancor the critical controversy between mimetic and autonomy
theories of the novel. (Some reviewers wished that he were more
combative.) Erich Auerbach's *Mimesis*† and Ian Watt's *The
Rise of the Novel*‡ discuss in great detail the novel's relation to
modes of perception. Harvey's implication that a changing world-
view alters art forms is developed further in his book, in John
Wain's essay in this volume, and in the closing pages of Scholes's
and Kellogg's *The Nature of Narrative.* Perhaps the most striking contrast to Harvey's commitment to liberalism and thus to
the novel is Joseph Frank's acceptance of changes in world-views
and art forms in "Spatial Form in Modern Literature." Harvey's view that autonomy theories are false and perhaps harmful
to the novel as well as to criticism is discussed in concrete terms
in Steven Marcus' essay.

---

* David Lodge, *Language of Fiction* (New York: Columbia Uni-
versity Press, 1966), p. 86.
† Translated by Willard Trask (Garden City, N.Y.: Doubleday &
Company, Inc., 1957).
‡ Berkeley: University of California Press, 1957.

Point of View in Fiction:
The Development
of a Critical Concept

NORMAN FRIEDMAN

*Let me only add that in this Art, as in the others, there is, and
will be always, whatever has been done already, something new
to discover, something new to express, something new to describe.*
—Walter Besant, *The Art of Fiction* (1885)

Aldous Huxley, speaking through Philip Quarles's "Notebook,"
questioned some twenty-five years ago the contemporary distaste for
the omniscient author in fiction: "But need the author be so retiring?
I think we're a bit too squeamish about these personal appearances
nowadays." Yet four years later Joseph Warren Beach could write:
"In a bird's eye view of the English novel from Fielding to Ford, the
one thing that will impress you more than any other is the disappearance of the author." Accordingly, Bradford A. Booth wrote in 1950:
"It has been said that the most significant change in the fiction of
our time is the disappearance of the author. Conversely, the trade
mark of the Victorian novel is the presence of the author, ever poised
to intrude a comment, to interpret the characters, or to write an essay
on cabbages and kings." For better or for worse, then, it seems that
our "squeamishness" has won the day.[1]

Reprinted by permission of the Modern Language Association. From *PMLA,*
LXX (1955).

---

[1] Huxley, *Point Counter Point* (1928), Ch. XXII; Beach, *The Twentieth
Century Novel: Studies in Technique* (New York and London, 1932), p. 14;
Booth, "Form and Technique in the Novel," *The Reinterpretation of Victorian
Literature,* ed. Joseph E. Baker (Princeton, 1950), p. 79.

The importance of this fastidiousness is conceived by many today, however, as of the highest. "This is the great outstanding feature of technique since the time of Henry James," claims Beach, "that the story shall tell itself, being conducted through the impressions of the characters. It is this which finally differentiates fiction from history and philosophy and science." Mark Schorer's concern is even more rigorous; it is time, he announces, that we read fiction as if technique were something more crucial than mere embellishment, for "technique is the only means [the writer] has of discovering, exploring, developing his subject, of conveying its meaning, and finally, of evaluating it." And he speaks chiefly of the aesthetic relationship between the author and his work. "We are no longer able to regard as seriously intended," he continues, "criticism of poetry which does not assume these generalizations; but the case for fiction has not yet been established." If fiction's case has not yet been established, there are strong forces at work in the process of establishing it. "Point of View" is becoming one of the most useful critical distinctions available to the student of fiction today.[2]

It is the purpose of this paper to sketch in the aesthetic background of this concept and its emergence as a critical tool, to outline and exemplify its basic principles, and finally to discuss its significance in relation to the problem of artistic technique generally.

I

The art of literature, as opposed to the other arts, is by virtue of its verbal medium both cursed and blessed with a fatal capacity for talk. Its vices are the defects of its virtues: on the one hand, its range and depth of significance far exceed the scope of painting, music, or sculpture; on the other, its ability to project the sensory qualities of person, place, and event is correspondingly less. While it can express more ideas and attitudes, it presents qualitatively weaker images. It is enough for the painter to attend to his palette, to get the proper shade in the proper place; but the writer is torn continually between the difficulty of showing what a thing is and the ease of telling how he feels about it. The sculptor can only show; the musician, program music notwithstanding, can never tell. But literature derives

---

2 Beach, ibid., pp. 15–16; Schorer, "Technique as Discovery," *Essays in Modern Literary Criticism,* ed. Ray B. West, Jr. (New York and Toronto, 1952), pp. 190–91 (reprinted from the *Hudson Review,* 1948).

its very life from this conflict—which is basic to all its forms—and the history of its aesthetic could in part be written in terms of this fundamental tension, to which the particular problem of point of view in fiction is related as part to whole. For the general distinction was being made, from Plato and Aristotle to Joyce and Eliot, in order that the specific one could take shape. From the ancient rhetorician's directions regarding "vividness" (*enargia*) to the modern aesthetician's study of "projection" (empathy), the relationship between the author's values and attitudes, their embodiment in his work, and their effect upon the reader, have been and continue to be of crucial concern.

For our purpose it will suffice to fix the two opposite points in time between which the history of this concept may be plotted. Plato, to begin with, made a distinction, when discussing the "style" of epic poetry,[3] between "simple narration" on the one hand and "imitation" on the other. When the poet speaks in the person of another we may say that he assimilates his style to that person's manner of talking; this assimilation of himself to another, either by the use of voice or gesture, is an *imitation* of the person whose character he assumes. But, if the poet everywhere appears and never conceals himself, then the imitation is dropped and his poetry becomes *simple narration*. Plato then illustrates this difference by "translating" a passage from the

---

[3] *The Republic* (Plato died 347 B.C.), III, 392–94. For some representative high spots in the history of aesthetics and criticism regarding this distinction, see the following: Aristotle, *Rhetoric* (ca. 330 B.C.), III, xi, 2–4; Quintilian, *Institutes* (fr. ca. A.D. 88), IV, ii, 63; VI, ii, 28–34; VIII, iii, 61–62; Sidney, *An Apology for Poetry* (ca. 1583, printed 1595), in *Elizabethan Critical Essays*, ed. G. Gregory Smith (London, 1904), I, 201; John Hoskins, *Directions for Speech and Style* (ca. 1600), ed. Hoyt H. Hudson (Princeton, 1935), p. 42; Bacon, *De Augmentis* (1623), V, v; Dryden, "A Letter to the Honorable Sir Robert Howard," prefacing *Annus Mirabilis* (1666); Alexander Gerard, *Essay on Taste* (London, 1759), Part III, Sec. vi, pp. 197–98, and *Essay on Genius* (London, 1774), Part II, Sec. iii, pp. 169–174; Henry Home, Lord Kames, *Elements of Criticism* (Edinburgh, 1762), Ch. XVII, pp. 483–84 (cf. Mihail M. Morozov, "The Individualization of Shakespeare's Characters through Imagery," *Shakespeare Survey 2*, Cambridge, Eng., 1949, pp. 83–106); Coleridge, "Shakespeare as a Poet Generally," first published 1836, but probably delivered as a lecture in 1818, or even 1808; Keats, Letter to Bailey, Sat., 22 Nov. 1817, Letter to George and Thomas Keats, Sun., 21 Dec. 1817; Hazlitt, "On Shakespeare and Milton," Lecture II, *Lectures on the English Poets* (1818); Arnold, preface to *Poems*, 1853 ed.; Meredith, Letter to Miss J- H-, 22 Nov. 1864, *Letters of George Meredith*, coll. and ed. by his son (New York, 1912), I, 163.

I am indebted to my colleague, Mr. Charles A. McLaughlin, for calling my attention to the first 7 of these references.

beginning of *The Iliad* out of the direct form of discourse into the indirect—chiefly by substituting "he said *that*" or "he bade him *to*" for quoted dialogue—thus changing an imitative passage to simple narrative. He goes on to note that the opposite extreme—dialogue only—approaches the style of the drama, which is wholly imitative (with the exception, we might add, of choral comment and messenger-narration). Homer, of course, mixes the two—as do most of his successors. We have, on the other hand, that form which uses the poet's voice only: for example, the dithyramb (lyric). As we shall see below, however, dialogue is not the only factor which distinguishes imitation from narration.

Coming now to the opposite end of the curve of history, we recall a similar distinction developed by Joyce in the person of Stephen, between the lyric and the dramatic forms, with the epic as intermediary, which in no way differs in its essential outlines from that of Plato. He is speaking here of the evolution of literature from the lyric cry to the impersonalized dramatic projection: "The narrative is no longer purely personal. The personality of the artist passes into the narration itself, flowing round and round the persons and the actions like a vital sea.... The dramatic form is reached when the vitality which has flowed and eddied round each person fills every person with such vital force that he or she assumes a proper and intangible esthetic life." There follows the by now famous passage about the disappearance of the author: "The personality of the artist, at first a cry or a cadence or a mood [lyric] and then a fluid and lambent narrative [epic], finally refines itself out of existence [drama], impersonalizes itself, so to speak."[4]

Let us now consider briefly the emergence of the specific application of this basic distinction to the analysis of point of view in fiction, for point of view provides a *modus operandi* for distinguishing the possible degrees of authorial extinction in the narrative art.

Regarding the particular problem of the relation between the author, the narrator, and the story subject, Edith Wharton complained

---

4 *A Portrait of the Artist as a Young Man* (dated Dublin 1904, Trieste 1914, published 1916), middle of Ch. V. Cf. Eliot, "Tradition and the Individual Talent" (1917), "Hamlet and His Problems" (1919). For technical discussion of "aesthetic distance" see Melvin Rader, *A Modern Book of Aesthetics*, rev. ed. (New York, 1952), pp. 381–465, where the work of Munsterberg, Bullough, Ortega y Gasset, Worringer, and Vernon Lee is presented and discussed.

in 1925, "It seems as though such a question must precede any study of the subject chosen, since the subject is conditioned by the answer; but no critic appears to have propounded it, and it was left to Henry James to do so in one of those entangled prefaces to the Definitive Edition from which the technical axioms ought some day to be piously detached."[5] As it turns out, she was more nearly correct than she knew, for not only have James's prefaces become the source and fount of critical theory in this matter but also no fewer than two full-length interpretations of them had already appeared before she wrote these words—that of Beach in 1918 and that of Lubbock in 1921. But first let us examine some of the pronouncements of the master himself.

James in his prefaces (1907–09) tells us he was obsessed by the problem of finding a "centre," a "focus," for his stories, and that it was in large measure solved by considering how the narrative vehicle could be limited by framing the action inside the consciousness of one of the characters within the plot itself. "A beautiful infatuation this," he comments, "always, I think, the intensity of the creative effort to get into the skin of the creature. . . ." Thus, since the irresponsible illusion-breaking of the garrulous omniscient author, who tells the story as *he* perceives it rather than as one of his characters perceives it, is eliminated by this device, the story gains in intensity, vividness, and coherence. "There is no economy of treatment without an adopted, a related point of view, and though I understand, under certain degrees of pressure, a represented community of vision between several parties to the action when it makes for concentration, I understand no breaking-up of the register, no sacrifice of the recording consistency, that doesn't rather scatter and weaken."[6]

Professor Beach undertook to organize the theory of this "method" and to apply it to James's own fiction. He distinguishes among several kinds of points of view and discriminates between James's calculated shifts in focus and "that arbitrary and unconsidered shift of point of view within the chapter, within the paragraph, that visible manipulation of the puppets from without, which is so great a menace to illusion and intimacy." The problem as a whole, however, "is a most complex and difficult one, and the practice of story-tellers is manifold. It would be impossible to give a brief summary of the common usage, even if one had made a sufficiently careful survey of the field to feel

---

[5] *The Writing of Fiction* (New York and London, 1925), pp. 43 ff.

[6] *The Art of the Novel: Critical Prefaces,* ed. R. P. Blackmur (New York and London, 1934), pp. 37–38, 300.

certain of all the facts."[7] The time was ripe, apparently, for the next step.

It remained to Percy Lubbock to apply the general distinction between direct and indirect presentation—a distinction common, as we have suggested, throughout the history of aesthetics and criticism—to a discussion of James's particular concern with point of view in fiction. "The art of fiction," he claims, "does not begin until the novelist thinks of his story as a matter to be *shown,* to be so exhibited that it will tell itself [rather than being *told* by the author]...the thing has to *look* true, and that is all. It is not made to look true by simple statement." If artistic "truth" is a matter of compelling rendition, of creating the illusion of reality, then an author speaking in his own person about the lives and fortunes of others is placing an extra obstacle between his illusion and the reader by virtue of his very presence. In order to remove this obstacle the author may choose to limit the functions of his own personal voice in one way or another: "The only law that binds him throughout, whatever course he is pursuing, is the need to be consistent on *some* plan, to follow the principle he has adopted; and of course it is one of the first of his precepts, as with every artist in any kind, to allow himself no more latitude than he requires." One of the chief means to this end, the one James himself not only announced in theory but followed in practice, is to have the story told as if by a character in the story, but told in the third person. In this way the reader perceives the action as it filters through the consciousness of one of the characters involved, yet perceives it *directly* as it impinges upon that consciousness, thus avoiding that removal to a distance necessitated by retrospective first-person narration: "the difference is that instead of receiving his report we now see him in the act of judging and reflecting; his consciousness, no longer a matter of hearsay, a matter for which we must take his word, is now before us in its original agitation."[8] Mental awareness is thus dramatized directly instead of being reported and explained indirectly by the narrator's voice, much in the same way that words and gestures may be dramatized directly (*scene*) rather than being summarized by the narrator (*panorama*).

Although one may find many shrewd observations on this point scattered throughout the writings of novelists and critics before the

---

7 *The Method of Henry James* (New Haven, 1918), pp. 56–71.
8 *The Craft of Fiction* (New York, 1921), pp. 62, 66–67, 71–72, 139–143.

prefaces of James served to crystallize the main issue—for his notions did not spring full-blown from the head of Jove[9]—we must perforce limit ourselves to a brief consideration of what happened to them after they were expounded by Beach and Lubbock. An exception may be made, however, for the work of Selden L. Whitcomb, entitled *The Study of a Novel* (1905), the first to my knowledge which devotes a formal section to the rubric, "The Narrator. His Point of View." Here it is claimed that "the unity of a passage or a plot depends largely on the clearness and stability of [the narrator's] position."[10] This notion, coming as it does a year or two before James's prefaces, seems remarkably prophetic of things to come, since from this point on almost every manual published on the art of fiction contains a similar section. During the next ten years or so we find a spate of such manuals which soon grows into an avalanche, and the specific analysis of point of view becomes common property.[11]

---

[9] See, e.g., the remarks of MacKenzie, Defoe, Richardson, Fielding, and Scott, in *Novelists on Novels,* ed. R. Brimley Johnson (London, 1928), pp. 13, 25, 41–45, 58–59, 94, 173, 180–84, 199–200; of Thackeray and de Maupassant in *The Writer's Art,* ed. Rollo Walter Brown (Cambridge, Mass., 1921), pp. 202–4, 271; Nassau William Senior, *Essays on Fiction* (London, 1864—written 1821–57), pp. 189 ff., 349–351, 391–92; Sidney Lanier, *The English Novel,* Centennial Ed., Vol. IV, eds. Clarence Gohdes and Kemp Malone (Baltimore, 1945), pp. 22, 172–73, 190, 220–22; Walter Besant, *The Art of Fiction* (Boston, 1885—a lecture delivered at the Royal Institution in 1884), p. 3; Henry James, *The Art of Fiction and Other Essays,* ed. Morris Roberts (New York, 1948), pp. 4–6; cf. "A Humble Remonstrance" (1884), by R. L. Stevenson; Daniel Greenleaf Thompson, *The Philosophy of Fiction in Literature* (London and New York, 1890), pp. 211–12; William Dean Howells, *Criticism in Fiction* (New York, 1891), pp. 19–21, 75–76; Brander Matthews, *Aspects of Fiction* (New York, 1896), pp. 185–86, 198–99, 223, 234; Bliss Perry, *A Study of Prose Fiction* (Boston, 1902), pp. 48–72; Frank Norris, *The Responsibilities of the Novelist* (New York, 1903), pp. 27–28, 206, 246.

[10] Boston, 1905, pp. 15–21, 31–38, 49 ff., 66–72, 101; cf. Evelyn May Albright, *The Short-Story* (New York, 1907), pp. 54–55, 66–70.

[11] Clayton Hamilton, *Materials and Methods of Fiction* (New York, 1908—reprinted as *A Manual of the Art of Fiction* in 1918), pp. 120–38; Charles F. Horne, *The Technique of the Novel* (New York and London, 1908), pp. v, 243–63; J. Berg Esenwein, *Writing the Short-Story* (Springfield, Mass., 1909), pp. 109–24; Walter B. Pitkin, *The Art and Business of Story Writing* (New York, 1912), pp. 174–187; Carl H. Grabo, *The Art of the Short Story* (New York, 1913), pp. 21–36, 159; Ethan Allen Cross, *The Short Story* (Chicago, 1914), pp. 80–86; Harry T. Baker, *The Contemporary Short Story* (New York, 1916), pp. 52, 111–12; Blanche Colton Williams, *A Handbook on Story Writing* (New York, 1917 [2nd ed. rev. 1930]), pp. 129–66; Henry Burrowes Lathrop, *The Art of the Novelist* (London, 1921), pp. 252–82.

The most significant work in the field after Beach and Lubbock, although as we have seen she seems curiously unaware of them, is that of Mrs. Wharton herself in 1925: "It should be the story-teller's first care to choose his reflecting mind deliberately, as one would choose a building-site...and when this is done, to live inside the mind chosen, trying to feel, see and react exactly as the latter would, no more, no less, and, above all, no otherwise. Only thus can the writer avoid attributing incongruities of thought and metaphor to his chosen interpreter." And from now on the manuals are always with us.[12]

The remainder of the second decade is distinguished by the demurral of E. M. Forster in 1927, who glances briefly at our problem only to pass it up as a trivial technicality. Allowing Lubbock full credit for his "formulae," he prefers to regard the novel otherwise: the novelist's chief specialty is unhampered omniscience whereby "he commands all the secret life, and he must not be robbed of this privilege. 'How did the writer know that?' it is sometimes said. 'What's his standpoint? He is not being consistent, he's shifting his point of view from the limited to the omniscient, and now he's edging back again.' Questions like these have too much the atmosphere of the law courts about them. All that matters to the reader is whether the shifting of attitude and the secret life are convincing."[13]

The third decade is graced chiefly by Beach's monumental study, in 1932, of the technique of the twentieth-century novel, which is characterized, he says, mainly by virtue of the fact that "the story tells itself; the story speaks for itself. The author does not apologize for his characters; he does not even tell us what they do but has them tell us, themselves. Above all, he has them tell us what they think, what they feel, what impressions beat in on their minds from

---

[12] Wharton, pp. 11–16, 43–46, 70–75, 86–95; Glenn Clark, *A Manual of the Short Story Art* (New York, 1922), pp. 89–95; Elizabeth A. Drew, *The Modern Novel* (New York, 1926), pp. 246–62; Michael Joseph, *How to Write a Short Story* (New York, 1926), pp. 47–56.

[13] *Aspects of the Novel* (New York, 1927), pp. 118–28. Cf. Grant Overton, *The Philosophy of Fiction* (New York, 1928), pp. 59, 131–35; Carl H. Grabo, *The Technique of the Novel* (New York, 1928), pp. 65, 81; Van Meter Ames, *Aesthetics of the Novel* (Chicago, 1928), pp. 177–93; Stewart Beach, *Short-Story Technique* (Boston, 1929), pp. 4–13, 103–20, 136–58; Mary Burchard Orvis, *Short Story Writing* (New York, 1928), pp. 111–21; Edith Mirrielees, *Writing the Short Story* (New York, 1929), pp. 81–121; John Gallishaw, *Twenty Problems of the Fiction Writer* (New York and London, 1929), pp. vii–x, 88–167.

the situations in which they find themselves." Apparently encouraged by the work of Lubbock, which followed shortly after his own early study of James, Beach now makes a concerted and massive onslaught upon the telling-showing problem as it appears in hundreds of modern novels.[14]

In an essay dated 1941 we find Allen Tate taking up the gauntlet cast down by Forster: "The limited and thus credible authority for the action, which is gained by putting the knower of the action inside its frame, is perhaps the distinctive feature of the modern novel; and it is, in all the infinite shifts of focus of which it is capable, the specific feature which more than any other has made it possible for the novelist to achieve an objective structure." Accordingly, Phyllis Bentley, in 1947, is constrained to remark: "The gradual decline in the use of direct comment, till at last heaved overboard with a splash by the twentieth century, is a fascinating study which should be attempted by a contemporary critic in the interest of...[that rather neglected aesthetics of fiction] I mentioned in my introduction."[15]

The really significant advance in the theory of point of view which occurred in the forties is the work of Mark Schorer in 1948. If Lubbock was concerned with the point of view as a means to a coherent and vivid presentation, Schorer takes it one step further by examining "the uses of point of view not only as a mode of dramatic delimitation, but, more particularly, of thematic definition." A novel, he says, normally reveals a created world of values and attitudes, and an author is assisted in his search for an artistic definition of these values and attitudes by the controlling medium offered by the devices of point of view; through these devices he is able to disentangle his own pre-

---

14 *The Twentieth Century Novel* (New York and London, 1932), p. 15, et passim. Cf. Ford Madox Ford, "Techniques," *Southern Review*, I (1935), 20–35; Gordon Hall Gerould, *How to Read Fiction* (Princeton, 1937), pp. 54–55, 66–67, 71–73; Douglas Bement, *Weaving the Short Story* (New York, 1931), pp. 169–73; John T. Frederick, *A Handbook of Short Story Writing*, rev. ed. (New York, 1932), pp. 34–35; Thomas H. Uzzell, *Narrative Technique*, 3rd ed. (New York, 1934), pp. 410–37, and "New Techniques in the Novel," *English Journal*, XXIV (1935), 355–63; Arthur Sullivant Hoffman, *The Writing of Fiction* (Boston, 1934), pp. 69, 317–67; James Weber Linn and Houghton Wells Taylor, *Foreword to Fiction* (New York and London, 1935), pp. 27–45, 57–60; Edward J. O'Brien, *The Short Story Case Book* (New York, 1935), pp. 13–32.

15 Tate, "The Post of Observation in Fiction," *Maryland Quart.*, II (1944), 61–64; Bentley, *Some Observations on the Art of Narrative* (New York, 1947), pp. 35–39.

judices and predispositions from those of his chararcters and thereby to evaluate those of his characters dramatically in relation to one another within their own frame. He has here the concurrence of Ellen Glasgow, who wrote in 1943: "To be too near, it appears, is more fatal in literature than to be too far away; for it is better that the creative writer should resort to imagination than that he should be overwhelmed by emotion." The novelist must "separate the subject from the object in the act of creation"; he does this by "total immersion" or "projection" into the materials of his story. Finally, that the telling-showing distinction is established as a commonplace of the criticism of fiction is evidenced by its latest reiteration in the work of Bernard De Voto in 1950, as well as in the current handbooks—not only of fiction writing and reading but also of freshman composition.[16]

II

Having traced the development of this key concept, we may now attempt a concrete and coherent definition of its parts and their relationships. Such a definition will, I think, be produced if we can

---

[16] Glasgow, *A Certain Measure* (New York, 1943), pp. 18–19, 41–43, 70, 99, 114, 150, 168, 180–83, 189–92; Schorer, "Technique as Discovery," loc. cit. Cf. W. H. Rogers, "Form in the Art-Novel," *Helicon,* II (1939), 1–17; DeVoto, "The Invisible Novelist," *The World of Fiction* (Boston, 1950), pp. 205–28; Arthur E. Dubois, "The Art of Fiction," *South Atlantic Quart.,* XL (1941), 112–22; Cleanth Brooks and R. P. Warren, *Understanding Fiction* (New York and London, 1943), pp. 588–96; William Foster-Harris, *The Basic Formulas of Fiction* (Norman, Okla., 1944), pp. 22–53; A. L. Bader, "The Structure of the Modern Short Story," *College English,* VII (1945), 86–92; Elizabeth Bowen, "Notes on Writing a Novel" (1945), *Collected Impressions* (New York, 1950), pp. 249–63; Kenneth Payson Kempton, *The Short Story* (Cambridge, Mass., 1947), pp. 82–145; Dorothy McCleary, *Creative Fiction Writing* (Boston, 1947), pp. 61–69, 70–85, 99–104; Mary Burchard Orvis, *The Art of Writing Fiction* (New York, 1948), pp. 70–91, 113–33, 135–51; Alex Comfort, *The Novel and Our Time* (Denver, 1948), pp. 33–43; Richard Summers, *Craft of the Short Story* (New York and Toronto, 1948), pp. 47–48; René Wellek and Austin Warren, *Theory of Literature* (New York, 1949), pp. 223–34; Brooks and Warren, *Fundamentals of Good Writing* (New York, 1949), pp. 267–88; Manuel Komroff, *How to Write a Novel* (New York and Boston, 1950), pp. 62–95; Mark Schorer, *The Story: A Critical Anthology* (New York, 1950), pp. 16–17, 65; Fred B. Millet, *Reading Fiction* (New York, 1950), pp. 14–25; Vincent McHugh, *Primer of the Novel* (New York, 1950), pp. 4, 16, 113–24; Caroline Gordon and Allen Tate, *The House of Fiction* (New York, 1950), pp. 621–34; A. A. Mendilow, *Time and the Novel* (London, 1952), pp. 96–115; Francis Connolly, *A Rhetoric Case Book* (New York, 1953), pp. 588–89.

manage to codify the questions of which these distinctions are answers, and if we can arrange these answers into some semblance of logical sequence.

Since the problem of the narrator is adequate transmission of his story to the reader, the questions must be something like the following: 1) Who talks to the reader? (author in third or first person, character in first, or ostensibly no one); 2) From what position (angle) regarding the story does he tell it? (above, periphery, center, front, or shifting); 3) What channels of information does the narrator use to convey the story to the reader? (author's words, thoughts, perceptions, feelings; or character's words and actions; or character's thoughts, perceptions, and feelings: through which of these or combination of these three possible media does information regarding mental states, setting, situation, and character come?); and 4) At what distance does he place the reader from the story? (near, far, or shifting). And since, further, our major distinction is between "telling" and "showing," the sequence of our answers should proceed by degrees from the one extreme to the other: from statement to inference, from exposition to presentation, from narrative to drama, from explicit to implicit, from idea to image.

EDITORIAL OMNISCIENCE

Regarding the modes of transmission of story material, we have first therefore to define concretely our major distinction: summary narrative (telling) vs. immediate scene (showing). Ben Franklin, on his way as a lad to Philadelphia, came across a copy of *Pilgrim's Progress* in Dutch, and commented somewhat unhistorically. "Honest John was the first that I know of who mix'd Narration and Dialogue, a Method of Writing very engaging to the Reader, who in the most interesting Parts finds himself, as it were, brought into the Company, and present at the Discourse. De foe [sic] in his Cruso [sic], his Moll Flanders, Religious Courtship, Family Instructor, and other Pieces, has imitated it with Success. And Richardson has done the same in his Pamela, etc.—" While this is our distinction, I am not so sure that, for our purposes, dialogue is the crucial factor. Edward Overton, the narrator in Butler's *The Way of All Flesh,* informs us in the opening chapter that "My father's face would always brighten when old Pontifex's name was mentioned. 'I tell you, Edward,' he would say to me, 'old Pontifex was not only an able man, but he was one of the very ablest men that I ever knew.' This was more than I as a young man was prepared to stand. 'My dear father,' I answered, 'what did he do?' "[17] It can hardly be said that the dialogue here constitutes a scene—other factors would seem to be required. Notice that the verb form is past imperfect, and that as a result the time and place are indefinite.

In order, then, that the event be placed immediately before the reader, there is required at least a definite point in space and time. The chief difference between narrative and scene is accordingly of the general-particular type: summary narrative is a generalized account or report of a series of events covering some extended period and a variety of locales, and seems to be the normal untutored mode of story-telling; immediate scene emerges as soon as the specific, continuous, and successive details of time, place, action, character, and dialogue begin to appear. Not dialogue alone but concrete detail within a specific time-place frame is the *sine qua non* of scene.

Butler again will supply us with an example of pure summary narrative: "Old Mr. Pontifex had married in the year 1750, but for fifteen years his wife bore no children. At the end of that time Mrs. Pontifex astonished the whole village by showing unmistakable signs of a disposition to present her husband with an heir or heiress. Hers had long ago been considered a hopeless case, and when on consulting the doctor concerning the meaning of certain symptoms she was informed of their significance, she became very angry and abused the doctor roundly for talking nonsense" (opening of Ch. II). Notice here that, in spite of the specific date (1765), it is the narrator's tone rather than the event itself which dominates—"unmistakable signs," "certain symptoms," and so on, reveal Overton's delight in the irony of the situation rather than the situation itself. We are not shown Mrs. Pontifex's appearance directly (although we can of course infer its general outlines), nor her visit to the doctor, nor her words of anger and abuse, and so on.

For an example of immediate scene we might as well select the obvious—Hemingway is its master: "The rain stopped as Nick turned into the road that went up through the orchard. The fruit had been picked and the fall wind blew through the bare trees. Nick stopped and picked up a Wagner apple from beside the road, shiny in the

---

[17] Franklin, *Autobiography* (fr. 1793 on, Franklin died in 1790); Butler, first published posthumously in 1903 (Butler died in 1902, but ceased work on this novel in 1884).

brown grass from the rain. He put the apple in the pocket of his Mackinaw coat."[18] Here, although no one has yet spoken, we have Hemingway's typically patient presentation of sensory detail: setting (weather: rain, wind; background: road, trees, apple, grass), action (Nick turned, stopped, picked up, put), and character (Nick and his Mackinaw coat). The event itself rather than the overt attitude of the narrator dominates.

These modes of rendering, the one second-hand and indirect, the other immediate and direct, rarely occur in their pure form. Indeed, the chief virtue of the narrative medium is its infinite flexibility, now expanding into vivid detail, now contracting into economical summary; yet one might hazard the loose generalization that modern fiction is characterized by its emphasis on the scene (in the mind or in speech and action), while conventional fiction is characterized by its emphasis on narration. But even the most abstract of narrations will have embedded somewhere within it hints and suggestions of scenes, and even the most concrete of scenes will require the exposition of some summary material. The *tendency,* however, in Editorial Omniscience is away from scene, for it is the author's voice which dominates the material, speaking frequently as "I" or "we."

Here "omniscience" signifies literally a completely unlimited—and hence difficult to control—point of view. The story may be seen from any or all angles at will: from a godlike vantage point beyond time and place, from the center, the periphery, or front. There is nothing to keep the author from choosing any of them, or from shifting from one to the other as often or rarely as he pleases.

The reader accordingly has access to the complete range of possible kinds of information, the distinguishing feature of this category being the thoughts, feelings, and perceptions of the author himself; he is free not only to inform us of the ideas and emotions within the minds of his characters but also of his own. The characteristic mark, then, of Editorial Omniscience is the presence of authorial intrusions and generalizations about life, manners, and morals, which may or may not be explicitly related to the story at hand. Thus, for example, Fielding in *Tom Jones* and Tolstoy in *War and Peace* have interpolated their essays as separate chapters within the body of the work, and hence they are easily detachable. Hardy, on the other hand,

---

18 "The Three-Day Blow," from *In Our Time* (1925).

makes no such formal distinction, commenting here and there in the midst of the action as he sees fit.

One may indeed investigate this sometimes ambiguous relationship between the author's commentary and the story itself. The results are almost always interesting, if not enlightening. Hardy is a case in point: in *Tess of the D'Urbervilles* he indulges in one of his characteristic editorializing passages: "In the ill-judged execution of the well-judged plan of things, the call seldom produces the comer, the man to love rarely coincides with the hour for loving." He continues on about the general unlikelihood of this uneven situation ever improving, and then attempts explicitly to relate this observation to the story at hand: "Enough that in the present case, as in millions, the two halves of an approximately perfect whole did not confront each other at the perfect moment. . . . Out of which maladroit delay sprang anxieties, disappointments, shocks, catastrophes—and what was called a strange destiny" (1891: end of Ch. V).

We may therefore expect the story to illustrate this cause and effect relationship: if Tess's misery has its source in plain bad luck, then it should properly have no cause in her temperament; either the fault is in ourselves or in our stars. Yet Hardy, in his analysis of the motivation of his people, seems at times to be implying something quite different. Tess has screwed up her courage, for example, to tell Angel the horrible truth, but ends (as usual) by ducking the issue: "At the last moment her courage failed her, she feared his blame for not telling him sooner; her instinct of self-preservation was stronger than her candor" (middle of Ch. XXX). There is an internal conflict, then; one which she cannot resolve. Apparently there is more here than mere clumsy mischance. Again, she decides to visit his parents in an effort to settle things, but again quails at the critical moment: "She went her way without knowing that the greatest misfortune of her life was this feminine loss of courage at the last critical moment" (middle of Ch. XLIV).

Things need not have been so bad for her, on the other hand, if Angel's character had been different: "Within the remote depths of his constitution, so gentle and affectionate as he was in general, there lay hidden a hard logical deposit, like a vein of metal in a soft loam, which turned the edge of everything that attempted to traverse it. It had blocked his way with the Church; it blocked his way with Tess" (middle of Ch. XXXVI). It is obviously an open question whether a novelist can create characters wholly devoid of significant motivation, even in the service of a naturalistic fatalism.

At any rate, it is a natural consequence of the editorial attitude that the author will not only *report* what goes on in the minds of his characters, but he will also *criticize* it. Thus Hardy depicts poor Tess wandering disconsolately about the countryside after her disastrous encounter with Alex, imagining natural sights and sounds as proclaiming her guilt. He then overtly informs the reader that the unfortunate girl was wrong in feeling this way: "But this encompassment of her own characterization, based upon shreds of convention, peopled by phantoms and voices antipathetic to her, was a sorry and mistaken creation of Tess's fancy—a cloud of moral hobgoblins by which she was terrified without reason" (end of Ch. XIII). Because *she* never discovers this, all we can say is that it is just too bad she has less perception than her creator.

Neutral Omniscience

Since the next step toward objectification differs from Editorial Omniscience only in the absence of direct authorial intrusions (the author speaks impersonally in the third person), we may continue our discussion of the various media available for the transmission of story material here. The absence of intrusions does not imply, however, that the author necessarily denies himself a voice when using the Neutral Omniscient frame: such people as Mark Rampion and Philip Quarles in *Point Counter Point* are obviously projections of one or another of Huxley's own attitudes (at that time), as we know from the external evidence, even though Huxley never editorializes in his own voice.

Regarding characterization, although an omniscient author may have a predilection for scene and consequently may allow his people to speak and act for themselves, his predominant tendency is to describe and explain them to the reader in his own voice. Thus Tess meets Alex for the first time, hesitating uncertainly before him: ". . . a figure came forth from the dark triangular door of the tent. It was that of a tall young man, smoking." Now, although Tess is standing there and observing, Alex is described as seen by Hardy and not by his heroine: "He had an almost swarthy complexion, with full lips, badly moulded, though red and smooth, above which was a well-groomed black mustache with curled points though his age could not be more than three- or four-and-twenty. Yet despite the touches of barbarism in his contours, there was a singular force in the gentleman's face, and in his bold rolling eyes" (middle of Ch. V).

By way of illustrating this characteristic indirection concretely, I have re-written the passage by placing this description more directly within Tess's sensory frame: "*She saw* a figure come forth from the dark triangular door of the tent. It was that of a tall young man, smoking. *She noticed* his swarthy complexion, his full lips, badly moulded though red and smooth, and above them a well-groomed mustache with curled points. Though he cannot be more than three- or four-and-twenty, *she thought.* Yet despite the apparent touches of barbarism in his features, *she sensed* a singular force in the gentleman's face and in his bold rolling eyes."

Similarly, the mental states and the settings which evoke them are *narrated* indirectly as if they have already occurred—discussed, analyzed, and explained—rather than presented *scenically* as if they were occurring now. If we return to the passage where Tess is wandering guiltily about the countryside, we read: "On the lonely hills and dales her quiescent glide was of a piece with the element she moved in. . . . At times her whimsical fancy would intensify natural processes around her till they seemed a part of her own story. . . . The midnight airs and gusts, moaning among the tightly wrapped buds and bark of the winter twigs, were formulae of bitter reproach." In contrast, I have again tried revising the scene by showing it occurring directly within Tess's mind: "At times *she felt* the scenery as part of her own story. *She heard* the midnight airs and gusts, moaning among the tightly wrapped buds and bark of the winter twigs, *reproaching her* bitterly."

Finally, since summary narrative and immediate scene are equally available (the latter largely for external speech and action), the distance between the story and the reader may be near or far, and it may shift at will—often whimsically and without apparent design. The prevailing characteristic of omniscience, however, is that the author is always ready to intervene himself between the reader and the story, and that even when he does set a scene, he will render it as he sees it rather than as his people see it.

"I" AS WITNESS

Our progress toward direct presentation charts the course of surrender; one by one, as the concentric rings of an onion are peeled, the author's channels of information and his possible vantage points are given up. As he denied himself personal commentary in moving from Editorial to Neutral Omniscience, so here, in moving to the "I" as Witness category, he hands his job completely over to another. Albeit the narrator is a creation of the author, the latter is from now on denied any direct voice in the proceedings at all. The witness-narrator is a character on his own right *within* the story itself, more or less involved in the action, more or less acquainted with its chief personages, who speaks to the reader in the first person.

The natural consequence of this narrative frame is that the witness has no more than ordinary access to the mental states of others; its distinguishing characteristic, then, is that the author has surrendered his omniscience altogether regarding all the other characters involved, and has chosen to allow his witness to tell the reader only what he as observer may legitimately discover. The reader has available to him only the thoughts, feelings, and perceptions of the witness-narrator; he therefore views the story from what may be called the wandering periphery.

What the witness may legitimately transmit to the reader is not as restricted as may at first appear: he can talk to the various people within the story and can get their views on matters of concern (notice how carefully Conrad and Fitzgerald have troubled to characterize Marlow and Carraway as men in whom others feel compelled to confide); particularly he can have interviews with the protagonist himself; and finally he can secure letters, diaries, and other writings which may offer glimpses of the mental states of others. At the utmost limit of his tether, he can draw *inferences* as to how others are feeling and what they are thinking. Thus Nick Carraway speculates, after Gatsby's solitary death, about what went on in his mind before he was shot: "No telephone message arrived.... *I have an idea* that Gatsby himself didn't believe it would come, and *perhaps* he no longer cared. If that was true *he must have felt* that he had lost the old warm world, paid a high price for living too long with a single dream. *He must have looked up* at an unfamiliar sky through frightening leaves and shivered as he found what a grotesque thing a rose is and how raw the sunlight was upon the scarcely created grass."[19]

But Butler wanders uncertainly beyond his limits in *The Way of All Flesh* more often than one could wish. His witness-narrator does, in fact, explicitly inform us of his boundaries: "But what were the feel-

---

[19] End of Ch. VIII (1925). Italics mine.

ings of Theobald and Christina when the village was passed and they were rolling [in their honeymoon carriage] quietly by the fir plantation?...For some time the pair said nothing: what they must have felt during their first half-hour, the reader must guess, for it is beyond my power to tell him." What, then, are we to make of this passage immediately preceding? "Christina and he [Theobald] had got on, *he thought to himself,* very nicely for a great number of years; why—why—why should they not continue to go on as they were doing now for the rest of their lives?" (beginning of Ch. XIII). Or again, " 'I hope,' said Theobald *to himself,* 'I hope he'll [Ernest] work—or else that Skinner will make him' " (beginning of Ch. XXIV).

It is true that Overton is a contemporary and close friend of Theobald, as well as the godfather and guardian of Ernest, and that Theobald in these instances might have told him later about what went on in his mind, but Overton too frequently gives us no clue whatever as to his authority for such information.

Since the witness-narrator can summarize his narrative at any given point as well as present a scene, the distance between the reader and story may be either near or far, or both. We may note here that the scenes are usually presented directly as the witness sees them.[20]

"I" as Protagonist

With the shift of the narrative burden from a witness to one of the chief personages, who tells his own story in the first person, a few more channels of information are given up and a few more vantage points are lost.[21] Because of his subordinate role in the story itself, the witness-narrator has much greater mobility and consequently a greater range and variety of sources of information than the protagonist proper, who is centrally involved in the action. The protagonist-narrator, therefore, is limited almost entirely to his own thoughts, feelings, and perceptions. Similiarly, the angle of view is that of the fixed center.

---

[20] One may speculate, if he wishes, as to the relation between the "I" as Witness frame in fiction and the convention of the messenger in Greek drama. E.g., the re-telling of the catastrophe at the end of *Oedipus Rex* or *Oedipus at Colonus* by an eye-witness.

[21] There is an intermediary category, albeit a minor one, to be mentioned here. It is characterized by the fact that, although the protagonist tells his own story, he tells it not to the reader but rather to someone of his acquaintance who thereupon relays it to the reader in his own person. Something of a combination "I" as Witness and "I" as Protagonist frame.

And, since the protagonist-narrator can summarize or present directly in much the same way as the witness, the distance may be near or far, or both. One of the best examples of this mode is to be found in *Great Expectations*.

Multiple Selective Omniscience

In spite of the fact that both the "I" as Witness and the "I" as Protagonist modes are limited to the narrator's mind, there is still *someone* doing the talking, *someone* is still narrating. The next step toward the objectification of the story material is the elimination of not only the author, who disappeared with the "I" as Witness frame, but also of any narrator whatsoever. Here the reader ostensibly listens to no one; the story comes directly through the minds of the characters as it leaves its mark there. As a result, the tendency is almost wholly in the direction of scene, both inside the mind and externally with speech and action; and narrative summary, if it appears at all, is either supplied unobtrusively by the author by way of "stage direction" or emerges through the thoughts and words of the characters themselves.

The appearance of the characters, what they do and say, the setting —all the story materials, therefore—can be transmitted to the reader only through the mind of someone present. Thus Mrs. Ramsay's age and appearance are rendered in Virginia Woolf's *To the Lighthouse:* "They must find a way out of it all. There might be some simpler way, some less laborious way, *she sighed.* When *she looked* in the glass and *saw* her hair grey, her cheek sunk, at fifty, *she thought,* possibly, she might have managed things better—her husband; money; his book."[22]

It might be questioned as to exactly how this mode of presentation, where the author *shows* us internal states, differs from normal omniscience, where the author peers into the minds of his characters and *tells* us what is going on there. It is chiefly that the one renders thoughts, perceptions, and feelings as they occur consecutively and in detail passing through the mind (scene), while the other summarizes and explains them after they have occurred (narrative). A "translation" of another passage from Mrs. Woolf will illustrate the precise point of difference: "Such was the complexity of things [thinks Lily Briscoe]. For what happened to her, especially staying with the Ramsays, was to be made to feel violently two opposite things at the

---

22 Harbrace Modern Classics ed. (1927), pp. 13–14. Italics mine.

same time; that's what you feel, was one; that's what I feel, was the other, and then they fought together in her mind, as now. It is so beautiful, so exciting, this love, that I tremble on the verge of it."[23] The shift to normal omniscience is effected by changing to indirect discourse, standardizing the personal pronouns to the third person (one often thinks of oneself in the first, second, or third person), and normalizing the syntax: "It seemed to Lily *that* things were quite complex. Staying with the Ramsays, especially, made her feel *that* she was being pulled in two opposite directions at the same time. On the one hand, *there were* the feelings of others; and, on the other, *there were one's own* feelings. Sometimes love appeared so beautiful and exciting *that she* trembled on the verge of it." A less patient omniscient author might simply remark: "Lily felt ambivalent about love, especially with the Ramsays."

SELECTIVE OMNISCIENCE

Here the reader is limited to the mind of only one of the characters. Instead, therefore, of being allowed a composite of viewing angles, he is at the fixed center. The other questions are answered as they were for the previous category.

It remains merely to illustrate. A vivid example of exactly how the story materials are transmitted directly to the reader through a character's mind is found in Joyce's *A Portrait:* "Consciousness of place *came ebbing back to him* [Stephen] slowly over a vast tract of time unlit, unfelt, unlived. The squalid scene *composed itself around him;* the common accents, the burning gasjets in the shops, odours of fish and spirits and wet sawdust, moving men and women. An old woman was about to cross the street, an oilcan in her hand. He bent down and asked was there a chapel near?"[24]

The abrupt beginnings and much of the distortion characteristic of modern stories and novels are due to the use of Multiple and Selective Omniscience, for, if the aim is to dramatize mental states,

---

23 Ibid., p. 154. Roman Fernandez, in *Messages* (1926), trans. from the French by Montgomery Belgion (New York, 1927), makes a very keen distinction, apparently independently, between the "novel" (showing) and the "recital" (telling), pp. 61–69.

24 End of Ch. III (1916). I am in fundamental agreement with Ellsworth Mason, who maintains that the Joyce canon is "dramatic" from beginning to end, displaying no progression from "lyric" to "epic" to "drama," as has commonly been supposed. See "Joyce's Categories," *Sewanee Review, LXI* (1953), 427–32.

and depending upon how far "down" into the mind you go, the logic and syntax of normal daytime public discourse begin to disappear. Of course, there is no necessary connection: Henry James, staying on the "upper" levels of his characters' minds, which are usually of the highly articulate type anyway, cannot be called a "stream-of-consciousness" writer. Woolf, who might be said to dwell on the "middle" level of her characters' minds (which are characteristically chaste), and Joyce, who knows no bottom, are correspondingly more difficult.[25]

THE DRAMATIC MODE

Having eliminated the author, and then the narrator, we are now ready to dispose of mental states altogether. The information available to the reader in the Dramatic Mode is limited largely to what the characters do and say; their appearance and the setting may be supplied by the author as in stage directions; there is never, however, any direct indication of what they perceive (a character may *look* out of the window—an objective act—but what he *sees* is his own business), what they think, or how they feel. This is not to say, of course, that mental states may not be *inferred* from action and dialogue.

We have here, in effect, a stage play cast into the typographical mold of fiction. But there is some difference: fiction is meant to be read, drama to be seen and heard, and there will be a corresponding difference in scope, range, fluidity, and subtlety. The analogy, however, does largely hold, in that the reader apparently listens to no one but the characters themselves, who move as it were upon a stage; his angle of view is that of the fixed front (third row center), and the distance must always be near (since the presentation is wholly scenic). Hemingway comes into his own here (mainly in short stories

---

25 Cf. Louis Hasley, "The Stream-of-Consciousness Method," *Catholic World*, CXLVI (1937), 210–13; Lawrence Bowling, "What is the Stream of Consciousness Technique?" *PMLA*, LXV (1950), 333–45; Robert Humphrey, "'Stream of Consciousness': Technique or Genre?" *PQ*, XXX (1951), 434–37. Bowling makes a very useful distinction between mental analysis, interior monologue, and stream of consciousness; the latter two represent the more and the less articulate manner of directly rendering internal states, the first the indirect omniscient manner. See also Gleb Struve, "Monologue Interieur: The Origins of the Formula and the First Statement of its Possibilities," *PMLA*, LXIX (1954), 1101–11; and Robert Humphrey, *Stream of Consciousness in the Modern Novel*, Perspectives in Criticism: 3 (Berkeley and Los Angeles, 1954)—both of which appeared after this article was completed.

such as "Hills Like White Elephants"), and mention might be made of James's *The Awkward Age* (1899), which is something of a tour de force—the gains in immediacy hardly compensating for the difficulties of sustaining a full-length novel within this mode.[26]

THE CAMERA

Largely for the sake of symmetry, our account of the kinds of points of view may be concluded with what seems the ultimate in authorial exclusion. Here the aim is to transmit, without apparent selection or arrangement, a "slice of life" as it passes before the recording medium: "I am a camera," begins Isherwood's narrator at the opening of *Goodbye to Berlin* (1945), "with its shutter open, quite passive, recording, not thinking. Recording the man shaving at the window opposite and the woman in the kimono washing her hair. Someday, all this will have to be developed, carefully printed, fixed."[27]

Perhaps, however, with the final extinction of the author, fiction as an art will become extinct as well, for this art, while requiring some degree at least of objective vividness, requires as well, it seems to me, a structure, the product of a guiding intelligence which is implicit in the narrative and which shapes the material so as to arouse the reader's expectations with regard to the probable course of events, to cross those expectations with an equally probable contrary course, and then to allay these expectations so that the resultant outcome seems after all the necessary one. Nor need this statement be taken as a plea for a return to novels in which "something happens," in the sense of melodramatic action; "events" refers equally, as we have argued above, to mental states as to overt action, and a writer—such as Mrs. Woolf, for example—can become infinitely subtle in these matters without entirely abandoning structure. To argue that the function of literature is to transmit unaltered a slice of life is to misconceive the fundamental nature of language itself: the very act of writing is a process of abstraction, selection, omission, and arrangement. But why,

---

26 For a discussion of the reverse of this problem, see Herman M. Weisman, "An Investigation of Methods and Techniques in the Dramatization of Fiction," *Speech Monographs*, XIX (1952), 48–59.

27 Tolstoy is reported to have recorded camera-style, as his first attempt at authorship in March 1851, everything that he saw and felt for one day. Cf. Prince D. S. Mirsky, *A History of Russian Literature* (New York, 1934 [1927]), pp. 329–30; and Janko Lavrin, *Tolstoy: An Approach* (London, 1944), p. 21. It is called *The History* [or *An Account*] *of Yesterday,* but I have not been able to obtain a copy.

finally, need we go to a novel for a slice of life when we can go to the nearest street corner for a much more vivid one which we can experience at first hand?

III

What, it may be asked, is the result of all this "squeamishness"? Does not all this fuss over technique by an author end in a cold detachment, a clinical, passionless objectivity? Thus Bradford Booth objects that "if the Victorian intrusive author failed, he failed on a grand scale, for he attempted much. In the eyes of many of us, however, he did not fail. It is charged that he does not maintain a consistent point of view. What matter, if his characters live? It is charged that he sees human nature only from the outside. What matter, if his view be not distorted?" Are not Scott and Dickens, after all, more delightful than James, with his obsessive scrupulosity? For Beach, the answer is relative, a matter of taste: "We cannot be the worse for the wisdom of these big men, these large souls [i.e., the Victorian novelists]. But, for better or worse, the fashion has changed; we like fiction unadulterated; we like the sense of taking part in an actual, a present experience, without the interference of an authorial guide."[28]

But is it really so largely a matter of "fashion"? And does not Booth beg some crucial questions? We have indicated above that it has been all along a commonplace of aesthetic theory that effective presentation and "impersonality" go hand in hand;[29] and the difference between Dickens and James regarding liveliness is also a function of their characteristic choice of materials, not merely of technique. But perhaps the whole question can be rephrased in terms of ends and means: has the novelist utilized the available techniques in such a way as to produce the effect intended? or has he allowed opportunities to pass and obstacles to arise between the reader and the desired illusion?

---

28 Booth, pp. 94–96; Beach, *Twentieth Century Novel,* pp. 15–16. Booth informs me that his stand in this matter has since undergone some modification.

29 See, e.g., Aristotle's *Poetics,* 1460a 5: "Homer, admirable as he is in every other respect, is especially so in this, that he alone among epic poets is not unaware of the part to be played by the poet himself in the poem. The poet should say very little *in propria persona,* as he is no imitator when doing that. Whereas the other poets are perpetually coming forward in person, and say but little, and that only here and there, as imitators, Homer after a brief preface brings in forthwith a man, or woman, or some other Character—no one of them characterless, but each with distinctive characteristics" (Bywater trans.).

The basic assumption, then, of those who are seriously concerned over technique, as James himself so long ago pointed out, is that the prime end of fiction is to produce as complete a story-illusion as possible. Given material potentially interesting, concentration and intensity, and hence vividness, are the results of working within limits, albeit self-imposed, and any lapse thereof is in all probability the result either of not establishing a limiting frame to begin with or of breaking the one already established. Surely this is one of the basic principles of artistic technique in general.

Thus the choice of a point of view in the writing of fiction is at least as crucial as the choice of a verse form in the composing of a poem; just as there are certain things which cannot get said in a sonnet, so each of the categories we have detailed has a probable range of functions it can perform within its limits. The question of effectiveness, therefore, is one of the suitability of a given technique for the achievement of certain kinds of effects, for each kind of story requires the establishment of a particular kind of an illusion to sustain it. Editorial Omniscience, for example, may be called the "free verse" of fiction: its limits are so wholly internal that an unwary novelist has more opportunities for illusion-breaking here than with the others. How much of Whitman, Sandburg, or Masters is flat and dull? And how much of *War and Peace*—to take the highest—could easily be dispensed with? On the other hand, when the personality of the author-narrator has a definite function to fulfill in relation to his story—say of irony, compassion, philosophical range and depth, and so on—he need not retire behind his work, so long as his point of view is adequately established and coherently maintained. It is more a matter of consistency than of this or that degree of "impersonality." But the author-narrator has a more complicated problem on his hands here, and had best look to his devices. Free verse is not "free" after all, as Eliot has somewhere remarked; but to establish a pattern within it is more difficult and hence more liable to disruption. In this respect, Fielding's *Tom Jones* is more successful than *War and Peace:* the intellectual tone and pedantic material of Tolstoy's interchapters are often at variance with the tenor and impact of the story itself, which has as its theme the glorification (in Pierre, Kutuzov, Karataev, Nikolay, Natasha) of the instinctive and intuitive forces in life. There is thus revealed, for all its majesty, a fatally unresolved ambiguity at the core of this novel: it is commonly agreed that Andrey and Pierre are symbolic projections of Tolstoy's own ambivalence, and it is as if, after having killed off Andrey, the author-narrator could not allow Andrey's attitude to disappear altogether from the story and so kept it alive, as it were, in the interchapters. However we may view them, they are basically undramatic.

Thus, if it is essential to an author's purpose that the minds of many be revealed freely and at will—to achieve, for example, the effect of a social milieu in the manner of Huxley—and if the author's superior and explanatory tone is to dominate the perception and awareness of his characters—to achieve that typical Huxleyan effect of smallness and futility and indignity—then Neutral Omniscience is the logical choice. If the element of suspense is to be foremost—as, say, in mystery stories and detective fiction—if a situation is to be gradually built up and revealed piecemeal—as, for example, in *Lord Jim*—then the witness-narrator seems more likely than any other. If the problem is one of tracing the growth of a personality as it reacts to experience, the protagonist-narrator will prove most useful—as in *Great Expectations*—assuming that he has sufficient sensitivity and intelligence to develop and to perceive the significance of that development (a naïve protagonist may, of course, be used for an ironic effect). If the author is concerned with the way in which personality and experience emerge as a mosaic from their impingement upon the sensibilities of several individuals, then Multiple Selective Omniscience provides a way—as in *To the Lighthouse*. If the intent is to catch a mind in a moment of discovery—as in *A Portrait of the Artist*—Selective Omniscience is the means. And finally, if the author's purpose is to produce in the reader's mind a moment of revelation—as in Hemingway's "Hills Like White Elephants"—then the Dramatic Mode, with its tendency to imply more than it states, provides the logical approach. The analysis of technique, then, is crucial, as Schorer maintains, when it is seen as revealing the author's purpose and, even more fundamentally, the basic structure of values which he has embodied by means of that technique.

Consistency and not cold-bloodedness is all, for consistency—within however large and diverse and complex a frame—signifies that the parts have been adjusted to the whole, the means to the end, and hence that the maximum effect has been rendered. It is, however, a necessary rather than a sufficient cause; the over-all consistency of a great but clumsy novelist may emerge *in spite of* his technical inadequacies, while the consistency of a lesser talent will not in itself produce masterpieces, succeeding within a smaller frame than that which genius may attempt. Sometimes a noble failure is more exciting than a petty victory. But how many of our most ambitious and brilliant novels would have been even more successful if closer attention had been directed toward these matters?[30] There is surely no necessary contradiction between genius and technical mastery.

D. H. Lawrence is a case in point, and Schorer has outlined the basic cause of the curious restlessness with which the reader is left after reading, say, *Sons and Lovers.* In spite of its "modern" concern with sex and the unconscious, this story is still narrated within the frameless frame of old-fashioned Editorial Omniscience, and the danger of authorial identification with the protagonist—and hence of partisanship and dice-loading—has not been obviated. The author-narrator thus analyzes Miriam's thoughts: "So in May she asked him [Paul] to come to Willey Farm and meet Mrs. Dawes. There was something he hankered after. She saw him, whenever they spoke of Clara Dawes, rouse and get slightly angry. He said he did not like her. Yet he was keen to know about her. Well, he should put himself to the test. She believed that there were in him desires for higher things, and desires for lower, and that the desires for the higher would conquer. At any rate, he should try." And then Lawrence adds, "She forgot that her 'higher' and 'lower' were arbitrary."[31]

Both Schorer and Diana Trilling point out that there is consequently a contradiction in the book's theme: Paul Morel cannot achieve a satisfactory sexual relationship either because of his enervating mother-fixation or because Miriam can encompass only the "spiritual" aspects of such a relationship. And these two themes are mutually exclusive—the fault is the mother's or Miriam's—and the trouble is that Lawrence has been unable sufficiently to dissociate himself from Paul to tell one from the other, with the result that he tries to have it both ways. But the reader remains frustrated; lack

---

30 I have in mind here, for example, the obvious inconsistencies in the narrative of *Don Quixote* as well as the often burdensome references to Cid Hamete, the author of the "original" MS. (cf. Wayne C. Booth, "The Self-Conscious Narrator in Comic Fiction before *Tristram Shandy,*" *PMLA,* LXVII [1952], 163–85) ; or Melville's continual bursting of his original witness-narrator frame in *Moby Dick;* or the frequent absurdities engendered in the course of the narrative by Richardson's epistolary technique in *Pamela;* or the curiously split structure of *Moll Flanders;* or the excesses and lapses in emphasis in Wolfe's bulky novels (cf. n. 32 below).

31 Schorer, "Technique as Discovery," op. cit., pp. 197–98; Lawrence (1913), Modern Library Edition, p. 269.

of consistency means loss of effect. Yet the irony is that Lawrence himself believed in the efficacy of dramatic projection as a way of clarifying and understanding his own emotional problems: "One sheds one's sicknesses in books—repeats and presents again one's emotions, to be master of them." E. T., however, the original of Miriam, knew that in this case he had failed: "...he burked the real issue. It was his old inability to face his problem squarely. His mother had to be supreme.... So instead of a release and a deliverance from bondage, the bondage was glorified and made absolute.... The best I could think of him was that he had run with the hare and hunted with the hounds."[32]

By way of contrast, we may note Joyce's presentation of Stephen in *A Portrait,* where, in spite of the common tendency to treat it as auto-biographical, the story of the hero's coming-of-age is completely objectified. Because Joyce has strictly limited the flow of information only to those scenes, perceptions, thoughts, and feelings which Stephen's mind records, he has eliminated the possibility of authorial partisanship which so vitiates the structure of *Sons and Lovers.* As a result, we get such a clear picture of the protagonist that one of his friends can say to him: "It is a curious thing, do you know—Cranly said dispassionately—how your mind is supersaturated with the religion in which you say you disbelieve." One cannot conceive of Lawrence, given his lack of control, as allowing Miriam to say to Paul: "It is a curious thing, do you know, how your rather excessive love for your mother causes you unwittingly to seek a sexual outlet with younger women which will be devoid of spiritual content. Passion and devotion are split in your mind by guilt, and therefore you react violently when a woman asks you for both together, accusing her of wanting to draw the soul out of you. Your soul has already been given to your mother. So you misconceive me completely when you say I want only your

---

[32] Trilling, Introd. to *The Portable D. H. Lawrence* (New York, 1947), pp. 19–20; Lawrence, quoted in the same place; E. T., *D. H. Lawrence: A Personal Record* (London, 1935), pp. 201–4. For another interesting firsthand account of the problem of objectivity in fiction, see Thomas Wolfe's *The Story of a Novel* (1936): "The nature of my method, the desire fully to explore my material had led me into another error. The whole effect of those five years of incessant writing had been to make me feel not only that everything had to be used, but that everything had to be told, that nothing could be implied." Penguin ed. of Wolfe's short stories (New York, 1947 [variously entitled *Short Stories* and *Only the Dead Know Brooklyn*]), pp. 117–18, 146.

spiritual love." (Due allowance will, I hope, be made for the fact that I am not a novelist; but I believe, from the evidence in E. T.'s book, that Miriam was fully capable of such penetration. Lawrence, however, renders her as agonizingly inarticulate.)

Such is the success of Joyce's projection that, in spite of the fact that both he and his hero deliberately rejected Catholicism, literary Catholics can nevertheless relish his portrayal of religious life in the book. Thus Thomas Merton comments regarding the famous Hell passages: "What impressed me was not the fear of hell, but the expertness of the sermon. . . . So then I continued to read Joyce, more and more fascinated by the pictures of priests and Catholic life that came up here and there in his books." Similarly, Caroline Gordon can say, "I suspect that this book has been misread by a whole generation. It is not primarily a picture of the artist rebelling against constituted authority. It is, rather, the picture of a soul that is being damned for time and eternity caught in the act of foreseeing and foreknowing its damnation."[33] While I think that this is perverse sophistry, I think also that it is a tribute to Joyce's dramatic genius that a Catholic can sympathize with the portrayal of Catholic values in the novel which the hero rejects.

All this is merely to say, in effect, that when an author surrenders in fiction, he does so in order to conquer; he gives up certain privileges and imposes certain limits in order the more effectively to render his story-illusion, which constitutes artistic truth in fiction. And it is in the service of this truth that he spends his creative life.

※※※※

Of all the essays in this collection, Norman Friedman's is the most obviously formal in tone and the most scholarly in method. Readers unaccustomed to work in this mode are likely to accord his essay either misapplied reverence or swift dismissal. Both attitudes ignore the real uses to which the essay should be put. Superficially, it may seem that Friedman is too formal; that he tells more about point of view than anyone would care to know; that he tends to categorize too rigidly; and that in his

---

[33] Merton, *The Seven Storey Mountain,* Signet ed. (New York, 1952 [1948]), pp. 255–56; Gordon, "Some Readings and Misreadings," *Sewanee Review,* LXI (1953), 384–407.

tendency to abstractness he fails to deal with the complexity of the novel and sometimes judges individual works from what may seem to be a very limited and arbitrarily chosen angle. On the other hand, it could be argued that Friedman's formality accompanies and is to some extent required by his presentation of premises and their implications; that in searching out, judging, and giving pattern to the theories of others he not only pays his scholarly debts but performs a valuable service for his successors; and that he intends to make readers aware of possible approaches to the novel—not to present full and final analysis, but to add to a continuing process of interpretation and evaluation. Readers who accept his essay as the final word, as a rigid scheme or exclusive method to be applied prescriptively to any novel, do him a disservice. An argument is honored by efforts to refute it, but it withers under misapplication. No formula can replace intelligence and sensitivity.

The best way to treat critical approaches is to understand them and attempt to transcend their limitations. Friedman's theories certainly can be questioned and developed. Thus, although he strives to avoid prescription, the structure of his essay, moving from the least to the most representational types of point of view, seems to imply progress from less to more perfect methods. His views that illusion demands consistency and that consistency implies limits are questioned by Wayne Booth, who asks how much consistency is needed for what kind of illusion, and why the limits set by James and his followers must be accepted as fixed and final. One might go even further and question the very concept of illusion. Certain modern dramatists, notably Peter Weiss in *Marat/Sade,* remind the audience again and again that what they are seeing is a play—and then challenge them to withhold their belief in and empathy for the situations and characters. Perhaps novelists can make analogous use of the inevitable illusion. The matter of limits is also open to further examination, for the struggle against limits, formal or merely conventional, can be regarded as one of the major sources of energy in a work of art, most notably the novel. Of course, not all struggle is fruitful, nor is all limitation sterile. Like the critic, the artist must be sensitive and self-critical.

The ensuing essay by Wayne Booth is one of the most valuable criticisms and extensions of Friedman's. The chapter on "Point of View" in Scholes and Kellogg's *The Nature of Narrative* provides a larger perspective than Friedman's, and these authors go even further in denying the availability of omniscience as a method to the modern novelist. Friedman's notes provide what amounts to an annotated bibliography on the subject; material published since 1955 is listed in the *PMLA* annual bibliography, particularly in the section devoted to "Themes and Types."

Distance and Point-of-View:
An Essay in Classification

WAYNE C. BOOTH

But he [the narrator] little knows what surprises lie in wait for him, if someone were to set about analysing the mass of truths and falsehoods which he has collected here.
—"Dr. S.," in *Confessions of Zeno*

Like other notions used in talking about fiction, point-of-view has proved less useful than was expected by the critics who first brought it to our attention. When Percy Lubbock hailed the triumph of Henry James's dramatic use of the "central intelligence," and told us that "the whole intricate question of method, in the craft of fiction," is governed by "the relation in which the narrator stands to the story," he might have predicted that many critics would, like E. M. Forster, disagree with him. But he could hardly have predicted that his converts would produce, in forty years of elaborate investigations of point-of-view, so little help to the author or critic who must decide whether this or that technique in a particular work is appropriate to this or that effect. On the one hand we have been given classifications and descriptions which leave us wondering why we have bothered to classify and describe; the author who counted the number of times the word "I" appears in each of Jane Austen's novels may be more obviously absurd than the innumerable scholars who have traced in endless detail the *"Ich-Erzählung,"* or *"erlebte Rede,"* or *"monologue intérieur"* from Dickens to Joyce or from James to Robbes-Grillet. But he is no more irrelevant to literary judgment. To describe par-

From *Essays in Criticism*, XI (1961). Reprinted by permission of the editors of *Essays in Criticism*.

ticulars may be interesting but it is only the preliminary to the kind of knowledge that might help us explain the success or failure of individual works.

On the other hand, our efforts at formulating useful principles have been of little more use because they have been overtly prescriptive. If to count the number of times "I" occurs tells us nothing about how many times "I" should occur, to formulate abstract appeals for more "showing" and less "telling," for less authorial commentary and more drama, for more realistic consistency and fewer arbitrary shifts which remind the reader that he is reading a book, gives us the illusion of having discovered criteria when we really have not. While it is certainly true that some effects are best achieved by avoiding some kinds of telling, too often our prescriptions have been for "the novel" entire, ignoring what James himself knew well: there are "5,000,000 ways to tell a story," depending on one's over-all purposes. Too many Jamesians have tried to establish in advance the precise degree of realistic intensity or irony or objectivity or "aesthetic distance" his work should display.

It is true that dissenting voices are now heard more and more frequently, perhaps the most important being Kathleen Tillotson's recent inaugural lecture at The University of London, "The Tale and the Teller." But the clichés about the superiority of dramatic showing over mere telling are still to be found everywhere: in scholarly journals, in the literary quarterlies, in the weekly reviews, in the latest book on how to read a novel, and in dust-jacket blurbs. "The author does not tell you directly but you find out for yourself from their [the characters] every word, gesture, and act," a Modern Library jacket tells us about Salinger's *Nine Stories*. That this is praise, that Salinger would be in error if he were found telling us anything directly, is taken for granted.

Since the novelist's choices are in fact practically unlimited, in judging their effectiveness we can only fall back on the kind of reasoning used by Aristotle in the *Poetics: if* such-and-such an effect is desired, *then* such-and-such points-of-view will be good or bad. We all agree that point-of-view is in some sense a technical matter, a means to larger ends; whether we say that technique is the artist's way of discovering his artistic meaning or that it is his way of working his will upon his audience, we still can judge it only in the light of the larger meanings or effects which it is designed to serve. Though we all at times violate our own convictions, most of us are convinced that we have no right to impose on the artist abstract criteria derived from other kinds of work.

But even when we have decided to put our judgments in the hypothetical "if-then" form, we are still faced with an overwhelming variety of choices. One of the most striking features of our criticism is the casual way in which we allow ourselves to reduce this variety, thoughtlessly, carelessly, to simple categories, the impoverishment of which is evident whenever we look at any existing novel. On the side of effect critics at one time had a fairly large number of terms to play with—terms like tragedy, comedy, tragi-comedy, epic, farce, satire, elegy, and the like. Though the neo-classical kinds were often employed in inflexible form, they did provide a frame of discourse which allowed the critic and artist to communicate with each other: "if the effect you want is what we have traditionally expected under the concept 'tragedy,' then your technique here is inadequate." If what we are working for is a first-rate comedy, Dryden tells us in "An Essay of Dramatic Poesy," then here are some rules we can count on; they may be difficult to apply, they may require painstaking discussion, and they will certainly require genius if they are to be made to work, but they can still be of help to artist and critic because they are based on an agreement about a recognized literary effect.

In place of the earlier kinds, we have generally substituted a criticism based on qualities that are supposed to be sought in all works. All novels are said to be aiming for a common degree of realistic intensity; ambiguity and irony are discussed as if they were always beauties, never blemishes. Point-of-view should always be used "consistently," because otherwise the realistic illusion will be destroyed.

When technical means are related to such simplified ends, it is hardly surprising that they are themselves simplified. Yet we all know that our experience of particular works is more complex than the simple terminology suggests. The prescriptions against "telling" cannot satisfy any reader who has experienced *Tom Jones, The Egoist, Light in August,* or *Ulysses* (the claim that the author does not address us directly in the last of these is one of the most astonishingly persistent myths in modern criticism). They explicitly contradict our experience of dozens of good novels of the past fifteen years which, like Joyce Cary's posthumous *The Captive and the Free,* have rediscovered for us how lively "telling" can be. We all know, of course, that "too much" of the author's voice is, as Aristotle said, unpoetic. But how much is too much? Is there an abstract rule applicable to "the novel," quite aside from the needs of particular works or kinds?

Our experience with the great novels tells us that there is not. Most novels, like most plays, cannot be purely dramatic, entirely shown as taking place in the moment. There are always what Dryden called "relations," narrative summaries of action that takes place "off-stage." And try as we will to ignore the troublesome fact, "some parts of the action are more fit to be represented, some to be related." But related by whom? When? At what length? The dramatist must decide, and his decision will be based in large part on the particular needs of the work in hand. The novelist's case is different mainly in that he has more devices to choose from; he may speak with all of the voices available to the dramatist, and he may also choose—some would say he is also tempted by—some forms of telling not easily adapted to the stage.

Unfortunately our terminology for the author's many voices has been inadequate. If we name over three or four of the great narrators —say Cervantes' Cid Hamete Benengeli, Tristram Shandy, the "author" of *Middlemarch* and Strether in *The Ambassadors* (with his nearly effaced "author" using his mind as a reflector of events)—we find again that to describe any of them with conventional terms like "first-person" and "omniscient" tells us little about how they differ from each other, and consequently it tells us little about why they succeed while others, described in the same terms, fail. Some critics do, indeed, talk about the problem of "authority," showing that first-person tales produce difficulties in stories which do not allow any one person to know all that goes on; having made this point, which seems so obvious, they are often then driven to find fault with stories like *Moby Dick,* in which the author allows his narrator to know of events that happen outside his designated sphere of authority.

We can never be sure that enriching our terms will improve our criticism. But we can be quite sure that the terms with which we have long been forced to work cannot help us in discriminating among effects too subtle—as are all actual literary effects—to be caught in such loose-meshed nets. Even at the risk of pedantry, then, it should be worth our while to attempt a richer tabulation of the forms the author's voice can take.

(1) Perhaps the most overworked distinction is that of "person." To say that a story is told in the first or the third person, and to group

novels into one or the other kind, will tell us nothing of importance unless we become more precise and describe how the particular qualities of the narrators relate to specific desired effects. It is true that choice of the first person is sometimes unduly limiting; if the "I" has inadequate access to necessary information, the author may be led into improbabilities. But we can hardly expect to find useful criteria in a distinction that would throw all fiction into two, or at most three, heaps. In *this* pile we see *Henry Esmond,* "A Cask of Amontillado," *Gulliver's Travels* and *Tristram Shandy.* In *that* we have *Vanity Fair, Tom Jones, The Ambassadors,* and *Brave New World.* But the commentary in *Vanity Fair* and *Tom Jones* is in the first person, often resembling more the intimate effect of *Tristram Shandy* than that of many third person works. And again, the effect of *The Ambassadors* is much closer to that of the great first-person novels, since Strether in large parts "narrates" his own story, even though he is always referred to in the third person.

Further evidence that this distinction is ordinarily overemphasized is seen in the fact that all of the following functional distinctions apply to both first- and third-person narration alike.

(2) There are *dramatized* narrators and *undramatized* narrators. The former are always and the latter are usually distinct from the implied author who is responsible for their creation.

The Implied Author (*the author's "second self"*).   Even the novel in which no narrator is dramatized creates an implicit picture of an author who stands behind the scenes, whether as stage-manager, as puppeteer, or as an indifferent God, silently paring his fingernails. This implied author is always distinct from the "real man"—whatever we may take him to be—who creates a superior version of himself as he creates his work; any successful novel makes us believe in an "author" who amounts to a kind of "second self." This second self is usually a highly refined and selected version, wiser, more sensitive, more perceptive than any real man could be.

In so far as a novel does not refer directly to this author, there will be no distinction between him and the implied, undramatized narrator; for example, in Hemingway's "The Killers" there is no narrator other than the implicit second self that Hemingway creates as he writes.

Undramatized Narrators.   Stories are usually not as rigorously scenic as "The Killers"; most tales are presented as passing through the consciousness of a teller, whether an "I" or a "he." Even in drama much of what we are given is narrated by someone, and we are often as much interested in the effect on the narrator's own mind and heart as we are in learning what *else* the author has to tell us. When Horatio tells of his first encounter with the ghost in *Hamlet,* his own character, though never mentioned explicitly as part of the narrative event, is important to us as we listen. In fiction, as soon as we encounter an "I" we are conscious of an experiencing mind whose views of the experience will come between us and the event. When there is no such "I," as in "The Killers," the inexperienced reader may make the mistake of thinking that the story comes to him unmediated. But even the most naïve reader must recognize that something mediating and transforming has come into a story from the moment that the author explicitly places a narrator into the tale, even if he is given no personal characteristics whatever.

One of the most frequent reading faults comes from a naïve iden-tification of such narrators with the authors who create them. But in fact there is always a distinction, even though the author himself may not have been aware of it as he wrote. The created author, the "second self," is built up in our minds from our experience with all of the elements of the presented story. When one of those elements is an explicit reference to an experiencing narrator, our view of the author is derived in part from our notion of how the presented "I" relates to what he claims to present. Even when the "I" or "he" thus created is ostensibly the author himself—Fielding, Jane Austen, Dickens, Meredith—we can always distinguish between the narrator and the created author who presents him. But though the distinction is always present, it is usually important to criticism only when the narrator is explicitly dramatized.

Dramatized Narrators. In a sense even the most reticent narrator has been "dramatized" as soon as he refers to himself as "I," or, like Flaubert, tells us that "we" were in the classroom when Charles Bovary entered. But many novels dramatize their narrators with great fullness. In some works the narrator becomes a major person of great physical, mental and moral vividness (*Tristram Shandy, Remembrance of Things Past,* and *Dr. Faustus*) ; in such works the narrator is often radically different from the implied author who creates him, and whose own character is built up in our minds partly by the way in which the narrator is made to differ from him. The range of human types

that have been dramatized as narrators is almost as great as the
range of other fictional characters—one must say "almost" because
there are some characters who are unqualified to narrate or reflect
a story.

We should remind ourselves that many dramatized narrators are
never explicitly labeled as narrators at all. In a sense, every speech,
every gesture, narrates; most works contain disguised narrators who,
like Molière's *raisonneurs,* are used to tell the audience what it needs
to know, while seeming merely to act out their roles. The most important unacknowledged narrators are, however, the third-person "centers
of consciousness" through whom authors filter their narrative. Whether
such "reflectors," as James sometimes called them, are highly-polished,
lucid mirrors reflecting complex mental experience, or the rather
turbid, sense-bound "camera eyes" of much fiction since James, they
fill precisely the function of avowed narrators.

> Gabriel had not gone to the door with the others. He was in a dark
> part of the hall gazing up the staircase. A woman was standing near
> the top of the first flight, in the shadow also. He could not see her face
> but he could see the terra-cotta and salmon-pink panels of her skirt
> which the shadow made appear black and white. It was his wife. She
> was leaning on the banisters, listening to something. Gabriel was
> surprised at her stillness and strained his ear to listen also. But he
> could hear little save the noise of laughter and dispute on the front
> steps, a few chords struck on the piano and a few notes of a man's
> voice singing. . . . He asked himself what is a woman standing on the
> stairs in the shadow, listening to distant music, a symbol of.

The very real advantages of this method, for some purposes, have
been a dominant note in modern criticism. Indeed, so long as our
attention is on such qualities as naturalness and vividness, the advantages seem overwhelming. It is only as we break out of the fashionable
assumption that all good fiction seeks these qualities in the same degree
that we are forced to recognize disadvantages. The third-person reflector is only one mode among many, suitable for some effects but
cumbersome and even harmful when other effects are desired.

(3) Among dramatized narrators, whether first-person or third-
person reflectors, there are mere *observers* (the "I" of *Tom Jones, The
Egoist, Troilus and Criseyde*), and there are *narrator-agents* who
produce some measurable effect on the course of events (ranging from
the minor involvement of Nick in *The Great Gatsby* to the central
role of Tristram Shandy, Moll Flanders, Huckleberry Finn, and—in
the third-person—Paul Morel in *Sons and Lovers*). Clearly any rules

we might discover about observers may or may not apply to narrator-agents, yet the distinction is seldom made in talk about point-of-view.

(4) All narrators and observers, whether first- or third-person, can relay their tales to us primarily as *scene* ("The Killers," *The Awkward Age*), primarily as *summary* or what Lubbock called "picture" (Addison's almost completely non-scenic tales in *The Spectator*) or, most commonly, as a combination of the two.

Like Aristotle's distinction between dramatic and narrative manners, the somewhat different modern-distinction between telling and showing does cover the ground. But the trouble is that it pays for broad coverage with gross imprecision. Narrators of all shapes and shades must either report dialogue alone or support it with "stage directions" and description of setting. But when we think of the radically different effect of a scene reported by Huck Finn and a scene reported by Poe's Montresor, we see that the quality of being "scenic" suggests very little about literary effect. And compare the delightful summary of twelve years given in two pages of *Tom Jones* (III, i), with the tedious showing of even ten minutes of uncurtailed conversation in the hands of a Sartre when he allows his passion for "durational realism" to dictate a scene when summary is called for. We can only conclude that the contrast between scene and summary, between showing and telling—indeed, between any two dialectical terms that try to cover so much ground—is not prescriptive or normative but loosely descriptive only. And as description, it is likely to tell us very little until we specify the kind of narrator who is providing the scene or the summary.

(5) Narrators who allow themselves to tell as well as show vary greatly depending on the amount and kind of *commentary* allowed in addition to a direct relating of events in scene and summary. Such commentary can, of course, range over any aspect of human experience, and it can be related to the main business in innumerable ways and degrees. To treat of it as if it were somehow a single device is to ignore important differences between commentary that is merely ornamental, commentary that serves a rhetorical purpose but is not part of the dramatic structure, and commentary that is integral to the dramatic structure, as in *Tristram Shandy*.

(6) Cutting across the distinction between observers and narrator-agents of all these kinds is the distinction between *self-conscious narrators,* aware of themselves as writers (*Tom Jones, Tristram Shandy, Barchester Towers, The Catcher in the Rye, Remembrance of Things Past, Dr. Faustus*), and narrators or observers who rarely if ever

discuss their writing chores (*Huckleberry Finn*) or who seem unaware that they are writing, thinking, speaking, or "reflecting" a literary work (Camus' *The Stranger*, Lardner's *Haircut*, Bellow's *The Victim*).

(7) Whether or not they are involved in the action as agents, narrators and third-person reflectors differ markedly according to the degree and kind of *distance* that separates them from the author, the reader, and the other characters of the story they relate or reflect. Such distance is often discussed under terms like "irony," or "tone," but our experience is in fact much more diverse than such terms are likely to suggest. "Aesthetic distance" has been especially popular in recent years as a catch-all term for any lack of identification between the reader and the various norms in the work. But surely this useful term should be reserved to describe the degree to which the reader or spectator is asked to forget the artificiality of the work and "lose himself" in it; whatever makes him aware that he is dealing with an aesthetic object and not real life increases "aesthetic distance," in this sense. What I am dealing with is more complex and more difficult to describe, and it includes "aesthetic distance" as one of its elements.

In any reading experience there is an implied dialogue among author, narrator, the other characters, and the reader. Each of the four can range, in relation to each of the others, from identification to complete opposition, on any axis of value or judgment; moral, intellectual, aesthetic, and even physical (does the reader who stammers react to the stammering of H. C. Earwicker as I do? Surely not). The elements usually discussed under "aesthetic distance" enter in of course; distance in time and space, differences of social class or conventions of speech or dress—these and many others serve to control our sense that we are dealing with an aesthetic object, just as the paper moons and other unrealistic stage effects of some modern drama have had an "alienation" effect. But we must not confuse these effects with the equally important effects of personal beliefs and qualities, in author, narrator, reader, and all others in the cast of characters. Though we cannot hope to deal with all of the varieties of control over distance that narrative technique can achieve, we can at least remind ourselves that we deal here with something more than the question of whether the author attempts to maintain or destroy the illusion of reality.

(*a*) The *narrator* may be more or less distant from the *implied author*. The distance may be moral (Jason vs. Faulkner; the barber vs. Lardner, the narrator vs. Fielding in *Jonathan Wild*). It may be intellectual (Twain and Huck Finn, Sterne and Tristram Shandy in the matter of bigotry about the influence of noses, Richardson and Clarissa). It may be physical or temporal: most authors are distant from even the most knowing narrator in that they presumably know how "everything turns out in the end"; and so on.

(*b*) The *narrator* also may be more or less distant from the *characters* in the story he tells. He may differ, for example, morally, intellectually and temporally (the mature narrator and his younger self in *Great Expectations* or *Redburn*), morally and intellectually (Fowler the narrator and Pyle the American in Greene's *The Quiet American,* both departing radically from the author's norms but in different directions), morally and emotionally (Maupassant's "The Necklace," and Huxley's "Nuns at Luncheon," in which the narrators affect less emotional involvement than Maupassant and Huxley clearly expect from the reader).

(*c*) The *narrator* may be more or less distant from the *reader's* own norms, e.g., physically and emotionally (Kafka's *The Metamorphosis*); morally and emotionally (Pinkie in *Brighton Rock,* the miser in Mauriac's *Knot of Vipers;* the many moral degenerates that modern fiction has managed to make into convincing human beings).

One of the standard sources of plot in modern fiction—often advanced in the name of repudiating plot—is the portrayal of narrators whose characteristics change in the course of the works they narrate. Ever since Shakespeare taught the modern world what the Greeks had overlooked in neglecting character change (compare *Macbeth* and *Lear* with *Oedipus*), stories of character development or degeneration have become more and more popular. But it was not until we had discovered the full uses of the third-person reflector that we found how to show a narrator changing *as he narrates*. The mature Pip, in *Great Expectations,* is presented as a generous man whose heart is where the reader's is supposed to be; he watches his young self move away from the reader, as it were, and then back again. But the third-person reflector can be shown, technically in the past tense but in effect present before our eyes, moving toward or away from values that the reader holds dear. The twentieth-century has proceeded almost as if determined to work out all of the permutations and combinations on this effect: start far and end near; start near and end far; start far, move close, but lose the prize and end far; start near, like Pip, move away but see the light and return close; start far and move farther (many modern "tragedies" are so little tragic because the hero is too distant from us at the beginning for us to care that he is, like Macbeth, even further at the end); start near and end nearer...I can think of no theoretical possibilities that haven't been tried; anyone who has read widely in modern fiction can fill in examples.

(*d*) The *implied author* may be more or less distant from the *reader.* The distance may be intellectual (the implied author of *Tristram Shandy,* not of course to be identified with Tristram, is more interested in and knows more about recondite classical lore than any of his readers), moral (the works of Sade), and so on. From the author's viewpoint, a successful reading of his book will reduce to zero the distance between the essential norms of his implied author and the norms of the postulated reader. Often enough there is very little distance to begin with; Jane Austen does not have to convince us that pride and prejudice are undesirable. A bad book, on the other hand, is often a book whose implied author clearly asks that we judge according to norms we cannot accept.

(*e*) The *implied author* (and reader) may be more or less distant from *other characters,* ranging from Jane Austen's complete approval of Jane Fairfax in *Emma* to her contempt for Wickham in *Pride and Prejudice.* The complexity that marks our pleasure in all significant literature can be seen by contrasting the kinds of distance in these two situations. In *Emma,* the *narrator* is non-committal toward Jane Fairfax, though there is no sign of disapproval. The *author* can be inferred as approving of her almost completely. But the chief *reflector,* Emma, who has the largest share of the job of narration, is definitely disapproving of Jane Fairfax for most of the way. In *Pride and Prejudice,* on the other hand, the narrator is non-committal toward Wickham for as long as possible, hoping to mystify us; the author is secretly disapproving; and the chief reflector, Elizabeth, is definitely approving for the first half of the book.

It is obvious that on each of these scales my examples do not begin to cover the possibilities. What we call "involvement" or "sympathy" or "identification," is usually made up of many reactions to author, narrators, observers, and other characters. And narrators may differ from their authors or readers in various kinds of involvement or detachment, ranging from deep personal concern (Nick in *The Great Gatsby,* MacKellar in *The Master of Ballantrae,* Zeitblom in *Dr. Faustus*) to a bland or mildly amused or merely curious detachment (Waugh's *Decline and Fall*).

In talk about point-of-view in fiction, the most seriously neglected of these kinds of distance is that between the fallible or unreliable narrator and the implied author who carries the reader with him as against the narrator. If the reason for discussing point-of-view is to find how it relates to literary effects, then surely the moral and intellectual qualities of the narrator are more important to our judgment than whether he is referred to as "I" or "he," or whether he is privileged or limited, and so on. If he is discovered to be untrustworthy, then the total effect of the work he relays to us is transformed.

Our terminology for this kind of distance in narrators is almost hopelessly inadequate. For lack of better terms, I shall call a narrator *reliable* when he speaks for or acts in accordance with the norms of the work (which is to say, the implied author's norms), *unreliable* when he does not. It is true that most of the great reliable narrators indulge in large amounts of incidental irony, and they are thus "unreliable" in the sense of being potentially deceptive. But difficult irony is not sufficient to make a narrator unreliable. We should reserve the term unreliable for those narrators who are presented as if they spoke *throughout* for the norms of the book and who do not in fact do so. Unreliability is not ordinarily a matter of lying, although deliberately deceptive narrators have been a major resource of some modern novelists (Camus' *The Fall,* Calder Willingham's *Natural Child,* etc.). It is most often a matter of what James calls *inconscience;* the narrator is mistaken, or he pretends to qualities which the author denies him. Or, as in *Huckleberry Finn,* the narrator claims to be naturally wicked while the author silently praises his virtues, as it were, behind his back.

Unreliable narrators thus differ markedly depending on how far and in what direction they depart from their author's norms; the older term "tone," like the currently fashionable "distance," covers many effects that we should distinguish. Some narrators, like Barry Lyndon, are placed as far "away" from author and reader as possible, in respect to every virtue except a kind of interesting vitality. Some, like Fleda Vetch, the reflector in James's *The Spoils of Poynton,* come close to representing the author's ideal of taste, judgment, and moral sense. All of them make stronger demands on the reader's powers of inference than does reliable narration.

(8) Both reliable and unreliable narrators can be *isolated,* unsupported or uncorrected by other narrators (Gully Jimson in *The Horse's Mouth,* Henderson in Bellow's *Henderson the Rain King*) or supported or corrected (*The Sound and the Fury*). Sometimes it is almost impos-

sible to infer whether or to what degree a narrator is fallible; sometimes explicit corroborating or conflicting testimony makes the inference easy. Support or correction differs radically, it should be noted, depending on whether it is provided from within the action, so that the narrator-agent might benefit (Faulkner's *Intruder in the Dust*) or is simply provided externally, to help the reader correct or reinforce his own views *as against the narrator's* (Graham Greene's *The Power and the Glory*). Obviously the effects of isolation will be radically different in the two cases.

(9) Observers and narrator-agents, whether self-conscious or not, reliable or not, commenting or silent, isolated or supported, can be either *privileged* to know what could not be learned by strictly natural means or *limited* to realistic vision and inference. Complete privilege is what we usually call omniscience. But there are many kinds of privilege and very few "omniscient" narrators are allowed to know or show as much as their authors know.

We need a good study of the varieties of limitation and their function. Some limitations are only temporary, or even playful, like the ignorance Fielding sometimes imposes on his "I" (as when he doubts his own powers of narration and invokes the Muses for aid, e.g. *Tom Jones* XIII, i). Some are more nearly permanent but subject to momentary relaxation, like the generally limited, humanly realistic Ishmael in *Moby Dick,* who can yet break through his human limitations when the story requires (" 'He waxes brave, but nevertheless obeys; most careful bravery that!' murmured Ahab"—with no one present to report to the narrator.) And some are confined to what their literal condition would allow them to know (first person, Huck Finn; third person, Miranda and Laura in Katherine Anne Porter's stories).

The most important single privilege is that of obtaining an inside view, because of the rhetorical power that such a privilege conveys upon a narrator. A curious ambiguity in our notions of "omniscience" is ordinarily hidden by our terminology. Many modern works that we usually classify as narrated dramatically, with everything relayed to us through the limited views of the characters, postulate fully as much omniscience in the silent author as Fielding claims for himself. Our roving visitation into the minds of sixteen characters in Faulkner's *As I Lay Dying,* seeing nothing but what those minds contain, may seem in one sense not to depend on an omniscient narrator. But this method is omniscience with teeth in it: the implied author demands our absolute faith in his powers of divination. We must never for a moment doubt that he knows everything about each of these sixteen minds, or that he has chosen correctly how much to show of each. In short the choice of the most rigorously limited point-of-view is really no escape from omniscience—the true narrator is as "unnaturally" all-knowing as he ever was. If evident artificiality were a fault—which it is not—modern narration would be as faulty as Trollope's.

Another way of suggesting the same ambiguity is to look closely at the concept of "dramatic" story-telling. The author can present his characters in a dramatic situation without in the least presenting them in what we normally think of as a dramatic manner. When Joseph Andrews, who has been stripped and beaten by thieves, is overtaken by a stage-coach, Fielding presents the scene in what by some modern standards must seem an inconsistent and undramatic mode. "The poor wretch, who lay motionless a long time, just began to recover his senses as a stage-coach came by. The postilion hearing a man's groans, stopped his horses, and told the coachman, he was certain there was a dead man lying in the ditch. . . . A lady, who heard what the postilion said, and likewise heard the groan, called eagerly to the coachman to stop and see what was the matter. Upon which he bid the postilion alight, and look into the ditch. He did so, and returned, 'That there was a man sitting upright, as naked as ever he was born'." There follows a splendid description, hardly meriting the name of *scene,* in which the selfish reactions of each passenger are recorded. A young lawyer points out that they might be legally liable if they refuse to take Joseph up. "These words had a sensible effect on the coachman, who was well acquainted with the person who spoke them; and the old gentleman above mentioned, thinking the naked man would afford him frequent opportunities of showing his wit to the lady, offered to join with the company in giving a mug of beer for his fare; till partly alarmed by the threats of the one, and partly by the promises of the other, and being perhaps a little moved with compassion at the poor creature's condition, who stood bleeding and shivering with the cold, he at length agreed." Once Joseph is in the coach, the same kind of indirect reporting of the "scene" continues, with frequent excursions, however superficial, into the minds and hearts of the assembly of fools and knaves, and occasional guesses when complete knowledge seems inadvisable. If to be dramatic is to show characters dramatically engaged with each other, motive clashing with motive, the outcome depending upon the resolution of motives, then this scene is dramatic. But if it is to give the impression that the story is taking place by itself, with the characters existing in a dramatic relationship vis-a-vis the spectator, unmediated by a narrator and decipherable only through inferential matching of word to word and word to deed, then this is a relatively undramatic scene.

On the other hand, an author can present a character in this latter kind of dramatic relationship with the reader without involving that character in any internal drama at all. Many lyric poems are dramatic in this sense and totally undramatic in any other. "That is no country for old men—" Who says? Yeats, or his "mask," says. To whom? To us. How do we know that it is Yeats and not some character as remote from him as Caliban is remote from Browning in "Caliban upon Setebos"? We infer it as the dramatized statement unfolds; the need for the inference is what makes the lyric *dramatic* in this sense. Caliban, in short, is dramatic in two senses; he is in a dramatic situation with other characters and he is in a dramatic situation over-against us. Yeats, or if we prefer "Yeats' mask," is dramatic in only one sense.

The ambiguities of the word dramatic are even more complicated in fiction that attempts to dramatize states of consciousness directly. Is *A Portrait of the Artist as a Young Man* dramatic? In some respects, yes. We are not told about Stephen. He is placed on the stage before us, acting out his destiny with only disguised helps or comments from his author. But it is not his actions that are dramatized directly, not his speech that we hear unmediated. What is dramatized is his mental record of everything that happens. We see his consciousness at work on the world. Sometimes what it records is itself dramatic, as when Stephen observes himself in a scene with other characters. But the report itself, the internal record, is dramatic in the second sense only. The report we are given of what goes on in Stephen's mind is a monologue uninvolved in any modifying dramatic context. And it is an *infallible* report, even less subject to critical doubts than the typical Elizabethan soliloquy. We accept, by convention, the claim that what is reported as going on in Stephen's mind really goes on there, or in other words, that Joyce knows how Stephen's mind works. "The equation of the page of his scribbler began to spread out a widening tail, eyed and starred like a peacock's; and, when the eyes and stars of its indices had been eliminated, began slowly to fold itself together again. The indices appearing and disappearing were eyes opening and closing; the eyes opening and closing were stars. . . ." Who says so? Not Stephen, but the omniscient, infallible author. The report is direct, and it is clearly unmodified by any "dramatic" context —that is, unlike a speech in a dramatic scene, we do not suspect that the report has here been in any way aimed at an effect on anyone but the reader. We are thus in a dramatic relation with Stephen only in a limited sense—the sense in which a lyrical poem is dramatic.

Indeed if we compare the act of reporting in *Tom Jones* with the act of reporting in *Portrait,* the former is in one sense considerably more dramatic; Fielding dramatizes himself and his telling, and even though he is essentially reliable we must be constantly on our toes in comparing word to word and word to deed. "It is an observation sometimes made, that to indicate our idea of a simple fellow, we say, he is easily to be seen through: nor do I believe it a more improper denotation of simple book. Instead of applying this to any particular performance, we choose rather to remark the contrary in this history, where the scene opens itself by small degrees; and he is a sagacious reader who can see two chapters before him." Our running battle to keep up with these incidental ironies in Fielding's narration is matched, in *Portrait,* with an act of absolute, unquestioning credulity.

We should note finally that the author who eschews both forms of artificiality, both the traditional omniscience and the modern manipulation of inside views, confining himself to "objective" surfaces only, is not necessarily identical with the "undramatized author" under (2) above. In *The Awkward Age,* for example, James allows himself to comment frequently, but only to conjecture about the meaning of surfaces; the author is dramatized, but dramatized as partially ignorant of what is happening.

(10) Finally, narrators who provide inside views differ in the depth and the axis of their plunge. Boccaccio can give inside views, but they are extremely shallow. Jane Austen goes relatively deep morally, but scarcely skims the surface psychologically. All authors of stream-of-consciousness narration attempt to go deep psychologically, but some of them deliberately remain shallow in the moral dimension. We should remind ourselves that any sustained inside view, of whatever depth, temporarily turns the character whose mind is shown into a narrator; inside views are thus subject to variations in all of the qualities we have described above, and most importantly in the degree of unreliability. Generally speaking, the deeper our plunge, the more unreliability we will accept without loss of sympathy. The whole question of how inside views and moral sympathy interrelate has been seriously neglected.

Narration is an art, not a science, but this does not mean that we are necessarily doomed to fail when we attempt to formulate principles about it. There are systematic elements in every art, and criticism of fiction can never avoid the responsibility of trying to explain technical successes and failures by reference to general principles. But the question is that of where the general principles are to be found. Fiction, the novel, point-of-view—these terms are not in fact subject to the kind of definition that alone makes critical generalizations and rules meaningful. A given technique cannot be judged according to its service to "the novel," or "fiction," but only according to its success in particular works or kinds of work.

It is not surprising to hear practicing novelists report that they have never had help from critics about point-of-view. In dealing with point-of-view the novelist must always deal with the individual work: which particular character shall tell this particular story, or part of a story, with what precise degree of reliability, privilege, freedom to comment, and so on. Shall he be given dramatic vividness? Even if the novelist has decided on a narrator who will fit one of the critic's classifications—"omniscient," "first-person," "limited omniscient," "objective," "roving," "effaced," and so on—his troubles have just begun. He simply cannot find answers to his immediate, precise, practical problems by referring to statements that the "omniscient is the most flexible method," or "the objective the most rapid or vivid," or whatever. Even the soundest of generalizations at this level will be of little use to him in his page-by-page progress through his novel. As Henry James's detailed records show, the novelist discovers his narrative technique as he tries to achieve for his readers the potentialities of his developing idea. The majority of his choices are consequently choices of degree, not kind. To decide that your narrator shall not be omniscient decides practically nothing. The hard question is, just how *inconscient* shall he be? To decide that you will use first-person narration decides again almost nothing. What kind of first-person? How fully characterized? How much aware of himself as a narrator? How reliable? How much confined to realistic inference, how far privileged to go beyond realism? At what points shall he speak truth and at what points utter no judgment or even utter falsehood?[1]

---

[1] I try to deal with some of these questions in *The Rhetoric of Fiction,* to be published this autumn by the University of Chicago Press. This article is an expanded version of one chapter from that book.

There are no doubt *kinds* of effect to which the author can refer—
e.g., if he wants to make a scene more amusing, poignant, vivid, or
ambiguous, or if he wants to make a character more sympathetic or
more convincing, such-and-such practices may be indicated. But it is
not surprising that in his search for help in his decisions, he should
find the practice of his peers more helpful than the abstract rules of
the textbooks: the sensitive author who reads the great novels finds
in them a storehouse of precise examples, examples of how *this* effect,
as distinct from all other possible effects, was heightened by the
proper narrative choice. In dealing with the types of narration, the
critic must always limp behind, referring constantly to the varied
practice which alone can correct his temptations to over-generalize.

The impact of Wayne Booth's *The Rhetoric of Fiction**
upon the criticism of fiction has been so great that it must be
taken into account by anyone who wishes to generalize about
fiction. Booth's book is valuable not merely for the theoretical
structure he advances but to a much greater degree for the
questions that he raises. Most important is his challenge to those
who accept without sufficient examination the critical tenets of
Henry James; a comparison of his essay with Norman Friedman's
demonstrates the practical effects of that challenge. By showing
that terms such as "dramatic" and "objective" have become
mere counters and by stressing the distinction between description and evaluation, Booth has forced others to examine their
premises more carefully.

Booth's positive thesis is less revolutionary but no less interesting. In the opening of the preface to *The Rhetoric of Fiction,*
he defines his subject as "the techniques of non-didactic fiction,
viewed as the art of communicating with readers—the rhetorical
resources available to the writer of epic, novel, or short story as
he tries, consciously or unconsciously, to impose his fictional
world upon the reader." The theory of the implied author, his
most important contribution to the concept of point of view, is
closely related to this purpose: the novel creates a persuader as it
presents a vision of reality to the audience. Thus the distinction
between showing and telling is blurred or abolished, and the
emphasis shifts to the process by which the audience is persuaded

---

* Chicago: University of Chicago Press, 1961.

(the novel is seen both as process and as embodiment of the whole conception) and to the audience for whom the novel has its being.

In this essay, Booth's schematization is much more complex in its distinctions than that of Friedman and less progressive in its structure. In practical terms, his discussion of Joyce's *A Portrait of the Artist as a Young Man,* considerably amplified in *The Rhetoric of Fiction* (pp. 323–36), makes an interesting contrast to the treatment accorded the novel by both Friedman and Schorer. Booth denies that the book's point of view is objective and detached in a technical sense and he argues that the lack of a clear moral standard is far from being a virtue. In the end, he says, after one has made all possible qualifications, "one must say that an author has an obligation to be as clear about his moral position as he possibly can be" (p. 389).

Although it would be a mistake to ignore the weight of "possibly" in this pronouncement, one might object to Booth's position. Scholes and Kellogg argue near the end of *The Nature of Narrative* (1) that Booth and other Aristotelian critics do not understand the cultural and social processes that produce inevitable changes in method; (2) and that, therefore, Booth's rejection of modern techniques of fiction is based upon nostalgia rather than logic; (3) and that he embraces a normative position. Some hints of this attitude, presented in moral terms, are evident in the essay printed here, particularly in Booth's discussion of the distance between implied author and reader. Toward the end of this essay, and in greater detail near the end of his book, Booth attempts to deal with the relationship of art to morality. "A bad book...," he says in this essay, "is often a book whose implied author clearly asks that we judge according to norms that we cannot accept." This may seem a valuable answer to the problem in practical terms—what strikes the reader as immoral does so because of a failure in art, which has become persuasion—but in theory as well as in practice it raises more questions than it answers. For one thing, it makes the reader's moral norms a primary source of artistic evaluation and therefore confuses ethical and aesthetic judgments. However, it is difficult to blame Booth for failing to solve a problem which seems clear only to those who take extreme positions.

The Rhetoric of Fiction provides not only theoretical justification for many of Booth's premises but an annotated bibliography of more than three hundred and fifty items. For analysis and criticism of Booth's argument, see Henry Sams, "Show and

Tell."* References to further comment on this and other works published since 1962—those by Lodge, Harvey, and Scholes and Kellogg among them—can be found in *Index to Book Reviews in the Humanities* (1961–1964), *Book Review Index* (1965–   ), and *Book Review Digest*.

* *Journal of General Education,* XVII (January 1966), 315–29.

Pattern and Rhythm

E. M. FORSTER

Our interludes, gay and grave, are over, and we return to the general scheme of the course. We began with the story, and having considered human beings, we proceeded to the plot which springs out of the story. Now we must consider something which springs mainly out of the plot, and to which the characters and any other element present also contribute. For this new aspect there appears to be no literary word—indeed the more the arts develop the more they depend on each other for definition. We will borrow from painting first and call it the pattern. Later we will borrow from music and call it rhythm. Unfortunately both these words are vague—when people apply rhythm or pattern to literature they are apt not to say what they mean and not to finish their sentences: it is, "Oh, but surely the rhythm..." or "Oh, but if you call that pattern...."

Before I discuss what pattern entails, and what qualities a reader must bring to its appreciation, I will give two examples of books with patterns so definite that a pictorial image sums them up: a book the shape of an hour-glass and a book the shape of a grand chain in that old-time dance, the Lancers.

Thais by Anatole France is the shape of an hour-glass.

There are two chief characters, Paphnuce the ascetic, Thais the courtesan. Paphnuce lives in the desert, he is saved and happy when the book starts. Thais leads a life of sin in Alexandria, and it is his duty to save her. In the central scene of the book they approach, he succeeds; she goes into a monastery and gains salvation, because she

192

has met him, but he, because he has met her, is damned. The two characters converge, cross, and recede with mathematical precision, and part of the pleasure we get from the book is due to this. Such is the pattern of *Thais*—so simple that it makes a good starting-point for a difficult survey. It is the same as the story of *Thais*, when events unroll in their time-sequence, and the same as the plot of *Thais*, when we see the two characters bound by their previous actions and taking fatal steps whose consequence they do not see. But whereas the story appeals to our curiosity and the plot to our intelligence, the pattern appeals to our aesthetic sense, it causes us to see the book as a whole. We do not see it as an hour-glass—that is the hard jargon of the lecture room which must never be taken literally at this advanced stage of our inquiry. We just have a pleasure without knowing why, and when the pleasure is past, as it is now, and our minds are left free to explain it, a geometrical simile such as an hour-glass will be found helpful. If it was not for this hour-glass the story, the plot, and the characters of Thais and Paphnuce would none of them exert their full force, they would none of them breathe as they do. "Pattern," which seems so rigid, is connected with atmosphere, which seems so fluid.

Now for the book that is shaped like the grand chain: *Roman Pictures* by Percy Lubbock.

Roman Pictures is a social comedy. The narrator is a tourist in Rome; he there meets a kindly and shoddy friend of his, Deering, who rebukes him superciliously for staring at churches and sets him out to explore society. This he does, demurely obedient; one person hands him on to another; café, studio, Vatican and Quirinal purlieus are all reached, until finally, at the extreme end of his career he thinks, in a most aristocratic and dilapidated palazzo, whom should he meet but the second-rate Deering; Deering is his hostess's nephew, but had concealed it owing to some backfire of snobbery. The circle is complete, the original partners have rejoined, and greet one another with mutual confusion which turns to mild laughter.

What is so good in *Roman Pictures* is not the presence of the "grand chain" pattern—anyone can organize a grand chain—but the suitability of the pattern to the author's mood. Lubbock works all through by administering a series of little shocks, and by extending to his characters an elaborate charity which causes them to appear in a rather worse light than if no charity was wasted on them at all. It is the comic atmosphere, but sub-acid, meticulously benign. And at the end we discover to our delight that the atmosphere has been externalized, and that the partners, as they click together in the marchesa's drawing-room, have done the exact thing which the book requires, which it required from the start, and have bound the scattered incidents together with a thread woven out of their own substance.

Thais and *Roman Pictures* provide easy examples of pattern; it is not often that one can compare a book to a pictorial object with any accuracy, though curves, etc., are freely spoken of by critics who do not quite know what they want to say. We can only say (so far) that pattern is an aesthetic aspect of the novel, and that though it may be nourished by anything in the novel—any character, scene, word—it draws most of its nourishment from the plot. We noted, when discussing the plot, that it added to itself the quality of beauty; beauty a little surprised at her own arrival: that upon its neat carpentry there could be seen, by those who cared to see, the figure of the Muse; that Logic, at the moment of finishing its own house, laid the foundation of a new one. Here, here is the point where the aspect called pattern is most closely in touch with its material; here is our starting point. It springs mainly from the plot, accompanies it like a light in the clouds, and remains visible after it has departed. Beauty is sometimes the shape of the book, the book as a whole, the unity, and our examination would be easier if it was always this. But sometimes it is not. When it is not I shall call it rhythm. For the moment we are concerned with pattern only.

Let us examine at some length another book of the rigid type, a book with a unity, and in this sense an easy book, although it is by Henry James. We shall see in it pattern triumphant, and we shall also be able to see the sacrifices an author must make if he wants his pattern and nothing else to triumph.

The Ambassadors, like *Thais,* is the shape of an hour-glass. Strether and Chad, like Paphnuce and Thais, change places, and it is the realization of this that makes the book so satisfying at the close. The plot is elaborate and subtle, and proceeds by action or conversation or meditation through every paragraph. Everything is planned, everything fits; none of the minor characters are just decorative like the talkative Alexandrians at Nicias' banquet; they elaborate on the main theme, they work. The final effect is pre-arranged, dawns gradually on the reader, and is completely successful when it comes. Details of intrigue, of the various missions from America, may be forgotten, but the symmetry they have created is enduring.

Let us trace the growth of this symmetry.[1]

Strether, a sensitive middle-aged American, is commissioned by his old friend, Mrs. Newsome, whom he hopes to marry, to go to Paris and rescue her son Chad, who has gone to the bad in that appropriate city. The Newsomes are sound commercial people, who have made money over manufacturing a small article of domestic utility. Henry James never tells us what the small article is, and in a moment we shall understand why. Wells spits it out in *Tono Bungay,* Meredith reels it out in *Evan Harrington,* Trollope prescribes it freely for Miss Dunstable, but for James to indicate how his characters made their pile—it would not do. The article is somewhat ignoble and ludicrous— that is enough. If you choose to be coarse and daring and visualize it for yourself as, say, a button-hook, you can, but you do so at your own risk: the author remains uninvolved.

Well, whatever it is, Chad Newsome ought to come back and help make it, and Strether undertakes to fetch him. He has to be rescued from a life which is both immortal [sic] and unremunerative.

Strether is a typical James character—he recurs in nearly all the books and is an essential part of their construction. He is the observer who tries to influence the action, and who through his failure to do so gains extra opportunities for observation. And the other characters are such as an observer like Strether is capable of observing—through lenses procured from a rather too first-class oculist. Everything is adjusted to his vision, yet he is not a quietist—no, that is the strength of the device; he takes us along with him, we move as well as look on.

When he lands in England (and a landing is an exalted and endur- ing experience for James, it is as vital as Newgate for Defoe; poetry and life crowd round a landing): when Strether lands, though it is only old England, he begins to have doubts of his mission, which increase when he gets to Paris. For Chad Newsome, far from going to the bad, has improved; he is distinguished, he is so sure of himself that he can be kind and cordial to the man who has orders to fetch him away; his friends are exquisite, and as for "women in the case" whom his mother anticipated, there is no sign of them whatever. It is

---

1 There is a masterly analysis of *The Ambassadors* from another standpoint in *The Craft of Fiction.*

Paris that has enlarged and redeemed him—and how well Strether himself understands this!

> His greatest uneasiness seemed to peep at him out of the possible impression that almost any acceptance of Paris might give one's authority away. It hung before him this morning, the vast bright Babylon, like some huge iridescent object, a jewel brilliant and hard, in which parts were not to be discriminated nor differences comfortably marked. It twinkled and trembled and melted together; and what seemed all surface one moment seemed all depth the next. It was a place of which, unmistakably, Chad was fond; wherefore, if he, Strether, should like it too much, what on earth, with such a bond, would become of either of them?

Thus, exquisitely and firmly, James sets his atmosphere—Paris irradiates the book from end to end, it is an actor though always unembodied, it is a scale by which human sensibility can be measured, and when we have finished the novel and allow its incidents to blur that we may see the pattern plainer, it is Paris that gleams at the centre of the hour-glass shape—Paris—nothing so crude as good or evil. Strether sees this soon, and sees that Chad realizes it better than he himself can; and when he has reached this stage of initiation the novel takes a turn: there is, after all, a woman in the case; behind Paris, interpreting it for Chad, is the adorable and exalted figure of Mme. de Vionnet. It is now impossible for Strether to proceed. All that is noble and refined in life concentrates in Mme. de Vionnet and is reinforced by her pathos. She asks him not to take Chad away. He promises—without reluctance, for his own heart has already shown him as much—and he remains in Paris not to fight it but to fight for it.

For the second batch of ambassadors now arrives from the New World. Mrs. Newsome, incensed and puzzled by the unseemly delay, has dispatched Chad's sister, his brother-in-law, and Mamie, the girl whom he is supposed to marry. The novel now becomes, within its ordained limits, most amusing. There is a superb set-to between Chad's sister and Mme. de Vionnet, while as for Mamie—here is disastrous Mamie, seen as we see all things, through Strether's eyes.

> As a child, as a "bud," and then again as a flower of expansion, Mamie had bloomed for him, freely, in the almost incessantly open doorways of home; where he remembered her at first very forward, as then very backward—for he had carried on at one period, in Mrs. Newsome's parlours, a course of English literature reinforced by exams and teas—and once more, finally, as very much in advance. But he had kept no great sense of points of contact; it not being in the nature

of things at Woollett that the freshest of the buds should find herself in the same basket with the most withered of the winter apples. . . . He nonetheless felt now, as he sat with the charming girl, the signal growth of a confidence. For she *was* charming, when all was said, and nonetheless so for the visible habit and practice of freedom and fluency. She was charming, he was aware, in spite of the fact that if he hadn't found her so he would have found her something he should have been in peril of expressing as "funny." Yes, she was funny, wonderful Mamie, and without dreaming it; she was bland, she was bridal—with never, that he could make out as yet, a bridegroom to support it; she was handsome and portly, and easy and chatty, soft and sweet and almost disconcertingly reassuring. She was dressed, if we might so far discriminate, less as a young lady than as an old one—had an old one been supposable to Strether as so committed to vanity; the complexities of her hair missed moreover also the looseness of youth; and she had a mature manner of bending a little, as to encourage and reward, while she held neatly in front of her pair of strikingly polished hands; the combination of all of which kept up about her the glamour of her "receiving," placed her again perpetually between the windows and within sound of the ice cream plates, suggested the enumeration of all the names, gregarious specimens of a single type, she was happy to "meet."

Mamie! She is another Henry James type; nearly every novel contains a Mamie—Mrs. Gereth in *The Spoils of Poynton* for instance, or Henrietta Stackpole in *The Portrait of a Lady*. He is so good at indicating instantaneously and constantly that a character is second-rate, deficient in sensitiveness, abounding in the wrong sort of worldliness; he gives such a character so much vitality that its absurdity is delightful.

So Strether changes sides and loses all hopes of marrying Mrs. Newsome. Paris is winning—and then he catches sight of something new. Is not Chad, as regards any fineness in him, played out? Is not Chad's Paris after all just a place for a spree? This fear is confirmed. He goes for a solitary country walk, and at the end of the day he comes across Chad and Mme. de Vionnet. They are in a boat, they pretend not to see him, because their relation is at bottom an ordinary liaison, and they are ashamed. They were hoping for a secret week-end at an inn while their passion survived; for it will not survive, Chad will tire of the exquisite Frenchwoman, she is part of his fling; he will go back to his mother and make the little domestic article and marry Mamie. They know all this, and it is revealed to Strether though they try to hide it; they lie, they are vulgar—even Mme. de Vionnet, even her pathos, once so exquisite, is stained with commonness.

It was like a chill in the air to him, it was almost appalling, that a creature so fine could be, by mysterious forces, a creature so exploited. For, at the end of all things, they *were* mysterious; she had but made Chad what he was—so why could she think she had made him infinite? She had made him better, she had made him best, she had made him anything one would; but it came to our friend with supreme queerness that he was nonetheless only Chad. The work, however admirable, was nevertheless of the strict human order, and in short it was marvellous that the companion of mere earthly joys, of comforts, aberrations —however one classed them—within the common experience, should be so transcendently prized.

She was older for him tonight, visibly less exempt from the touch of time; but she was as much as ever the finest and subtlest creature, the happiest apparition, it had been given him, in all his years, to meet; and yet he could see her there as vulgarly troubled, in very truth, as a maidservant crying for a young man. The only thing was that she judged herself as the maidservant wouldn't; the weakness of which wisdom too, the dishonour of which judgment, seemed but to sink her lower.

So Strether loses them too. As he says: "I have lost everything— it is my only logic." It is not that they have gone back. It is that he has gone on. The Paris they revealed to him—he could reveal it to them now, if they had eyes to see, for it is something finer than they could ever notice for themselves, and his imagination has more spiritual value than their youth. The pattern of the hour-glass is complete; he and Chad have changed places, with more subtle steps than Thais and Paphnuce, and the light in the clouds proceeds not from the well-lit Alexandria, but from the jewel which "twinkled and trembled and melted together, and what seemed all surface one moment seemed all depth the next."

The beauty that suffuses *The Ambassadors* is the reward due to a fine artist for hard work. James knew exactly what he wanted, he pursued the narrow path of aesthetic duty, and success to the full extent of his possibilities has crowned him. The pattern has woven itself with modulation and reservations Anatole France will never attain. Woven itself wonderfully. But at what sacrifice!

So enormous is the sacrifice that many readers cannot get interested in James, although they can follow what he says (his difficulty has been much exaggerated), and can appreciate his effects. They cannot grant his premise, which is that most of human life has to disappear before he can do us a novel.

He has, in the first place, a very short list of characters. I have already mentioned two—the observer who tries to influence the action, and the second-rate outsider (to whom, for example, all the brilliant opening of *What Maisie Knew* is entrusted). Then there is the sympathetic foil—very lively and frequently female—in *The Ambassadors.* Maria Gostrey plays this part; there is the wonderful rare heroine, whom Mme. de Vionnet approached and who is consummated by Milly in *The Wings of the Dove;* there is sometimes a villain, sometimes a young artist with generous impulses; and that is about all. For so fine a novelist it is a poor show.

In the second place, the characters, beside being few in number, are constructed on very stingy lines. They are incapable of fun, of rapid motion, of carnality, and of nine-tenths of heroism. Their clothes will not take off, the diseases that ravage them are anonymous, like the sources of their income, their servants are noiseless or resemble themselves, no social explanation of the world we know is possible for them, for there are no stupid people in their world, no barriers of language, and no poor. Even their sensations are limited. They can land in Europe and look at works of art and at each other, but that is all. Maimed creatures can alone breathe in Henry James's pages— maimed yet specialized. They remind one of the exquisite deformities who haunted Egyptian art in the reign of Akhenaton—huge heads and tiny legs, but nevertheless charming. In the following reign they disappear.

Now this drastic curtailment, both of the numbers of human beings and of their attributes, is in the interests of the pattern. The longer James worked, the more convinced he grew that a novel should be a whole—not necessarily geometric like *The Ambassadors,* but it should accrete round a single topic, situation, gesture, which should occupy the characters and provide a plot, and should also fasten up the novel on the outside—catch its scattered statements in a net, make them cohere like a planet, and swing through the skies of memory. A pattern must emerge, and anything that emerged from the pattern must be pruned off as wanton distraction. Who so wanton as human beings? Put Tom Jones or Emma or even Mr. Casaubon into a Henry James book, and the book will burn to ashes, whereas we could put them into one another's books and only cause local inflammation. Only a Henry James character will suit, and though they are not dead —certain selected recesses of experience he explores very well—they are gutted of the common stuff that fills characters in other books, and ourselves. And this castrating is not in the interests of the Kingdom of Heaven, there is no philosophy in the novels, no religion (except an occasional touch of superstition), no prophecy, no benefit for the superhuman at all. It is for the sake of a particular aesthetic effect which is certainly gained, but at this heavy price.

H. G. Wells has been amusing on this point, and perhaps profound. In *Boon*—one of his liveliest works—he had Henry James much upon his mind, and wrote a superb parody of him.

> James begins by taking it for granted that a novel is a work of art that must be judged by its oneness. Someone gave him that idea in the beginning of things and he has never found it out. He doesn't find things out. He doesn't even seem to want to find things out. He accepts very readily and then—elaborates. . . . The only living human motives left in his novels are a certain avidity and an entirely superficial curiosity. . . . His people nose out suspicions, hint by hint, link by link. Have you ever known living human beings do that? The thing his novel is *about* is always there. It is like a church lit but with no congregation to distract you, with every light and line focused on the high altar. And on the altar, very reverently placed, intensely there, is a dead kitten, an egg shell, a piece of string. . . . Like his *Altar of the Dead* with nothing to the dead at all. . . . For if there was, they couldn't all be candles, and the effect would vanish.

Wells sent *Boon* as a present to James, apparently thinking the master would be as much pleased by such heartiness and honesty as was he himself. The master was far from pleased, and a most interesting correspondence ensued.[2] Each of the eminent men becomes more and more himself as it proceeds. James is polite, reminiscent, bewildered, and exceedingly formidable: he admits that the parody has not "filled him with a fond elation," and regrets in conclusion that he can sign himself "only yours faithfully, Henry James." Wells is bewildered too, but in a different way; he cannot understand why the man should be upset. And, beyond the personal comedy, there is the great literary importance of the issue. It is this question of the rigid pattern: hour-glass or grand chain or converging lines of the cathedral or diverging lines of the Catherine wheel, or bed of Procrustes—whatever image you like as long as it implies unity. Can it be combined with the immense richness of material which life provides? Wells and James would agree it cannot, Wells would go on to say that life should be given the preference, and must not be whittled or distended for a pattern's sake. My own prejudices are with Wells. The James novels are a unique possession and the reader who cannot

---

2 See the *Letters of H. James*, Vol. II.

accept his premises misses some valuable and exquisite sensations. But I do not want more of his novels, especially when they are written by someone else, just as I do not want the art of Akhenaton to extend into the reign of Tutankhamen.

That then is the disadvantage of a rigid pattern. It may externalize the atmosphere, spring naturally from the plot, but it shuts the doors on life and leaves the novelist doing exercises, generally in the drawing-room. Beauty has arrived, but in too tyrannous a guise. In plays—the plays of Racine, for instance—she may be justified because beauty can be a great empress on the stage, and reconcile us to the loss of the men we knew. But in the novel, her tyranny as it grows powerful grows petty, and generates regrets which sometimes take the form of books like *Boon*. To put it in other words, the novel is not capable of as much artistic development as the drama: its humanity or the grossness of its material hinder it (use whichever phrase you like). To most readers of fiction the sensation from a pattern is not intense enough to justify the sacrifices that made it, and their verdict is "Beautifully done, but not worth doing."

Still this is not the end of our quest. We will not give up the hope of beauty yet. Cannot it be introduced into fiction by some other method than the pattern? Let us edge rather nervously towards the idea of "rhythm."

Rhythm is sometimes quite easy. Beethoven's Fifth Symphony, for instance, starts with the rhythm "diddidy dum," which we can all hear and tap to. But the symphony as a whole has also a rhythm— due mainly to the relation between its movements—which some people can hear but no one can tap to. This second sort of rhythm is difficult, and whether it is substantially the same as the first sort only a musician could tell us. What a literary man wants to say though is that the first kind of rhythm, the diddidy dum, can be found in certain novels and may give them beauty. And the other rhythm, the difficult one— the rhythm of the Fifth Symphony as a whole—I cannot quote you any parallels for that in fiction, yet it may be present.

Rhythm in the easy sense, is illustrated by the work of Marcel Proust.[3]

Proust's conclusion has not been published yet, and his admirers

---

[3] The first three books of *A la recherche du temps perdu* have been excellently translated by C. K. Scott Moncrieff under the title of *Remembrance of Things Past,* A. & C. Boni.

say that when it comes everything will fall into its place, times past will be recaptured and fixed, we shall have a perfect whole. I do not believe this. The work seems to me a progressive rather than an aesthetic confession, and with the elaboration of Albertine the author was getting tired. Bits of news may await us, but it will be surprising if we have to revise our opinion of the whole book. The book is chaotic, ill-constructed, it has and will have no external shape; and yet it hangs together because it is stitched internally, because it contains rhythms.

There are several examples (the photographing of the grandmother is one of them) but the most important from the binding point of view is his use of the "little phrase" in the music of Vinteuil. It does more than anything else—more even than the jealousy which successively destroys Swann, the hero, and Charlus—to make us feel that we are in a homogeneous world. We first hear Vinteuil's name in hideous circumstances. The musician is dead—an obscure little country organist, unknown to fame—and his daughter is defiling his memory. The horrible scene is to radiate in several directions, but it passes, we forget about it.

Then we are at a Paris salon. A violin sonata is performed and a little phrase from its andante catches the ear of Swann and steals into his life. It is always a living being, but takes various forms. For a time it attends his love for Odette. The love affair goes wrong, the phrase is forgotten, we forget it. Then it breaks out again when he is ravaged by jealousy, and now it attends his misery and past happiness at once, without losing its own divine character. Who wrote the sonata? On hearing it is by Vinteuil, Swann says, "I once knew a wretched little organist of that name—it couldn't be by him." But it is, and Vinteuil's daughter and her friend transcribed and published it.

That seems all. The little phrase crosses the book again and again, but as an echo, a memory; we like to encounter it, but it has no binding power. Then, hundreds and hundreds of pages on, when Vinteuil has become a national possession, and there is talk of raising a statue to him in the town where he has been so wretched and so obscure, another work of his is performed—a posthumous sextet. The hero listens—he is in an unknown rather terrible universe while a sinister dawn reddens the sea. Suddenly for him and for the reader too, the little phrase of the sonata recurs—half heard, changed, but giving complete orientation, so that he is back in the country of his childhood with the knowledge that it belongs to the unknown.

We are not obliged to agree with Proust's actual musical descriptions (they are too pictorial for my own taste) : but what we must admire is his use of rhythm in literature, and his use of something which is akin by nature to the effect it has to produce—namely a musical phrase. Heard by various people—first by Swann, then by the hero—the phrase of Vinteuil is not tethered; it is not a banner such as we find George Meredith using—a double-blossomed cherry tree to accompany Clara Middleton, a yacht in smooth waters for Cecilia Halkett. A banner can only reappear, rhythm can develop, and the little phrase has a life of its own, unconnected with the lives of its auditors, as with the life of the man who composed it. It is almost an actor, but not quite, and that "not quite" means that its power has gone towards stitching Proust's book together from the inside, and towards the establishment of beauty and the ravishing of the reader's memory. There are times when the little phrase—from its gloomy inception, through the sonata into the sextet—means everything to the reader. There are times when it means nothing and is forgotten, and this seems to me the function of rhythm in fiction; not to be there all the time like a pattern, but by its lovely waxing and waning to fill us with surprise and freshness and hope.

Done badly, rhythm is most boring, it hardens into a symbol and instead of carrying us on it trips us up. With exasperation we find that Galsworthy's spaniel John, or whatever it is, lies under the feet again; and even Meredith's cherry trees and yachts, graceful as they are, only open the windows into poetry. I doubt that it can be achieved by the writers who plan their books beforehand, it has to depend on a local impulse when the right interval is reached. But the effect can be exquisite, it can be obtained without mutilating the characters, and it lessens our need of an external form.

That must suffice on the subject of easy rhythm in fiction: which may be defined as repetition plus variation, and which can be illustrated by examples. Now for the more difficult question. Is there any effect in novels comparable to the effect of the Fifth Symphony as a whole, where, when the orchestra stops, we hear something that has never actually been played? The opening movement, the andante, and the trio-scherzo-trio-finale-trio-finale that composes the third block, all enter the mind at once, and extend one another into a common entity. This common entity, this new thing, is the symphony as a whole, and it has been achieved mainly (though not entirely) by the relation between the three big blocks of sound which the orchestra has been playing. I am calling this relation "rhythmic." If the correct musical term is something else, that does not matter; what we have now to ask ourselves is whether there is any analogy to it in fiction.

I cannot find any analogy. Yet there may be one; in music fiction is likely to find its nearest parallel.

The position of the drama is different. The drama may look towards the pictorial arts, it may allow Aristotle to discipline it, for it is not so deeply committed to the claims of human beings. Human beings have their great chance in the novel. They say to the novelist: "Recreate us if you like, but we must come in," and the novelist's problem, as we have seen all along, is to give them a good run and to achieve something else at the same time. Whither shall he turn? not indeed for help but for analogy. Music, though it does not employ human beings, though it is governed by intricate laws, nevertheless does offer in its final expression a type of beauty which fiction might achieve in its own way. Expansion. That is the idea the novelist must cling to. Not completion. Not rounding off but opening out. When the symphony is over we feel that the notes and tunes composing it have been liberated, they have found in the rhythm of the whole their individual freedom. Cannot the novel be like that? Is not there something of it in *War and Peace?*—the book with which we began and in which we must end. Such an untidy book. Yet, as we read it, do not great chords begin to sound behind us, and when we have finished does not every item—even the catalogue of strategies—lead a larger existence than was possible at the time?

❈❈❈

First delivered as a series of lectures, *Aspects of the Novel* is informal and seemingly diffident, but the book is deceptive in its simplicity, for it seizes upon some of the major critical controversies about the novel. Most important in this chapter is the opposition of pattern to rhythm, of a novel regarded as a fixed structure, a thing—James uses architectural metaphors in speaking of *Portrait of a Lady,* for example—as opposed to a novel regarded as a process, a fluid shifting state, as in the essay by Walter O'Grady.

The frames of reference do not coincide exactly, but those who see the novel as a process tend to hold mimetic theories and thus stress the life-likeness and sometimes, like Forster, the liveliness of fiction. Forster's argument that the novel cannot be developed as artistically as drama because of "its humanity or the grossness of its material" is implied and sometimes stated in the essays of Rahv, Harvey, and Marcus. Those who see the novel as a structure, an object, tend to favor aesthetic and formal approaches. Whether or not the theories overlap, the distinction between structure and process is both real and theoretically significant.

Of course, a novel is both process and construct, and it draws from life as well as art. Forster is too canny to polarize these terms, and his concept of rhythm is intended to resolve the conflicts by positing a kind of structure built up from within the work rather than imposed upon it. The result would be an organic form that permits life to enter the work but at the same time allows for shape—not just a slice of life or a sprawling vitalism such as might accommodate Tom Jones to Emma and both to Mr. Casaubon—and enables the whole to be greater than the sum of its parts. Forster does not pursue the matter in this book, but a theory that has such promise for reconciling disparate theories deserves further discussion.

An important contribution to the discussion is E. K. Brown's *Rhythm in the Novel,** a book so tightly planned that excerpting, even of chapters, would do violence to the argument. Brown develops Forster's concepts at much greater length, and holds that Forster's own novel, *A Passage to India,* illustrates the difficult kind of rhythm that is also structure. One of the major criticisms of Forster's use of terms and of his general approach is Edwin Muir's *The Structure of the Novel.*†

* Toronto: University of Toronto Press, 1950.
† London: The Hogarth Press, Ltd., 1928.

On Plot in Modern Fiction : Hardy, James, and Conrad

WALTER O'GRADY

E. M. Forster distinguishes between story and plot.[1] Story he calls the narrative of events arranged in their time sequence, while plot is likewise a narrative of events, but with the emphasis falling on causality. "The King died and then the Queen died" is a story, but "the King died and then the Queen died of grief" is a plot. The difference is that while each contains two incidents, the second contains the reason for one of the incidents. But Forster does not examine closely enough. "The King died because he was old" is not of the same order as "the Queen died because of grief," nor even of "the litmus paper turned red because the solution was acidic." The difference seems to lie in the fact that the grief of the queen is an internal, non-physical human event. What Forster has given us is one external event causing a change in an internal situation, which internal event causes another external event. Thus what we have in plot is two exterior events, one interior event, an interior situation and change. We may say that this is merely the interaction of character and plot, yet this phrase has meaning only if the plot is considered as the totality of external events. But why should the emotion of love be considered less an event than the action of marrying? Why is a new perception not considered as happening to a character in the same way as inheriting a fortune is considered as happening to him? The difference does not lie in the fact that one is an incident and the other a state, for being rich is as much a state as being in love, and inheriting

From *Modern Fiction Studies,* © 1965 by Purdue Research Foundation, Lafayette, Indiana. Reprinted by permission of the Purdue Research Foundation and the author.

[1] E. M. Forster, *Aspects of the Novel* (London: Edward Arnold, 1958), pp. 82–83.

206

a fortune will no more, or perhaps no less, direct our actions than a new perception or awareness. In the novel there is a given interior situation, and grief or a thunderstorm, love or a car accident operate on this interior situation in the same way. All that we can say now is that some events are external and some are internal. The relationship between them will be examined in more detail later.

If we return to Forster's example of a story, that is "the King died and then the Queen died," we note that this is something more than "the cat died and then the dog died." It is more even than "John died and then Joe died." There are degrees of interest here, with the highest degree appertaining to the first story. This cannot be because of the external events, which are the same. It cannot be because of the interior situation or the interior events, for they are not given. It must therefore reside in the exterior situation. By making the people who died a king and queen, Forster postulates for us a situation which, although exterior, has a direct bearing on the interest of the story. At the beginning of his novel, an author may postulate whatever exterior situation he wishes. There may be war or peace, drought or rain; the characters may be poor or rich, married or single, urban or rural; they may have a physical disability or be involved in any kind of relationship with other characters. For the novelist, all probable situations exist. The exterior situation might be said to stand in the same relationship to the working out of the plot as oxygen to fire. It is necessary for it to exist, but it is used up in that working out. It can never return in exactly the same form.

These two given situations, the interior and the exterior, are the beginning point of any novel. This does not mean that the novel starts with a delineation of them. They may never be made explicit by the novelist, and may only become apparent as the plot works out. The exterior situation may have been created by the interior situation of the character or characters, and conversely, the interior situation may have been created by the exterior situation. It is not the business of the novel to examine this, for we must grant the novelist his given situations. His characters may involve themselves in an external state because of their makeup, as Verloc does in *The Secret Agent*. They may be thrust into some situation merely because of the power of that situation, and through no activity of their own, as Tess Durbeyfield is. Or the exterior situation may exist with its own power, which combines with the interior situation of the character to provide the given situation of the novel, as is the case with Lambert Strether. We should note that the process by which the author arrives at the opening situation does not involve one of these three possibilities to the exclusion of the others. All opening situations result from a combination of these. It is more a question of whether the author puts the emphasis on the characters involving themselves, or on the characters being involved by circumstances. Of the three writers whom we shall consider, Henry James comes closest to striking a balance between the power of the internal situation and the power of the external situation. In all novels, the juxtaposition of these two states is the spark which sets the plot in motion. It might be said that given a certain interior state, and given a certain exterior state, it is impossible that things remain the same; the novel is the working out of the process of change.

When we examined Forster's plot, we noticed that it implied the existence of five things: an external situation, an internal situation, an external event, an internal event, and change. Up to now we have examined the external and internal situations and their relationship. We turn back now to examine the external and internal events and their relationship. An external event we shall call an incident, an internal event we shall call an event.

Both incidents and events are part of what may be called the action of the novel. We have seen earlier that one is not more important or significant than the other, that they are, in fact, of the same order. An incident may be caused by a combination of an event and an exterior situation, or it may happen to a character and be caused by fate or circumstance. What is important to notice is what the incident does. It seems to me that an incident can either reveal character or form it, and that in fact all incidents do both of these in varying degrees. Likewise, an incident may reveal or form a situation. Depending upon the weight which the author puts on the revelatory or formative aspects of the function, we may call an incident indicative or formative. Thus, when Strether meets Chad and Madame de Vionnet on the river, we have an incident which is caused by chance, which reveals the true situation existing, and which helps to re-form Strether's perceptions and sensibilities. In this case, the weight of the incident is thrown upon the revelation of the situation, and we could call it an indicative incident.

What stands out from a consideration of these four aspects of a plot, is the interrelationship of all of them, the fact that each works upon the other to produce the fifth aspect, change. Here we can see that the concept of structure, indeed the very term structure, is mis-

leading when applied to the novel. Structure implies a static relationship, whereas the novel is concerned with fluid relationships. I do
not mean fluid relationships between characters, but between the component parts of the novel. We might more correctly use the concept
of molecular structure to indicate this relationship: just as the form
of any molecular structure is determined by the rate and direction of
flow of the molecules, so the final form or meaning of the novel is
determined by the rate and direction of the flow between the inter-
related parts of the novel. Plot I take to be this flow. This is only
another way of saying that plot is the interflow between external
situation, internal state, incident, event, and change. It is revealing
to examine a novel from the point of view of what force and direction
an author gives to his plot. Does the novelist give more weight to
the interior state or the exterior situation as the generator of events?
Does the flow of events turn back upon itself to modify the external
situation, or does it produce some change in the internal situation? Or
are the events and incidents indicative rather than formative? According to Robert Liddell, "The process of working out one's conception
in fiction is not at all like arranging flowers, putting this here, that
there, and giving a pull or a twist to a leaf or a spray in order to make
it stand out. It is very much more like giving birth to a baby."[2] I do
not know if Mr. Liddell has ever arranged flowers. But this quotation
illustrates how difficult it is to talk of the novel without using metaphorical language, and how far many modern critics are stretching for
metaphors. It seems to me that we must try to refrain from indulging
in comparisons which only apparently clarify, and examine the work
as critics. This critical examination of the novel may require an
entire new terminology. In defining Henry James's conception of art,
R. P. Blackmur writes: "The subject of art was life, or more particularly someone's apprehension of the experience of it, and in
striving truly to represent it art removed the waste and muddlement
and bewilderment in which it is lived and gave it a lucid, intelligible
form."[3] If we stop the flow of the plot of *The Ambassadors* at two or
three points in the novel, and determine what direction and weight
James is giving to that flow, we may perhaps perceive something of
how his art truly represents his apprehension of life, and of how that

---

2 Robert Liddell, *A Treatise on the Novel* (London: Jonathan Cape, 1947),
pp. 85–86.
3 Henry James, *The Art of the Novel*, Introduction by Richard P. Blackmur
(New York: Charles Scribner's Sons, 1947), p. xv.

art becomes part of our experience of life. We are not concerned with judging whether James's apprehension of life is good or bad, valid or invalid. We are concerned solely with the art or craft involved. We can then apply the same method to *Tess of the D'Urbervilles* and *The Secret Agent*.

If a certain exterior situation had not existed, Lambert Strether would never have gone to Paris. Had he not gone to Paris, he would never have changed. But if anyone other than Lambert Strether had gone to Paris, that person would not have changed in the same way, and perhaps would not have changed at all. John Verloc could not react to such a situation, nor could Angel Clare, nor John D'Urberville. This is obvious, but it serves to point up the fact that James gives equal weight to the interior and exterior situation in the production of incidents and events. There is no mechanism in this novel such as we can find in Conrad and to a greater extent in Hardy. Two situations interact to produce a few incidents and a great number of events. The only real incident in the first two books is Strether's meeting with Maria Gostrey, and here James throws the entire weight not on the incident of meeting, but on the events which it triggers in Strether: "...and what he finally sat there turning over was the strange logic of his finding himself so free. He felt it in a manner his duty to think out his state, to approve the process, and when he came in fact to trace the steps and add up the items they sufficiently accounted for the sum."[4] The flow here is forward, the incident causes the event, it does not change the situation. It is, moreover, a formative rather than an indicative incident.

In the same way, Strether's first meeting with Chad is an incident which causes an event. Chad has changed, and this change changes Strether: "The phenomenon that had suddenly sat down there with him was a phenomenon of change so complete that his imagination, which had worked so beforehand, felt itself, in the connection, without margin or allowance. It had faced every contingency but that Chad should not *be* Chad, and this was what it now had to face with a mere strained smile and an uncomfortable flush" (pp. 136–37). It is indicative of the direction of this incident that Waymarsh is oblivious of the change: "The social sightlessness of his old friend's survey [of Chad] marked for him afresh, and almost in a humiliating

---

[4] Henry James, *The Ambassadors* (New York: Charles Scribner's Sons, 1909), I, 81.

way, the inevitable limits of direct aid from this source" (p. 137). This is an example of an incident being both formative, or event causing, and indicative. Even Maria Gostrey is not aware of the change in Chad, and because we conceive of her internal situation as being one of perception and awareness, in spite of her ignorance of Chad we might expect her to notice the shock to Strether. Here James obviously directs the incident towards the internal event of Strether's changing awareness. Throughout the novel Strether is learning, or rather, he is being taught, even how to enter a theater box at ten o'clock at night: "he had on the spot and without the least trouble of intention taught Strether that even in so small a thing as that there were different ways" (p. 140). That everything else in the novel flows into this stream of the events in Strether's mind is indicated by Chad's remark to him, "I haven't put you through much—yet" (p. 154).

A third and revealing incident is the accidental meeting of Strether with the two lovers at the country inn. This is an incident caused by accident or chance. It does not change the original external situation; it merely completes the revelation of that situation to Strether. James does not allow the confrontation to affect either Chad or Madame de Vionnet, beyond a momentary disaccommodation; it does not change their relationship. But the incident does trigger a series of events in Strether until finally it and the original situation become unimportant to him. In Strether's perceptions Madame de Vionnet loses some of her luster, indeed begins to seem old; Chad begins to seem unworthy of what he has, or at least of the concern which Strether had shown for him. Again James directs the incident toward events in Strether's consciousness; "He was, at that point of vantage, in full possession, to make of it all what he could."[5]

Thus we see that the entire direction of the flow of *The Ambassadors* is inward. The external situation, the internal situation, the incidents are all directed to the internal event. The change in the novel is an internal change, the growing awareness of Strether; it might be said that Strether does not cause incidents which change the situation, but that incidents and situation cause Strether. Perhaps this is what is meant by the novel of "character," but surely such a term destroys the idea of the organic relationships existing in a novel.

When we look at *Tess of the D'Urbervilles* we see that Hardy has

---

5 Henry James, *The Ambassadors* (New York: Charles Scribner's Sons, 1909), II, 262.

the novel moving in a different direction. Here the internal and external situations combine to cause an incident, but this incident turns back upon its direction of flow and modifies the external situation. The incidents in the novel are, therefore, formative, but have a different function than those of *The Ambassadors*. Tess is deposited in one situation after another, none of them really of her own choosing, for the most important incidents are accidental.

The death of Prince is one of the generating happenings in the novel; it is an accident arising out of the given situation, and Hardy throws the whole weight of the incident on the sense of the modified situation arising out of the incident. Tess must make the trip with the hives because of the poverty of the family, because of her father's drunkenness and illness, and because of her own pride. The result of the accident is the worsening of this situation: "The haggling business, which had mainly depended on the horse, became disorganized forthwith. Distress, if not penury loomed on the distance."[6] Tess must make the decision to go to the D'Urbervilles, but there is little opportunity to not make it. The situation forces her, and introspection and examination will not change that. Hardy scarcely mentions Tess's mind: "Having at least taken her course, Tess was less restless and abstracted, going about her business with some self assurance in the thought of acquiring another horse for her father by an occupation which would not be onerous. She had hoped to be a teacher at the school, but the fates seemed to decide otherwise" (p. 56). The movement to the D'Urbervilles is a change from one bad situation to a potentially worse one. Her seduction is another accidental incident, from her point of view, which again changes her situation more than it changes her. The internal event is, really, contained in the chapter head, "Maiden No More." Once again the incident is directed to the change in situation and Tess's attempt to come to terms with that situation, and to live some kind of peaceful life within the terms offered by her environment. She suffers, but the internal events are not re-presented as they are in James. She changes internally, but Hardy does not choose to focus on this: "Almost at a leap Tess thus changed from simple girl to complex woman. Symbols of reflectiveness passed into her face, and a note of tragedy at times into her voice. Her eyes grew larger and more eloquent...her soul that of a woman

---

6 Thomas Hardy, *Tess of the D'Urbervilles* (London: Macmillan and Co., Ltd.), p. 40.

whom the turbulent experiences of the last year or two had quite failed to demoralize" (p. 127).

The actual function of Tess in the novel is to be always looking for a new departure, a way out of the situation in which she finds herself through no fault of her own. Even her final desperate condition, in which she is living with Alec when Angel Clare returns, is forced upon her by the necessity of looking after her mother and family. The stabbing is a last fierce outcry against being forced into situations, positions into which she did not put herself and over which she has no control.

We might say, then, that if the direction of flow of *The Ambassadors* is forward and inward, the flow of Hardy's novel is outward and backward. The incidents in both are formative, but James directs them ahead to the formation of a new consciousness, while Hardy directs them backward to the modification of an old situation.

In *The Secret Agent* Conrad orders and directs all situations and incidents to one climactic incident, the attempt to blow up the Greenwich Observatory and the consequent destruction of Stevie. The given combination of Verloc's interior situation and the exterior situation in which this has involved him combine to produce the interview with Mr. Vladimir. This interview does not change Verloc's interior state, it does not cause an event, it merely stirs up that state. There is no real change in Verloc, only an increase of anxiety. The exterior situation does not change, it becomes more pressing. This is an example of an incident being directed not towards change, but toward the production of another incident. There is a difference in the nature of incident as used by Conrad and as used by James and Hardy. For the latter two, incident is generally formative as well as indicative. In *The Secret Agent* incident is generally indicative only. In this sense, this novel is the most uncharacteristic of Conrad's work. After the interview with Vladimir, Verloc is still the pragmatic anarchist, the seeker after security and comfort, the good provider. His relationships with his wife, mother-in-law, brother-in-law and fellow anarchists remain on the same uninvolved plane as before. His situation is more precarious but essentially the same; his attitude towards anarchy and government is unchanged. Anarchy is a way of making a living, while government is something that is not thought about.

It is interesting that in all three of our authors accident plays an important part in the working out of the plot. The accident of Stevie stumbling produces the major incident in the novel. In what direction does Conrad point this incident? Verloc remains morally uninvolved and unchanged by it; it was "as much an accident as if he had been run over by a bus while crossing the street."[7] He conceives of himself as not being responsible, of merely trying to do his job and to be a good provider. He cannot understand Winnie's withdrawal from him, and even tries to woo her when he thinks he has made her see reason. There has been no interior change, no event within the consciousness of Verloc. Nor has Winnie changed, despite Conrad's protestation to the contrary. Her violent reaction against Verloc and the ultimate act of stabbing him are merely the obverse side of the coin of her love for Stevie. This love had previously led her to give up the man she wanted to marry, and now it forces her to commit a deed which will make her give up her life. What has changed is the exterior situation of Verloc, both as an anarchist and in relation to his wife. Whether or not he is caught by the police, he will never again be able to function in the world of Vladimir. Whether or not he knows it, his relationship with his wife has turned to one of hatred. Conrad has directed the given interior situation, the exterior situation, the incidents which their combination produces, to a complete destruction of the exterior situation. In this sense he is closer to Hardy than James, although there is a very great difference in degree of emphasis. The flow of his plot, like Hardy's, is backward and outward.

There is no attempt here to judge the relative values of the different kinds of plot. How an author determines the direction and flow of his incidents, what weight he gives to value and situation, will depend on what he is trying to do. In spite of my strictures against metaphor, I have been forced to use one throughout. As in all writing on the novel, this is a dangerous oversimplification. An author may direct his plot toward the internal event, but this does not mean that there is no modification of the external situation. In most novels all things will coexist. It is a question of determining where the main emphasis has been placed, that is, to return to the metaphor, which is the main stream and which are tributaries. What this is, perhaps, is a suggestion of a different way of looking at a novel, a way which will not explain the novel away, but which will help to make it seeable. I do not know if it could be applied to all novels; I doubt it, but at least in the rejection of this concept of plot as the interacting flow, we would be

---

7 Joseph Conrad, *The Secret Agent* (London: William Heinneman, 1921), p. 291.

forced to examine the relationships between the parts of the novel, and to determine the kind of change which it conveys.

❋❋❋

    Besides offering new and clearer distinctions between critical terms, Walter O'Grady's essay shows that the work of younger critics of fiction—O'Grady was a graduate student when he wrote it—depends upon and develops the work of their predecessors. O'Grady's debt to E. M. Forster is obvious: the definition of plot and the stress on the internal and, in the strict sense, nondramatic quality of fiction are major theses in Forster's chapter on plot, and the view of fiction as process rather than object pervades "Pattern and Rhythm." However, rigid distinctions must not be insisted upon. Too often forgotten is the support that Henry James gives to such views in "The Art of Fiction": "I cannot imagine composition existing in a series of blocks, nor conceive, in any novel worth discussing at all, of a passage of description that is not in its intention narrative, a touch of truth of any sort that does not partake of the nature of incident, or an incident that derives its interest from any other source than the general and only sources of the success of a work of art—that of being illustrative. A novel is a living thing, all one and continuous, like any other organism, and in proportion as it lives will it be found, I think, that in each of the parts there is something of each of the other parts."

    Working independently of O'Grady, both Alan Friedman and Malcolm Bradbury have discussed the novel as process in much the same terms. In "The Stream of Conscience as a Form in Fiction"* and in *The Turn of the Novel*,† Friedman argues that "By looking at events as an onrushing confrontation (of tensions contained internally in character, externally in the world), we sacrifice something—the convenience of considering events as closed 'units' in a separable 'construction'—but we come closer to a dynamic and true sense of structure in the novel....the event is the fundamental unit of fiction...[and] the stream of events is the fundamental form of fiction" (p. 544). Approaching the novel from the writer's rather than the reader's point of view in "Towards a Poetics of Fiction: 1) An Approach

---

* *Hudson Review*, XVII (Winter 1964–65), 537–46.
† New York: Oxford University Press, 1966.

through Structure,"* Malcolm Bradbury shows "how the novelist limits, by formalizing it, the total environment offered by life, how he creates a conditioned world...a world in which experience can only assume certain shapes and characters only assume certain dimensions, in order that 'structure' may have its existence. By this view structure would be that devised chain of events that, presented by narration, conditions the successive choices, made sentence by sentence...and constitutes not only an entire narrative but an attitude towards it..." (p. 51).

O'Grady's essay is less comprehensive in scope and less ambitious in aim than these, but its self-imposed limitations do not necessarily work to his disadvantage. He is able to define his terms exactly and illustrate his points clearly, and he is careful to limit himself to description—these is no implied or concealed scale of values. However, his arguments can be expanded. For example, his directional metaphors "forward" and "backward" are not defined or described as clearly as they might be, and his discussion of Hardy's and Conrad's methods could be usefully supplemented by Wayne Booth's discussion of authorial attitude and distance. Finally, O'Grady admits that his method needs to be tested. Perhaps the most useful kind of test would be novels with points of view at the extremes of Norman Friedman's scale—for example, *Tom Jones* and *Ulysses*.

---

* *Novel,* I (Fall 1967), 45–52.

Fictional Chapters
and Open Ends

PHILIP STEVICK

Normally, a chapter in fiction is, in a limited sense, a formal unit. Of course the main conflicts and tensions must continue from chapter to chapter or a novel will seem to be only a collection of related short stories. Nevertheless, most chapters are arranged in such a way that they will appear to end, even though the novel continues. This appearance of conclusion is induced in a number of ways: stylistically by a particularly weighty series, for example, or by periodicity; substantively by the completion of an action or by a summary or by preparation for a change of scene or, on occasion, simply by saying that the chapter is over. George Eliot ends one of the chapters of *Middlemarch* in this way.

> Miss Brooke, however, was not again seen by either of these gentlemen under her maiden name. Not long after that dinner-party she had become Mrs. Casaubon, and was on her way to Rome. (I, X.)

With its marking of the end of a "stage" in Dorothea's life, with its summary and its anticipation of a change of scene, the paragraph represents a thoroughly conventional way of making a chapter seem to end.

A good many chapters, however, contain no devices which suggest finality. They do not effect, at their conclusions, a "cadence," a formal movement, that is, by which the chapter of fiction is analogous to the movement in music in the capacity of both to achieve at their ends a kind of repose. Such chapters, in other words, simply stop, as if the convention of dividing long prose fictions into chapters were only the most mechanical of exigencies, a meaningless convention against

From *Journal of General Education,* XVII (1966). Reprinted by permission of The Pennsylvania State Universty.

which the novelist were obliged to oppose himself by making the units of his narrative, despite the fact that they physically end, seem not to end at all. A chapter of James's *The Awkward Age,* for example, ends thus:

> She was instantly gone, on which Mrs. Brook had more attention for her son. This, after an instant, as she approached the sofa and raised her eyes from the little table beside it, came straight out. "Where in the world is that five-pound note?"
>
> Harold looked vacantly about him. "What five-pound note?" (VI, XXIII.)

So ends not only the chapter but an entire book of James's novel.

Harold is one of those precocious and vicious children who turn up from time to time in James. He steals from his mother elsewhere in the novel, although elsewhere he acknowledges the theft. Here the reader must assume that Harold has committed the theft. James nowhere says that he does; but for the reader not to assume Harold guilty is surely to make nonsense of the passage. The reader also must make what he can of the theft. Is it a clever gesture intended by Harold to demonstrate a kind of superiority over his mother? Is it an act so essentially neurotic as to defy motivational analysis? Is it a kind of child-like revenge for one of those characteristically Jamesian scenes where the adults go on with their adult talk, unaware of the perceptive but apparently innocent child nearby? Is it less an act significant in itself than a judgment of Mrs. Brook? Mrs. Brook is certainly judged in the next-to-last paragraph, where her "more attention for her son" turns out to be concern for a stolen bill. Is the theft an expression of the quintessence of Harold, or is it an expression of a different Harold, a culmination? With a summary sentence, James could have settled his chapter with both certainty and finality, something, say, about Harold's sense of satisfaction, or his mother's moral obtuseness, or the insight of either of them into what is going on. But such a sentence James will not provide.

In the case of a chapter that ends with a setting sun, one can be reasonably sure of the author's intention, as the characters fade away into the cosmic twilight; readers will respond to the ending in rather similar ways. Such an ending as James's is baffling by comparison. Nevertheless, it is possible, however tentatively, to find some aesthetic principles behind the efforts of writers of fiction to subvert the very chapter divisions which they feel compelled to make, to protest against these breaks in continuity, and to ignore the conventions which the making of chapters seems to demand. Generally, these aesthetic principles are of two kinds, the comic and the mimetic. That is, the reader's expectation that the chapter will end is violated in such a way as to produce an effect that is ludicrous, or satiric, witty, or grotesque. On the other hand, the abruptness of the chapter ending and the disregard for the conventions of seeming to end may be a calculated attempt to render fictionally some aspect of the way in which the novelist views the world at large, a view, perhaps, of the operation of the mind or of the metaphysical continuity of the world or of social disintegration, views which may make the tradition of cadence, with its tranquil enclosure and its suggestion of philosophical certainty, unusable. These two categories, of course, are not mutually exclusive. A novelist may achieve comic effects by means of his formal manipulations at the same time that he is attempting to get his imaginative vision down on paper as accurately, and if need be as unconventionally, as possible.

James's ending in *The Awkward Age* is more nearly an example of the mimetic than the comic open end. It is largely a result of a view, adopted for purposes of the novel, in which only so much of experience matters as can be rendered scenically; and it is a result of a search for a formal expression of certain shallow social relations and certain rather petty states of mind. Still, James's passage is not devoid of comedy. Mrs. Brook is not only ineffectual, and comically so, gulled as she is by a small boy; she is doubly ineffectual because of the very form of the chapter. She is forever paralyzed, unable to find "that five-pound note," since James will not let the chapter continue. In a similar way, Harold, his guile written on his vacant look, is forever frozen on page 273 with his question "What five-pound note?" unanswered.

A poetic prototype for the comic possibilities in manipulating the narrative break occurs in Pope's *The Rape of the Lock*.

> "Uncurled it hangs, the fatal shears demands,
> And tempts once more, thy sacrilegious hands.
> Oh, hadst thou, cruel! been content to seize
> Hairs less in sight, or any hairs but these!"
> Canto V
> She said; . . . .

Nothing could diminish the gravity of Belinda's speech more than the physical detachment of "She said." Such a delayed attribution has, of course, its epic analogues, the long speech in Homer or Virgil, followed by white space, followed by something like "Thus spoke the noble Aeneas." But in Pope "She said" lacks the elevation of epic diction and the summary quality of the epic attribution. It is the barest, simplest attribution possible in English; and thus it contributes to the mockery of epic pretentions which is the spirit of the poem. But it is, as I suggest, not only its flatness but its position that makes "She said" comic since the phrase cannot carry with it, as the epic attribution can, justification for that momentous pause which the reader must make. A large part of the comic force of the passage, in other words, is not directed toward Belinda but toward Pope. It is as if what must be enclosed within Canto IV cannot be managed there so that it hangs out, dangles into Canto V, as if a carpenter, building two houses, finished the first only to find some windows left over and so put them gratuitously onto the second house. It is a pretense, in other words, of formal ineptitude, all the more ironic because of Pope's cool brilliance in the management of his formal structures. Trollope, in *Barchester Towers,* ends a chapter with something rather like Pope's comic use of the narrative division. "Mr. Slope, however, on his first introduction must not be brought before the public at the tail of a chapter." (Ch. III.) Of course, if Mr. Slope must not be introduced until the next chapter, then there is no point, except a comic one, for bringing up his name in the present chapter. As in the case of Pope, the comedy is directed both toward the subject matter and toward the narrator, who is eagerly trying to adjust his subject matter to his physical form.

A classic example, as well as the most outrageously comic example, of such technical play with the chapter break occurs in *Don Quixote.* "But the unfortunate thing," Cervantes begins one of his last paragraphs, "is that the author of this history left the battle in suspense at this critical point, with the excuse that he could find no more records of Don Quixote's exploits than those related here." The author, however, persuaded that further records exist, has found some more, and promises to relate their contents as the chapter ends. The next chapter begins, with Don Quixote and the Basque frozen, their swords in the air. And for four pages, Cervantes describes his quest for the records, his motives for the search, and the veracity of Benengeli. At last the narrative resumes: "The trenchant swords of the two valorous and furious combatants, brandished aloft, seemed to threaten the heavens, and earth, and the pit of hell, such was their courageous aspect." (Cohen translation, Penguin edition, pp. 74–78.) Cervantes' formal manipulations here permit him to mock the convention of cliffhanging chapter endings and the conventional management of suspense. They enable him to induce in the reader a comic distance at a potentially bloody point in the narrative. Finally, they enable him to assert the fictive truth of his novel at the same time that he denies its literal truth by discrediting Benengeli.

Alice in Wonderland suggests still another way in which the chapter break can become a comic device. "Alice watched the White Rabbit as he fumbled over the list, feeling very curious to see what the next witness would be like, '—for they haven't got much evidence *yet,*' she said to herself. Imagine her surprise, when the White Rabbit read out, at the top of his shrill little voice the name 'Alice!' Chapter XII   'Here!' cried Alice, quite forgetting. . . ." Bergson has constructed an elaborate theory of laughter on the discovery, at the basis of the comic, of "something mechanical encrusted on the living." In Lewis Carroll, the transition from chapter to chapter is so immediate and continuous that to have made a chapter break at all is to have made a particularly apt example of Bergsonian comedy.

If, as I have suggested, the purposes for avoiding the appearance of an ending at the points at which the parts of a novel physically end are comic and mimetic, then Sterne, in *Tristram Shandy,* accomplished a remarkable fusion of the two. The raw materials of life are so formally intractable for Tristram that the conventions of chapter construction violate Sterne's mimetic obligations; for Sterne to transfer the raw materials of experience onto the page is for him to make chapters that inevitably collide with the reader's formal expectations. And this collision is comic. "A sudden impulse," writes Sterne in his chapter on chapters, "comes across me—drop the curtain, Shandy— I drop it—Strike a line here across the paper, Tristram—I strike it— and hey for a new chapter." (IV, 10.) The conventional wisdom regarding the making of chapters, Sterne continues, is "a story of a roasted horse." Do chapters "relieve the mind"? Do they "assist—or impose upon the imagination"? These are "cold conceits, enough to extinguish the fire which roasted" the horse. Indeed, in order to understand such matters, one had better read Longinus, and if one doesn't understand, then one can read him again. "How my father went on, in my opinion," writes Sterne, or rather Tristram, some pages later, "deserves a chapter to itself." The next chapter begins: "—And a chapter it shall have, and a devil of a one too—so look to yourselves." (V, 3.) Part of Sterne's bag of tricks is to end a chapter now and then with a conventional, indeed a virtuoso, cadence. "My uncle Toby never felt the consciousness of his existence with more complacency than what the corporal's, and his own reflections, made him do at that moment;—he lighted his pipe, Yorick drew his chair closer to the table,—Trim snuffed the candle,—my father stirred up the fire,—took up the book,—coughed twice, and began." (V, 30.) Such a cadence is an image of order which. Tristram rarely permits himself, with its unanimity of purpose in Tristram, Yorick, Trim, and Walter Shandy, with its clarity of beginning, and with its perfect conventionality of time sequence. A more characteristically Shandean ending is this one: "...—for as he opened his mouth to begin the next sentence,   Chapter 15   In popped Corporal Trim with Stevinus." (II, 14–15.) Other comic novels are "inventive" or "witty," suggesting that comic fiction often involves a heightening of the comedy latent in experience itself. Sterne, on the other hand, suggests the possibility that fiction is most comic when it is least arranged. Simply by seeming to attempt an earnest, truthful imitation of experience, the novelist inevitably writes comedy. In a sense, of course, the stance of Sterne-Tristram is misleading; he contrives and arranges as much as any comic novelist. But in another sense, Sterne is perfectly right. His time scheme and his vision of the inner life are undertaken with a sense of mimetic fidelity; insofar as they succeed mimetically, they are funny; and his endlessly virtuoso endings are functions of this double purpose.

With a slightly different variety of the comic open end, Thomas Love Peacock ends a chapter of *Crotchet Castle* with a speech by Lady Clarinda. "So you will see, some morning, that my novel is 'the most popular production of the day.' This is Mr. Puffall's favorite phrase. He makes the newspapers say it of everything he publishes. But 'the day,' you know, is a very convenient phrase; it allows of three hundred and sixty-five 'most popular productions' in a year. And in leap year one more." (Ch. V.) It is difficult to say whether Lady Clarinda possesses a penetratingly comic, indeed a Shandean, imagination, or whether she is an idiot. In any case, the last sentence is so petty, so irrelevant in all but the technical sense in which it is true, so anticlimactic that it mocks the convention of the cadence, which one expects to be, if not resounding, at least reasonably climactic. And thus the ending, by diminishing its own function as ending, adds to the comic force of Peacock's novel.

Mimetically, the technical manipulations of the novelist at the point at which his chapters come together is a result of the conflicting claims of continuity and discontinuity. These conflicting claims find a remarkable treatment in Gide, where the problem involves Gide and his characters not so much in exploration and intellection as in a visceral reaction. In *The Counterfeiters* Edouard visits La Perouse, and their conversation ends this way.

> "Have you observed that the whole effect of modern music is to make bearable, and even agreeable, certain harmonies which we used to consider discords?"
>
> "Exactly," I rejoined. "Everything must finally resolve into—be reduced to harmony."
>
> "Harmony!" he repeated, shrugging his shoulders. "All that I can see in it is familiarization with evil—with sin. Sensibility is blunted; purity is tarnished; reactions are less vivid; one tolerates; one accepts. . . ."
>
> "But you don't pretend to restrict music to the mere expression of serenity, do you? In that case, a single chord could suffice, a perfect and continuous chord."
>
> He took both my hands in his, and in a burst of ecstasy, his eyes rapt in adoration, he repeated several times over:
>
> "A perfect and continuous chord; yes, yes; a perfect and continuous chord . . . . But our whole universe is a prey to discord," he added sadly.
>
> I took my leave. He accompanied me to the door and as he embraced me, murmured again:
>
> "Oh! How long shall we have to wait for the resolution of the chord?" (Modern Library, p. 151.)

In his "Journal of '*The Counterfeiters*,'" Gide writes:

> This novel will end sharply, not through exhaustion of the subject, which must give the impression of inexhaustibility, but on the contrary through its expansion and by a sort of blurring of its outline. It must not be neatly rounded off, but rather disperse, disintegrate. . . .(p. 415.)

Here the problems of continuity and resolution, conclusion and "disintegration," life and art, are given a kind of definitive statement. In fact, in the two passages, taken together, there is a remarkably complementary breadth. The tension between continuity and resolution is felt emotionally and intellectually, with spontaneity and detachment, as an abstract philosophical problem and as an intimate question of fictional craft. The subject, Gide writes, "must give the impression of inexhaustibility." In different ways, all fictional subjects do just this.

Although a piano sonata or a Chinese vase may seem evocative of nothing beyond its own limits, a Breughel tableau suggests an even wider scene than it portrays. No one assumes, in looking at a painting by Breughel, that all of the rustics visible on the day in which Breughel painted his picture are captured within his frame. Part of the effect of such a painting must be the suggestion that the scene would have continued if the frame were larger, that there is an infinite number of little fat Dutchmen available to Breughel, only a small but crowded portion of whom could be squeezed within his frame. That Breughel should suggest such continuity where a Chinese vase does not, makes Breughel especially analogous to the novelist. For among all of the novelist's commitments, one commitment which he cannot escape is his obligation to the surface of life. No one expects to find amplitude of physical detail and "reality" of surface in, say, Lucian's *True History* or Bunyan's *Pilgrim's Progress*. But the novel since Defoe can almost be defined by its attempt to contain or at least to refract the empirical data of ordinary experience. Even in Virginia Woolf, time can be suspended but sensations cannot. Those solid blocks of "materialistic" detail which she protested against in Bennett may be absent from her own fiction; but no one conveys a sense of the landscape of London, the experience of the sea, and the look of certain people more forcefully than Virginia Woolf. Fiction, then, even at its most anti-realistic, is capable of imitating the passage of ordinary experience in a way that most other art forms are not. At its most realistic, fiction can come remarkably close to what seems like unmediated scene, transcript, literary photography, without forfeiting its claim to be art. When fiction tends to pursue a nearly total illusion of reality, abruptness of ending can become a positive virtue, suggesting, as it may, a minimal contrivance by the author. But in any fiction, including the least photographic, the bulk of sensory detail must suggest continuity and inexhaustibility (except perhaps for those mystery novels in which every detail is related to a crime, the solution of which explains every detail and dispels all interest in the characters). This suggestion of continuity and inexhaustibility, which is almost unavoidable in an art so potentially close to the chaos of experience, is a quality which a writer may exploit if he wishes.

At its simplest level, this compulsion to continue results in a continuity between chapters rather like the comic fusions of Lewis Carroll and Sterne.

> In fine, Hester Prynne resolved to meet her former husband, and do what might be in her power for the rescue of the victim on whom he had so evidently set his gripe. The occasion was not long to seek. One

afternoon, walking with Pearl in a retired part of the peninsula, she beheld the old phsyician, with a basket on one arm, and a staff in the other hand, stooping along the ground, in quest of roots and herbs to concoct his medicines withal.

Hawthorne's next chapter, "Hester and the Physician," begins:

> Hester bade little Pearl run down to the margin of the water, and play with the shells and tangled seaweed, until she should have talked awhile with yonder gatherer of herbs. So the child flew away like a bird. (*The Scarlet Letter,* Chs. XIII and XIV.)

There is structural justification for a new chapter, as Hawthorne's title "Hester and the Physician" suggests. But the narration is continuous—continuous, moreover, in such a way not only as to seem entirely serious but perhaps even to make the substance of the new chapter all the more urgent. It is only when a novel as a whole is comic that a reader is predisposed to find the open ends of Sterne and Lewis Carroll comic. But, what is more to the present point, Hawthorne's narration gives the impression of perfect control. Whatever the stylistic success of the passage I have quoted, Hawthorne is in charge, and the words do what he wants them to do. James, Pope, and Sterne are all three probably greater craftsmen than Hawthorne. But in those comic examples which I have quoted, there is a carefully induced appearance of a lack of control—in James, with his ironic ignorance of what it all means, in Pope, with his apparent failure to get all of Canto IV said before Canto V begins, in Sterne, with his apparent inability to arrange the chaos of his imagination. Thus, the same formal movement is capable of carrying great comic force and of suggesting the immense pressure of the continuity in a deeply felt and deadly serious narrative.

I have suggested previously the possibility of abruptness in the scenic method, specifically in the case of *The Awkward Age,* where the conventional rhetoric of narrative management is scrupulously abjured and where every effort contributes to an illusion of a chunk of life almost arbitrarily carved out of the interminable whole of experience. This is not to say that James, even at his most scenic, does not write cadences; he often does. But James, and writers with a similar fondness for scene, inevitably find occasion to make chapters in which people interact, not toward some Q. E. D., not toward a dramatic resolution, but so as to be on display. The second chapter of Book II of *Tender Is the Night,* for example, ends with this speech. " 'We wanted to warn you about getting burned the first day,' she continued cheerily, 'because *your* skin is important, but there seems to be so darn much formality on this beach that we didn't know whether you'd mind.' " There is more to Fitzgerald's chapter than manners alone, but it is toward the display of manners that the chapter directs its main effort. It is entirely appropriate that the chapter should conclude with an example of characteristic talk, fragmentary, inconclusive, but quintessentially illustrative of those qualities of manners and mind that Fitzgerald wishes to illustrate.

Evelyn Waugh divides so frequently that he seems almost to be making a parody of novelistic structure. *A Handful of Dust* contains, as a subtitle for Chapter Two, "English Gothic—I"; this chapter is divided into four subsections; and the first subsection is divided eleven times by white space. The whole thing suggests, for a moment, one of those endlessly divided outlines that school children are sometimes induced to write. What Waugh's chapter seems to be, finally, is a collection of brilliant miniatures, none of which really ends, none of which really begins, all of which make a kind of progressive narrative sense only in their totality. One such subsection, for example, begins thus: " 'I should have thought it was very nice to be called a tart,' John argued, 'and anyway it's a word Ben often uses about people.' " The section ends thus: " 'Hooray. Thunderclap went very well today. We jumped a big post and rails. She refused to first time but went like a bird after that.' 'Didn't you come off?' 'Yes, once. It wasn't Thunderclap's fault. I just opened my bloody legs and cut an arser.' " As with Fitzgerald, the section exists not so much to get somewhere as to display manners and shared states of mind, displayed, in Waugh, so that the very fragmentary abruptness of the scene reinforces the ironic detachment. There is something redeeming about a scene of stylish, shallow conversation that leads somewhere; there is something satirically devastating about such a scene that merely stops; and there is something satirically appalling about a novel which contains dozens of such scenes.

A final example, this one extreme, of the usefulness of abruptness when the substance of a chapter strives for a bizarre approximation of the surface of life occurs in Dos Passos' *Manhattan Transfer*. The title of Dos Passos' chapter, "Nickelodeon," suggests something of the harsh vulgarity of the contents. The chapter is deliberately discontinuous and fragmentary. Such a passage as this is a fair sample: "HELP WANTED MALE. That's more your speed you rummy. Addressers, first class penmen...Lets me out.... Artist, Attendant,

Auto, Bicycle and Motorcycle repair shop. . . . He took out the back
of an envelope and marked down the address. Bootblacks. . .Not yet.
Boy; no I guess I aint a boy any more. Candystore, Canvassers, Car-
washers, Dishwasher. EARN WHILE YOU LEARN." For a chapter
whose whole substance is want ads, subway posters, popular songs,
smells, and fragmentary conversation, the only aesthetically satisfying
ending must be one that is jarringly abrupt and quite unfinished.

> "What time's it?" she asks a broadchested wise guy. "Time you
> an me was akwainted, sister. . . ." She shakes her head. Suddenly the
> music bursts into Auld Lang Syne. She breaks away from him and
> runs to the desk in a crowd of girls elbowing to turn in their dance-
> checks. "Say Anna," says a broadhipped blond girl. . ."did ye see
> that sap was dancin wid me?. . .He says to me the sap he says See you
> later an I says to him the sap I says see yez in hell foist. . .and then
> he says, Goily he says. . ."

It is, of course, both a surface and a philosophical interpretation that
Dos Passos offers by the shape of his ending.

Finally, very little in fiction is not contained in those two compen-
diums of how things can be done, *Tristram Shandy* and *Ulysses*.
Significantly, both novels exploit the possibilities of enclosure and
openness as well. Something rather like the fragmented urban world
of Dos Passos occurs in Joyce's Wandering Rocks episode, for example, and in the same novel occur some of the most graceful cadences
in prose fiction. The open end is useful in a hundred ways, as Joyce
and Sterne surely knew, and for that matter as Chaucer knew before
them, because the convention of enclosure, elusive as that convention
may be, is one of the most firmly established in fiction. No matter how
many times a novelist may leave us in mid-air, the avoidance of
enclosure is a formal manipulation which few readers can ever entirely
adjust to. The open end, in other words, is a formal shock, demanding
of the reader an assimilation of the unexpected in a way which can
challenge responses all the way from the reader's sober expectation
of continuity to the reader's metaphysic; and the open end is nearly as
great a shock the tenth time it occurs in a novel as it is the first.
In a genre so ill-defined and flexible as the novel, shocks to our sense
of formal propriety are rarely possible. If, as I argue, such a shock is
possible at the point at which the reader expects a chapter to seem
to end, then the open end must surely be one of the most inexhaustibly
rich of all the rhetorical possibilities available to the novelist.

✖✕✖✕

Although other critics in this volume have touched on the matter, Philip Stevick's primary concern is the relationship between convention and form. In another essay, "The Theory of Fictional Chapters,"* he explores the necessity behind the convention: "the need for limiting the size of the fictional unit to the reader's gestalt-making faculty" (pp. 237–38). "Fictional Chapters and Open Ends" examines the individual artist's fruitful struggle against convention.

Like many of the critics in this volume, Stevick focuses on a single aspect of technique but remains aware of other elements— rhythm in style, dynamics in plot, and control or lack of it exercised by the author—and sees the relationship of all these elements to the author's total vision. Moreover, his essay corroborates and is supplemented by the work of others: the discussion of authorial control is related to Booth's concept of rhetorical strategy in the novel; the distinction between chapters aimed at dramatic resolution and those that display character recalls O'Grady's contrast between formative and illustrative incidents and events; and the attempt to discover the basic unit of fiction is parallel but not identical to Handy's.

Although Stevick leans toward mimetic theories and toward a view of the novel as process, his approach may seem eclectic, for the critics whom he parallels have widely different premises about the novel. A desire for theoretical consistency should not, however, blind the critic to the value of particular strategies of analysis; Stevick's approach is all the more valuable for being applicable to all forms of narrative and for fitting within the framework of the mimetic, the rhetorical, and—with some reservations—the autonomy schools of criticism.

---

* *Western Humanities Review,* **XX** (Summer 1966), 231–41.

Time and Space

EDWIN MUIR

Up till now I have had to simplify everything. I have spoken as if the divisions of prose fiction were pure categories; as if any example of the character or the dramatic novel were absolute and unmixed. There are of course no novels purely of character or merely of conflict; there are only novels which are predominantly the one or the other. This predominance, however, is always salient and always sufficient. The principle of *Wuthering Heights* is dramatic, though it contains a few characters, like old Joseph and Mrs. Dean; the principle of *Vanity Fair* is not dramatic, though it contains several highly dramatic scenes, such as Rawdon Crawley's quarrel with the Marquis of Steyne. Nobody is likely to dispute this distinction, or to insist that it is absolute; and trusting to this, I can now go on to my next generalization, which is that the imaginative world of the dramatic novel is in Time, the imaginative world of the character novel in Space. In the one, this roughly is the argument, Space is more or less given, and the action is built up in Time; in the other, Time is assumed, and the action is a static pattern, continuously redistributed and reshuffled, in Space. It is the fixity and the circumference of the character plot that gives the parts their proportion and meaning; in the dramatic novel it is the progression and resolution of the action. The values of the character novel are social, in other words; the values of the dramatic novel individual or universal, as we choose to regard them. On the one hand we see characters living in a society, on the other figures moving from a beginning to an end. These two types of the novel are neither opposites, then, nor in any important sense complements of each other; they are rather two distinct modes of seeing life: in Time, personally, and in Space, socially.

From Edwin Muir, *The Structure of the Novel* (London: The Hogarth Press, Ltd., 1957). Reprinted by permission of Mrs. Willa Muir and the publisher.

As stated, this thesis may seem full of difficulties. How can a story have a spatial construction, seeing that in it certain things must happen, and some time, however short, must be consumed? How can time be subordinate in any sense, seeing that every novel necessarily records the passing of time? But to say that a plot is spatial does not deny a temporal movement to it, any more, indeed, than to say that a plot is temporal means that it has no setting in space. Here, once more, it is all a question of the predominating element. The main object of the one plot is to proceed by widening strokes, and to agree that it does so is to imply space as its dimension. The main object of the other is to trace a development, and a development equally implies time. The construction of both plots will be inevitably determined by their aim. In the one we shall find a loosely woven pattern, in the other the logic of causality.

A more vivid sense of the meaning of this distinction can be evoked by calling to mind the different feeling of time and space in various novels. In the dramatic novel in general the articulation of space is vague and arbitrary. London might be a thousand miles away from Wuthering Heights or Casterbridge. But from the London of *Vanity Fair* and *Tom Jones,* on the other hand, every place has its just geographical distance, and no part of England, no small town, no country estate or remote parsonage is inaccessible; the gentry, the tradesmen, the peasantry, the post-boys, the innkeepers—the classes, rich and poor, are there, or at least some hypothetical provision is made for them. *Wuthering Heights* and *The Return of the Native,* on the contrary, blot out all that portion of England which lies beyond the concentrated scene of their action; the world outside is ghostly and remote, and the countless figures peopling it are quite forgotten, wiped out, as if the intensity and swiftness with which time consumes itself in the action had wasted them too. We are conscious of England in *Tom Jones* and *Vanity Fair*; we are only aware of the Yorkshire moors and Egdon Heath in *Wuthering Heights* and *The Return of the Native.*

Or consider another difference. By what seems at first a paradox we shall find in the dramatic novel a far more intense visual realization of the scene than in the novel of character. No doubt this is partly because the scene in the former becomes colored and dyed by the passions of the chief figures, because we always see them against it, and closed in by it. But it is more essentially because the scene here—

the scene in Hardy's novels and in *Wuthering Heights*—is not an ordinary and particular scene at all, like the Sedley's drawing-room, or Sir Pitt Crawley's country estate, but rather an image of humanity's temporal environment. The Yorkshire moors and Wessex are not places differentiated and recognizable like Mr. Bennett's Five Towns or Trollope's Barchester; they are universal scenes where the drama of mankind is played out. As this drama, seen thus, is independent of temporal fashions, as the period with its manners, costumes, and habits, and all the other properties of changing civilization, are in a sense irrelevant to it, the scene will be primitive: Egdon Heath, or "the harebells and limestone" of Emily Brontë's Yorkshire moors, or the oceans over which Ahab pursues the White Whale. When we think of Thackeray's characters we think of them in the costume and against the background of their time; their clothes, the houses they live in, and the fashions they observe, are part of their reality; they exist in their period as in a suddenly fixed world. But we recall Hardy's figures as we recall things which are amenable to no fashions save those of nature; as we remember heaths, rocks, and trees. The scene against which he sets his men and women has not essentially changed since the time when figures capable of the few universal emotions with which he endows them might have lived in it. Space here, then, is undifferentiated and universal, though apparently narrow, an image of the world itself, and moreover unchangeable, for no matter what fashions may alter the surface of human life, in this way, a mind like Hardy's will always be able to see the world. The scene here, in short, is the earth, as in the novel of character it is civilization. The power which Hardy's landscapes exercise is drawn from nature directly, and his characters are bound by as strong ties to the earth as to each other.

But those natural potencies which have such influence over Hardy's characters will be little felt in Thackeray's scenes, which are cut off from nature, as by a wall, by the observances of society. To the social parlors of Barchester, to the prosperous middle-class villas of the Five Towns, they will reach with difficulty. But, on the other hand, we will be shown by the character novelist that the human scene, that world in itself, is infinitely various and interesting; that Queen's Crawley is a very different place from Russell Square, and that there is an inexhaustible diversity of places and states of life in the Five Towns. We shall see the universal becoming particularized; humanity in all its varieties of prison-house, ornamental or plain; and if we are no longer conscious of the earth, we become free citizens of society, with a pass to all sorts of places.

Or take another striking difference, between the feeling of time in the character and the dramatic novel; how it seems to linger in the one and fly in the other. If we open *Vanity Fair* at the first chapter and listen to Becky Sharp, and then take it up toward the end, when we know that a great number of things have happened and many years elapsed, we shall have a curious feeling of having marked time, of still being on the same spot; somewhat the same feeling one might have if one were to fall asleep in a room where people were discussing some question, and wake up to find the discussion at exactly the same stage. In the last chapters of *Vanity Fair* Becky is still talking very much as she did in the first. Let us turn next to the passage which introduces Catherine Earnshaw, and to her last interview with Heathcliff. There the shock we receive is of a different kind. We know at once that while we have been sleeping something extraordinary has happened; Time, almost like a physical process, has passed over the figure of Catherine. This test may be applied to any great dramatically conceived figure except for a few like Captain Ahab in *Moby Dick*. For Ahab does not change; the action of the whole book, indeed, hardly moves for a while; there is only the long stretch of description, reverie, waiting, and then the fatal combat described in the last few chapters; a combat which we do not see approaching, which could only come suddenly, absent one moment, unconditionally present the next; neither to be courted in its absence, nor when it is there avoided. With its static characters and sudden calamitous movement, *Moby Dick* occupies a place somewhat apart from the ordinary dramatic novel. But it is an exception which throws light on the point we are considering. In *Moby Dick* Melville was not dealing with the ordinary world where good and evil are mixed, where passion is both noble and sordid, and there is right on both sides, as there is in *Wuthering Heights*. He was portraying a world purged as nearly as possible of the intermediate and the mixed; and on the most inhuman of arenas, the sea, he set two absolute forces against each other, the symbolical figures of Ahab and the White Whale. The enmity between these two is not human; it is not a thing which could arise through some accident of Time, and develop and suffer enhancement or diminution, like everything of this world; it is there from the beginning, not a feeling which must be fed if it is to grow, but a force which cannot be altered. The drama in *Moby Dick* is, then, a drama of opposites, and as neither can yield, the conflict had to be simple, catastrophic, and without a development. There is a very strong sense of time in the book, it is true, but not the sense of time which we find in Hardy or Emily Brontë. For an age the action stands still, with an almost intolerable vacancy of expectation and deferred crisis, as if the ship's company were foundering in a stagnant sea of Time; then in the last few chapters all seems to burn away in a breath-space.

As this urgency of time in the dramatic novel is one of its essential characteristics, we must consider it a little further. The scenes in a dramatic novel postulate an end, as we have seen, and in the greatest we have a sense that the end is known. In other words, we have a prescience of something *definite* to come; and it is this alone that articulates and vivifies future time for us, so that it no longer seems a mere impersonal process, or a vacant succession, but becomes a presence, hostile or auspicious, capable of destroying our peace, or of bringing us happiness. In a story like *The Return of the Native,* first we have a vague apprehension of the end towards which things are moving. Eustacia Vye's ambition and passion will lead her to some exceptional destiny, brilliant or calamitous; but everything is undetermined as yet. With the arrival of Clym Yeobright her destiny begins to take shape; for a moment it seems to be leading her to happiness; then Clym's blindness and fanaticism alter everything. As yet the end is in the distance; but time has begun to accelerate, and only something extraordinary can slow it down. There follows the scene where Mrs. Yeobright walks over the heath to visit Eustacia, and turned away while Clym is sleeping, dies on her way back. This is the turning point in the story; the end is brought close to Eustacia, and after her last interview with Clym there is nothing between her and the moment toward which all her life she has been moving. Up to the last phase only the creator of Eustacia has known this moment and when it would come, but now we know it too. And in this brief interval between our knowledge of the end and its coming all Eustacia's transit through life is realized as if for the first time, and in our realization has been ended.

In the beginning of a dramatic novel such as this, then, we see Time gradually gathering itself up; then beginning to move, its end still unknown to us; then as its goal becomes clearer, marching with a steady acceleration; and finally fate is there and all is finished. This end may coincide with the end of the book, as in *Tess of the D'Urber-*

villes, or it may come before, leaving a pause, as in *The Mayor of Casterbridge,* or it may be the main crisis, as in *Wuthering Heights,* where Heathcliff is no longer completely there after the last interview with Catherine in the middle of the book; the drama is over, and only his suffering remains.

No one, perhaps, has understood better than Dostoevsky this naked manifestation of Time at the moment when it is slipping away; and a passage in *The Idiot* describing the feelings of a man condemned to death explains it with great force, and gives at the same time the reason why those scenes in the dramatic novel should have such extraordinary power. Prince Muishkin is describing an execution he had seen at Lyons. "Well, at all events," someone says, "it is a good thing that there's no pain when the poor fellow's head flies off."

"Do you know, though," the Prince replies, "you made that remark now, and everyone says the same thing, and the machine is designed with the purpose of avoiding pain, this guillotine, I mean; but a thought came into my head then: What if it should be a bad plan after all? You may laugh at my idea, perhaps—but I could not help its occurring to me all the same. Now with the rack and tortures and so on—you suffer terrible pain of course; but then your torture is bodily pain only (although no doubt you have plenty of that) until you die. But here I should imagine the most terrible part of the whole punishment is, not the bodily pain at all—but the certain knowledge that in an hour—then in ten minutes, then in half a minute, then now—this very *instant*—your soul must quit your body and that you will no longer be a man—and that this is certain, *certain!* That's the point—the certainty of it. Just that instant when you place your head on the block and hear the iron grate over your head—then—that quarter of a second is the most awful of all."

Here Dostoevsky shows in what ways the knowledge of something to come can change and at the same time bring out the values of time. In the instance he describes the knowledge is certainty, and the thing to come is death. The end of a dramatic novel is very seldom known with certainty, however, either to the actors or to the reader. The effect of the acceleration of time in it is therefore at once less painful and more complex than here. No doubt the author's foreknowledge contributes something to that effect; seeing what is to come he will communicate his forebodings of the event before it is revealed; and his utterance will warn us, while the protagonists are still unconscious of their fate.

Or the characters may for long foresee their fate as an incredible possibility; fearing it and yet not crediting their fears. It is the expectation of this event dreaded and yet inconceivable that gives *The Idiot* its painful tension, and makes the conclusion so powerful, at once an exposure and a fulfilment of the whole action. Again and again throughout the book there are hints prefiguring the end, which, as everyone knows, is the murder of Nastasia by Rogojin; there are perhaps too many of these, indeed, and in places the symbolism becomes clever and obvious. But in the scene where Prince Muishkin returns from Moscow and goes to see Rogojin at his Petersburg house, there is an admirable foreshadowing incident. Only a third of the story has been told, but the end is already throwing wild shadows over the action.

Muishkin and Rogojin have been talking of various things.

"Let go of it!" said Parfen, seizing from the prince's hand a knife which the latter had at that moment taken up from the table, where it lay beside the history book. Parfen replaced it where it had been.

"I seemed to know it—I felt it, when I was coming back to Petersburg," continued the prince. "I did not want to come, I wished to forget all this, to uproot it from my memory altogether! Well, good-bye —what is the matter?"

He had absently taken up the knife a second time, and again Rogojin snatched it from his hand, and threw it down on the table. It was a plain looking knife, with a bone handle, a blade about eight inches long, and broad in proportion; it did not clasp.

Seeing that the prince was considerably struck by the fact that he had twice seized this knife out of his hand, Rogojin caught it up with some irritation, put it inside the book, and threw the latter across to another table.

"Do you cut your pages with it or what?" asked Muishkin, still rather absently, as though unable to throw off a deep preoccupation into which the conversation had thrown him.

"Yes."

"It's a garden knife, isn't it?"

"Yes. Can't you cut pages with a garden knife?"

"It's quite new."

"Well, what of that? Can't I buy a new knife if I like?" shouted Rogojin furiously, his irritation growing with every word.

The prince shuddered, and gazed fixedly at Parfen. Suddenly he burst out laughing.

"Why, what an idea!" he said. "I didn't mean to ask you any of these questions; I was thinking of something quite different! But my head is heavy, and I seem so absent-minded nowadays! Well, good-bye—I can't remember what I wanted to say—good-bye!"

There the vague suspicion that Rogojin will try to murder him is accompanied in the prince's mind by the shadowy prescience of some act farther away which he cannot catch; it is the premonition that this knife will be used to kill Nastasia. This shadow of knowledge in his mind is like something he has dreamt of and dismissed without being able to unriddle it. The whole passage is masterly. Dostoevsky's intention seems to be to suggest so often and so openly that Rogojin will end by murdering Nastasia that it becomes the one thing that nobody expects because everybody says it. One such scene as this would have prepared us for the murder; but Dostoevsky gives us scene after scene until a mood almost of security is built up. Yet at the same time, more and more unbelievable the oftener it is mentioned, the fear remains; and it is from this double tension of incredulity and fear, too painful almost, that the murder at last gives us relief. One or two of the characters actually experience in advance those moments of fascinated terror which come from foreknowledge of murder; but then those moments become part of their memory of the past, and therefore no longer to be dreaded; and so they continue to say in security, as if it were an old story, that Rogojin will murder Nastasia. The end, which comes suddenly and unexpectedly, lights up everything which led up to it; fate which had been playing hide-and-seek for so long manifests itself, and shows the action in one instant as it is. Into this instant all the time traversed by the action seems to fly, transformed and ended by the same stroke.

In *The Idiot* the sense of the urgency of time is given by a particular fear, by the knowledge, sometimes hidden, but always revealed again, of a definite event that will happen. In *Wuthering Heights* it is given by a fear more vast and shadowy; by the apprehension of something terrible, but unknown. In *The Idiot* the characters and the reader foresee the definite act of violence which lies in wait; the action consequently awakens a painful emotion somewhat similar to that of the condemned man whose story Dostoevsky, with marvelous art, introduces in the first few pages. But in *Wuthering Heights* the end is foreseen by a consciousness neither ours nor that of Heathcliff or Catherine. In so far as it is foreseen it is definite; but to us it is not yet in the realm of Time; it is rather something which at a predestined moment will appear in Time, when it will be as palpable as the last action in *The Idiot,* and as luminously as that will light up the action, during its progress dark and only in part manifest. We know that

Heathcliff's and Catherine's love will end in disaster; yet that disaster has no recognizable shape for us, and is limited by no one significance. Until it falls it is an image of every potentiality of disaster, and we are given a sense of possibility, of freedom, which is absent in Dostoevsky's novel. In *Wuthering Heights* Heathcliff and Catherine seem to be freely choosing their fate without knowing it; in *The Idiot* Rogojin, Muishkin, and Nastasia are driven helplessly towards a fate they foresee and cannot escape. The sense of Time in the two novels is accordingly very dissimilar; in *The Idiot* the characters wander in a daze, living in that nightmare state, known sometimes in our dreams, in which there are innumerable things which we must do, but we cannot remember them, or we do not know which to do first. Almost from beginning to end Muishkin, Rogojin, and Nastasia are fighting against time, and it is this that gives the book its hurried and urgent movement. In *Wuthering Heights,* on the other hand, Catherine and Heathcliff, unconscious of their fate, fly toward it with a single unhesitating flight. Time passes in both novels swiftly, but in the one with a rush of freedom, in the other with an unwilling haste.

The feeling of time may be vastly dissimilar in different dramatic novels, then; our apprehension of the end toward which it is moving may be definite or indefinite; the march of the action may be slower or faster; but enough, perhaps, has been said to show that the sense of time running out gives the real edge to the dramatic emotion.

In the dramatic novel, then, as in all dramatic literature, time moves and will therefore move to its end and be consumed. In the novel of character at its best we feel that time is inexhaustible. The great character creations, Uncle Toby, Parson Adams, Lismahago, Mr. Collins, Cuddie Headrigg, Micawber, are beyond time and change, just as the great dramatic figures are completely enclosed in them and subject to them. In no novel of character, of course, is time quite stationary, though certain of the characters may remain so; but the more time is slowed down or ignored—the more all urgency is taken from it—the more favorable does it become for the emergence of characters. There is something humorous, something giving a sense of security, in the very slowing down of time, as may be seen in *Tristram Shandy, Ulysses,* and the slow-motion picture. Marvell's often-quoted poem, "To his Coy Mistress," is an admirable illustration of this. Thinking how he would woo "Had we but world enough, and time," he uses images which involuntarily become humorous:

> I would
> Love you ten years before the Flood,
> And you should, if you please, refuse
> Till the conversion of the Jews.

Then comes the turning-point in the poem, and all becomes urgent and dramatic:

> But at my back I always hear
> Time's winged chariot hurrying near...
> Now let us sport us as we may;
> And now like amorous birds of prey
> Rather at once our Time devour
> Than languish in his slow-chapped power...
> Thus, though we cannot make our Sun
> Stand still, yet we will make him run.

If one wanted an image of the world of character one might without extravagance see it in the first part of this poem, just as one might see the world of dramatic action in the second.

We must not separate these worlds too rigidly, however. In all dramatic novels we shall find visitors from the world of character; in all character novels dramatic scenes. Hardy's peasants, Emily Brontë's old Joseph, change as little as Uncle Toby or Andrew Fairweather. But they do not hold the stage like these. They exist in a secondary world; they inhabit a sort of stationary dream. They look out; they see the altering scene around them; and this scene is the dramatic action, which to them, in the same way, has the appearance of a swiftly changing dream. For this reason Falstaff, as we recreate him in our imagination, remains quite unthreatened by the violent events in the two parts of *Henry IV*; the world in which Prince Henry and Hotspur fight and the king dies is not his world, but only a dream which passes over it. Time is the central reality in that dream, and Time passes him by.

It is this imperviousness to time, this almost mythical permanence, which deepens our delight in such figures as Falstaff, Uncle Toby, Cuddie Headrigg, and Mr. Micawber. To admit that they were capable of change would be to limit their significance, not to enrich it; changed, they would no longer be universal in their place, which is a stationary spatial world in which time has reached an equilibrium. This is the reason why, when Dickens fits out Micawber with a new existence at the end of *David Copperfield*, the effect is so displeasing. Not only is a term set to a delight which seemed unending, but

Micawber himself is at one stroke robbed of his eternal validity. We still think of him as everlastingly "waiting for something to turn up," it is true, for our imagination ignores the last transformation, and gives him back to us as he was. Yet Dickens' mistake harms Micawber, as Shakespeare's, marvelous as it is, harms Falstaff. Our imagination gives us back Falstaff, too, as he lived, in spite of the pathos of the death scene. His death is less a part of his life than a term set to it; and the shadow that mortality casts back upon him is so imperceptible that he seems as unthreatened by it as Uncle Toby, or Mr. Collins, who do not die at all. We know that like these he will always exist, and always be the same.

This, then, is the mark of all the principal creations of the character novelist; it is of their life, and of that alone, that we are aware, not of their life and death, not of that double fate which colors all dramatic figures. The true character seems to exist equally in all time, and untouched by time. *Vanity Fair* is no more a picture of Victorian society than of society itself; it does not show us only how people lived in Victoria's reign, but how people live in civilized society. It can justly, therefore, be called a picture of life or of manners; but the definition does not apply to the other divisions of the novel. The dramatic novel is rather a development reproducing the organic movement of life; and if we may take up an analogy without following it too far, is more like a movement in a symphony than a picture.

So much for the temporal vacancy of the novel of character; its spatial vitality, if this analysis should be accepted by anyone, will appear as obvious. There is in the great character novels a feeling of intensely filled space as extraordinary in its way as the feeling of crowded time in the dramatic novel. The almost nightmare luxuriance of life in Dickens' London; the mob of characters who jostle one another in his books, so that the scene seems crammed to bursting-point: this intensity of spatial reality, which can only be found in the character novel, is the counterpart of the intensity of time in the chief scenes in *Wuthering Heights* and the conclusion of *Moby Dick*. When we think of the world of characters, the picture that comes before us is something like those crowded frontispieces which used to adorn the collected editions of Dickens' novels, where we see standing side by side, and one behind the other, the forms of Mr. Pickwick, Pecksniff, Micawber, Dick Swiveller, Uriah Heep, Sam Weller, Sairey Gamp, Montague Tigg, The Artful Dodger, The Fat Boy, and a host of minor figures, until the page seems to be unable to hold any more. This crowded effect, this sense of living and moving space, is produced, once more, by the unchangeability of the characters. None of them ceases to occupy his place when another appears; all existing permanently, all exist contemporaneously; and even if they have their places in separate novels, we think of them together. It is as if the talent of the character novelist could only propagate itself by fission, where the dramatic genius observes the narrower limitations of reproduction; the variety of the first remaining purely spatial, where that of the other, being organic, can only be manifested in time. We think of Dickens' and Thackeray's characters as all living at the same time, and as all living forever, and we think of them, therefore, as a crowd. But Emily Brontë's figures appear to us singly; Space may from out its distances throw them together, but one by one they disappear from it, and at last they leave it vacant.

Why should those two forms of the novel be bound by the limitations which we have been discussing? Why should not the action develop with equal freedom in Time and in Space?...

❦❦❦❦

Intended in part as an answer to Forster's *Aspects of the Novel,* Muir's *The Structure of the Novel* is an important complement to its predecessor because it provides the critic with a viable alternative to Forster's method. Forster classifies with apparent reluctance, and he begins with the simplest element of the novel—story, the mere succession of events that appeals to the audience's vulgar curiosity—and moves to the most general, most complex, and least definable—pattern and rhythm. Muir begins by classifying novels in the most general terms and then moves, in the chapter reprinted here, to a discussion of the novelist's vision, the means of giving configuration to his imaginative world, and, though he does not use the terms, of the interrelationship of form and content. In fact, though Muir dismisses Forster's terms "pattern" and "rhythm," his analogies between the novel of character (in the special sense in which he uses the term) and a picture and between the dramatic novel and a symphony correspond closely to Forster's contrast between spatial pattern and temporal rhythm. This is not to say that different approaches reach the same end, but that criticism which searches far enough must ask similar questions.

Although he is not often cited, Muir anticipates a number of problems that concern recent critics. His use of the term "character"—it parallels Forster's "flat character"—as description rather than judgment is developed by W. J. Harvey from somewhat different premises and with a clearer view of philosophical implications. In *The Plot of Satire,** Alvin Kernan uses visual analogies to describe the movement of satiric works and to defend them against charges that they are incoherent or plotless. Both he and Muir help the critic to evaluate works written in the comic and satiric mode in their own terms. Muir's discussion of structure in the novel of character might help to answer the question that O'Grady raises at the end of "On Plot in Modern Fiction": a method which uses "change" as a primary concept may not apply to such books. Last, though by no means finally, Muir's theory that slowing time is humorous because it is reassuring should be compared to Eric Bentley's view in "The Psychology of Farce"† that farce depends upon speeded-up motion. This distinction may provide a means of discriminating between methods and effects that have sometimes been confused.

One of the tests of Muir's theories—as of any criticism—is their adequacy in dealing with contemporary literature. Muir's book seems less satisfactory when he attempts to treat the major fiction of the twenties, and one must ask whether his theories or his application of them is at fault. If his theories are adequate, the critic must show their relevance not only to the novels of Joyce, Woolf, and Huxley, but to those of such contemporaries as John Barth, Joseph Heller, and Saul Bellow; for the changing nature of fiction makes the process of theorizing and discriminating a continuous one.

---

* New Haven: Yale University Press, 1965.
† *Let's Get a Divorce! and Other Plays* (New York: Hill and Wang, Inc., 1958).

The English Novel
and the
Three Kinds of Time

JOHN HENRY RALEIGH

It is a truism that both the form and the content of the novel are bound up, more than is the case in any other of the major literary forms, with the dialectic between man and time and/or history. Upon this primordial fulcrum, which leans, in one direction, toward the private, the individual, the subjective and, in another and opposite direction, toward the public, the collective, the objective, the novel rests, achieving grandeur, like all art, only insofar as it maintains an equivocal synthesis, constantly breaking down and knitting together, between these two diametrically different but interacting areas of human experience. "Thus," writes Santayana, "two concomitant yet strangely different streams would seem to compose human life: one the vast cosmic flood of cyclic movements and sudden precipitations, in which man has his part like other animals; and the other, the private little rivulet of images, emotions, and words babbling as we move, and often hidden underground in sleep or forgetfulness." Santayana's aphorism, which sounds like a capsule-description of *Finnegans Wake,* is saying, like *Finnegans Wake,* that human experience is simultaneously a public nightmare and a private dream. And it is precisely this perspectivist observation post over the life of man that the great novelists have commanded, from Cervantes to Joyce. But the exact artistic formulation differs from author to author, and, more importantly, from century to century.

"A nous deux maintenant," says Rastignac (the private dream)

From *Sewanee Review,* LXII (July–September 1954). Copyright © by The University of the South, Reprinted by permission of The University of the South and the author.

to Paris (the public nightmare). This is the classic nineteenth-century formulation of the dialectic between man and time-history: the individual (here conceived of not as a psychic unit but as a whole, sociobiological person) clashing and coalescing with the city (contemporary history). But the twentieth-century purview of Stephen Dedalus includes not only the city and contemporary history but the nightmare of universal time-history as well. So that the major movement in the novel over the last one hundred years consists of a successive radicalizing of the two sides of the antithesis, with the individual becoming more and more a purely psychic entity, finally turning into a literal private dream, and time-history becoming more and more all-embracing until it eventually becomes a literal, public, multi-encompassing nightmare. *Finnegans Wake* formulates the dialectic in terms at once the most minute and grandiose: the ego dreaming on the history of the universe. The basic categories in the two centuries remain the same, but, whereas the nineteenth-century novel filled them out normatively, prosaically, the twentieth-century novel fills them out violently, grotesquely.

It is the purpose of this essay to trace out the broad outlines, using for illustrative material the history of the British novel of the last one hundred years, of this movement from man-social history to ego-universal history, in terms of the differing conceptions of and differing metaphors for the idea of time-history, with final remarks concerning, first, the bearings of these metaphors upon the conventions symbolizing personality and, secondly, the relationships between the idea of man and the idea of time-history.

The Platonic tradition held that time was "the moving image of eternity." This definition, while it may well be philosophically unsound, is just artistically and imaginatively if we grant that Everyman must somehow come to terms with time-history and evolve for it an emotionally satisfying metaphor which then constitutes an emblem of things ultimate. This is one of the things that literature attempts to do. But if we say that the time-sense and the historical-sense of a work of art is "the moving image of eternity" and is, as Spengler and others have held, profoundly axiological, we must still have more precise categories for more specific analysis. The categories most often used, of course, are the time-space antitheses. Yet to hypostasize time as a discrete entity is to pass over precedent aspects of the problem, for there are, in life and art and anterior to the space-time antithesis, several divergent metaphors for describing time-history itself.

According to the late Nicholas Berdyaev there are three basic categories and symbols for describing time-history (Berdyaev makes no distinction between the time-sense and the historical-sense, taking them both to be specific manifestations of the general attitude toward temporal experience). First, there is cosmic time, which can be symbolized by a circle and which refers to the endless recurrence of things: night following day, season following season, the cycle of birth, growth, and decay; in short the circular character of human and natural experience. Secondly, there is historical time, symbolized by a horizontal line, and referring to the course of nations, civilizations, tribes (i.e., mankind in the mass) through time. Likewise the individual has a linear as well as a circular relationship to time. The line, for man or men, may slant upward, to indicate progress, or downward, to indicate regress. Third, and symbolized by a vertical line, there is existential time, referring to a notion of time somewhat like Bergson's *duree,* only religious or mystical in nature. This concept of existential time is actually an extreme form of individualism, or in Berdyaev's words, "personalism," and presupposes the individual's ability to free himself from either cyclic or historical time. Existential time, in effect, denies the validity of time-history. Historically, this idea of time manifested itself in the apocalyptic tendencies of early Christianity; in secular terms it still survives in certain anarchist doctrines. Popularly, it receives prosaic expression in the old wives' tale about a drowning man's whole life flashing before him in an instant, and, generally, in the common notion that, in all men's psychological experience, time has differing speeds and, at certain critical moments, seems, almost, to stop.

The time-sense of the Victorians was, of course, the linear one, which for twentieth-century man, so accustomed to the idea of "recurrence," seems to be almost equivalent to having no time-sense at all. In fact what appears, for us, to be absent in most Victorian novels—this despite the preoccupation of the nineteenth century with the past—is precisely an acute sense of time and a deep sense of history. And we do not need to go all the way up to Joyce, Proust, and Mann to see the difference between the central Victorians and us in these matters. Hardy and James will do.

In the work of neither Dickens nor Trollope, to take them as our examples, is there any what you might call "metaphysical" concern with time. Both authors, of course, were signally unintellectual and uninterested in such matters. They did use time for a certain shock

value, for it was "in time" that the convolutions of plot were un-
raveled, the hero restored, and so on. But their time convention was
vague and loose as compared, for example, to the rigorously observed
"continuous present" of the late James. Trollope was given to suspending novel time altogether, by dropping the narrative and candidly
predicting future events. In *The Eustace Diamonds* the diamonds at
one point mysteriously disappear, as far as most of the characters in
the novel are concerned, but Trollope informs the reader thus:

> In the mean time, the Eustace diamonds were locked up in a small
> safe fixed into the wall at the back of a small cellar beneath the
> establishment of Messrs. Harter and Benjamin, in Minto Lane, in the
> City. Messrs. Harter and Benjamin always kept a second place of
> business. Their great shop was at the West End; but they had accom-
> modations in the city.
> The chronicler states this at once, as he scorns to keep from his
> reader any secret that is known to himself.

In other words novel time to Trollope was a joke. Generally he
assumed that a convention of time existed and that the essence of
his art, along with delineation of character, was temporality and that
only by the passage of time would events unfold. But Trollope, like
the rest of the Victorians, practiced a narrative method which
explicitly allowed the author to see before and after, and hence for
him as for God, there was no time and eternity lay spread before him.
Thus every so often, banteringly (and Thackeray did the same thing),
Trollope told the reader that novel time was his, and the reader's,
sport, to be suspended at will, as the novelist desires. With how little
seriousness novel time was taken by Trollope and the other Victorians
can best be realized by comparing the above novelistic convention,
which is not at all uncharacteristic of the Victorians, with the intricate
"time-shift" of Ford and Conrad, where time is a cross to bear.

What is also absent in both Trollope and Dickens, and in most of
the other Victorians, George Eliot perhaps excepted, particularly in
the Jewish passages of *Daniel Deronda,* is a sharp sense of history.
Of course practically all of the Victorians, following Scott, wrote historical novels, and, as a rule, failed to recapture and reconstruct a
valid representation of the age they were concerned with. Yet their
lack of historical sense is not best exemplified by these partial failures,
although one might say that they were bound to fail, given their
general attitude toward human history. What is absent in the Victorians is that more profound sense of the past (deeper than any

fascination for the past as picturesque or the past as more attractive socially, in the fashion that Thackeray was intrigued by the eighteenth century)—the obsession of modern man that the past is continually impinging on the present and assuming the proportions of a nightmare.

The classic Victorian attitude toward history and the attitude which underlay most of its literary conventions is presented most unequivocally by Dickens, whose opinion of his collective heritage was negative, to say the least. Dickens had only pity and contempt for those unfortunates who had been born at other times and in other places than nineteenth-century England (although this is not to imply that he thought that he himself was living in paradise). It is reported that he had, in his library at Gadshill, a set of false backs which purported to be a history of Western civilization and which bore the following general and specific titles: "The Wisdom of our Ancestors—I. Ignorance. II. Superstition. III. The Block. IV. The Stake. V. The Rack. VI. Dirt. VII. Disease." So much for the past.

Turning now to James and Hardy, one finds quite a different situation. Both James and Hardy, in different ways, represent the ingress of temporal and historical preoccupations in the British novel. James was one of the first novelists to take time seriously and to make it an implicit part of his work. Pre-eminently in James things happen in time. In the typical James novel, meaning a late novel, all the psychic action is seen as the relentless unfolding of time, minute by minute, hour by hour, year by year, within the mind or sensibility of an individual.

History or the sense of the past likewise begins to appear in the novels of James. James, of course, did not have the historical imagination of his friend Henry Adams with its conception of man's past as a construct of great forces bearing down on the present. Nevertheless, it is history that plays, generally, a major role in the motivation of all James's novels and it is history that became an obsessional preoccupation in his late works. In James's abiding theme—the American in Europe—the sense of the past is one of Europe's most subtle blandishments, something that pierces the soul and makes one laugh and weep simultaneously. Thus Isabel Archer on seeing the Eternal City for the first time:

> She had always been fond of history, and here was history in the
> stones of the street and the atoms of sunshine. She had an imagina-
> tion that kindled at the mention of great deeds, and wherever she
> turned some great deed had been acted. These things strongly moved

her, but moved her all inwardly. . . . By her own measure she was very happy; she would even have been willing to take these hours for the happiest she was ever to know. The sense of the terrible human past was heavy to her, but that of something altogether contemporary would suddenly give it wings that it could wave in the blue. Her consciousness was so mixed that she scarcely knew where the different parts of it would lead her, and she went about in a repressed ecstasy of contemplation, seeing often in the things she looked at a great deal more than was there, and yet not seeing many of the items enumerated in her Murray.

This sense of the past became successively more acute in James's works and is the explicit and sole concern in some of the late tales and novels. In *The Altar of the Dead* the protagonist perpetually lights candles in commemoration of the dead, or the past; the hero of *The Jolly Corner* symbolically recaptures his own past; and, most bizarrely, Ralph Pendrel of the late unfinished novel *The Sense of the Past* actually changes place with a dead ancestor. And here, in this novel, James gave his most magniloquent testimony to the force of human history:

> On the day he disembarked in England he felt himself as never before ranged in that interest [the past], counted on that side of the line. It was to this he had been brought by his desire to remount the stream of time, really to bathe in its upper and more natural waters, to risk even, as he might say, drinking of them. No man, he well believed, could ever so much have wanted to look behind and still behind—to scale the high wall into which the successive years, each a squared block, pile themselves in our rear and look over as nearly as possible with eye of sense into, unless it should be called out of, the vast prison house. . . . If his idea in fine was to recover the lost moment, to feel the stopped pulse, it was to do so as experience, in order to be again consciously that creature that had been, to breathe as he had breathed and feel the pressure he had felt.

In Hardy too time is taken seriously and becomes, in fact, dramatized as a malignant Fate, lying ominously in the future, waiting to strike down humans. Likewise everything in Hardy, natural or human, reverberates with history. The background for Hardy's Wessex series is provided by an immemorial community, the peasantry, who are, in a literal sense, the past, and who surround the main characters with an aura of ancient custom, legend, and myth, and the landscape itself mutely speaks for and of the ages.

But if time and history had become more pressing and more of a concern in the later nineteenth-century novel, they had also become something quite different, in their very nature; and a new set of literary conventions arose to symbolize the new attitudes. Dickens and Trollope were committed, by their unconscious assumptions and by the literary conventions which they inherited, to historical time, or time as a straight line, from the past into the future. In their case the idea of time was tied up with the idea of progress; so that the line of history led upward and receded downward, with the result that one looked forward to a pleasant but indefinite future and shunned a definite but unpleasant past. This attitude—rationalistic, progressive, secular—is, of course, the heritage of the eighteenth century and is known as liberalism. But what is noteworthy about the liberal attitude toward time-history is that, while it is generally confident about the future, it is vague about the concrete content of the future, as compared, say, to a Marxist, a conservative, or a cyclist. The key here is the ending of a novel, which is a specific and concrete manifestation of the general sense of time-history underlying the novel as a whole. At the end of a Dickens novel, for example, the leading characters are briefly projected into the future. But as the late George Orwell said, although the reader is assured of the infinite happiness of all parties, he is never quite sure as to why they are happy or what they are happy at, save that there is a childbirth every year and a Christmas spirit all the time. The assumption about futurity here is that these happy few will continuously but mistily compound their happiness, piling cheer on cheer, for the rest of their mortality. In short, the Victorian convention of the "happy ending" was not simply the result of a solid society wishing to have its sense of the fitness of things reaffirmed, for there is plenty of evidence to prove that the Victorian was anything but the stable and unworried cultural group that it is often supposed to have been. The "happy ending" does make sense if it be regarded as a literary convention metaphorically expressing the Victorian time-sense; i.e., man projected into an imprecise but, nevertheless, happy future. And for the Victorian novelist, before the "happy ending" happened, the substance of things and the material for his novel was a reality composed of an historically-emptied conjunction of the present and the future.

With Hardy and James it is precisely this concept of time and history as a straight line, leading upward, that begins to break down. Hardy's sense of the past is, partially anyway, a metaphorical expression of cosmic time, whose essence is the endless recurrence of things. In *The Return of the Native* an entire cycle of nature takes place, while the humanity in the foreground works itself out into an unhappy and ambiguous ending. Likewise in so many of the other Wessex novels, the one immutable certainty is that nature will continue her ceaseless cycle, no matter what sad fate besets man. As in nature so in man: the only solidity that man possesses is that which he inherits from the past, and Hardy's natives, like Faulkner's negroes, "endure." For the moderns, the civilized, the rationalists, the dependents on a liberalist future, the type who in the Victorian novel had the "happy ending," there is only tragedy, or misery, waiting in the future. In other words the universe of Thomas Hardy has only one certitude, the cyclic character of existence, and only one prop for humans, an allegiance to the past.

James's time-sense was obviously different from Hardy's and is, in effect, a secular version of existential or subjective time. Ralph Pendrel of *The Sense of the Past* literally fulfills Berdyaev's definition of existential time—he escapes from history. Less obvious is the implicit sense of existential time in all of James's late work, where there is no objective reality, and thus no real time, outside of the mind of the individual. Moreover, this internal time, while it flows continuously, does not always move at a constant rate. What happens in James is that time is extricated from history, as, with the clock stopped, James explores, often for pages, the infinity of implications arising from an instantaneous impression, and, in a sense, James's late works constitute a long essay on the potential infinity of individual psychological moments.

As in the case of the Victorians, the key to Hardy's and James's time-sense is the manner in which each ends his novels. They both wrote "happy endings" but their most characteristic novels end either tragically (Hardy) or ambiguously (James). This is to say that man's future is either dark or unsure. In Hardy and in James, then, simple historical time, built along the idea of progress, is breaking down and cosmic and existential time are becoming the province of the novelist, who is, simultaneously, developing an historical sense and an immortal desire for an immersion in the past. It should be added that with James, at least, the novel is turning away from the objective world of society toward the inner world of the self for its subject matter.

Of Joyce's preoccupation with time-history, nothing need be said. He had, said Wyndham Lewis in paying the highest insult he could think of, a "time-mind." Nor do I propose to unravel the incredibly elaborate time-history structures underlying *Ulysses* and *Finnegans*

Wake. For the purpose of this essay, however, *Ulysses* and *Finnegans Wake* may be taken as the uttermost extensions of the movements in the British novel being sketched here. As compared to Hardy, where a cosmic vision of time-history appeared only in regard to nature, the cycles in Joyce are all-inclusive, embracing human experience in its entirety, from personal, to social and natural, to, finally, divine history. As compared to James, where a limited existentialist time is employed at certain times, in Joyce the moment actually becomes infinity. "I hear," thinks Stephen Dedalus, "the ruin of all space, shattered glass and toppling masonry, and time one livid final flame." Thus in *Finnegans Wake* every moment is infinity and everything in history happens in every moment. Existential and cosmic time here coincide, producing a continuous, multileveled present which, by the principle of infinite regress, constantly recapitulates the key events of human and divine history, preeminently the Fall of Man. This concept of time-history could be symbolized in Berdyaev's categories as follows: time-history is a series of concentric circles; at dead center is H.C.E. (Man) who rays out vertical lines of existential being in all directions and through all levels of the cyclic experiences. Joyce has made incommensurables—the circular and the vertical—complement one another.

Likewise the implication for human destiny of the endings of *Ulysses* and *Finnegans Wake* is neither the vague happiness of the Victorians nor the ambiguous tragedy of James and Hardy. Joyce had the concrete circular vision—everything that has happened before will happen all over again—and it is this assumption that makes Joyce's work the true "tower beyond tragedy." At the end of *Ulysses* we know that Bloom will arise the next day and, with slight and unessential differences, will repeat his day-cycle once more. At the end of *Finnegans Wake* the cycle is made even more explicit by the famous broken sentence whose end can be found at the beginning of the book.

At this point the novel has turned from its Victorian standing-ground at a conjunction of the present-future to a conjunction of the past-present; and time-history, formerly a prosaic segment in the life of the city, in the linear image, has become a giant nimbus of exfoliating circles, shot through with existential lines of being.

While the concept and metaphor for time-history were expanded and elaborated, the concept and metaphor for characterology contracted and intensified. Thus Dickens' eccentrics with their diamond-hard outlines turned, finally, into Joyce's blurred and fluxial egos, into their shadowy archetypal bases. In both the line of expansion and contraction, James's late novels appear to be a critical stage, for here the novel, in matters of character, is narrowing down, simultaneously decreasing the number in the cast of characters and turning away from the world into the self; at the same time there is an elaborate burgeoning of the idea of time-history into a complex metaphor which affords a glimpse of eternity and provides a bizarre vision of life, under which man, now time-obsessed, is, at certain moments, free of time and, at other moments, bears the whole of human history, like a cross, upon his back.

And the case of James points out too the intimate interconnection between these two lines of contraction and expansion, in fact, their cause-and-effect relationship. James's methods and interests led straight to the central convention of the early twentieth-century novel, that is, "the stream of consciousness" or "interior monologue." And this device, while its most obvious function was to body forth the inner life in a fashion impossible within the nineteenth-century novelistic conventions, was also a way of objectifying time-history in a manner unavailable to the Victorians: first it permitted the illusion of a continuous present (the existential), and, second, it permitted by reverie and memory, exploration of the past and the juxtaposition and confounding of past with present (the cosmic). It is only one more step for the individual memory, with which the "stream of consciousness" was initially concerned, to step over into collective memory and thus pass out into history.

Historically this is about what happened, for as the novel turned inward and contemporary history became thinned and abstracted (the late as opposed to the early James, for example), universal history began to emerge. In Thomas Mann's words, "the bourgeois and individual passes over into the mythical and typical." As in the children's fable, one digs a hole in the ground, to turn away from the world, but finally emerges in China, and, as a matter of fact, when one thinks of James's famous pagoda and caravan images or the orientalism of *Finnegans Wake,* the analogy is apt.

What has happened, then, in the novel is that the two sides of the basic antithesis of the novel (the private dream and the public nightmare) have had their respective time-schemes changed. Whereas both once traveled the linear line of historical time, in the twentieth-century novel the individual's time-sense has been, in great part, existentialized and the time-scheme of the universe has been circular-

ized. *Finnegans Wake* carries these twin, complementary movements
to their highest and most equivocal pitch, into an area, in fact, where
they are breaking down, one into the other, and where the parallels of
development are beginning to curve and cross: a subjectivity, on
the side of the individual, so complete, minute, and intense that it
is constantly verging into the most broad and representative kind of
archetypism; a vision of time-history so elaborate, so all-encompassing,
so grandiose that it threatens, continually, to turn into a private,
esoteric, mystagogic poem. Yet *Finnegans Wake* achieves the balance
between the private and the public, the "perspectivism" which the
great novel, since *Don Quixote,* has always achieved, albeit here in a
radical, almost desperate fashion. And the success of this equivocal
equation is, in great part, due to the organic blend of two kinds of
time: the existential being the most extreme form of individualism;
the cosmic being the most impersonal and objective way of describing
the incessant tick, whose meaning is a circle, that sounds throughout
Finnegans Wake and in all our ears.

❦❦❦❦

The contrast between the essay by Edwin Muir and the
one by John Henry Raleigh reveals the importance of both
perspective and the kind of evidence on which an inductive
critical argument is based. Although later chapters of *The Structure of the Novel* discuss recent fiction, Muir's basic position is
derived from a study of the pre-twentieth-century novel. Furthermore, whether because of a lack of perspective in depth or, more
likely, because of his desire to contrast what seem to him basic
and static types, Muir sees only the formal differences between
such novelists as Dickens and Hardy. He does so, apparently,
because he conceives of time in only one way—what Raleigh
would call linear—and because he sees time almost as an
independent entity, going so far as to personify it in "we see
Time gradually gathering itself up...." Raleigh's concept of
time is more fluid and dynamic: he perceives a shift in conceptions of it and he is more interested in the relationship of time
to personality and to the author's and the age's concepts of
time, personality, and history than, like Muir, in its relationship
to plot and to the imaginative configuration of the novel. The
major difference between their positions, however, lies in their
attitudes towards myth. In the discussion of *Ulysses,* Muir denies

the relevance and significance of the Homeric parallels and regards their use as artificial, pedantic, and incapable of vivifying and illuminating the plethora of realistic detail in the novel. Raleigh accepts mythic structure as a normal and valuable means of giving depth and significance to a work. He would understand, as Muir would not, the distinction made in Charles Bernard O'Hare's "Myth or Plot? A Study in Ways of Ordering Narrative."*

Although Raleigh's essay is written from a later and broader perspective than Muir's, it shares some of the same kinds of limitation. It is clear that Santayana is not saying "that human experience is simultaneously a public nightmare and a private dream"; Raleigh uses the distinction to make an important point about the modern attitudes and the literature they produce, but one might ask whether he accepts the modern as normative, whether, in fact, his perspective is too narrow. Further, it is possible to accept his view that *Finnegans Wake* is the culmination of a process without accepting the corollary—strongly implied for rhetorical purposes—that it is the end of that process. Critics of more recent novels will have to make their own formulations unless, like some prophets of the death of the novel, they take an elegiac tone about all prose fiction published after 1939.

Despite its limitations—and most of them are dictated by the length and purpose of the essay—Raleigh's approach has important relationships to major trends in modern theory. His view that the novel changes in focus and even in genre falls between the definitions of Shroder and Freedman and helps to explain the process of interiorization. His concern for the novel as an art both developed in time and concerned with the problem of time parallels the work of those, like W. J. Harvey and Alan Friedman, who see the novel as process and as a mimetic reproduction of the world of our experience, particularly the world as defined by the liberal tradition.

The problem of time has been discussed at greater length in Harvey's chapter, "Time and Identity," in *Character and the Novel* (see p. 140n); in A. A. Mendilow, *Time and the Novel*,† concerned largely with questions of form; and in Hans Meyerhoff, *Time in Literature*,‡ concerned with philosophical and social questions.

---

* *Arizona Quarterly*, XIII (1957), 238–50.
† London: Peter Nevill, Ltd., 1952.
‡ Berkeley: University of California Press, 1955.

Mixed and Uniform Prose Styles in the Novel

LEONARD LUTWACK

A distinction may be made between a novel in which more than one prose style is used and a novel which is written in a single, uniform style throughout. *Tom Jones* and *Ulysses* are mixed style novels, *Pamela* and *The Ambassadors* are uniform style novels. The object of this paper is to define the distinction and to work out some of the implications it may have in the study of the novel.

Tom Jones is an early specimen of a novel with mixed prose styles that originate from the author's ironical attitude toward his material and from his compartmentalized treatment of the three genres of which fiction is composed: narrative, essay, and drama. At least three narrative styles are used by Fielding. Tom's rescue of Mrs. Waters from Northerton is a passage of "mere narrative":

> He had not entered far into the wood before he beheld a most shocking sight indeed, a woman stripped half naked, under the hands of a ruffian, who had put his garter round her neck, and was endeavouring to draw her up to a tree. Jones asked no questions at this interval, but fell instantly upon the villain, and made such good use of his trusty oaken stick that he laid him sprawling on the ground before he could defend himself, indeed almost before he knew he was attacked; nor did he cease the prosecution of his blows till the woman herself begged him to forbear, saying, she believed he had sufficiently done his business.

Although excrescences of abstract diction slip into these lines, they are few and do no injury to the narrative force of the style. This prose is almost purely objective, with only the slightest suggestion of authorial attitude toward its content; it is prose that takes its subject

From *Journal of Aesthetics and Art Criticism,* XVIII (March 1960). Reprinted by permission of The American Society for Aesthetics and the author.

seriously. The syntax is a matter of the simple compounding of short clauses that make absolutely clear the persons, objects, and time sequence of the action.

Against this plain narrative style Fielding sets his "Homerican style," which parodies the heroic manner of narration in epic poetry and romance:

> Now the dogs of war being let loose, began to lick their bloody lips; now Victory, with golden wings, hung hovering in the air; now Fortune, taking her scales from her shelf, began to weigh the fates of Tom Jones, his female companion, and Partridge, against the landlord, his wife, and maid. . .

In Fielding's third narrative style, the formal, periodic manner of the eighteenth-century essay is used to overlay the plain narrative contents. After Tom's rescue of Mrs. Waters, the two repair to an inn where the landlady is not anxious to receive them:

> Now it required no very blamable degree of suspicion to imagine that Mr. Jones and his ragged companion had certain purposes in their intention, which, though tolerated in some Christian countries, connived at in others, and practised in all, are however as expressly forbidden as murder, or any other horrid vice, by that religion which is universally believed in those countries. The landlady, therefore, had no sooner received an intimation of the entrance of the above-said persons than she began to meditate the most expeditious means for their expulsion. In order to do this, she had provided herself with a long and deadly instrument, with which, in times of peace, the chamber-maid was wont to demolish the labours of the industrious spider. In vulgar phrase, she had taken up the broomstick, and was just about to sally from the kitchen, when Jones accosted her with a demand of a gown and other vestments to cover the half-naked woman up-stairs.

Both the essay and the heroic styles of narration, besides being amusing in themselves as burlesque and mock-heroic, are the result of Fielding's ambiguous attitude toward the material used in a novel. They also effectively point up the unsuitability in the novel of the "elevation of style" used in more traditional forms of narrative writing. By comparison the plain style is made to appear without question to be the best for the novel. The variety of narrative styles at the disposal of the novelist is succinctly illustrated by Fielding in *Joseph Andrews* on the occasion of one of the many beatings suffered by Parson Adams, whose assailant this time "belaboured the body of Adams till he was weary, and indeed till he concluded (to use the language of fighting) that he had done his business; or, in the language of poetry, 'that he had sent him to the shades below'; in plain English, 'that he was dead.' " And yet Fielding cannot take quite seriously the behavior of the "comic class" which his plain narrative style is so well calculated to report; his parodies and burlesques, like those of Joyce in *Ulysses*, exhibit the risibility of the world he is rendering and restore the ironical viewpoint of the author.

In addition to the three different narrative styles in *Tom Jones*, the style of the eighteenth-century essay is put to normal use in the well-known introductory chapters, "composed of observation and reflection," as well as in the course of the story itself when authorial comment seems appropriate. And to make the variety of styles even richer, Fielding, borrowing the principle of verisimilar speech from the drama, makes liberal use of many different speaking styles: the learned jargon of Square and Thwackum, the tiresome commonplace chatter of Mrs. Honour, the local dialects of barmaids, servants, and Squire Western.

Fielding's practice suggests the principle that the more independently the three genres composing the novel are developed, the more sharply differentiated will be the several prose styles of a novel, or the greater divergence there will be between the language that conveys the story, the language that conceptualizes and analyzes, and the language in which the characters speak. The structure of such a novel will tend to be episodic, the pattern of styles, paratactic: that is, blocks of varied material will be set beside each other without much coordination and modulation, and prose styles of sharply differing character will be juxtaposed. *Moby Dick*, even more than *Tom Jones*, is a prime example of a novel with mixed styles growing out of unassimilated genres and the divided mind of the author who regarded his material as both common whale blubber and rare mythic poetry. The narrative is presented in prose that is economical, concrete, and direct; exposition and authorial observations and reflections are presented ironically in a mixture of the "hopping," intimate style of the whimsical essay and the public style of oratory; the dialogue has the quality of heroic poetry, which Melville takes seriously as imitation, not parody, of Elizabethan blank verse. While all of these styles make a remarkable blend in *Moby Dick*, the special quality of each is preserved.

Being itself a compound of genres, each with a more fixed character than the novel and each having a different stylistic potential, the novel has always offered opportunities for a mixture of styles. And yet the novel has never imposed the necessity of being written in mixed styles. Indeed, from the very beginning, novelists have easily avoided the mixture of styles that the hybrid form and uncertain status of the novel seem to encourage. Far from being the rule, the mixed style novel has been the anomaly in the history of fiction, the kind of work that it is so difficult to justify as belonging at all to the genre.

The concentration on one of the component genres of the novel to the exclusion of the others has been one method to avoid a mixture of styles. Uniformity of style in *Clarissa* was made possible by the adaptation of the moral essay to fictional purposes; in *Tristram Shandy,* by the exploitation of that aspect of the personal essay that lends itself to facetious rhetoric and parenthesis. Concentration on the essayistic or analytic potential of prose produced uniform style in the later James and Proust, just as the scrupulous avoidance of analytic prose and an almost complete dependence upon narrative and drama yielded a uniform plain style in Hemingway.

In *The Ambassadors,* Maria Gostrey and Strether discover that they have in Waymarsh a mutual acquaintance:

> "Oh yes," he replied, "my very well-known friend. He's to meet me here, coming up from Malvern, and I supposed he would already have arrived. But he doesn't come till later, and I'm relieved not to have kept him. Do you know him?" Strether wound up.
> It was not till after he had spoken that he became aware of how much there had been in him of response; when the tone of her own rejoinder, as well as the play of something more in her face—something more, that is, than its apparently usual restless light—seemed to notify him. "I've met him at Milrose—where I used sometimes, a good while ago, to stay; I had friends there who were friends of his, and I've been at his house. I won't answer for it that he would know me," Strether's interlocutress pursued; "but I should be delighted to see him. Perhaps," she added, "I shall—for I'm staying over." She paused an instant, while our friend took in these things, and it was as if a good deal of talk had already passed. They even vaguely smiled at it, and Strether presently observed that Mr. Waymarsh would, no doubt, be easily to be seen. This, however, appeared to affect the lady as if she might have advanced too far. She was frank about everything. "Oh," she said, "he won't care!"—and she immediately thereupon remarked that she believed Strether knew the Munsters; the Munsters being the people he had seen her with at Liverpool.

The speeches of the characters, the motions of Strether's consciousness as it begins to play on a new phenomenon, and the author's objective record of the scene are all of a piece stylistically. There is no break

from one kind of material to another; stiff-jointed syntax carries the
burden of meticulous analysis. Colloquial usage gets into the recording
prose of the author ("our friend took in these things"), and the
formality of the author's manner gets into the speeches ("I supposed
he would already have arrived").

A different kind of uniformity is achieved by Hemingway. The
ambulance of Lieutenant Henry is bogged down in the mud:

> The thing to do now was to dig out in front of the wheels, put in
> brush so that the chains could grip, and then push until the car was
> on the road. We were all down on the road around the car. The two
> sergeants looked at the car and examined the wheels. Then they started
> off down the road without a word. I went after them.
> "Come on," I said. "Cut some brush."
> "We have to go," one said.
> "Get busy," I said, "and cut brush."
> "We have to go," one said. The other said nothing. They were in
> a hurry to start. They would not look at me.
> "I order you to come back to the car and cut brush," I said. The
> one sergeant turned. "We have to go on. In a little while you will be
> cut off. You can't order us. You're not our officer."
> "I order you to cut brush," I said. They turned and started down
> the road.
> "Halt," I said. They kept on down the muddy road, the hedge on
> either side. "I order you to halt," I called. They went a little faster.
> I opened up my holster, took the pistol, aimed at the one who had
> talked the most, and fired.

The same style is used for both action and dialogue and never varies
throughout the book. No differentiation is made between the speeches
of the narrator, an American who is presumably speaking simple
Italian, and the speeches of the sergeant, a native Italian. No analysis
is made of the characters' thought; it must be deduced from what
they do and say: Lieutenant Henry "aimed at the one who had
talked the most." There is no attempt in *A Farewell To Arms* to go
beyond the plain recording of simple action and speech, except on
one occasion when the mind of Lieutenant Henry is rendered as it
succumbs to sleep and on another when an unspoken prayer for
Catherine's recovery passes through the mind of the narrator.

Although competition among the three original genres of the novel
has always been a condition in the writing of fiction, it is to be
noted that in the earliest and latest years of the history of the novel
this competition has been more pronounced than in the middle
period, the nineteenth century. At that time the principle of assimila-

tion prevailed: that is, the narrative, essayistic, and dramatic ingredients of the novel were not treated independently, each with a different potential fully realized, but were combined in a single genre and presented under a single aspect of language. Henry James stated the principle of assimilation when he wrote:

> I cannot imagine composition existing in a series of blocks, nor conceive, in any novel worth discussing at all, of a passage of description that is not in its intention narrative, a passage of dialogue that is not in its intention descriptive, a touch of truth of any sort that does not partake of the nature of incident. . . .A novel is a living thing, all one and continuous, . . . in each of the parts there is something of each of the other parts.

In a novel of such closely articulated parts—and the works of James's middle phase are among the best examples—the essayistic material ("a touch of the truth"), the dramatic material, and the narrative ("incident") have no existence as independent genres and are presented in a prose style that is essentially uniform. Moreover, the elements of narrative, essay, and drama are held in more or less equal proportions: there is not more essay material than dramatic, no more dramatic material than narrative. The balancing of novelistic ingredients and the presentation of all in a uniform style characterize the greatest achievements in the novel of the nineteenth century. A uniform style was thus the result of the assimilation of the component genres of the novel, and uniform style was also the means by which assimilation was helped.

Concentration on the essayistic element in fiction is likely to result in a complex prose style of a personal rather than conventional quality. Conversely, the assimilation and balancing of the novel's three component genres more readily leads to a plain style of conventional character, the language of narrative and drama acting as correctives to the tendency of essayistic prose to become syntactically complex and verbally abstract. The prose style of nineteenth-century English, French, and Russian fiction is distinguished by its plainness and by its lack of literary distinction. It was not far removed from the common style used in all sorts of contemporary writing that made a close approach to the plain facts of existence. Being close to the style of journalism, it was an easy and a popular style, well suited to the purposes of realism.

Whatever variety there was in this unspecialized and general style for fiction was gained by differentiating the speeches of characters.

Such variety places most nineteenth-century fiction somewhere between the pure extremes of mixed and uniform style novels. It was of course the spirit of realism and the principle of verisimilar speech practiced in the drama that had prompted novelists as early as Fielding to contrive a mixture of speaking styles appropriate for various character types: dialect speakers, exotics like Scott's Highlanders and Cooper's Indians, and eccentrics whose peculiarities were better displayed in their speech than in their behavior. All of these speakers had numerous prototypes in Shakespeare and the contemporary stage, and most spoke in the novel "for the jest-sake," as Fielding put it, and for the purpose of injecting into the plain prose of the nineteenth-century novel a touch of "quaint," strange, or poetic language. Their varied speaking styles were not to be taken quite seriously, however, never to be accorded the same high value associated with the speaking style of the proper heroes and heroines. Since these spoke in the same style used in the essay and narrative material of the novel, the general effect of uniform style thus remained in spite of the speeches of amusing and exotic characters, whose divergent styles supplied only occasional color to the common fabric of the prose.

The normative or base style of the typical nineteenth-century novel can be described as polite, "literary," book prose, greatly relaxed and loosened by the influence of journalism—what Carlyle contemptuously labeled "ready-writing" and Thoreau "fluent writing." Undistinguished as such a style was, it served the purpose of the best fiction of the time. It had two important advantages for the novel of that time: its fluency and prolixity supported the sense of continuous and detailed existence that the novel tried to render, and its gentility constituted a valuable means of reader edification and reader identification with the point of view of the author. An equable and consistent view of reality was presented in a consistent and unpointed flow of language. Every narrative incident, every authorial comment was assured of a respectful response by reason of its being conveyed in a style common to both writer and reader. Characters of irregular habit or disposition were easily identified and evaluated according to their degree of departure from the normative style of the hero and the author.

Uniform style in fiction employing first-person narration is of course a formal requirement to reflect limited point of view. Some variety of style is secured by the narrator's total recall of the speeches of characters he encounters. When partial recall is used, as in *Huckleberry Finn,* the recorded speaking styles are accommodated to the style of the narrator, so that while there is some difference between the style of the narrator and other characters, it is not as great as in a novel like *David Copperfield,* in which the narrator preserves exactly the strikingly different qualities of Micawber and Mrs. Mowcher. Absolute uniformity of style in a first-person novel is achieved simply by making no concessions whatever to individual differences. Interest is made to center so exclusively on the narrator's particular response to reality and on a set of charaters closely resembling the narrator, that no expectation of stylistic variation has to be met by the writer. Walter Shandy and his guests are rhetoricians of the same school as Tristram; the narrators of James and Hemingway present worlds that are closed to any character and any style that is not of a piece with the narrator's.

While verisimilar speech was widely used for amusing and exotic characters in novels before the last quarter of the nineteenth century, little attempt was made to have the first-person narrator deliver his fiction in a verisimilar speaking style. Convention required that the narrator "write" his account in the style generally expected in all fiction rather than "speak" it in a special personal style. The prose of a narrator like David Copperfield differs not at all from the prose used by Dickens in his third-person novels. David Copperfield's personality is of course revealed, but not through the kind of prose style he employs. The manner in which he tells his story is calculated less to individualize his character than to supply the stabilizing and evaluative function of a conventional style. *Tristram Shandy* and *Moby Dick* represent early attempts to depart from the conventional style for first-person narration by exploiting the idiosyncrasies of the narrator's language. Tristram drives traditional rhetorical devices to unconventional extremes, and Ishmael resorts to archaic essay styles. Neither uses a verisimilar speaking style, although this is speciously suggested by their addressing the reader on almost every page. In neither case is a new style for fiction developed or even intended; the striking effect in each book depends upon the highly mannered application to fiction of prose styles that are outrageously unsuited for fiction.

It was not until the latter part of the nineteenth century, when the fully developed theory of realism embraced the serious use of dialect styles, that verisimilar speech was considered appropriate for first-person narrators. Mark Twain proved that a special dialect style could support a masterpiece, and Hemingway later proved that a general colloquial style is equally capable of sustaining a novel. But these are singular achievements of stylistic imitation and hold no promise either for the continued creativeness of a writer or for the novel in general.

Uniform style is characteristic of the naturalistic novel that specializes in the breadth rather than the depth of its *tranche de vie*. Since the naturalist takes no commanding view of his fiction, narrative and essay materials are presented in a style not far removed from the dull, unpointed speaking style of the characters, who are representative of average humanity. The result is a monolithic dullness of language. In the later development of naturalism, however, the limitations of simple syntax and colorless diction became an intolerable burden, and we find naturalists resorting to a modified mixed style novel. By the use of "interchapters" that range in style from the newspaper headline to the stream of consciousness, Dos Passos sought ways of varying the uniform dullness of his prose and gaining access to subjective and even poetic expression. Steinbeck, in *The Grapes of Wrath*, carries his tribe of Joads into Canaan almost entirely in the low dialect style of their speech, but, quite appropriately for a story that is a latter-day Exodus, his interchapters reflect the style of the King James Version.

The tendency toward mixed styles in the naturalistic novel proves the inadequacy of a prose style based exclusively on the low tone of ordinary speech, or what Henry James called the "unutterable depths" of the "bastard vernacular" of modern communities. An uncommon dialect speaker like Huck Finn commands interest, and his speech may even rise to heights of poetic expressiveness; a common colloquial narrator, like Frederick Henry in *A Farewell To Arms*, attracts because of his artful selection from the common store of colloquial diction and rhythm. But the unrelieved, common slush of prose characteristic of Studs Lonigan cannot fail to be dull. The naturalists as well as their critics recognized this, and their interchapters suggest the close of another period of uniform prose and the return of the novel to a mixture of styles.

In naturalistic novels that specialize in depth, the stream of consciousness technique constitutes an extreme development of the earlier principle of verisimilar speech. When the content of a character's consciousness is composed of ideas, of thought, it must be conveyed in language that approaches closer to the quality of speech than to the style of either essay or narrative. It is speech without the use of syntax, or speech in which conventional syntax is replaced by a personal rhetoric of associations employed just below the level of communication. The style of such passages must be an appropriate imitation of potential or incipient speech, just as speaking style in conventional fiction imitates actual or achieved speech. When the content of a character's consciousness is composed of sensations, however, the style cannot be modeled upon speech patterns but must depend upon the non-imitative imagination of the novelist working with the syntax and vocabulary of poetry. In either event, opportunities for mixed style novels have been immeasurably increased by the stream of consciousness technique; for in a single novel there may be as many styles as there are characters, and a single character may have more than one style assigned to him, depending upon the levels of consciousness in which he is revealed.

No historical or evolutionary principle explains the incidence of mixed and uniform styles in the novel. The possibilities of both methods were realized in the earliest novels, and both methods are in use today. The least one can safely say is that between *Moby Dick* and *Ulysses* the novel was committed to a uniform plain style. *Moby Dick* is the last specimen of the early mixed style novel, and *Ulysses* begins the return of the contemporary novel to mixed styles. In the period between these two works, the novel attained a degree of stylistic stability that made possible the perfection of the genre in that time.

Uniform style novels may result from the operation of some formal principle such as first-person narration, the assimilation of the three component genres of fiction, or the exclusive dependence upon one. Uniform style in a novel generally depends upon the writer's settled conviction of the single, unambiguous nature of his materials and of the novel's adequacy as a vehicle for their serious presentment. In so far as style is a means of shutting out many possible views on a subject and directing attention to a few selected views, a uniform style has the effect of better narrowing the scope to a single, unified view of reality. A uniform style is assimilative in that it helps to create under a single aspect of language a single vision of the multiplicity of reality; it is a bond between author and reader, insuring that no different adjustment to language and viewpoint will be demanded from the reader than that established at the outset. In the nineteenth century it was confidently expected—and sometimes rigorously demanded as in the case of Melville and James—that every work of a novelist be in the same style as his first success. Our contemporary taste is just the reverse: it finds fault with a writer like Hemingway because his style repeats itself from one work to another, while nothing now creates more respect and attention than a change of style, as was evidenced in the recent stir in critical circles over Cozzens' *By Love Possessed.*

A mixed style novel may proceed from the variety that can be gained from exploiting the different potentials of the three genres composing the novel. It is the ideal vehicle for the writer who is motivated by the spirit of irony and parody and who finds it impossible to remain committed to a single vision of reality. A mixture of styles has the effect of making the reader pass through a succession of contradictory and ambiguous attitudes; it offers no sure stylistic norm by which the reader may orient himself permanently to the fiction and to the point of view of the author. He is conditioned to expect to change his position of witness as the style changes. Instead of being assimilative, the mixed style method is mimetic, or imitative of the inherent qualities of things and of the diverse attitudes with which reality may be viewed.

※※※※

Lutwack's classification of prose styles and their effects not only provides a useful descriptive approach to the novel but supports Raleigh's contention that nineteenth-century novelists had a clear and stable world-view and, in the discussion of stylistic exceptions to the uniform style, echoes Muir's theory of the "character." Yet it is obvious, however much he resists prescription, that some of Lutwack's terms are normative: "unassimilated genres and the divided mind of the author," "the kind of work that it is so difficult to justify as belonging at all to the genre," "the perfection of the genre." In these judgments and in the view that plain style without ornament is the norm for the novel, Lutwack is allied with Rahv, Harvey, and Ian Watt (*The Rise of the Novel* [1957]). Most of these critics feel that the novel resists categorization, that it is an a-generic form. Others, notably Frye and Scholes and Kellogg, work from the idea of genre, and for them there is no need to justify *Moby Dick* as a novel, since it is rather a combination of romance and anatomy, and there is less a question of unassimilated genre or divided authorial mind than of the effects that can be achieved by an artful mixture of forms.

In the discussion of the nineteenth-century novel's style as a bond between author and reader, Lutwack raises another question that students of the novel should answer in terms of the modern situation. In their books more than in their essays included in this volume, Booth and Harvey seem to regard the audience's attitude as a norm that the novelist, no matter how rhetorical his method, must finally satisfy, while Fiedler seems to think that the novelist must shock the sensibilities of the general public. Steven Marcus feels that the novel's audience is diminishing and assumes that the decline can be halted, while Wain regards it as inevitable and irreversible. These positions, based on deduction or impression, need to be clarified by more exact studies.

For an approach to the problems of style in the novel and for the fullest bibliography on the subject, see Harold C. Martin, ed., *Style in Prose Fiction,* English Institute Essays, 1958.*

---

* New York: Columbia University Press, 1959.

The Novel Again

STEVEN MARCUS

I

Fifteen years ago, in a penetrating essay called "Art and Fortune," Lionel Trilling undertook to discuss the state of the novel. Although he willingly conceded that the novel was, so to speak, the sick man of literature, he nonetheless affirmed his disbelief in the widespread opinion that the novel was either moribund or dead and went on to discuss what he thought to be an important, though disregarded, matter—the place of ideas in the novel. In the course of this essay, Mr. Trilling found occasion to make two predictions. He first asserted that "the novelist of the next decades will not occupy himself with questions of form," explaining himself to mean that "a conscious preoccupation with form at the present time is almost certain to lead the novelist, particularly the young novelist, into limitation." His second prediction, which emerged as a corollary of the first, was that "the novel of the next decades will deal in a very explicit way with ideas." Mr. Trilling had in mind not merely the embodiment of ideas in character and dramatic action, but ideas as themselves, ideas represented in discourse as ideas; and he claimed it was the right and the necessity of the novel to deal with ideas "as directly as it deals with people or terrain or social setting."

Now predictions about the future of art are as a rule so much whistling in the wind. Correct prophecy is likely to be a function of genius, and genius doesn't habitually go with criticism. In any event, the combination when it does appear often proves equivocal. T. S. Eliot's criticism, for example, has a strong predictive strain, but it requires no great effort to discover that in his essays Eliot was largely predicting the poetry he had already written or was about to write. One instance of true prediction comes from Toqueville. Twenty-five years before the event, he foresaw not only what the character of the American poet would be but what his poetry would be like as well. If an ancient doctrine of biology could be revived one might remark that Toqueville had been privileged to examine the homunculus that was to become Walt Whitman. But predictions of this kind occur about as often as works like *Democracy in America.* Toqueville's description of the American poet, moreover, followed directly upon his general theory of American society and was an authentic prediction in the sense that it took the form of an inference: certain conditions having been observed, such and such was most likely to be the outcome. Mr. Trilling's prediction, on the other hand, was more in the way of a prescription, though it did not announce itself as one: given the present state of the novel (and the symptoms were distressing—spasms in the prose, compound fracture of the novelistic will, cirrhosis of the point of view), such and such *had* to happen if the novel were to be restored to health. And like most specifics, Mr. Trilling's contained a considerable dosage of hope.

In one sense at least I find myself in sympathy with Mr. Trilling's argument. If his prediction had been fulfilled the novel today would probably be in a much improved state, and we might all have a more definite sense of where we are and what we are, simply because the novelist would have been telling us—presuming he retained his traditional genius for making order and sense out of chaos and nonsense. In fact, the reverse of what Mr. Trilling envisaged has taken place. With all due respect, with certain exceptions to be noted presently, and without prejudice to whomever it may concern, it may be said that within the last fifteen years the novel almost has achieved that curious condition of fineness which T. S. Eliot once ascribed to the mind of Henry James: not an idea violates it. In the presence of such chastity it may be useful to inquire into what has happened and attempt to determine how whatever it is has come about.

The governing tendency in the novel during the last fifteen or twenty years has, I think, been in the direction of poetry. I do not mean by this that novelistic prose has become increasingly poetic and less able to sustain a narrative with all its freight of events and swiftness of movement—although this is probably true. I mean that the novel today seems more and more to be acquiring the formal characteristics of poetry, that novels are now being written according to what we can describe as a poetic conception both of experience and of the shape which experience must take.

Of course the novel has almost since its beginning employed certain elements or devices that are recognizably poetic in origin and function. It is important to note, however, that such recognition has become an articulate force only during recent years. Today's student of literature, for example, can hardly read *Wuthering Heights* without at some point being made aware that this novel's true affinities are with the Greek drama and Shakespeare, and not, as twenty-five years ago he would have been taught, with the Gothic romance or the Minerva Press thriller. Nor is anything more striking about the current revival of interest in Dickens than the fact that his novels are regularly being discussed as if they were actually poems. When a number of years ago F. R. Leavis undertook to praise Dickens, the highest tribute he could accord was to call him a great poet. And that is indeed true. All the images of fog and confusion in *Bleak House,* the endlessly varied representations of imprisonment in *Little Dorrit,* the continual presence of the river and the dust-heaps in *Our Mutual Friend*—all of these we now understand not only as part of the narrative design of these novels, but as infusing the most casual of details and bringing into confluence the most wayward and disparate events. Criticism today, in other words, regards these novels as utterances of a mind which has been seized by certain large plastic images, just as a poet's mind is thought to be seized. And it considers the dramatic statement of these novels as being made not primarily through the course of narrative or the conflict of characters, but—to use the dismal terminology—through the elaborate, organic development of a thematic structure of images. *Great Expectations* is now discussed as if it belonged to the same genre as *Timon of Athens* or "The Canonization" or "To His Coy Mistress." And today *Paradise Lost* resembles a novel—or what was once thought of as a novel—more than *Hard Times* does.

But most modern novelists are now seen in this light. We read the novels and stories of Melville and Conrad and Hemingway as we have learned to read lyric poems. We naturally read Flaubert in this manner, since Flaubert was the first novelist to write in deliberate approximation of a poetic principle. We even—God help us—read Stendhal and Dostoevsky in this way. We analyze the ideas in Dostoevsky's novels as if they were images; which is to say that we tend to discuss their strictly dramatic function and emphasize their internal coherence, their symmetry, their configurations of resonance. We tend less and less to think of these ideas as having an autonomous existence within the work, or as directing us toward something beyond it, as referring to reality in the way that the ideas in Plato or Hegel or Freud refer to it. At the other end of the spectrum, we find that even Jane Austen, once the most prosaic and genteel of novelists— it used to be said of her in the bad old days that she was a novelist of manners—is now written of as a poet. Much recent criticism of her novels has to do with just such formal considerations of structure and imagery, with their techniques of analogy and complex patterns of irony. It is only a matter of time, I suppose, before "the little bit (two Inches wide) of Ivory," on which she described herself as working "with so fine a Brush, as produces little effect after much labour," will itself be proposed as a metaphysical conceit to be put alongside Donne's "bracelet of bright hair about the bone." The possibilities which will at this point disclose themselves we had better leave unexplored.

Although these poetic elements exist abundantly in the great novels of the past, we cannot disregard the fact that it has not been until recently that they were discovered and placed in the forefront of critical discussion. In fact, both the novel and literary criticism have recently been going through an analogous development, though by way of introduction I am describing changes in our critical attitude toward the novel before turning to changes within the novel itself. This analogy is not surprising since the novel and literary criticism exist in close and reciprocal relation. Historically both forms have been characterized by their discursiveness, their impulse to moralize, and their topicality. And throughout their complex and highly sophisticated development into complex and highly sophisticated kinds of discourse both the novel and literary criticism continued to share an insistent concern with the topical and ephemeral, with the immediate social and cultural situation. The novel customarily dealt with that situation directly, whereas criticism dealt with its refracted appearance through literature—which meant that criticism has taken its direction from the literature of the recent past.

Nevertheless, we should recall that the novel has itself regularly demonstrated its affinities to literary criticism. And as we know, the novel first exercises its imaginative autonomy in connection with a question of literary criticism. *Don Quixote* begins, middles, and ends by asking the primitive, the classical, and the unanswerable critical question: how for good or bad does literature influence our lives? This question, though it is seldom asked so baldly, lurks behind a majority of important critical judgments. It is the only question that can modify, confuse, or overturn "literary" judgments about general considerations and excellences, although it cannot be said simply to take precedence over such judgments. And if we can consider that the modern novel finds a beginning in this question, then it might also be seen bringing itself almost to the end over this same question. It is at the bottom of an incessant debate in Joyce's writings. I refer not only to the theoretical discussions of literature in *Portrait of the Artist as a Young Man* and *Ulysses* and to the fact that Stephen and Bloom embody different answers to the question, but to the style of *Ulysses,* which in part represents a heroic effort to transcend that question. The virtual hero of *Ulysses* is its style, and by attempting to equate moral heroism with the heroism of literary style, Joyce attempted to put the question I have been referring to aside once and for all, to make it irrelevant. *Ulysses* does not, however, entirely achieve this. *Finnegans Wake* appears to, on the other hand; and it may be that, apart from its intrinsic difficulties, readers continue to be puzzled and disturbed by *Finnegans Wake* because it is the first important work of fiction to which the old, primitive question really seems irrelevant.

One might supply a variety of explanations for these changes in the way we have come to regard the novel. And we could demonstrate in detail how they coordinate with recent developments in the novel itself. For the present, however, I should like to look at two questions. First, the historical identity of the novel continues to change in time. As the great novels of the nineteenth century recede from us—and every circumstance of modern society conspires in accelerating that recession—their character inevitably is modified. What were once burning questions of dispute in the novel no longer possess what can be called an extra-novelistic dimension. The ideas of Rousseau as they are dramatized in Stendhal, the problem of the Napoleonic will corrupted by the social values it originally set out to overthrow—the very substance of Balzac's fiction—these can no longer appeal with anything like the directness or relevance they could still command even twenty-five years ago either to the personal interests of readers or to their larger social interests. The passion against social injustice which illuminates Dickens's novels, and which for a hundred years made them an actual force for good in the civilized world, is bound to leave readers less moved as the particular institutions and abuses which he satirized disappear or change or grow more remote. It is even a question, at least for certain groups within our society, whether the passion against injustice is not itself an emotion that has become anachronistic, that belongs to the unenlightened past—and to backward nations like the Soviet Union, for example! Again, for more than two hundred years the English novel may be understood as chafing under a single preoccupation: what it means to be a gentleman. No social, moral, personal, sexual, or political issue was irrelevant to this question or could not be brought into focus by it. Indeed it would not be excessive to suggest that the gentleman is the totemic figure that presides over the major phase of the English novel. In America, the idea of the gentleman could never, naturally, command such monolithic powers of organization; but until recently, I should say, there was still sufficient class feeling, and, perhaps more important, sufficient class memory, to make it possible to discuss this figure without undertaking the work of historical translation—of finding analogies to the past in the present— which now seems necessary. Even in England the question has become musty and remote, at least to the more interesting current novelists. Nevertheless, if the gentleman has at length paid his final tribute to nature, we may trust that—like the late Elia—he will continue his remarkable communications from the far side of the grave. The humor of the thing would be missed.

Similarly, the ideological life of the nineteenth century was dominated by the French Revolution. Under the irresistible power of this cataclysm—it was as Matthew Arnold simply put it, the greatest, the most animating event in human history—the nineteenth century novel was wrought into its distinctive shape and developed its distinctive subject. That subject was the relation of individual persons to authority, to established social and personal power—the subject, one might say, of the French Revolution itself. And the attitude of the great nineteenth century novelists toward this question, and toward the society at which it was pointedly directed, seems in most important respects an attitude favorable to the creation of a high art. It was an attitude of passionate ambivalence and contradiction. In Jane Austen and Dostoevsky, in Stendhal and Dickens, in Flaubert and Henry James, the depth to which society is criticized, hated, regarded with derision and disgust, and judged as unworthy to survive is consistently responded to by a desperate affection, a nostalgia for old, passing values, and an often touching weak willingness to compound with the existing world and all its rotten glories. The continuity of the first part of the twentieth century with the nineteenth is evident when we reflect that the attitude of modern writers toward the two great events of the first part of the present era, the first World War and the Russian Revolution, is of a similar ambivalence. Such an attitude seems no longer possible, although we cannot with any certainty attribute this either to the "betrayal" of the Russian Revolution— after all, half the significance of the French Revolution had to do with its "betrayal"—or to the nature of the second World War. Nevertheless, that an interruption in the continuity of attitude has occurred seems unmistakable.

It would be mistaken, however, to consider this inevitable change in the historical character of the nineteenth and early twentieth century novel as pure loss. The wars of the Guelphs and Ghibellines and of the Houses of Lancaster and York are lost to us forever, insofar as any immediacy of interest is concerned. And although one dare not anticipate the day when the arguments in *The Possessed* or the episode of "The Grand Inquisitor" will seem no different in kind from the arguments in *The Republic* or in *Gargantua and Pantagruel,* this too is certain to happen. For some writers, the change will pretty surely lead to redemption. Kipling is a case in point. For some thirty years Kipling has been, from the point of view of a balanced critical appraisal, next to inaccessible. Even the best essays on his writing—those by Edmund Wilson and George Orwell— reveal embarrassment in the very act of praise. Some day, however, Kipling's imperialism will have little more bearing on the reader's feeling for him than Virgil's imperialism has on our attitude toward *The Aeneid,* and readers will take Kipling's intermittent racist beliefs in stride, as they take Balzac's royalism or Dostoevsky's pan-Slavism. At that distant date, when current doctrines and passions will have receded into history, Kipling's writings might re-emerge, though their lineaments and proportions will be different from what they seem today. And although it is safer to reserve judgment, one may speculate that *Kim* and *Stalky & Co.* and *The Jungle Books* will then be recognized as minor classics of the language. They will, as we say, receive due recognition as works of art.

Clearly such an affirmation runs the risk of seeming to look down on things from Mount Olympus, when in fact we are peering up at them from the moral sewer that goes by the name of modern civilization. Detachment so-called is a critical virtue and necessity, but there is a point at which even detachment attaches. Detached as he may be, the critic lives in his own time. He is free to deplore and denounce it, but as a critic he is not free to renounce it or to assert that its clamors and confusions—unlike the golden clamors of Periclean Greece or the tapestried confusions of Renaissance Italy—are a mere passing show. He is not free to pontificate against his age by claiming for another age, past or future, a superior degree of reality. This is especially true for the critic of the novel, who must faithfully remind himself that of all the sovereign forms of art, the novel has been the least "artistic," the most dependent upon its extra-artistic powers of immediacy, involvement, and appeal. In one sense the novel may be described as a representation of life in which the loose ends regularly fail to get tied up. This crude co-extensiveness with experience is in fact a traditional point of pride for the novelist; it was a point of pride even for Henry James. In its changing historical identity, then, the novel can often be seen to gain as a work of art to the extent that it loses its connection with immediate and topical experience. And though a similar process takes place in all art and all forms of literature, the novel probably loses most by it. It loses most by virtue of its origins, its historical development and form, and by virtue of its relation to its audience.

My second point concerns what I have represented as the new conventions under which both the great novels of the past and current fiction have come to be read. Briefly we can observe that the last decade and a half has witnessed the complete and final domestication of what was once called the New Criticism. The techniques of close reading and analysis of poetic texts originally developed from a two fold interest—an interest in reclaiming for the present an important tradition of English poetry that had lapsed, and an interest in the new modern poetry which had itself established the first references to that tradition. The New Criticism dramatically altered the nature of reading and the nature of teaching literature in England and America. It created a revolution and has had to suffer a successful revolution's fate—institutionalization, assimilation to older, antithetical habits of thinking, and general dilution of potency. And no critic in his senses, I think, will deny that our university departments of literature, and even the tone of intellectual life in our universities,

have not been improved by it.[1] That the New Critical devices have
been directed to the novel recently should be obvious. Such a development was to be expected, as was the fact that in the hands of the
New Criticism's epigones—the new technicians, we may call them—
the modern novel, in all its fearful symmetry, should seem to have
had its fangs drawn and become just another academic tabby cat.
Still what has occurred during the last decade and a half would
scarcely appear so plain and intelligible, I think, had not the novel
developed its own refinements and restrictions.

II

If we examine the novels of interest written both in England and
America during the past fifteen years or so, certain diagnostic features
seem evident. Beginning with what may appear trivial, we can
observe that the length of the novel seems to have contracted. There
are, naturally, any number of exceptions, but until rather recently,
the usual optimum length of a novel was somewhere in the vicinity
of three hundred pages. Today that limit is closer to two hundred
pages. Such a reduction in size does not necessarily imply a diminution in intrinsic content; it does indicate, I think, a systematic win-
nowing out of related but extraneous matter, a disciplined effort of
compression, and an almost exclusive direction of skill toward the
dramatic rendering of theme through form. In the writing of William
Golding, the most interesting imaginative novelist to have appeared
in England during the last decade and a half, this development is
strikingly represented.

It hardly seems an accident that Golding began his career as
a poet; his first published work was a volume of verse. His novels
all develop what for want of a better description we may call the
structure of fantasy. They are suspended with considerable uncertainty in space and time; they are all in one way or another parables
or fables; and they have become progressively internal and lyrical.
Golding's prose is strenuous, compact, angular, extremely oblique
and elliptical. It is not to be mistaken for the sort of thing we are

---

[1] As for the older, historical scholarship, as it continues to become increasingly rare its virtues will continue to appear increasingly substantial. Its arrogant
disrespect for intellect, its stubborn and gratuitous overvaluation of fact, will
seem in comparison with what is replacing them to have had at least a semblance
of authentic masculine stupidity—and authority as well, authority having traditionally availed itself of the privilege of mindlessness.

familiar with in Virginia Woolf, however, or in Henry Green. These two writers are instances of highly "poeticized" novelistic sensibilities. The distinctive character of their work is that of a single, acutely responsive sensibility operating as a medium in which accidentally related events are registered. In this regard, however, Henry Green's writing apparently suffers from a divided intention; it is often doubtful whether he is trying to achieve the purely fortuitous or the merely inchoate. Some of his novels have either no shape or a purely accidental one; they are typically inconsequent, and sometimes have no discernible beginning, middle, or end. When Green does manage to impose a form on his material, as in *Nothing,* the upshot is likely to be a joke or burlesque of form itself, or as in *Back,* either arbitrary or destructive of what preceded it. But despite his efforts to achieve brilliance and vividness of registration, to liberate the novel from the drudgery of its own conventions, Green's writing still belongs to the older tradition; it represents the traditional novelistic sensibility in an extreme phase of disintegration.

Golding's novels share few of these qualities. They are rigorously organized and heavily controlled: they vex the reader with little that is gratuitous. Whatever freedom or spontaneity may be discovered in them resembles the freedom we find in a dramatic poem—it is the result of a deftly executed conception, refers dialectically to that conception, and if it is successful ultimately subserves and enriches it. In Golding's novels there is scarcely a local touch or detail of prose which does not perform humble service toward this proud and absolute end. When Coleridge objected to Wordsworth's "matter-of-factness" and "accidentality" as contravening the essence of poetry, he implied that these were the qualities of a writer of prose, a biographer or novelist. Golding's novels escape these strictures: so that makes him more of a poet than Wordsworth, though less of a novelist. Such are the uses of critical theory, and the usages of history.

Golding's first novel, *Lord of the Flies,* is set on an imaginary island in the South Seas at some unspecified time in the future; an atomic war has begun and the inhabitants of the island consist solely of boys who have been evacuated from England—their plane, we gather, had crash-landed, killing only the crew. The action of the novel concerns the way in which the boys go about arranging their island life together; it describes in vivid, poignant detail how the conventions, restraints, and taboos of civilized society are gradually sloughed off. That the boys have just been saved from a world destroying itself is a choice ironic background—and has the effect of a silent, invisible Chorus of Furies. Inexorably the boys revert to primitive habits of thought and belief, and to primitive, savage customs, though there is no external necessity for their doing so. In this connection it may be remarked that Golding is perhaps the first English novelist to use with entire naturalness the findings and doctrines of modern anthropology and psychoanalysis; they have been thoroughly assimilated to his vision of experience. They function, however, in poetic terms and not as ideas in the explicit sense referred to at the beginning of this discussion; there seems no compelling reason why they should.

At the end of *Lord of the Flies,* and after a number of dreadful things have happened, the boys are rescued. The naval officer who has arrived to take them off the island quickly grasps the situation and, in a grave state of shock, mutters, "I should have thought that a pack of British boys—you're all British aren't you?—would have been able to put up a better show than that—I mean—" and he trails off into inarticulateness. The extreme irony of this last page shifts the focus of the novel and reminds us that the narrative has been developing along several related lines of meaning. The conclusions of Golding's novels, in fact, like the conclusions of many poems, turn our attention back upon the work that has just been completed and present us with still another means of contemplating it. Yet *Lord of the Flies* is Golding's most "novelistic" work of fiction. It is also the only recent novel of imaginative originality that I am aware of which implies that society, insane and self-destroying as it undeniably is, is necessary. Despite its striking freshness and serious-ness, however, Golding's notion of society, in this novel and in his others, is rudimentary, restricted, and strangely abstract. In Golding's novels society as we know it is largely an idea, a confused memory recollected in the midst of catastrophe; while the pre-social and the post-social have become the paramount actualities.

From the post-historic future of *Lord of the Flies,* Golding turned to the pre-historic past, and his second novel, *The Inheritors,* is about a family of pre-historic creatures. The conception is daring, since it could so easily lapse into the ludicrous or maudlin. (Consider what it would be like were the last book of *Gulliver's Travels* written from the point of view of one of the Yahoos. On second thought, consider the same from the point of view of a Houyhnhnm). It is a measure of Golding's artistic sincerity and his virtuoso talents that he makes this story credible and touching. His ancient group of "people," as they call themselves, are food-gatherers, have only the rudiments of a language—though they seem to possess a kind of group consciousness—have only fragmentary powers of memory, and are unaggressive, affectionate, and innocent in the radical sense. They are brought into contact with another group of creatures who are equipped with a primitive technology, weapons, art, and even liquor, and who thereupon proceed to exterminate the brutes. Prepared as we are, it still gives us a jolt to realize that the pre-human creatures are being exterminated by the "Inheritors," who are our ancestors and ourselves, human beings.

Golding's third novel, *The Two Deaths of Christopher Martin* (published in England as *Pincher Martin*) moves still further in this a-historical, a-temporal direction. It is about a man thrown off a torpedoed destroyer into the North Atlantic and then cast up on a single, bare rock in the midst of the ocean, where he is slowly driven by exposure and illness into delirium and insanity. In the course of his disintegration, fragments of his past heave themselves up into consciousness, and though we are given no sense of the chronological shape of his life, certain images and symbols which recur obsessively in his recollections reveal a familiar kind of unpleasant character. Eventually he seems to be swept off the rock by a storm and is presumably drowned. The final chapter of the story, however, throws everything into reverse again. Martin's body is swept on shore, and we learn that he is still wearing the seaboots which we had been led to believe he took off shortly after he was first thrown into the sea. It suddenly appears that the entire novel takes place in the mind of a drowning man, and that this elaborate story of survival, retrospection, and madness, which covers about two hundred pages, occupies the interval of time between his first sensations of drowning on page one and his last twitch of delirious memory or sensation—whatever brief interval of time that may be.

Impressive as it is, *The Two Deaths of Christopher Martin* seems less successful than Golding's first two novels. And though it is altogether clear that the ending is no mere trick, there is perhaps something of the grand trick in it. It suggests an excessive reliance on technique or form, as if either of them could finally do the work of the intelligence. It reminds one of how in an earlier phase of the novel's history, Conrad or Ford, when they needed to extricate themselves from some difficulty of moral judgment, occasionally resorted to a clever manipulation of point of view. But it reminds one even more of how poets sometimes try to resolve what they have set in motion by introducing at the end of their poems a new consideration which turns the poem upside down, or ask some question which casts the whole enterprise into doubt or ambiguity.

Golding's fourth and most recent novel, *Free Fall*, strikes off on a new course. Though still exploiting virtuoso devices for the direct presentation of experience, for bringing conscious and unconscious processes simultaneously before the reader, and for rendering past and present as co-existent, it attempts to deal with the life history of a single man, an artist named Samuel Mountjoy. The representation of a complex, continuously developing person, however, turns out to be a labor that Golding is unequal to. He fails because his imagination seems unable to encompass society as we know it now and because those parts of experience which we think of as developing or developmental are almost impossible to deal with apart from the experience of society. In a sense they *are* our experience of society. Thus, although the theme of *Free Fall* is development, its style is essentially discontinuous, and the discrete episodes of which it is made float about in interstellar darkness. It is as if Wordsworth had tried to write *The Prelude* in the style of Blake's prophetic books, or Dickens had tried to write *David Copperfield* in the style of *Watt*. Nevertheless, Golding's failure in this novel is no discredit, for he was aspiring to a difficult achievement: to create for the present post-modern era a work which would also satisfy the traditional novelistic purpose. That failure suggests again, however, the rather narrow limits of his range.

Before turning to the American scene, I should mention Muriel Spark, whose elegantly compact and highly wrought fantasies—such as *Momento Mori, The Ballad of Peckham Rye,* and *The Go-Away Bird*—are examples of this development, though they are much more modest and altogether less serious works than Golding's. It has been said in praise of her fictions, by the way, that they curiously resemble metaphysical religious poems. It may be replied that if John Donne's poems were praised as curiously resembling modern novels, one might not be so prepared to accept this as a good thing, either for John Donne, poetry, or the modern novel. Nevertheless, if for purposes of contrast we consult the work of Kingsley Amis or Angus Wilson, two novelists whose allegiances go to the older fictional idea, our sense of the precariousness of the current situation is renewed.

In America the same tendencies exist, and one can find no better instance of them than the writings of Bernard Malamud. Malamud's first novel, *The Natural,* is nominally about baseball, but it has about the same relation to *You Know Me Al* as *Lord of the Flies* does to *A High Wind in Jamaica.* In this first novel, baseball, as one might expect, is represented as a legendary kind of behavior. Moreover, *The Natural* is written with reference to the myth of the Holy Grail, and in particular out of an elaborate system of references to Jesse Weston's *From Ritual to Romance* and, secondarily, to *The Waste Land.* Although this sounds as if *The Natural* were cooked up in the literary pot, it must be added that the allusions are in no way obtrusive and that the novel reads freshly and directly, though something at its center remains obscurely unrealized.

Malamud's second novel, *The Assistant,* is equally representative even though it takes place in a grocery store in Brooklyn during the depression. These tough sociological facts, however, are handled with utmost delicacy and circumspection by the author, as if they were marked "fragile." And as an expert on the matter once observed, the Jews who people Malamud's fiction bear a very special and indirect relation to the actual historical Jewish character. Malamud abstracts them from their historical circumstances and treats them poetically and mythically. The theme of *The Assistant* is equally mythical and is in fact the theme of all Malamud's novels to date. These novels are about the experience of re-birth; in each of them a prematurely oldish young man, whose earlier life is cloaked in darkness, but has included a dismal or tragic experience of failure, is given a second chance to make something of his life and redeem his disreputable past. In this connection the analogy between Golding's writing and Malamud's takes an odd dialectical turn. Golding's novels all deal with experiences of regression, disintegration, and death, and are violent fantasies of an unregenerate world, whereas the imaginative impulse behind Malamud's writing has attached itself to the idea of redemption and resurrection through suffering. Consider: in the year 1961 a former Oxonian, officer in the Royal Navy, and school-master, whose main interest outside of writing is sailing, writes novels under the influence of *Totem and Taboo* and *Civilization and Its Discontents;* while a New York Jew discovers *Pilgrim's Progress* in a grocery store, creates Jews who are dead-ringers for Christian saints, and finds the Chapel Perilous in Ebbetts Field. The wonders of nature never cease.

Like Golding's *Free Fall,* Malamud's recently published third novel attempts to deal with areas of experience that his earlier writing avoided. In *A New Life* Malamud has undertaken to represent the life of a provincial college community and to record its qualities of absurdity and unreality. But he has done so almost solely by attempting to register its banal actualities rather flatly most of the time, without transfiguring them in his magical distorting-mirror. Now the life of academic society is beyond doubt fantastic, and it is true that the fantasy, the wildness, the astounding irreality of it spring out of the multitude of dreary and humdrum details and duties that constitute its daily existence: the nightmare of academic life is inseparable from its terrible ordinariness. In the past this fantasia of the prosaic—society itself—was the meat and drink of novelists. But in Malamud it seems precisely the commonplace, daily reality that is elusive; his highly developed and specialized gift seems as yet unable to reproduce the reality out of which the fantastic takes shape, although it is almost always able brilliantly to do the reverse—that is, to render the fantasy in which the reality takes shape. No novel by Malamud could be without its serious interest, but the parts of *A New Life* that are most impressive, most "real," are the more private, claustral, and interior relations.

Malamud's first two novels were short and compact, and it is no coincidence that some of his best writing has been done in the medium of the short story. His justly celebrated "The Magic Barrel" is a kind of lyric poem in prose—by which I do not mean that it is any less a work of fiction, any less a story. If we compare Malamud's stories to Joyce's, the distinction I wish to make is at once clear. The stories of *Dubliners* are often spoken of as being constructed on formally poetic principles, and Joyce's notion of the epiphany is properly enlisted in support of this interpretation. Yet the prose of *Dubliners* somehow resists that idea. In its harshness, its flatness, its general, deliberate tonelessness, it imposes itself on the reader with impersonal masculine force, calling attention to itself as prose and nothing more, and identifying itself with the naturalistic tradition. Joyce himself called it "a style of scrupulous meanness." Moreover, the great poetic leaps and illuminations in certain of these stories are to a considerable degree validated by the aggressive, unpoetical insistence of their prose. Similar observations might be made about the writing of Kafka. In Malamud's stories on the other hand, the prose, though spare, is spare in a lyrical way, gracefully compact of metaphor, and of a piece with the poetic intention of their author's idea.

Another instance of this development in America can be found in the writing of Flannery O'Connor. In theme, style, and structure, Miss O'Connor's fantastic accounts of primitive religion and violence in the South seem to belong to this tendency in fiction.

Let me state at this point that these observations make no pretense to inclusiveness; any number of important writers cannot be accounted for or understood by the general argument they advance. Saul Bellow, for example, a writer whose gift is as considerable as his range, is among the few novelists today who are masters of several imaginative styles. Yet Bellow's finest piece of writing, the work in which his remarkable talents are most fully realized, is one which most resembles the kind of fiction I have been discussing. His superb short novel, *Seize the Day*, may in the present context be taken as an exception which proves the miserable rule.

III

That this development is not altogether new but has its roots in the tradition of the novel should be sufficiently clear. Nevertheless, this kind of fiction has never before occupied so prominent a part of the field nor claimed so large a proportion of the better writers. The novelists whom I have mentioned are writers of vitality and intelligence, and I do not want to disparage their achievement or discredit anyone's admiration of it. And yet it must be recognized, I think, that they are writing in what can only be judged as a minor mode. The very qualities of exquisiteness, restraint, and propriety of form which distinguish their writing from that of other and lesser figures also serve to set them off from what has been the major tradition of the novel. If the type of fiction I have been describing were currently competing with other types, either traditional or equally innovating, which gave evidence of similar vitality, then the situation would be quite different.

But what is apparent is that a break in the tradition of the novel seems to be taking place. Opinions will of course differ over the date at which the break begins and over the reasons for its continuance, but at this late hour few will question the fact that an interruption has occurred. It may even have persisted long enough to have affected the novel's audience and to have brought about a change in what can be thought of as the sociology of novel-reading— at least in America, which does not have the English advantage of a firm tradition of intelligent but second-rate fiction.

In this connection, I should like to speak from personal experience, for I first became aware of what seemed to me a change in the ranks of novel-readers in the course of my duties as a teacher. In my classes during the last few years I have noticed that when I chose to illustrate a point by comparing or contrasting it to something in a modern novel, I met a curious response. It is nearer the truth to say that I met no response, and that my students of recent years, unlike their predecessors, have been unfamiliar with the general range and canon of the modern novel. Since I like to think of myself as a conscientious teacher—which means, I suppose, that I become nervous when students seem to respond in new and mysterious ways—I instituted an unsystematic inquiry into the matter. What I learned was that my students—almost all of them seniors planning careers having something to do with literature—no longer read novels as a matter of course. The novels they do read are by and large either assigned reading for classes in English literature or collateral reading for some other field of study, such as history and sociology. (I might add that a similar poll among graduate students at the School of Letters in Indiana University yielded similar results. And many colleagues have had the same experience with their students.)

If this were to represent anything of a general tendency, and if it were to persist, then it is possible that we will have reached a new stage in the novel's long crisis. For more than one hundred and fifty years the novel has been the natural mode of reading in our culture. And though there has been intermittent talk of the novel's decline—and with increased frequency over the past forty-odd years—such talk has never been known to interrupt the widespread habit of reading novels. I say habit, but I really think it more accurate to say that our culture was addicted to the reading of novels. The causes of addiction naturally varied. There was, for example, the old, unmodern passion, as we find it represented in Colonel Newcome, who invariably took *The Spectator, Don Quixote,* and *Sir Charles Grandison* on his travels because, as he said, he liked to be in the company of gentlemen. A more advanced phase of addiction is confessed by Henry Tilney in *Northanger Abbey,* who excuses away his illicit passion by describing novels as works "in which the greatest powers of the mind are displayed, in which the most thorough knowledge of human nature, the happiest delineation of its varieties, the liveliest effusions of wit and humor are conveyed to the world in the best chosen language." Which of us has not mouthed a similar piety and then turned to read some piece of fictional trash with shameless and undiscriminating appetite? But of course such ritual perversity is possible only if the novel is a going thing, only if the conventions which inform popular and vulgar fiction maintain a vital connection with that fiction which is art.

Then the novel was read as much for its quality of truth as for its quantity of fantasy—truth being, as Jane Austen once observed, very excusable in an Historian. The novelist was looked to as historian, biographer, and sociologist: he was an explorer in the *terra incognita* of modern society. And his fantastic reports on life among the cannibals—whether these were the very rich or the very poor, the criminal or the insane, the blessed or the damned, the physically beautiful or the spiritually lame, halt, and blind—these reports were read with what amounted to infant credulity. For the novelist's fantasy of truth corresponded to the reader's fantasy of vicarious liberation. When Flaubert said, *"Madame Bovary, c'est moi,"* he affirmed not only an essential condition of the novelist's relation to his work, but one of the reader's relation to the novel as well. Finally, the novel was read for the largest moral and spiritual reasons. Lawrence once said that he wrote because he wanted "folk—English folk—to alter, and have more sense." And many folk read the novel in order to alter their lives. This is the most modern of demands made upon the novel—a demand for nothing less than salvation. And as such it is no less excessive and impossible than the demand made during the nineteenth century that the novel include within its purpose the reformation of society. Absurd and excessive as they are, these demands at least recognized the fact that we and our civilization unquestionably need saving. And so long as the novel was able to embody such demands, to envisage a life beyond our present condition of mortal terror and blank dismay—even to the extremity of an apocalypse, if there was hope of being purified in the destruction—so long could it be assured of its own perpetuation and its readers' fanatic loyalty.

This seems not to have happened, as we all know. If it is true that even the habit of novel-reading is becoming attenuated, then it may be inferred that this is a response to what the novel has not been able to do. For readers today to maintain a living connection with Proust and Gide and Mann and Joyce and Fitzgerald, with all the figures who fifteen or twenty years ago were still current in their own right, there will have to be more novelists who are capable of keeping that connection alive. I do not mean novelists who write like Lawrence or Kafka or Joyce, or write novels like theirs; the kind of novelist I have in mind would in some sense reject the great moderns, just as the great moderns rejected their nineteenth century predecessors. The paradox that only through the opposition of generations can civilization advance seems to hold true for its art, its literature—in the modern world, at least, continuity with the past is maintained only through the continual rejection of it. "Drive your cart and your plow over the bones of the dead," writes Blake, and then "The road of excess leads to the palace of wisdom"—and we believe it. There is, in other words, no short cut to beatitude; before the past can be reclaimed it must be repudiated. Whatever may prevent this process from taking place—whether it be the scarcity of genius or some convergence of historical or cultural events or all of these—the failure of creative repudiation entails the failure of continuity. The present condition of the novel, I believe, can be roughly described in these terms. Continuity may have been broken— at the very least it appears to be seriously damaged—and it is impossible to foresee how or when a connection will resume. One thing that seems clear is that the novel has nearly ceased to give us what we need: an adequate notion of what it is like to be alive today, why we are the way we are, and what might be done to remedy our bad situation.

What has prevented the novel from doing this is a perplexing question: the causes are obscure and for that very reason it is tempting to speculate upon them. But my speculations will have to be unargued, perfunctory, and merely suggestive.

There are, to my knowledge, two major explanations of the novel's deteriorating state. The first was proposed almost forty years ago by Ortega y Gasset, and states that with the great nineteenth and early twentieth century figures the novel fulfilled itself and was thus exhausted of further possibilities. To offer up the novel as dead of its own success is an elegant plausibility—like having your baked funeral meats and eating them too. The second explanation has been cogently set forth by Mary McCarthy in a recent essay called "The Fact in Fiction." This argument maintains that the reality of contemporary experience is so monstrous and aberrant, and so annihilates the merely human, that the novel has no way of reducing or accommodating it to a comprehensible vision of life. There is much to be said for this view, including the curious irony that a century ago

Balzac used similar language to argue an opposite case. Prose, Balzac wrote, "has no other resource than the actual." But in the modern world, he continued, "the actual is so terrible that in itself it is able to wrestle with the sublimity of poetry." Such a paradox makes comment not only on changes in actuality but on changes in attitudes toward that actuality.

Both these theories carry a large share of truth, I think, but no single explanation of a historical process so complex can achieve a persuasiveness commensurate to our sense of that complexity. Without wishing to oppose or dismiss either theory I should like to put them aside now and address the problem from another perspective.

Novels are not written out of thin air, and novelists, unlike God, do not generate their ideas *ex nihilo*. If we complain that novels fail to provide an adequate description and interpretation of contemporary experience, or that they have ceased to deal with ideas, we must also admit that they are not alone in their barren and unfed condition but reflect the general state of intellectual culture in our time. But so does the fact that we must remind ourselves of such time-worn truths as Matthew Arnold's notion that the precondition for a vivid and healthy culture and a morally significant literature is a strong and continuous exercise of the critical intellect—and it should be remembered that Arnold did not exclude general criticism of society from the intention of criticism. Some years ago Randall Jarrell wrote that we live in an age of criticism, but he wrote wryly and meant literary criticism, an enterprise which may be said to have prospered through lack of competition. In addition, the dominant form which literary criticism chose for itself in recent years was distrustful of ideas or interests which might be though of as "extrinsic" to the work under scrutiny. As for a coherent body of serious and significant critical thinking about modern culture, the closer one looks the less one finds. And as in the case of the novel, we cannot regard this situation from fancy moral postures, as if it were a simple failure of nerve or will, or a sudden depravity of intelligence, such as capitulation to the favors of an affluent society: it is a general condition we are faced with.[2]

A good example of this state of affairs is the most widely read

---

[2] The reader will note that the argument in the last part of this essay is phrased in terms which refer more immediately to the situation in America than in England. It is probably not so different, although the vigorous assertion of difference which is general in England today must be taken into account.

work of sociology written during the past fifteen years, David Riesman's *The Lonely Crowd*. As far as criticism goes, one might say of
this highly original and intelligent study that the most critical thing
about it is its title. At some point during its preparation a decision was
reached which seems to sum up the tone of the following years. For
alongside the impressive description and analysis of the two basic
types of modern character, the inner-directed and the other-directed,
there ran an elaborate refusal to judge between the two. There were
certainly all kinds of useful reasons to be advanced for this decision,
but the net effect of it, I think, was to deny the evidence of the
senses and the intellect. The escape hatch was found, as it so often is,
in a third term, "autonomy," and in the idea of an autonomous man.
This distinguished personage was a synthetic creation transcending
both types, was projected as a hopeful vision of the future, and was
in short a bit incredible, less an ideal than a myth. One might do
better by betting blindly at a horse race—the horses at least exist.
But such are the consequences of suspending critical judgment, for
whatever reasons and in whatever cause.

But lest we be misguided into supposing that in such times as
these the simple and stalwart determination to be critical will inspire
the triumph of intelligence, we might remind ourselves of such a book
as Norman O. Brown's *Life Against Death*. Coming a decade after
The Lonely Crowd and being actuated by very different impulses,
it expresses all the bitter, negative and apocalyptic wisdom of the
era, just as ten years before Mr. Riesman's work had revealed the
disposition toward compromise, reconciliation, and justification in
relation to society which intellectuals at that moment wanted to
affirm. And again, after a brilliant and moving analysis of the
manifold afflictions which characterize the malady we call modern
society, Mr. Brown, like Mr. Riesman before him, makes a leap in
the direction of some fantastic, unrealizable future–though it is to his
credit that he warns us to willingly suspend our common sense.
He looks forward to "the abolition of repression," and to a society
in which there will be a general "resurrection of the body." The new
man who thus walks erect will also simultaneously crawl on all fours,
since he will still inhabit the "polymorphously perverse body of
childhood." This creature is not simply incredible; he is almost un-
thinkable, not to say inconceivable. And yet there is a sad correspondence of opposites between him and Riesman's autonomous man.
Between these two mythical diagrams of the human future—auton-

omous character on the one hand, and resurrection into infantile sexuality on the other—the mind of the age oscillates in bleak and sickened discontent.

I have been implying that recent developments in the novel— the movement toward poetic form, the inability to deal with society, the poverty of ideas—are deeply connected with a general weakening of the critical function in recent years. And although both conditions have extensive histories, both have been exacerbated by the larger circumstance in which all our cultural transactions now take place. I refer, of course, to the Cold War, conceiving it not as a catch-word of journalism but as the new phase of Western culture.

Sooner or later, I suppose, the Cold War is going to be charged with everything, but I trust she will not mind if at this point I attach my small share of blame along with that of others. A Cold War is the continued pursuit of war by other means. Critical thinking, straitened, arduous, and problematical under the best of conditions, becomes under conditions of war, and especially under the autarchy of modern war, that much more so. When a society finds itself in a state of siege, when it discovers itself really threatened for the first time from the outside, it necessarily organizes itself to engage the forces that oppose it. Its intellectual and critical energies are mar- shalled as a matter of course, to the inevitable detriment of the central tradition of criticism. It is a rare society indeed which will in such circumstances continue to support a current of thinking whose historic purpose has been to point out the flaws, inadequacies, and contradictions of that society—and particularly if such criticism appears to coincide with the enemy's accusations. I am not alluding to specific episodes or manifestations but have in mind those massive and insidious pressures, conscious and unconscious, within any society so beset to turn its energies of mind and passion away from examining itself. Even those who argue the necessity of this process should remain aware that certain necessities can prove fatal. That this kind of necessity is fatal to culture is almost certain, culture and art having regularly been the first luxuries to go under conditions of protracted tension and war; that it tends to make the complex, critical attitude of mind seem indecisive, irrelevant, and even traitor- ous is equally undeniable; and that it may be causing grave damage to the spirit of the society ostensibly being protected seems likely.

However we regard the Cold War, there should be little need to buck ourselves up with pride in it. Since the effect of the Cold

War has been to syphon off a considerable amount of critical intelligence for the struggle against Communism and in defense of our own system, then there should be little wonder over the failure of criticism to produce, in Arnold's phrase, "a current of ideas in the highest degree animating and nourishing to the creative power." And there should be equally little wonder over the present state of the novel. American novelists, unfortunately, cannot be expected to write novels which are critical of the Soviet Union. Rastignac looks down on his own Paris—not a foreign capital—and says, "It's war between us now" and then descends to conquer those corrupt splendors which are in turn to destroy him. And the dilemma of *1984* was that it *had* to be about England. For the novelist's quarrel is by its nature with his own society, as is the critic's—and their function, like that of all frustrated lovers, is to prosecute that quarrel. When that quarrel is, for whatever resaon, suspended, diverted, or thwarted, there will inevitably follow, to use the words of a great American critic, the failure of distinction, the failure of style, the failure of knowledge, the failure of thought.

It is certainly true that the current state of the novel and of critical thinking originate in conditions which long antedate the last fifteen or twenty years; the history of their distress is depressingly rich and complex. The Cold War has in all probability served mainly to intensify and accelerate earlier tendencies, a development which might not in any event have been stopped. Nor am I saying that the contemporary situation is monolithic; my effort has been to describe a certain general tone and tendency. Seen from the inside any culture is apt to resemble gang-warfare, and as far as ours is concerned it is becoming apparent that the uneasy truce of the last fifteen years is in the process of suffering minor violations.

At one point, however, the Cold War has acted upon the novel directly. To put it simply, the Cold War is cold, it freezes things up, it fixes them in place. In particular it tends to freeze ideas, and (witness the work of David Riesman and Norman O. Brown) one of the ideas it has stopped dead in its tracks is the idea of the future. Under the conditions of the Cold War we perforce think of the future—our future, that is—as essentially unchanged: barring disaster, we are in for more of the same, which is to say that we cannot think of a future at all. No situation could be more subversive of the novel. Historically the novel came into existence as a major form of expression at the same time that the idea of the future, a different and possible human future, began to be realized. One of the enduring generic images of the novel is that of a young man forging madly ahead, intent upon grasping the newness, the novelty, the novel-ness that lies before him. When Hegel looked out of his window in Jena and saw Napoleon riding by, he thought he beheld the world-spirit on horseback; until recently, most novelists have had the same vision, or believed they did. And though novels end in numberless ways, they have favored one image consistently. How many novels can we recall which end with the hero, his back turned to the reader, walking off into the distance. That distance is of course his future, his unrealized possibilities, and those of the reader and society. No idea has had greater moral power in modern civilization than the idea of the fulfillable, earthly future: and its destructive power has been as wild as its power to create. And no idea has been more substantive to the modern novel. It is a fact which supplies us with one more reason for regarding *Finnegans Wake* with what amounts to the anxiety of premonition. It is the first important work of fiction to expel the future, for it runs in a circle.

Thomas Hardy once confessed to an admirer that it doesn't take very much intelligence to be pessimistic. The temptation to think or write under the assurance of pessimism is at the present moment acute—and is on that account to be resisted. Our embattled society still exists, novelists and critics are alive, and all have their appointed work to do. We live in our own times and cannot foresee the future, though we are all hostages to it. And our best hope of redemption still lies in the degree to which we can commit ourselves to the intelligent assessment of the world we inhabit—whether interested or disinterested. Only then, I think, can we resume working out those lines which will help the future, when it comes, to find its direction. "That promised land it will not be ours to enter, and we shall die in the wilderness: but to have desired to enter it, to have saluted it from afar, is already, perhaps, the best distinction among contemporaries; it will certainly be the best title to esteem with posterity."

❅❆❅❆

In "The Novel Again," Steven Marcus attempts two of the most difficult and most essential functions of a critic: first, to discover what is happening to art both in itself and in its relation to society and, second, to evaluate new artists both in terms of their continuity or discontinuity with tradition and in terms of an a priori critical theory. Neither task is for the cautious; both require a coherent position, wide reading, and the courage to generalize.

Although Marcus' discussion of recent trends in criticism and fiction corresponds in many of its details to the arguments advanced by Mark Schorer and Joseph Frank, his basic critical premise seems to be that the novel is primarily *about* something, that the novelist is valuable primarily for his vision rather than for his art. Marcus' arguments frequently correspond with those of Philip Rahv and W. J. Harvey—not surprisingly, for he worked with Rahv on the *Partisan Review* and, like Harvey, Marcus is influenced by the criticism of Lionel Trilling. Basic to all of these critics is the theory that the novel not only reflects society—both in its observable details and its current of ideas— but can and should serve as an instrument of enlightenment as well as of information, of change, even of salvation; as Marcus writes, the novel should give its readers "an adequate notion of what it is like to be alive today, why we are the way we are, and what might be done to remedy our bad situation." This group of critics exhibits the "novelistic bias" in its extreme form, and it could be argued that their historical and literary perspectives are too limited. (Marcus' remarks on poetry and meaning provide a good illustration). On the other hand, this limitation might be regarded as a strength; Marcus argues that the critic necessarily "lives in his own time" and must partici- pate in it, willingly or not. Like the debate between mimetic and autonomy theories of art, which it overlaps in many instances, this debate about the role and necessary perspective of the critic is not likely to be resolved. In Marcus' terms, it is one of "the primitive, the classical, the unanswerable" critical questions.

than the custom-bound, ritualistic feudal nobility: and from these beginnings, the novel developed as the instrument of a new candor, a new self-awareness, and a new preoccupation with the interest and variety of "average" experience.

An agricultural and feudal society, broken down into semitribal groups isolated from each other by poor communications, offers no encouragement to the novel. Everyday experience is too similar and too predictable; except at the level of the *fabliau,* it cannot hold attention; the mind craves marvels and far-off settings. England evolved from this kind of society into a recognizably modern society during (roughly) the lifetime of Daniel Defoe, who figures so prominently in our history as the first major writer of realistic fiction and also the first reporter to exploit the journalistic possibilities of the printing press (he had a syndicated column, for instance). After that, the novel moved into high gear and then into overdrive. By 1800 it already had a dozen masterpieces to its credit in English alone, and an impressive array of great names scattered over Western Europe. But this was nothing to what was to come. Within the next fifty or sixty years, a series of great writers arose who captured for the novel virtually every strategic point. And in doing so they advanced from the simple claim to realism, verisimilitude and clear-sightedness to the exalted ambition of the middle and late nineteenth century, when the novel, broken free at last from the stigma of being a commonplace and inferior form, took all truth for its province. With Stendhal and Flaubert, with Gogol, Dostoevsky and Tolstoy, with the later Dickens, George Eliot and Henry James, the novel attained something close to a religious prestige. It stood for a degree of awareness and under-standing that could—so it seemed to its awe-struck devotees—raise all human life to a higher level. From about 1860 onward, everyone who wrote seriously about the novel started with the assumption that it stood at the very center of the world. Thus Flaubert wrote to Louise Colet in 1852,

> I have glimpsed sometimes (in my great days of sunlight) the glimmerings of a rapture which sends a shudder over my flesh, from my nails to the roots of my hair, a spiritual state thus far above life in which fame would be nothing and even happiness without point.

And Conrad, in *A Personal Record,* described the writing of *Nostromo* in similar terms:

> All I know is that, for twenty months, neglecting the common joys of life that fall to the lot of the humblest on this earth, I had, like the

prophet of old, "wrestled with the Lord" for my creation, for the head-lands of the coast, for the darkness of the Placid Gulf, the light on the snows, the clouds in the sky, and for the breath of life that had to be blown into the shapes of men and women, of Latin and Saxon, of Jew and Gentile.

No task was too important for the novel to attempt. Its adepts saw it as the one form which, having cast away all binding and hampering conventions, had the freedom and strength to deal illumi-natingly with any subject. Indeed, they now and then spoke as if all other literary forms had been a mistake, or a mere transitional stage in the march toward fulfilment, and could now be scrapped—as when D. H. Lawrence remarked that if *Hamlet* had been a novel there would have been no mystery about why Hamlet behaves as he does.

These claims, extravagant as they occasionally became, were on the whole fairly justified. In the hands of its greatest practitioners, the novel climbed, between about 1850 and 1925, to every one of the highest peaks. It showed itself able to take over the functions of epic poetry, of lyric, of oratory, of drama, of pamphleteering. The part played by the novel in the life of every European nation, and of the United States, during these years is so important that their history is unintelligible without it. And it was not only an exalted but a humbly useful part. It crops up in every department of life. As new knowledge was gathered, and new vistas opened up which demanded new skills and attitudes, the novel, in its simpler forms, was there, ready to provide a channel whereby this new material could enter the popular imagination. As Scott had made the Middle Ages humanly intelligible by providing living and moving images of knight and villein, priest and churl, so the Victorian writer of fiction domesticated new scientific and geographical knowledge by assigning each new discovery a part in the endless succession of simply understood narratives that were read, aloud or silently, by every fireside in the civilized world.

The novel, in short, was important to nineteenth-century society on two levels: in its higher reaches, it sought an ever more precise adjustment to truth, both in the individual and the collective life: at its humbler levels, it acted as a binding agent, diffusing new ideas evenly throughout the mass of society, steadily countering the tendency of minority groups to break away on their own. It simplified the discoveries of the wise so that they could be appreciated by the popular mind: it held up before the comfortable middle class a picture of the sufferings of the poor; it contributed, on every level, to that consciousness of itself, that pride in its own individuality, that characterized the culture of every major nation in those days. And this multiple task was made easier for the novel by its realistic tradition. Novels have always come in many shapes and sizes, but only a very slender minority of them have been anything but realistic—using the word "realism" in its everyday literary sense, to indicate a credible setting in ordinary life, characters drawn from observation, and a general faithfulness to the externals, at any rate, of the familiar world. The novel could make room for thick slabs of detail about such things as railway journeys, business deals or domestic arrangements; unlike poetry and drama, which have to be careful what they eat, it had the digestion of an ostrich. Small wonder that the newspaper office has always been a recognized *carrière ouverte aux talents,* so that scores of major writers from Dickens to Hemingway have graduated from reporter to novelist.

So much for the situation of the novel as it was, during the years when it was unchallenged as the dominant form. If we look at the situation of the novel today, the first thing we notice is a radical loss of confidence. The social tasks which the novelist was once so able and so willing to perform have been split up and distributed among a number of his most powerful rivals—rivals who did not, in those old happy days, exist at all.

As popular entertainer, to begin with, he has been swept aside by radio, cinema and television. Television in particular, in the last ten years, has taken over almost entirely the documentary function that used to belong to popular fiction. Instead of reading novels about hospital life, or conditions among merchant seamen, or the Yukon, people now watch television documentaries about them. And this means that the old dependence on the novel as binding-material for the disparate elements of society has gone also. On that simple level, the anonymous teams who put together radio and television programs have supplanted the individual mind that invented stories. Further, the old relationship between the novel and the newspaper, between the reported "hard" news and the imagined "soft" news, has been thrown out by the complete change in the nature of the newspaper. News-reporting is now only one, and that not the most important, function of the newspaper. Comment and analysis (if the paper is a serious one), or entertainment (if it is aimed at a mass public)—these are now the primary aims. The news itself can be more efficiently supplied by radio.

If anyone doubts that the novel has been forced to abandon its mundane social usefulness, the essential documentation is there in modern science fiction, which purveys an imaginative vision profoundly hostile to art and indeed to anything specifically human. Victorian fiction acclimatized the populace to new knowledge by introducing this knowledge in stories of human interest. Modern science fiction does exactly the opposite. It projects its human characters into a universe which permits of no emotional response, no self-awareness or insight into others, at anything above the novelette level. The characters in a science fiction story cannot engage with emotional and moral problems because their attention is incessantly directed toward phenomena. Wells and Jules Verne placed the human reaction at the center; the conquistadores of *Astounding Science Fiction* place it at the periphery just because their main object is to astound. Theirs is a literature which must abandon once and for all the maxim that "men more often require to be reminded than informed." Its implication is that once humanity has advanced into the future and technology has solved all its problems, nothing as obsolete as emotional or moral problems will remain—a point of view significantly shared by the scientific fraternity, otherwise great readers of whodunits, and journalists with a grudge against literature.

The popular novelist has not disappeared. But he has become one of a crowd. Instead of being welcomed eagerly by a public starved of entertainment, he now fights for his diminishing share of attention in a world glutted with diversions of every kind. This leaves the nonpopular minority, "serious" novelist. Surely his position is unchanged?

In some respects, yes. The more immediate mass forms of entertainment do not rob him of his public as they rob the popular writer. And yet his position, too, is shaky. The mere fact that he is no longer at the apex of an enormous pyramid, no longer the fine blossom that breaks out at the top of a large and solid tree, is already disconcerting to him. Further, he is aware that the challenge to the printed page is being made at all levels: it is not confined to the popular. The novel, as I have said, is a product of the age during which the printing-press was the only means of reaching a large public quickly, and it is perfectly adapted to such an age. Silent and comparatively rapid reading is what the novel, for the most part, requires. The spoken arts of drama and poetry, as long as they depended on the human lungs and the human ear, were necessarily dwarfed by the printed sheet.

But now they have their own technical means of diffusion, and all at once the picture is different. In the race to capture an audience, the novel no longer has a colossal advantage. Everyone starts fair.

The contemporary novelist, then, faces a challenge from the dramatist and even—wonder of wonders!—from the poet. His only possible response is to do what the dramatist did in the face of the advancing cinema, what the poet did as the power of prose writing increased, what the newspaper has done before the challenge of radio and electronics: to redefine his function to decide what he can most profitably attempt. And, as we might expect, there has been no common, unified answer to this question. The novel has splintered so completely that there is no longer any question of picking out a main tradition. In this situation, the novel is rendered vulnerable by the very feature that used to be its strength: its amorphous, Protean nature, its ability to assume any shape. Drama must always consist basically of dialogue, spoken by performers who are deliberately assuming a character other than their own; poetry must always remain a heightened and rhythmic form of language, no matter what startling changes of idiom it may undergo. But the novel, once its documentary underpinning has been kicked away, crumbles into a score of minor forms. Its informative function has gone, and the one feature that sets it apart from journalism or biography—the fact that it offers an account of events that did not in fact take place—it shares with a dozen different forms of drama, human or mechanized. In this chaos, there is no chance for anything like a tradition to develop. If one writer influences another, the transaction takes place in so much a vacuum that it appears as simple imitation.

W. H. Auden's poem "The Novelist" opens with the memorable line "Encased in talent like a uniform." And indeed when one looks at the novelists who are most widely respected in England today, one has a feeling that each one of them is walking about in a perfectly fitting suit of some thick insulating material such as asbestos, within which he has his entire being. English novelists, like English actors, have brought their art to a very high degree of finish and skill; the American novel, by comparison, appears as more energetic but less disciplined and with unrealized possibilities everywhere. It is like comparison with the landscape of the two countries; every inch of England is cultivated and has been for a long time. Mr. Graham Greene, for instance, writes beautifully constructed tales in which he places his characters exactly halfway between two powerful magnets, one religious and the other sexual, and then has them perform a series of gyrations expressive of indecision and anguish—gyrations which, though highly predictable, are fascinating to read about. In everything that concerns style, characterization and setting, Mr. Greene's novels are entirely conventional—only less so than those of Sir Charles Snow, who is quite satisfied to take over, entirely unaltered, the machinery devised by Trollope. Sir Charles's interests are those of a practical man; he is concerned primarily with how the world works and how things get done. Since this kind of preoccupation has not altered very much in the last century, there is no reason why Sir Charles should trouble himself to adapt the Trollopian form; it will do as it stands; Galsworthy in *The Forsyte Saga* found that form perfectly suited to the task of describing the Edwardian social scene and Sir Charles finds it equally suited, for his own special purposes, to the mid-twentieth century. And indeed it may be that this kind of copious realistic novel, generously inventive as to episode and detail but entirely uninventive in regard to everything that concerns the art of the novel, can usefully be written in each generation. But there seems to be no possibility of any give and take between Snow and any other contemporary English novelist; he, like them, is "encased" in his talent; it is perhaps significant that he finds less affinity with anything in contemporary English literature than with the literature of Soviet Russia, which he seems to admire with strikingly few reservations. Again, Mr. Kingsley Amis has made himself into a master of his own kind of social comedy, exploiting to the full both his gift for original comic idiom and his disenchanted sharpness of observation: but there seems to be nothing here that any other novelist can usefully adapt to his own purposes. Amis's style is very easy to imitate, at a certain level, because it is highly idiosyncratic—but this very idiosyncratic quality seems to make it impossible to use as an ingredient. To jump to another extreme, the work of Mr. William Golding, which is quite rightly held in very high regard in England, exists in complete isolation. Mr. Golding is, except in the most loose sense, not a novelist at all; he is a writer on themes ultimately religious, whose work, when it is successful, has the authority of myth. Then again, England, like all countries, has a number of writers who use the novel as a means of presenting a social or political message to a large number of readers, and in particular those in which the writer communicates his vision of the future. Books of this kind, if they are successful at all, tend to have a very wide public—naturally, since everyone is interested in what will happen next. The success of Aldous Huxley's *Brave New World* and Orwell's *1984* has been approached recently by Mr. Constantine Fitz Gibbon's nightmarish novel about the even more immediate future, *When the Kissing Had to Stop*. But this brilliant and important book has curiously little to say for itself as a novel. Incident and character are real enough, but they so obviously exist not for their own sake but as the wrapping for an urgent political message that a certain impatience comes over the reader: the pill is necessary, but we would like to be considered grown-up enough to take it without a spoonful of jam. The same applies to the highly successful documentary novels of Mr. Colin MacInnes, which read like animated versions of his intelligent and observant articles in the weekly and monthly press. Perhaps Miss Iris Murdoch comes nearest to an idiom central enough to be visited, departed from and returned to again, by other writers intent on their own concerns. She writes about emotional and moral problems common to sensitive people in every society, and if she sometimes seems to construct her books rather from the outside, so that the story pivots on rather contrived pieces of symbolism, this is more than compensated for by the sense of a shared experience which she is able to give to her readers. But all in all, the picture is of a parade of individuals, each offering something entirely his own which draws on no central reservoir of strength. And, I must repeat, this has not always been the case.

Twenty years ago there was something approaching a common idiom among young English novelists. Christopher Isherwood's *Mr. Norris Changes Trains* came out in the same year (1935) as George Orwell's *A Clergyman's Daughter* and Graham Greene's *England Made Me;* Anthony Powell's *From a View to a Death* was two years earlier, Evelyn Waugh's *A Handful of Dust* two years later [sic]. Without juggling with dates, and without ironing out the essential differences between these writers, I am trying to suggest that there was a language they all used—each in his individual way, of course—and a situation they all faced. All the books I have just named were, in one way or another, putting the same question: given that we, as Englishmen, live in an old-established, liberal, habit-ridden and prosperous country which is shortly to be attacked by a modern, streamlined, unfree but ruthlessly efficient country, Nazi Germany, is there anything we can do about it? What kind of criticisms can we usefully make, that might help our society to become more workable? What, in any case, is worth trying to save in English life, and what would be better destroyed?

These novels were not, of course, tracts. But I believe that they were all motivated, at the deepest level, by the kind of concern I have indicated. If not, then the deep similarities between them would have to be assigned to mere coincidence, and there are some coincidences so great that they cannot happen. Isherwood set the figure of Arthur Norris, the pathetic old swindler with his toupee and scent, his Edwardian airs, his fundamental dishonesty and self-indulgence that could nevertheless go with an affectionate interest in other human beings, against the ruthlessly emerging and opportunistic Nazi state: a perfect emblem of the democratic countries, surviving by shift and compromise in a world that was increasingly going over to *Realpolitik*. Waugh drew a poignant sketch of the kindly, unambitious country squire, living only to take care of his house, his estate and his tenants, and pass his world on to the next generation with its values intact, being brutally deprived and humiliated by the forces of modern rootless cosmopolitanism. Orwell explored the hell that, in a country as prosperous as England, awaited those who ran out of money. Powell's story is really an inside-out version of Waugh's: the ambitious social-climbing artist, Zouch, tries to break in and plunder the world of the country houses, but is repulsed and destroyed by the very fact that the world he is trying to get into is one of terrifying mania and solipsism, too mad to be conquered because unable to recognize a conqueror. And so on. The problems are seen from many different angles and tackled in many different ways, but these writers, all of the same generation, evidently see the novel in much the same way, as having a function in which they all believe. If we look for a similar grouping in the nineteen-sixties we shall be disappointed. Not only are the problems facing England, and Western Europe generally, less clear-cut: the novel of satirical analysis and comment, as those writers practiced it and believed in it, no longer exists. In confirmation of which, look at the work those same writers have produced in the last decade or two. All of them, except Orwell, are still alive. Powell has retreated into a vast *roman fleuve*, possibly the most unreadable work of our time, about growing up in the interwar years. Waugh has also constructed a long reminiscence—of the war years, in his case—running into a number of volumes, interrupting the series only with odds and ends of biography, travelogue and—significantly—a book about a middle-aged writer having a severe nervous breakdown.

Isherwood has drifted away into film-script writing. Greene, though he has kept more vitality than the others, has tended to withdraw into that preoccupation of his with religious and sexual problems, gnawing away at the same questions in novel after novel, like a dog with a very old and very hard bone.

I do not want to exaggerate the way these writers have moved apart. All writers, like all human beings, become more idiosyncratic as they move into middle age; young writers tend to start from something like the same point and gradually move out of hailing-distance of each other: it is happening to my own generation. But what strikes me about the writers I have mentioned is that they seem to have given up the idea of the novel as a means of illuminating the society they are living in. They have withdrawn either into reminis-cence, into personal problems or into silence. This has not happened to the poets of the same generation: Auden, Spender and MacNeice, for instance, are all still writing poetry which, without resembling what they were writing in the thirties, is nevertheless still guided by the same kind of impulse. The mortality rate among novelists is higher than among poets, perhaps because the novel is too amorphous to give a man anything definite to cling to. Being a novelist isn't, any longer, a vocation like being a poet.

Naturally we come back to the question, "Why should this be so?" Granted that the novel has had its popular underpinning taken away, granted that it has been driven back on its final justification as imaginative literature, that it can no longer find safety in numbers by traveling in convoy with journalism, history, or pamphleteering, is this sufficient reason for its basic failure of nerve in the last few years?

It is impossible, of course, to find a final answer to a question like this. But I believe we can go some way toward one. This is an age in which all the arts have retreated into their own undisputed territory. They have been forced to do so by the sheer mass and variety of the technical means of communication which have become available. The old mixed forms, moving in a relaxed way cross a broad sweep of function and purpose, have become impossible. Painting, for instance, has become more concerned with purely visual values, more concentrated in color and line. It no longer has any mixture of the anecdotal. This is not to say that it is concerned with some mysterious set of painterly values that have no bearing on everyday life. All the great painters of the twentieth century have commented very directly on what has been happening about them; Picasso's "Guernica" is as overt in its social message as Hogarth's "Gin Lane." But the comment has been made in a language that borrows no terms from outside the pictorial. The vocabulary is drawn from colors and shapes and the emotions that they arouse. Modern art criticism is generally regarded as beginning with the declaration of Maurice Denis in 1890: "Remember that a painting—before being a horse in battle or a naked woman or an anecdote of any kind—is essentially a plane surface covered with colours assembled in a certain order." The reverberations of this statement can still be heard everywhere today, notably in modern criticism of poetry with its insistence on the primacy of "the words on the page." The picture is not an illustration to a text that we don't happen to possess. It is both text and illustration. And the new independence also means that the modern painter has a much freer use of image and symbol. Once photography had made it pointless for painters to strive after complete representational realism, the art of painting was thrown back on its resources as an art; and the result was a new stimulus. What initially appeared as a menace was quickly seen as a liberation—but only by painters with the courage to trust their art and to go forward rather than back. The cows-in-a-stream painter has never recovered from the invention of photography because he was trying to be the camera himself. Similarly, modern sculpture has withdrawn into a nonrepresentational world of pure mass and form. It has ceased to be journalism in stone and in doing so has rediscovered its own possibilities as three-dimensional draughtsmanship, as tangible geometry. Modern music, too, has shed its merely illustrative elements and moved inward to a world of pure musical values. It is as if all the arts had decided to cultivate their own ground by mining deeply for mineral resources rather than expanding outward. In the literary arts we can see this most clearly in poetry, but it is also very evident in drama, where, as we have seen, theater and cinema have ceased to compete and moved on their own divergent paths. Within the cinema itself, those who care for the film primarily as an art are much given to saying that the advent of sound was a disaster which set the cinema back many years, since what was formerly accomplished by purely cinematic means could now be explained in words. And certainly the best contemporary directors have moved back toward the pure cinema practiced by all the early directors from D. W. Griffith to Mack Sennett; they treat the spoken word with suspicion and employ it only where it is essential.

Now the novel cannot do this, because it is the child of an age which delighted in mixed forms—anecdotal painting, program music and the rest—and it has no "pure" identity to withdraw into. The novel is "pure," i.e., entirely self-reliant, when it reaches the point at which it contains no extraneous material; everything is dramatized, presented through characterization, or from incident that arises naturally from the characterization. With James, with Flaubert, with Chekhov, with Joyce, this ideal is completely realized. The novel cannot be purified beyond the point to which its major practitioners had brought it by 1920.

The chief cause of badness in novels is externality: the author wishes to communicate something to the reader, and to this end he makes his puppets, the characters, utter certain words and perform certain actions; but all the time it is obvious to both parties that the characters are ciphers: the only real people in the relationship are the author who has the ideas and the reader who absorbs them. Even novels written at a very high level of energy and inventiveness can show this fault. Dickens, for instance, until well on in his career, saw himself primarily as a journalist, bringing various scandals into the public eye by putting them into his fiction; as when he went on a tour of the notorious boarding-schools of Yorkshire in the disguise of a parent looking for a place to send his son, or asked to be smuggled into the Law Courts so that he could observe the mannerisms of a certain over-harsh judge whom he wished to pillory. The whole *raison d'être* of such fiction is precisely that it is not taken as fiction at all, but, in every sense that matters, as documentary: the author appears before the reader and harangues him with the object of stirring his conscience: the characters are puppets, though unforgettable ones, and the plot a mere sequence of contrived metaphors.

To revert for a moment to Mr. Fitz Gibbon's *When the Kissing Had to Stop,* let us consider the following extract:

> The monthly death roll at Camp 82 (Females), Dartmoor (Devon) included:
>
> > Sackville-Stuart, Lady Edwina, 56, Pneumonia.
> > Seligman, Mrs. Nora, 30, Cancer.
> > Simpson, Mrs. Patricia, 25, Pneumonia.
> > Sturtevant, Mrs. Olive, 83, Cancer.
>
> Throughout this list the cause of death was alternately cancer and pneumonia. It was known in Princeton, however, that the women had staged a hunger strike that had lasted for four weeks, their principal demand being that those with children should be allowed to live with

them in the prison. When this hunger strike proved unavailing, they marched, arm in arm, to the house of the prison governor. He, however, had already warned the Russians of this probable development, and tanks had been summoned. As had happened with the Latvian women at the Kingir camp, in Central Asia, on 26th June, 1954, the tank crews waited until the prisoners were crowded together outside the governor's house. Then the tanks crushed the women.

What ruins this passage as fiction is precisely the thing that makes it as political admonition—the sudden introduction of a fact from contemporary history. "You think this couldn't happen?" the author is saying to his readers. "But it did happen, on 26th June, 1954, and why should Soviet tank crews be any more merciful with English women than they were on that day with Latvian ones?" The point is made, the reader shudderingly assents—but the fiction is ruined. The brass pitcher and the china one have collided, and the frailer vessel is in fragments. Not that the imagination, by its very nature, is frailer than the news-story. But Mr. Fitz Gibbon, writing to persuade his readers (and here one recalls the first-night audience of *Waiting for Lefty* with their cries of "Strike! Strike!") keeps his eye so firmly on the documentary proof, on the fact that events similar to those he describes have happened, that it comes to seem natural to him, and to the reader, that his story should lean on documentary evidence, that it should seek in outside corroboration that conviction which it should carry by its own strength. The reference to Kingir camp amounts to an admission that he expects his readers to be more interested in fact than in fiction; and, having made this admission, why write a novel at all? We know the answer to that question— a novel, by dressing up the political warning in an exciting yarn, can reach more readers than a straight political book: but this is a decision taken at the administrative and strategic level, not the literary. And any form which is taken up for administrative reasons is not in a good state of health....

The pure novelist...writes fiction that is intended to be taken as fiction; its relevance to actual life is not less, but more, than that of documentary fiction, since its engagement with experience is at a much deeper level. Both author and reader step back from the limelight; the relationship between them is no longer a matter of simple give-and-take; this is life, and they are sharing in the experience of contemplating it.

This lesson, as I have said, was thoroughly learnt before 1920 or thereabouts. That is, at the very time when all the other arts were defining their territories with a new austerity, and settling down to dig more and more deeply for the riches contained in those territories, the novelist faced only a task that had been accomplished to perfection. Even for the most Herculean writer of fiction, there were no more stables to clean. Technical experiments could be made, but the results could never be as far-reaching as the results of that great movement toward complete dramatization, complete imaginative possession, which had been made by the generation of 1860 to 1910. There was only one major step left to be taken, and Joyce duly took it in *Ulysses* when he wrote a novel which dispensed with the central point of view and made each of his three main characters contemplate the same reality from different standpoints. If this was to be anything more than a play written for the page rather than the stage, it had to explore the nature of those standpoints by taking into consideration the characters' inner lives, their dreams and thought-processes. The result was a masterpiece because it combined the late nineteenth-century achievement of complete dramatization with the twentieth-century shift from outer to inner landscape.

Since then, there has been very little experimental novel-writing that strikes one as serious, or motivated by anything more than faddishness or the irritable search for new gimmicks. Occasionally a novelist aimed at putting an even higher polish on some aspect of technique that had already been developed satisfactorily. Thus Hemingway carried the principle of dramatization so far that he would hardly ever allow himself as narrator to say anything directly. Everything must be conveyed through the speech or action of the characters. His self-imposed austerity demanded that the situation must be absorbed entirely within the dialogue, and presented by no other means.

That style, heavily trade-marked, recognizable instantly as the Hemingway method, has nevertheless been imitated by countless writers who were so strongly under Hemingway's spell that they had no objection to appearing before the world as imitators. And the reason, I suspect, is that Hemingway had made the one technical advance that could still be recognizable as an advance. He gave the illusion of having purified the method of poetry, as Klee the method of painting, or Pirandello the method of the theater. But it was never more than an illusion. The same total dramatization, though less obsessively insistent on taking care of all the details, is already there in Flaubert, in Chekhov, in James. The apparent advance is a mere refinement in craftsmanship, just as it is in Miss Compton-Burnett's trick of presenting her narratives almost entirely in dialogue and making every character speak in exactly the same manner. There is novelty, but it is novelty of the surface. In reality the experimental novel died with Joyce. Its last undeniable success was scored by the Irish writer Flann O'Brien in *At Swim Two Birds* (1939), a Gargantuan comic novel which makes a simultaneous exploration, on four or five levels, of Irish civilization. Samuel Beckett, another Irishman and equally exposed to the example of Joyce, has written novels which seemed at first to be significantly experimental, but which are actually nothing more than adaptations of the method he has made so much his own in the theater, as we see if we compare *Malone Dies* with *Krapp's Last Tape*. The play is better than the novel simply because it is more securely itself.

Thus, if I am right, the present depressed and dispirited state of the novel has been foreseeable for some time. In an age when all the arts have been busily engaged in stripping themselves down to a new leanness, shedding extraneous matter and concentrating on those powers and purposes which were their own and not taken over from one another, when painting gave up the implied narrative as rapidly as music gave up the pictorial, when poetry drew away from prose and declared once and for all that its laws were not those of discourse, the novel was forced to stay where it was because its essential development was over. There is no such thing as "pure" novel form as there is "pure" poetic or dramatic or musical form. When novelists began cultivating their own individual plots in depth, the differences between them became more and more apparent, till finally the ground under their feet broke up like an ice-floe in spring. What novelists are now facing—or trying not to face, according to their temperaments—is the knowledge that "the novel," as a category within which one could feel a certain gregarious warmth, has gone. . . .

❋❋❋❋

Parallel, indeed identical, in many respects, the essays by Marcus and Wain are the best commentaries on each other, especially upon the kind of evidence that each uses and the perspective in which that evidence is viewed. Marcus points to the influence of recent literary criticism upon the reading and writing of novels and shows that the novel's concern for the immediate social situation results in a certain ephemerality or a change in meaning over the years; these historical and critical perspectives Wain lacks. However, Wain is far more aware of developments in the means of communication, so that he focuses less exclusively upon the novel as the means of informing, enlightening, and inspiring its audience; he shows that the decline of the novel is not necessarily a result of failure of nerve or of inadequate criticism but is a consequence of a shift in and purification of forms. Essentially, then, Marcus's argument is moral; Wain's, technical and technological.

Although Wain does not mention Marshall McLuhan, his arguments supporting the theory that changes in media produce changes in content and audience response resemble those in *Understanding Media** and McLuhan's other books. McLuhan holds that not only the novel but typographical, linear, eye-oriented Western civilization is changing radically under the influence of media such as radio and television. Not all McLuhan's judgments need be accepted, but his emphasis on the importance of media clearly deserves attention.

---

* New York: McGraw-Hill, Inc., 1964.

No! in Thunder

LESLIE FIEDLER

That the practice of any art at any time is essentially a moral activity I have always believed; indeed, I do not know how to begin to make a book or talk about one without moral commitment. Yet for a long time I tried to keep this secret from myself as well as from others, since in the critical world in which I grew up, a "moralistic approach" to literature was considered not only indecent but faintly comic. Most of my best literary friends, at any rate, considered it strategically advisable to speak of novels and poems *purely* (the adverb is theirs) in terms of diction, structure and point of view, remaining safely inside the realm of the formal. But an author's choice of—or a critic's preference for—one point of view, or type of diction, or kind of structure, or even his emphasis on one of these elements at the expense of the others, involves a judgment of the experience he is rendering; and such a judgment is, implicitly at least, a moral one.

One of the special strengths of modern fiction has been its awareness of the moral dimension of form; and the seminal greatness of Flaubert lies in his willingness to entrust judgment primarily to style: to transform style, in effect, from a social grace to a tool of ethical analysis. The author of *Madame Bovary* seldom comments directly on the social concerns which most deeply vex him; he has, indeed, an almost fanatic resolve *not* to admonish or preach, but his style is his surrogate in this regard. And his style judges—judges Emma and Homais, the clichés of Romanticism and Revolution, the formlessness and falsity of bourgeois life. By the same token, that style judges and condemns, as all serious style continues to judge and condemn, the literature of the marketplace and those misguided books dedicated to antistyle.

There are, of course, certain counterfeits of style, quite unlike Flaubert's, which are symptoms of the decay of their world rather than judgments of it; for there can be no neutrality in the area of technique. The form of a book represents either a moral critique of man and society, or a moral surrender. The pseudo-styles—which are called, a little misleadingly, "naturalist" and which have been practiced from the time of Émile Zola to that of James Jones—have represented such capitulations before the collapse of discrimination and sensitivity in the world around them; even as earlier Scott's manly carelessness and Dickens' hasty improvisations represented a retreat from moral engagement, and the ecstatic schoolgirl antistyle of Jack Kerouac projects a more recent sort of cowardice. Such writers as Zola, Jones, and Kerouac are guilty not only of moral weakness but of hypocrisy as well, for they proffer their sloppiness and their submission to the decay of language as tokens of their sincerity and belongingness. To seem "one of the boys" is especially an American temptation, eternally offered and eternally accepted. But it is not only the principled antistylists, populist or Beat, who stand condemned in the court of high art for flagrant immorality, an immorality of form which all their avowed (and guilt-compelled) dedication to quite moral ideas and causes cannot mitigate. Those responsible for books like *Exodus,* or *Advise and Consent,* or whatever improbable contender is currently fighting its way up the best-seller lists, must also be adjudged guilty; since ignorance is no excuse, and good will merely aggravates the crime.

In the realm of fiction, to be inept, whether unwittingly or on purpose, is the single unforgivable sin. To be inept is to lie; and for this, time and the critics grant no pardon. Yet the contemporary audience forgives the liar in art, even adulates him. It knows he is lying, but it needs his lies. In our Do-It-Yourself Age, when no one can really do anything for himself unless provided a kit and instructions, men are plagued by the failure of self-deceit itself, afflicted with a fatal incapacity to believe themselves happy. If happiness is, as Swift insisted, the faculty of being well-deceived, most men can no longer achieve it on their own. They must be lied to every day, and they are willing to pay well for the service.

Our culture is organized around the satisfaction of this demand, and the moral artist, who is the truthteller, is subject (not invariably, but with distressing frequency) to one of two indignities, the first of which is called success, the second failure. Either he is admired, like

Faulkner, for the wrong reasons: bought and unread because he is a living "classic" (in the United States, everything is speeded up to a bewildering tempo), his works posthumous before he is laid in the grave; or he is even more enthusiastically bought and *mis*read—like Pasternak, whose *Doctor Zhivago* became the very symbol of being one up on the Russians, or like Nabokov and D. H. Lawrence, the happy authors of once-banned books! Or the moral artist may be condemned out of hand, like Pasternak in Russia or Lawrence in the United States (until only the other day).

The customary charge leveled at the serious writer, until he is ripe for the even more deadly one of being a classic, is that of having written a dirty book. The Russians apparently believe this of all successful American writers who do not sympathize with Soviet objectives; but ironically, the charge is also believed in America of many of the same authors. It is, indeed, part of what has almost assumed the status of a ritual—the standard initiation of the truthteller into the culture of his country, inflicted at the moment when his truth still hurts. One is not startled, perhaps, to discover that Walt Whitman was once called "the dirtiest beast of the age," but it is a little disconcerting to learn that Hawthorne's *The Scarlet Letter* was accused of representing "the beginning of the era of French immorality" in American letters.

Yet it will not do to ignore the difference in the level of hysteria with which such charges were leveled at serious art one hundred years ago and that with which they were made of the first great books in the "modern" tradition at the point when the first of the Great Wars was about to begin. Whatever offense great art has always given and given with particular effect in America seems to have been compounded when, in what is still called, after nearly fifty years, "modern art," that offense was confessed in nonconventional form. Apparently the common man can more easily forgive an attack on home and mother than a flagrant disregard for harmony, or punctuation, or representation. Perhaps it is simply because technical offenses are less easy to overlook or to cancel out by misreading.

I have a clear memory of myself at fourteen or fifteen, struggling for an education in the public libraries of Newark, New Jersey, and having to fight to get Joyce's *A Portrait of the Artist as a Young Man* out of a locked room where it was kept with other dangerous material. Proust's *Remembrance of Things Past* was on the open shelves, but it was no easy matter to get it past the vigilance of a certain librarian who, in her spare time, went through the photography magazines stamping all female nudes three times with the official library stamp (to keep, I suppose, the minds of adolescents pure) and who regarded me as a special challenge. This experience has always seemed to me an archetypal one, my personal myth of The Intellectual Life as Moral Combat; for certainly (to a temperament for which, and in a time when, struggle seemed as necessary as eating) the library became for me an arena in which my morality was pitted against theirs in a war to end all wars! It was not dirty books I was after, I wanted to protest; it was. . . . But I did not know how to explain what it was I sought.

Only a long time afterward did I realize that I had been completely misled by the rationalizations of the guardians of the library, that it was not really the "dirtiness," the frank sexuality, of certain novels that irked the censors, but something quite different. Best sellers—in our country at least—have always been books which exploit sex as far as (and a little farther than) contemporary taboos will permit. From *The Monks of Monk Hall* to *Peyton Place* or the latest paperback by Richard S. Prather, the really popular book has talked of sex on the level of broad suggestion; it has spoken the last common language bearing on the last link (as Moravia has argued) between us and the world of nature. It seems to me now that what must be insisted upon is that even a good book can be a popular success if it can be thought of as dirty, like Nabokov's *Lolita* and Faulkner's *Sanctuary*.

No, the problem of the nonacceptance of serious fiction lies elsewhere: in the fact that *to fulfill its essential moral obligation, such fiction must be negative.* There is a dim sense of this in the popular mind, reflected in the over-the-bridge-table charge that certain great books, whatever their merits, are too "morbid" and responded to by the publishers' defensive assurances on the book jackets: "But beneath the shattering events of that book. . .lies a passionate affirmation" or "This is a book of great themes, of life, death and regeneration, of the dignity and triumph of man." Like the more particular religious reassurances of another age, these vaguely pious assertions are rooted in a profound distrust of art itself; and before them I am moved to resentment and anger. I can never read one without remembering a favorite anecdote of my old teacher, William Ellery Leonard, about how, one night in an inn, he had to share a bed with a man whom he had never met before. He felt no qualms until his bedmate kneeled down beside the bed to pray. "At that point," he liked to say, "I grabbed my wallet and ran!" So I before the book whose jacket assures me that the author is committed to affirmation, or love, or a belief in the dignity of man.

Insofar as a work of art is, as art, successful, it performs a negative critical function; for the irony of art in the human situation lies in this: that man—or better, some men—are capable of achieving in works of art a coherence, a unity, a balance, a satisfaction of conflicting impulses which they cannot (but which they desperately long to) achieve in love, family relations, politics. Yet works of art are *about* love, family relations, politics, etc.; and to the degree that these radically imperfect human activities are represented in a perfectly articulated form, they are revealed in all their intolerable inadequacy. The image of man in art, however magnificently portrayed—indeed, precisely when it is most magnificently portrayed—is the image of a failure. There is no way out.

The self-conscious writer, realizing this irony, feels a demand to make explicit the essentially negative view of man implicit in his work insofar as it is art at all. He is driven to make his avowed attitudes and allegiances congruous with the meaning that his techniques cannot help declaring. Especially in recent times, when the obligations of self-consciousness are imposed on us with a rigor unheard of in the past, the writer becomes aware that his Muse is more like the *Daimon* of Socrates (who appeared only to say *No!*) or the God of Job than like any of those white-draped Ladies of the genteel mythologists. The spirit which speaks to him conveys no reassurances or positive revelations; only the terrible message that what his best friends—in newspaper offices, or the pulpit, or Congress —have been, like Job's, telling him is "the thing which is not right." And that spirit addresses him from the whirlwind, directing his attention from himself to those absurd beasts, the Behemoth and the Leviathan.

Demonic, terrible, and negative: this is the Modern Muse—"Bluff'd not a bit by drain-pipe, gasometers, artificial fertilizers," as Walt Whitman had the wit to see; but in his euphoric, comic vision the sense of terror is dissipated. It is to such a writer as James Joyce (who chose for his slogan the device of Satan himself: *Non serviam*, "I will not obey!") or to Henrik Ibsen (whose final words were "On the contrary...") or to Whitman's contemporary, Herman Melville, that we must turn for the decisive clue. The secret motto of *Moby*

Dick was, Melville once confided: "I baptize you not in the name of the Father, the Son and the Holy Ghost, but in the name of the Devil." Even better, perhaps, because less theatrically gothic, is the phrase Melville attributes to Bartleby the Scrivener, his portrait of the writer in the modern world—a phrase in which there is already implicit Bartleby's insanity and death: "I would prefer not to." Most explicit of all is the comment in a letter to Hawthorne, in which Melville pretends to describe the essence of his beloved contemporary's art, while in fact revealing the deepest sources of his own:

> There is the grand truth about Nathaniel Hawthorne. He says No! in thunder; but the Devil himself cannot make him say *yes*. For all men who say *yes*, lie; and all men who say *no*,—why, they are in the happy condition of judicious, unincumbered travelers in Europe; they cross the frontiers into Eternity with nothing but a carpetbag,—that is to say, the Ego.

It pays to be clear about the nature of the "No! in thunder," which is quite different from certain lesser *no*'s in which a thriving trade is always done: the *no* in newsprint, for instance, and the *no* on manifestoes and petitions. A play written in the 1950's about the Salem witch trials, or a novel of the same period celebrating the revolt of the Maccabees, despite their allegorical intentions, are cheats, exploitations of the pseudo-*no*. Even the attack on slavery in Twain's post-Civil War *Huckleberry Finn*—or, for that matter, in Mrs. Stowe's pre-Civil War *Uncle Tom's Cabin*—like an anti-McCarthyite fiction in the recent past or an excoriation of segregation right now, carry with them a certain air of presumptive self-satisfaction, an assurance of being justified by the future. They are Easy No's, merely disguised *yes*'s, in varying degrees sentimental and righteous; they are *yes*'s by anticipation, tomorrow's *yes*'s. The "No! in thunder" remains a *no* forever; like the *no* implicit in the whole work of the Marquis de Sade, or the deeper *no* of *Huckleberry Finn*—Huck's *no* to womankind, the family, and organized society, which remains to this very day a *no*.

The "No! in thunder" is never partisan; it infuriates Our Side as well as Theirs, reveals that all Sides are one, insofar as they are all yea-sayers and hence all liars. There is some evidence that the Hard No is being spoken when the writer seems a traitor to those whom he loves and who have conditioned his very way of responding to the world. When the writer says of precisely the cause that is dearest to him what is always and everywhere the truth about all causes—that it has been imperfectly conceived and inadequately represented, and that it is bound to be betrayed, consciously or unconsciously, by its leading spokesmen—we know that he is approaching an art of real seriousness if not of actual greatness. The thrill we all sense but hesitate to define for ourselves—the thrill of confronting a commitment to truth which transcends all partial allegiances—comes when Dante turns on Florence, Molière on the moderate man, de Sade on reason, Shaw on the socialists, Tolstoy on the reformers, Joyce on Ireland, Faulkner on the South, Graham Greene on the Catholics, Pasternak on the Russians, and Abraham Cahan or Nathanael West on the Jews. What people, what party, what church needs an enemy when it has a great writer in its ranks?

Unless he bites the hand that feeds him, the writer cannot live; and this those who would prefer him dead (so they can erect statues of him) can never understand. I remember Faulkner's coming once, rather improbably, to Missoula, Montana, and getting engaged in conversation with a lady Montanan, who cried out at one point, "Why can't So-and-so write a novel that would do for this part of the world what you've done for Mississippi? He *loves* Montana so!" To which Faulkner, of course, answered (maybe I only dreamed it; it all seems so pat), "To write well about some place, you've got to *hate* it." A pause, and then, "The way a man hates his own wife." But this is scandalous in a way with which the righteous cannot seem to come to terms. Not only the Great Audience but also, and even especially, the Little Elite Audiences demand of the writer its disavowal in the name of a kind of loyalty which is for him death. The first attack on me as a critic ever to appear was launched because I had made some rather drastic qualifying remarks about, I think, Thomas Mann—a small god, at any rate, of the avant-garde church to which I was presumably applying for admission. "Aid and comfort to the enemy" was the implicit charge; but this charge the sayer of the Hard No must be willing to face; for he knows that the writer who rejects the negative obligation perishes even as he pleases, perishes though he please only a handful of the very best people—those, for instance, whom he has begun by admiring and whom he never ceases to admire.

It has not always been necessary for the writer to be aware of his denial; his work will do it for him anyhow, if it is honest work. Indeed, at certain periods in the past, it seemed almost better that the writer deceive himself as well as his contemporary audience about his intent: that Dickens, for example, believe himself to be glorifying the purity of woman and the simple heart of the child, while giving us in fact his mad, black-and-white nightmares, in which things live the life of men, and men perform with the lifeless rigidity of things. In the same way, Dostoevsky could think himself the apostle of a revived orthodoxy, and Samuel Richardson considered his essential task the defense of bourgeois virtue. But these days the writer cannot afford to lose for an instant his sense of himself in opposition to the world; let him pretend, however briefly, that his *no* is a *yes,* and he will end up writing *A Fable* or *The Town,* travesties of his own best work.

Naturally, not all writers in our time accept the negative obligation; and, indeed, its rejection separates the purveyor of commodity-fiction from the serious artist in the novel. There are certain pseudo-novels which are, in fact, transitional stages on the way to becoming movies or substitutes for going to the movies; and these books are obliged to be cheerful, positive, affirmative: to sustain the belief in endurance, piety, hard work and a deliberately maintained, blessed stupidity. Here is the giveaway! Nothing can, after all, be wholly positive; and even the most affirmative of subnovels (say, *Marjorie Morningstar*) must end by denying something: dirt, disorder, eccentricity, non-conformism, skepticism, intelligence—in short, the negative obligation itself! Conversely, the nay-saying writer is not wholly negative; he is in favor of one thing by definition: telling the truth (*Madame Bovary* will do as the counterexample) and accepting the tragic implications of that truth, the vision of an eternal gap between imagined order and actual chaos.

But it is not enough, in our time, for the serious writer to confess *in general* the inevitable discrepancy between dream and fact, between the best man can imagine and the best he can achieve. The artist must be willing specifically to comment on the defeat of a particular dream. The antiartist, on the other hand, incurs only the most general obligation; despite the particulars in which he apparently deals, he is in fact composing parables, pseudo-myths, to express not wonder and terror but sentimental reassurance. What life refuses, the antiartist grants: the dying catcher hits a three bagger, and everyone loves him; the coward, at the last moment, finds the courage to fight the segregationist and his hired thugs; the girl in the office takes off her glasses and wins the heart of the boss's playboy son. That these are prefabricated, masturbatory dreams almost everyone (including, I suspect, the authors) would be prepared to admit, yet they do not stir in most of us the moral indignation we feel at the distribution of other habit-forming drugs. They seem more benign than marijuana, which is banned, or tranquilizers, which may soon be sharply regulated; because we accept the fantasies they promote as finally truer than those born of "pot" or happiness pills. Assuring us that man is OK, that men are OK, that we are all—despite our mistakes and the machinations of others—OK, they feed into (at least they do not contradict) the last widely held *Weltanschauung* of the West: the progressive and optimistic, rational and kindly dogma of liberal humanism.

Yet, as some of us are rather disturbedly aware, many if not most of the eminent writers of the twentieth century have found themselves in conflict with this dogma, not always *despite* its nobility, but often because of it. The fact that such otherwise ill-assorted writers as Shaw, Joyce, Faulkner, Yeats, Pound, Eliot, Wyndham Lewis, and Samuel Beckett are arrayed against the liberal tradition indicates that it represents for our age the belief against which the serious artist must define himself, the official "Yea!" to which he must say his private "Nay!" As earlier poets had to say "Nay!" to the fifth-century Greeks' belief that their world was really explicable in terms of the Homeric gods, or the Christians' assumption that their society was Christian, or the Enlightenment's conviction that its passion and politics were finally rational, so the artist today must deny the liberal view of the possibilities of man. But liberalism is essentially different from earlier official faiths, religious or secular, in that its ideal is "openness" rather than orthodoxy; and the writer striving toward the Hard No is likely to discover that his most ardent denial is met with a disconcerting "Yes, yes, though all the same..." or "I don't finally agree with you, of course, but still..."

Nietzsche's assertion that God is dead once shook half the world, and Ibsen's attack on marriage left northern Europe trembling, but they find us merely confused or indifferent—or, as we say when confusion and indifference reach their highest pitch, "tolerant." Only an assault on tolerance itself is able to stir us as Goethe's assault on the ban against suicide once stirred his readers. The very advocacy of adultery, which from the time of the troubadours to that of D. H. Lawrence possessed an almost magic potency to provoke, has now become fashionable and meaningless. The recent redemption of *Lady Chatterley's Lover* in the courts represents not a triumph of literary taste over taboo but a failure of the moral imagination; and Lillian Smith can suggest in her novel *One Hour,* an essentially middlebrow book, that an Episcopalian priest's moment of vision and truth comes when he is in bed with his friend's wife. Who can *épater la bourgeoisie* when the bourgeoisie regards even the grossest scandal as a test of its capacity for understanding and forgiveness?

Yet there is finally a liberal view of man, to deny which is to risk blasphemy: an image of the human situation which persists very like a dogma beneath the undogmatic "openness" of which contemporary society is so proud. This view sees man as the product of a perhaps unplanned but rationally ordered and rationally explicable universe, a product which science can explain, even as it can explain the world which conditions him. The first fictionists who accepted this view of man thought of themselves as protoscientists and of their books as scientific reports on how vice and virtue are produced in the great laboratory of society. Such books, with their blend of rationalism, determinism, and quasi-scientific objectivity, were variously hailed when they appeared as examples of Realism, Naturalism, Verism, etc.; and whatever the inadequacy of their styles, they performed in the beginning the essential function of art, the negative one of provocation and scandal. Novelists like Zola and de Maupassant—in America, even so belated a representative of the school as Dreiser—horrified the genteel by exposing the self-delusions of sentimental Christianity. They soon fell victim to the fallacy of imitative form (realism-naturalism did not *have* to eschew style, as the example of Flaubert should have made clear) and proffered antistyle as evidence of their honesty. But even their very bad writing served temporarily a good cause, exposing the pretensions of academic rhetoric.

Purveyors of the old realistic article still circulate among us (James T. Farrell, for instance, and Nelson Algren), but they tell no truths that are not clichés, and they give no valuable offense. Indeed, they have become indistinguishable from the producers of chic Italian movies and from TV entertainers like Paddy Chayefsky—second-rate artists, purveyors of the scandal of the day before yesterday. The day is gone when the tradition of realism-naturalism was so deeply accepted as *the* mode of serious literature that a mannered and artificial stylist like Hemingway, or an exploiter of backwoods rhetoric and gothic nightmare like Faulkner, had to pretend to be a "naturalist" in order to seem respectable. In the first place, realism-naturalism has become an academy itself, sustaining a triumphant orthodoxy instead of challenging one; and meanwhile, certain contraband, smuggled into the presumably objective laboratory report from the beginning, has come to seem more and more essential: political propaganda, heavy-handed symbolism, righteous pornography, and sentimentality.

The latter two especially have assumed a disheartening importance in the standard subforms of post-realism, first clearly defined in the United States in the 1930's: the Popular Front Novel, on the one hand, and Regionalist or Protest Pornography on the other. John Steinbeck is the father of the first, having established in *The Grapes of Wrath* the prototype of the pious tract disguised as a sociological report, in which the cruel exploiters of labor are contrasted with simple and kindly men who give candy to children, and women of the people who offer their swollen breasts to the starving unemployed. Erskine Caldwell is the founder of the other, having created in *Tobacco Road* a genre capable of providing all the forbidden thrills of a peep show together with the conscientious satisfactions of deploring the state of the (more exotic) poor. It is hard to remember that Caldwell was considered a serious "proletarian" writer before he became a paperback best seller; one reads with surprise the accounts of his current reception in places like Turkey, where he is still regarded as a pattern for "village literature." In this country, his example has occasioned lately only such bootleg high-school literature as Grace Metalious' *Peyton Place*.

Steinbeck's prototype, however, continues to provide inspiration for the prevailing upper middlebrow form of our time: the serious pseudo-novel as practiced by certain not-quite-first-rate authors, committed equally to social conscience and success, and sure that these are not mutually exclusive goals. There is scarcely a moment these days when such authors of the Sentimental Liberal Protest Novel as Irwin Shaw, John Hersey, Budd Schulberg, and James Michener are not fighting for slots on the list of best sellers; since in our time left-of-center politics has become, by virtue of converting all its political content to sentiment, the reigning belief of the educated middle classes. In our genteel age, the class struggle has been translated from a confrontation of workers and bosses on the barricades to a contest between certain invisible or remote exploiters and all the rest of us— a contest in which more tears are shed than blood. The writer dedicated to portraying that struggle is no longer the man in the work shirt rolled to the elbow and open at the neck, but the man ashamed of his gray flannel suit—the searcher out and defender of Victims. For the image of man which possesses the genteel conscience is the image of the Victim: the snubbed Jew, the oppressed Negro, the starving Chinese, the atom-scarred Japanese, the betrayed Hungarian, the misunderstood paraplegic. For each Victim there is an appropriate book, a last indignity: *Gentlemen's Agreement, The Wall, The Bridge at Andau, The Last Pebble, One Hour.* Even the War Novel is recast in the prevailing form, captured, like *The Young Lions,* for piety, protest, and self-pity. In the end, we are left with the sense that wars are fought and armies organized (in representative platoons, with all minorities duly represented) so that the persecuted Jew or tormented Italian can shame his fellows by proving his unforeseen valor in the end.

Having only a single theme, of a rather simple-minded sort, the Sentimental Protestors are driven to eke it out, to conceal its stereotypical bareness with up-to-date details and topical references. Their eyes are constantly on the headlines; and before the ink is dry, Michener and Hersey are already embarked for the scene of the latest indignity—or at least racing for their typewriters! It is a somewhat comic contest, with the whole reading world breathlessly waiting to discover who will get Little Rock first, who the Puerto Ricans. But what is the ersatz morality which sustains the protest fictionists, from Hersey-Shaw to Jones-Algren, from the soft-sell defenders of the dark-skinned peoples to the tough apologists for maximum security prisoners and minor hoods? It is the theory that the "Little Man" must be defended against the great and powerful, merely because he is little and "wants only to be let alone." Little! Surely no more degrading label has ever been invented for the exploited, none which has so combined pathos and condescension: the little Jew, the little shopkeeper, the little mixed-up kid, the bewildered little pusher of dope, the little pimp trying to establish himself against the competition of the big operators....Against so abject a surrender to sentiment, one wants to cry out in the terrible words of the Old Testament, "Thou shalt not honor the poor man in his cause." But who could be heard over the voices of those storming their book counters for copies of *Exodus* and *Hawaii?*

What, then, of serious literature in our time? What counterimage of man does it proffer? Not, as so often in the past, an image of man struggling (and failing) to fulfill some revealed or inherited view of himself and his destiny; but of man learning that it is the struggle itself which is his definition. In a time when answers are the business of professional answer men (cheats and delusions carefully rehearsed before the show is put on the air), we have been forced to learn that our humanity is dependent not on the answers we hope for but on the questions we are able to ask. Like Job, we are granted no response except from the apparition which tells us it is time to be still, time to know that man is he who asks what man is. And like Melville's "unincumbered travelers," we must be prepared to leave our Encyclopedia Britannicas and Oxford English Dictionaries behind us, to cross the frontiers of Eternity with no baggage except the Ego. This the most serious writers of our day have taught us, insisting that we endure uncertainty, not as a stage on the way to knowledge, but as our essential condition. Now we see as through a glass darkly. There is no "then."

This view of man opens into a world not of melodrama but of ambiguity, not of the polemical but of the problematical. Saul Bellow's *The Victim,* for instance, will survive *Focus, Gentlemen's Agreement, The Professor's Umbrella,* and all the other earnest and humane tracts on anti-Semitism because, despite its title, it is not a protest novel at all. In Bellow's view, both Jew and gentile are simultaneously Victim and Victimizer; he renders their mutual torment in terms of their common desire to discover what it means to be human, their common need to *be* what is human. Our Jewishness or gentileness, Bellow leaves us feeling, is *given;* our humanity is what we must achieve. There is no more room for sentimentality in such a travesty of the liberal Jewish novel than there is in Robert Penn Warren's similar recasting of the political novel, or Malamud's of the novel about baseball, or James Baldwin's of the standard Negro novel, or Mary McCarthy's of fictional protests against the restriction of academic freedom. Reading, say, *All the King's Men,* one need only think of *The Last Hurrah* or *Advise and Consent*—or picking up *The Natural,* one need only recall Mark Harris' *Bang the Drum Slowly*—to realize how we ordinarily lust to be lied to, and how seldom we are granted the privilege of hearing the truth.

Ambiguity is the first resource of the serious novelist, tempted like all the rest of us to clichés of simplicity; but to say that the good novel is ambiguous is not to say that it is difficult and confused (this is optional), merely to insist that it is *about* moral ambiguity and that it cannot betray its theme. I distrust the writer who claims to know black from white, left from right, Hip from Square, Them from Us—no matter which of the sides he chooses. And I distrust especially the characters in whom he embodies his presumable insights. The protagonists of the best recent books are not self-righteous, long-suffering, diminished prigs, who want only to live in peace and are sure they know what peace is. From the most sympathetic to the least, they are troublemakers like their authors, who will not let the world rest until it acknowledges that they exist. We have by now quite a gallery of such types, including Joyce's insufferable Stephen, too stiff-necked to grant his mother's deathbed wish; Kafka's K., guilty as charged though no one knows quite what the charge is; Nathanael West's Miss Lonely-hearts, trying in vain to be the Christ in whom he does not believe; Ralph Ellison's Invisible Man, vainly striving to escape the myth of his color; and Faulkner's Popeye, counterfeiting manhood with a bloody corncob.

The contemporary novel through which such characters stalk—bringing harm to those around them, even as they court destruction for themselves—is terror-ridden, dreadful; but it is not humorless. In the midst of Faulkner's grimmest book, *Sanctuary,* a couple of rustics play out a humorous scene in a whorehouse. West's bleakest novel is his funniest, *A Cool Million,* whose title comes from the "Old Saying": "John D. Rockefeller would give a cool million to have a stomach like yours." Kafka, we are told, used to laugh until the tears ran down his cheeks, reading aloud from *Amerika.* Joyce, one sometimes feels, would do anything for a laugh, and Beckett has thought of some things to do which even his master could not imagine; Bellow can be a clown; Mary McCarthy insists on compelling our titters in the midst of our deepest shame; and the British "Angries" have us guffawing like a pack of fools. In this sense, Mark Twain is the true ancestor of the modern writer, and his *Pudd'nhead Wilson* a storehouse of the sort of humor which is not dated by changes of fashion. *"October 12, the Discovery.* It was wonderful to find America, but it would have been more wonderful to miss it." This is our kind of joke, proper to a world in which we may all die laughing—as we like to say.

Such humor is not incompatible with negation, or even terror, for it is not party or factional humor, with which the *in's* satirize the *out's,* and the "normal" put the eccentric in their places. It is total humor, through which men laugh not at their foibles but at their essential selves. The vision of man shared by our greatest writers involves an appreciation of his absurdity, and the protagonists of our greatest books are finally neither comic nor tragic but absurd. To the modern writer, the distinction between comedy and tragedy seems as forced and irrelevant as that between hallucination and reality; his world partakes of both, and he would be hard put to it to say where one ends and the other begins. The conventional definitions of the comic and the tragic strike him as simplifications, falsifications of human life, appropriate to a less complex time. To insist that we regard man, even for the space of three acts or five, as *either* horrible or funny; to require us, through four or five hundred pages, *either* to laugh or to cry we find offensive in an age when we can scarcely conceive of wanting to do one without the other. For us, the great works of the past are those which occupy an intermediate position between comedy and tragedy: the *Bacchae* of Euripides, the *Misanthrope* of Molière, Shakespeare's *Measure for Measure,* Ibsen's *An Enemy of the People,* Twain's *Pudd'nhead Wilson,* and Melville's *The Confidence Man.* And the writers of our own time whom we most admire—West, Faulkner, and Beckett, among others—pursue a third genre, which suggests that the ludicrous is the source of pity and terror, and that pity and terror themselves are the heart of the ludicrous.

The vision of the truly contemporary writer is that of a world not only absurd but also chaotic and fragmentary. He tries in his work to find techniques for representing a universe in which our perceptions overlap but do not coincide, in which we share chiefly a sense of loneliness: our alienation from whatever things finally are, as well as from other men's awareness of those things and of us. Rapid shifts in point of view; dislocations of syntax and logic; a vividness more like hallucination than photography; the use of parody and slapstick at moments of great seriousness; the exploitation of puns and of the vaudeville of dreams—these experiments characterize much of the best work of recent decades, from Joyce's *Ulysses* through Djuna Barnes's *Nightwood* to Wright Morris' *Field of Vision,* whose winning of the National Book Award so incensed the guardians of middlebrow standards. At the present moment, Morris is almost alone in the United States in his continuing devotion to the themes and techniques of the negative novel. (There is, to be sure, the young novelist John Barth, strangely ignored.) For we have been suffering a general loss of nerve, or a waning of talent, which has persuaded writers of such different origins and generations as Hemingway, Faulkner, Saul Bellow, and Mary McCarthy to pursue affirmation in the place of art—disconcerted, perhaps, as they pass from being ignored to relative degrees of fame and victimized by a perverse sort of *noblesse oblige.*

The unearned euphoria of *Henderson, the Rain King;* the shapeless piety of *A Fable;* the sentimental self-indulgence of *Across the River and into the Trees;* the maudlin falsity of *The Town;* the heavy-handed symbolism and religiosity of *The Old Man and the Sea,* destined from its inception for the pages of *Life*—such failures make over and over the point that the contemporary American writer can abjure negativism only if he is willing to sacrifice truth and art. For major novelists and minor, the pursuit of the positive means stylistic suicide. Language itself decays, and dialogue becomes travesty; character, stereotype; insight, sentiment. The Nobel Prize speech destined for high-school anthologies requires quite another talent from that demanded by the novel; and the abstract praise of love requires another voice from that which cries *No!* to the most noble temptations, the most defensible lies.

Yet one must not forget, in the face of their recent decline, the successes of Bellow and Hemingway and Faulkner: the terrible impact of *The Victim, The Sun Also Rises,* and *The Sound and the Fury.* The last, in particular, remains the exemplary American novel, perhaps the greatest work of fiction produced in the United States in the twentieth century. And it is no accident that its title comes from the bleakest passage in Shakespeare, or that its action begins inside the mind of an idiot. The point is insisted upon bluntly, almost too obviously: life is a tale told by an idiot, full of sound and fury, signifying nothing. Here is the ultimate negation, the Hard No pressed as far as it will go. Yet "nothing" is not quite Faulkner's last word, only the next to the last. In the end, the negativist is no nihilist, for he affirms the void. Having endured a vision of the meaninglessness of existence, he retreats neither into self-pity and aggrieved silence nor into a realm of beautiful lies. He chooses, rather, to render the absurdity which he perceives, to know it and make it known. To know and to render, however, mean to give form; and to give form is to provide the possibility of delight—a delight which does not deny horror but lives at its intolerable heart.

❦❦❦

Leslie Fiedler is essentially a critic in Marcus' and Matthew Arnold's sense, one who evaluates and judges not only literature (as a literary scholar or theorist would) but the whole culture. However, it seems appropriate to conclude this volume with a critical essay because it reminds us that the critic must begin where the scholar and the theorist end. He must be both scholar and theorist, unaided by the perspective of centuries or decades; he must judge the new in terms of the old, and vice versa; and he must be interesting as well as accurate, for art must evoke a vital response from its audience, which the critic both represents and helps to create. Seen in these ideal terms, Fiedler, like most critics, both succeeds and fails. He is capable of intense personal response to literature, but at times he is more flamboyant and rhetorical than intense. He judges, as a critic must, but sometimes he does so by fiat rather than by analysis, or by a set of disjunctions—style and antistyle, real *no* and pseudo-*no*— that are not clearly defined and that are used to bludgeon rather than to dissect. Some would say that Fiedler makes criticism more interesting than fiction by making it even more remote from the facts. And he is undeniably interesting; the energy manifested in all his essays is frequently in refreshing contrast to more abstract theorizing.

Fiedler's difference in tone and method from most of the other critics in this volume should not be allowed to conceal the fact that he is dealing with many of the same issues. Although he says that art is essentially a moral activity, his view of the moral function of form is closer to Mark Schorer's than to Philip Rahv's position. And in his rejection of the arguments of critics like Marcus who want the novel to tell us not only where we are but where we should go (and in fact of all critics who believe that liberal humanism is the basic world-view of the novel and, by extension, of all fiction), he is closer to the position of Frye and of Scholes and Kellogg. Yet he seems to be neither formalist nor mimetic in his approach, perhaps because he takes a position that both embodies and attacks features of each extreme.

A supplement to and possibly an implied criticism of Fiedler's approach is provided by the last chapter of Murray Krieger's *The Tragic Vision.** Published in the same year as *No! in Thunder,* Krieger's essay presents an argument that, while parallel to Fiedler's, has premises that are more carefully reasoned and implications that are more consciously and more thoroughly explored. Direct criticisms of Fiedler's approach are made by Robert Gorham Davis, "The Writer Must Say No,"† and Philip Rahv, "Plain Critic and *Enfant Terrible*" (Fiedler is the *enfant terrible*).‡

---

* New York: Holt, Rinehart and Winston, 1960.
† *New York Times Book Review,* January 8, 1961, p. 6.
‡ *The Myth and the Powerhouse* (New York: Farrar, Straus and Giroux, 1965).